THE CAMBRIDGE ILLUSTRATED HISTORY OF

Archaeology

Edited by

PAUL G. BAHN

CAMBRIDGE
UNIVERSITY PRESS

PUBLISHED BY THE PRESS SYNDICATE OF THE UNIVERSITY OF CAMBRIDGE
The Pitt Building, Trumpington Street, Cambridge, United Kingdom

CAMBRIDGE UNIVERSITY PRESS
The Edinburgh Building, Cambridge CB2 2RU, UK   http://www.cup.cam.ac.uk
40 West 20th Street, New York, NY 10011–4211, USA   http://www.cup.org
10 Stamford Road, Oakleigh, Melbourne 3166, Australia

First published 1996
First paperback edition 1999

Editorial management by Seven Dials Publishing,
38 Barrons Way, Cambridge CB3 7DR
Picture research: Paula Granados
Layout: David Seabourne
Imagesetting by HiLo Offset, Colchester

Printed in the United Kingdom at the University Press, Cambridge

A catalogue record for this book is available from the British Library

Library of Congress cataloguing in publication data
The Cambridge illustrated history of archaeology/edited by Paul G. Bahn.
p.   cm.
Includes bibliographical references (p. 379) and index.
ISBN 0 521 45498 0 (hardcover)
1. Archaeology – History.   I. Bahn, Paul G.
CC100.C28   1996
930.1–dc20   95-36172   CIP

ISBN 0 521 45498 0 hardback
ISBN 0 521 66946 4 paperback

Half-title: early excavations at Herculaneum. Sponsored by Charles III of Spain, King of the Two Sicilies, army engineer Rocco Gioacchino de Alcubierre began digging in March 1748 in search of antique sculptures for the Spanish court. The solidified mud that engulfed the city in AD 79, in places 8 metres deep, was mined by convict labour to form tunnels, steps and access ramps. Engraving by Louis-Jean Desprez from Saint-Non's *Voyage pittoresque* (1781).

Title page: 'The Ruins of the Palace of Karnak at Thebes', 1856, by Jacob Jacobs (1812–79).

Contents

Contributors

Paul G. Bahn   Western Europe (Palaeolithic)

Gina Barnes *University of Durham*   Far East

Caroline Bird *La Trobe University, Melbourne*   Australia and the Pacific

Peter Bogucki *Princeton University*   Central and Eastern Europe

Philip Duke *Fort Lewis College, Durango*   North America

Christopher Edens *Harvard University*   Near East; Central Asia; India

David Gill *University College of Swansea*   Classical World

John Hoffecker *Argonne National Laboratory*   Central and Eastern Europe (Palaeolithic)

Christopher Mee *University of Liverpool*   Greece and the Aegean

Christopher Scarre *McDonald Institute, University of Cambridge* Western Europe

Katharina Schreiber *University of California, Santa Barbara*   Latin America

Steven Snape *University of Liverpool*   Egypt and the Levant

Anne Thackeray *University of the Witwatersrand*   Africa

with

Claudine Cohen *Ecole des Hautes Etudes en Sciences Sociales, Paris*

Andrew Foxon *Hull City Museums*

Alice Kehoe *Marquette University, Milwaukee*

Carl Lamberg-Karlovsky *Harvard University*

Mary Ann Levine *University of Massachusetts, Amherst*

Foreword

We are all shaped by the past. The discovery of that past is therefore in some senses a voyage of self-discovery. For the past is today the last great unknown continent, whose vast territories remain largely untrodden by the modern investigator. Every archaeological excavation is an expedition into a world still largely unexplored: the world of the origin of ourselves and of human culture. It is the mapping of one more pathway in time, extending back from the present to the mysterious lands where humankind was formed.

The history of archaeology holds many fascinations. There are innumerable great discoveries: the bulls of Altamira and the recognition of palaeolithic art; the tomb of Tutankhamen and the fabled wealth of the Egyptian pharaohs; Easter Island and its mysterious *rongo rongo* writing. Every continent and territory of the globe has its own archaeology, and the development of the discipline in every area is for the first time allowing the construction of a true world history – or world prehistory.

The most exciting thing about this book is that it is telling a story which is still in its early stages. For although it takes us back to Nabonidus, the monarch of ancient Babylon with his antiquarian curiosity, and to the connoisseurs of ancient Rome and of early imperial China, the story begins in earnest only with the realization – generally dated to the year 1859 – that the human species is of great antiquity, with an origin extending far back beyond the date of 4004 BC established in the seventeenth century by zealous biblical scholars. The realization that came then upon the scholarly world – like 'stout Cortés' with his first view of the Pacific Ocean, 'silent upon a peak in Darien' – that there were vast tracts (in this case of time, of human existence) unimagined and unexplored, was the true birth of archaeology, if we see that subject as the investigation of the human story.

That story continues to unfold. Today many of the exciting discoveries come not simply from new excavations, but from the discovery of new research techniques, such as radiocarbon dating or molecular genetic research, which are transforming our ability to investigate and to understand the past. Moreover, the development of archaeological theory has made us more aware that we do not simply rediscover the past: we create it. For the raw materials dug up from the earth do not tell us much directly. They have to be interpreted. And it is *we* who do the interpreting. The past as we understand it is thus, in a sense, our own creation, although it is built up out of all the great discoveries made by the archaeologist's spade. The history of archaeology is therefore a complex one – a story not only of discovery and of new research techniques, but also of new interpretive frameworks. For if we are shaped by our past, we also, in a very real sense, through the practice of archaeology, create that past for ourselves. The history of archaeology is the history of self-awareness.

Lord Renfrew of Kaimsthorn ScD FBA FSA
Disney Professor of Archaeology, Director of the McDonald Institute for Archaeological Research, and Master of Jesus College, University of Cambridge

Preface

The term 'archaeology' today means literally 'the study of the ancient'. It has come to denote the investigation of the remains of the human past, from the very first artifact all the way to yesterday's garbage. First coined, naturally enough, by the Greeks (*arkhaiologia*, or discourse about ancient things), it was originally applied to remote periods of history: for example, in the reign of the emperor Augustus, Dionysius of Halicarnassus wrote a great history of Rome from its beginnings to the Punic Wars, and called it *Roman Archaeology*.

The term 'archaeologist', however, appeared in the first centuries AD, with a somewhat specialized meaning. In Greek lands it denoted a category of actors who recreated ancient legends on stage through dramatic mimes. Subsequently, both words disappeared, and were not reinvented until Jacques Spon, a seventeenth-century doctor and antiquary in Lyon with a great interest in Roman antiquities, introduced not only 'archaeology' but also 'archaeography'. The former persisted, and entered the international vocabulary.

It may seem amusing to imagine 'archaeologists' as players, cavorting on stage and enacting ancient legends, but in fact little has really changed. The modern phenomenon of archaeology, as outlined in this book, can arguably be considered as two separate but parallel soap operas. The first involves the archaeologists themselves – their different personalities, their influences, friendships and alliances, their rivalries and hatreds – and of course, as in any soap, the constant deaths and the arrival of new characters who breathe refreshing new life into the

Too close a study of the past has long been thought to breed eccentricity and it is no coincidence that the history of archaeology is rich in notable characters, always independent-minded, occasionally obsessive. This 'Congress of the best antiquaries of Rome' was caricatured in 1728 by Piero Leone Ghezzi, a painter and antiquary who was one of Rome's foremost eighteenth-century scholars. Apparently the most sober of the participants, Ghezzi is taking notes at the back. The seated figure in the foreground is Baron von Stosch, a famous collector.

storyline. There are cliques, power-groups and mafias, saints and scoundrels, bores and bullies, insiders and outsiders, just as in any other walk of life.

The second is archaeology's view of the past, constantly changing as new evidence arises or as old evidence is reinterpreted, and always closely interwoven with the personalities and interactions of the archaeologists themselves. As in any good serial, there are sudden surprises, plot twists and red herrings. Neither soap opera will ever end, but they both require a perpetual stream of novelties – eccentric characters, glamorous or spectacular finds – to maintain the all-important interest of their audience, without which they might be in danger of cancellation when times are hard.

The first soap, that of the archaeologists and their personalities, is all too factual; the second, the account of the past they put together, is inevitably fictional. Most archaeologists strive to be objective about the past, to discover the 'truth' about what went on, but the best that can be achieved without a time-machine is an accepted fiction – one deduced from, and perhaps even tested against, the data, but a fiction nonetheless. We can never *know* what happened in the past – even for historic periods the written sources are always subjective and often mutually contradictory – but for periods before writing, archaeology is our only means of producing even an informed guess.

The accounts presented by archaeologists are often supported and enhanced by pictorial reconstructions of the past, and in recent years we have become aware that many such images – for example, those of different kinds of fossil humans, like the Neandertals – have not only entertained and instructed the public but actually played an important role in influencing archaeological debate and in promoting favoured interpretations.

This 'literary bias', where science proceeds by telling stories both verbal and visual, has allowed a number of conventional myths to take hold, in which powerful words or vivid pictures are found to be more romantic and inspiring than the plain facts. For example, when little Maria de Sautuola first spotted the great bison painted on the ceiling of Altamira (p. 124), she did not cry out 'Toros, toros!' – if anything, she cried 'Mira, Papa, bueyes!' ('Look, Father, oxen!'). The dramatic image of horses being driven over the cliff-top at Solutré was created for the first prehistoric novel, and never appeared in the factual account of the site (p. 122). Howard Carter's reply to Lord Carnarvon, who asked at the entrance of Tutankhamen's tomb (p. 241) if he could see anything, was not 'Yes, wonderful things' – according to Carter's own notes, he replied 'Yes, it is wonderful' (the more famous version was actually written later by Arthur Mace from Carter's notes). Heinrich Schliemann was not fired by an image of Troy in flames in a book given to him as a child – his interest in the subject arose far later and more deliberately (p. 145); nor did he dash off a telegram from his dig at Mycenae to the king of Greece, claiming 'I have gazed upon the face of Agamemnon' – that was invented later. The moving and heroic mass suicide of the defenders of Masada was more likely a massacre, later adapted by the Jewish historian Josephus for his own ends; ironically, it was the archaeological excavations at the site which revealed his artistic licence, although Yigael Yadin, the excavator, tried hard to fit the archaeological data to the ancient historian's more inspiring version of events (p. 313).

This book chronicles the slow development of archaeology, from the crude fumblings of early antiquaries to the sophisticated multidisciplinary projects of the present day; from the days of the polymath to those of extreme specialization; from a scramble for curiosities to the search for answers to specific questions. It is the story of the growing realization that evidence can survive, be recovered, and be made to reveal its secrets; of a steady increase in the care with which the evidence has been sought and interpreted; and of the close relationship between archaeology's progress and that of technology – from aerial photography to dating methods and computers. One overriding development has been the ability to do more with less: consider, for example, the wide variety of information that can now be extracted from a single potsherd – its date and decoration, its raw materials and their source, the temperature of its firing – perhaps even identification of the food the vessel once contained.

Archaeology is no longer just about finding things – though that can still be of great importance. Archaeology today focuses more on finding out things. This book, therefore, tries to strike a balance between spectacular discoveries and the equally important developments in ideas: in how archaeologists have tried to make sense of the past, from the naive assertions and speculations of the beginnings to today's post-modern navel-gazing and lack of confidence in 'facts'.

Dignifying the present. Dated 1584, this painting by Hendrik III van Cleve of Cardinal Federico Cesi's palace and garden in Rome depicts part of the cardinal's important collection of Roman antiquities, a notable example of the Renaissance taste for the classical. Social rank and wealth are implicitly legitimized in this type of cultural appeal to antiquity.

At the same time, it attempts to set many of the leading characters in the story against the background of their time, since it is self-evident that all archaeologists are heavily influenced by their social milieu, their political or religious beliefs, their teachers, and their friendships and enmities. This is by no means a new concept: many of the prejudices of early historians have been explained in terms of dependence on the largesse of their rulers, and all writers' views inevitably derive from the times in which they live. This should not necessarily be seen as a negative phenomenon: inherent biases can greatly stimulate creativity as scholars strive to uphold or, conversely, to demolish a cherished position.

Although this is the first book to provide a truly worldwide survey of archaeology's development, some readers may still find it excessively Eurocentric in its emphasis on the discipline in terms of the 'Western experience'. We make no apologies for this. Archaeology was not created by non-Western experience. It was initiated predominantly in Europe, as people tried to make sense of the most distant past of which they were aware. Europeans strove to understand the Greeks and Romans through study of the classical world; and they originally turned to Egypt and the Near East in order to find traces of the civilizations that touched the classical world and the history of Christianity. These areas were seen as the cradle of the intellectual and spiritual life of the West. Only much later did that archaeological interest spread to other areas. The emphasis on Europe is therefore inevitable, the result of historical accident. In the same way, western and eastern Europe have to be considered separately in most of the book because of the very different paths they took over past centuries.

The first 'underwater excavation', 24 August 1854. This watercolour shows Bern geologist Adolphe von Morlot (1820–67), armed with pick and butterfly net, in the Genfersee at Morges among wooden posts of the Swiss lake dwellings discovered the previous winter (p. 94).

His helmet, of sheet zinc with a glass panel, was attached to his shoulders by straps and fed with air by a force-pump operated in the boat above by Frédéric Troyon, curator of Lausanne Museum, and F. Forel. The air escaped in big bubbles beneath his chin as the helmet was not fixed to his body.

It was, wrote Morlot to Ferdinand Keller shortly after, 'strikingly poetical to stand amid those ancient posts in the bluish twilight'.

The greatest difficulty in putting the volume together was in choosing what to include and what to leave out. It goes without saying that the history of world archaeology is so vast a subject that it could not possibly be encompassed adequately in a book of this length: all the contributors could easily have filled it with material from their own period or region. Instead we have sought a balance between the well-known and the unfamiliar, between archaeology's 'greatest hits' and the events or finds which, though sometimes unspectacular, were of the greatest importance to the subject's progress. With some notable exceptions, there is less emphasis on sites and individuals in the final chapters, since it is not yet possible to achieve an adequate perspective on recent events and assess their true importance and significance for the overall history of archaeology.

It is hoped that one result of the book may be to encourage readers, and especially students, to delve into the old and neglected writings of the discipline. One can understand that, faced with an ever-growing literature, students are reluctant to look at material that seems hopelessly outdated and irrelevant, and much of which may even be in a foreign language. Yet, lurking in the dusty tomes of nineteenth-century scholarship, they will find untold riches in terms of concepts and pioneers which will show them that there is really no such thing as a new idea, and that ideas evolve through a constant compilation of older notions rather than come into being through sudden discoveries or leaps of the imagination. Much can be learned from a serious study of the formative phases of the discipline. Many autodidacts and polymaths of the Victorian era were utterly remarkable scholars.

In my own case, I found the nineteenth-century French archaeological literature a total revelation when I began my research on the Pyrenees twenty years ago. Names I had never heard mentioned in lectures became my heroes as I read their insights and enjoyed their frank, and often downright rude, exchanges with colleagues. I was astonished too by their pioneering achievements. For example, the abbé Pouech, in 1847, digging for bear bones in the cave of L'Herm, divided the excavated surface into metre squares and gave them each a letter, in order to see if the bear skeletons were complete. In 1870, Emilien and Charles Frossard took some sediment from the Magdalenian cave of Aurensan and subjected it to a crude but effective kind of flotation, recovering carbonized strawberry and raspberry seeds. In 1878 Félix Regnault was already trying to differentiate smashed bones from gnawed bones at the palaeolithic cave of Gargas, and studying the bone-crushing behaviour of big menagerie carnivores to help him in distinguishing the two. Edouard Piette was a pioneer in numerous domains, not only in finding important sites by systematically searching in suitable parts of the landscape, but also in the scale and care of his excavations, as well as in the many broad-minded interpretations he brought to the Upper Palaeolithic – the semi-domestication of animals, the possible cultivation of plants and so on. There was even a British pioneer in the Pyrenees in the unlikely form of Sabine Baring-Gould, future writer of 'Onward Christian soldiers', who, while on holiday in Pau in 1847, at the age of thirteen, dug

Opposite. Since the nineteenth century archaeology has provided an outlet – usually innocent, occasionally sinister – for national pride. Epitomizing the 'heroic Gaul', this bronze statue of Ambiorix, chief of the Celtic Eburones, presides over the marketplace at Tongres in Belgium. The origin of the Gallic attitudes guyed by Asterix, Obelix and Getafix in Goscinny and Uderzo's renowned comic strip is not hard to find.

Iron Age burial mounds; three years later he also excavated an important
Roman villa with magnificent mosaic floors. If such a wide variety
of exploits can be found merely in the Pyrenean region, what
others remain to be rediscovered in the literature from other parts
of the world?

In a book on the history of archaeology published in Cambridge it
is only fitting that tribute be paid to the late Professor Glyn Daniel
whose superb books and entertaining lectures gave generations of
readers and students an appreciation of the fascinating characters
and insights to be found in the development of this field of
study. This volume is dedicated to his memory; we hope that
he would have approved of – and enjoyed – its contents.

Paul G. Bahn

The Archaeology of Archaeology

Like any area of study, archaeology has no fixed point of origin. Curiosity about the past seems to be widespread among human beings, and is by no means a new phenomenon. People have always been aware that others came long before them. Before archaeology or even antiquarianism had come into existence, knowledge of these past times came only from written records, oral histories, religious beliefs, legends and superstition: in many rural areas this remained true even into the twentieth century. The most obvious relics of the past were standing monuments or ruins, often shrouded in mystery and folklore. These stimulated the imagination and were often attributed to the fabulous heroes of mythology, to demons or elves, with the larger ones naturally being ascribed to giants. In some Christian communities, ancient monuments were eventually linked with the devil, while prehistoric rock art sites and megalithic tombs in southwest Europe were often given names linking them with the Moorish conquerors of the early medieval period.

Until the twentieth century the fact that most people travelled little, and lived and worked in the same place for generations, engendered a strong sense of lineage and continuity, and a firm attachment to native soil. But neither in ancient times nor in the medieval world was there any grasp of the fact that this soil could be a source of information about the past. Most antiquities came to light accidentally, through ploughing or construction work; any digging for objects involved a search for treasure, or – in medieval Europe – for saints' relics.

The first glimmerings of archaeology lay with the pioneers who not only took a closer interest in the past but also realized that a history different from that of classical texts could be gleaned from traces left behind in the ground – indeed in the entire landscape.

PRE-MODERN VIEWS OF THE PAST

The earliest known archaeological probings are reckoned to be those of Nabonidus, king of Babylon, who, in the sixth century BC, excavated a temple floor down to a foundation stone laid nearly 2,000 years earlier. He was concerned with tracing the floor plans of ruined temples and collecting artifacts from these 'excavations'. Nabonidus' efforts were directed towards the correct restoration of these temples in line with his cultic reforms and his emphasis on the lineal descent of imperial power from earlier kings. His inscriptions report that:

> He beheld a statue of Sargon, father of Naram-Sin, within the foundations [of the Ebabbar temple]. Half of its head was broken and it was so worn that its face could not be recognized. Because of reverence for the gods and respect for kingship, he summoned the skilled craftsmen, renovated the head of that statue and restored the face of it. He did not alter its location but placed it in the Ebabbar …

CHAPTER 1

Opposite. Buried treasure. In this scene from a French illuminated manuscript of 1477, the burial and discovery of treasure in the ground are the pretext for a lesson in morality. The seated figure, representing ill-gotten wealth, is a magistrate whose treasures are displayed at his feet; below, a man digs a hole in the ground with a mattock.

Nabonidus was not an early archaeologist, however much his techniques may have resembled those of nineteenth-century excavators. However, his interest in the past is clear. His daughter's home had a special room to house her collection of local antiquities.

In the eastern Balkans a fifth-century Thracian princess had a collection of Stone Age axes in her grave. And even divine emperors were not immune to the attractions of 'archaeology': the historian Suetonius informs us that the Roman emperor Augustus, in the first century BC, 'had collected the huge skeletons of extinct sea and land monsters popularly known as "giants' bones"; and the weapons of ancient heroes.' This interest in 'ancient heroes' can be traced back to Homer, often considered the father of archaeology. It was Homer who was instrumental in turning people's eyes to the past through his descriptions of the Trojan War in the *Iliad*, and of peoples from different lands in the *Odyssey*.

The Near East

Mesopotamia, the region of western Asia defined by the Euphrates and Tigris rivers, enjoyed a 2,500-year literary 'stream of tradition', with another 1,000 years encoded in myth and oral tradition. The ancient prestige of Mesopotamia ensured that many of its traditions passed into the literature of adjoining regions, including the Bible. This literary tradition included ostensibly historical documents such as king-lists, chronicles, annals, epic poems and lamentations. Accumulated from third millennium BC beginnings, it was repeatedly copied as part of the training of scribes and disseminated through libraries. By the time of the great Assyrian kings (in northeast Mesopotamia) and of Nebuchadnezzar in the first millennium BC, educated Mesopotamians were heirs to a long historical consciousness.

A common attitude towards the past in western Asia involved the divine creation of the social world and the need for a just king to preserve social order. Heroic and just kings like Gilgamesh (p. 158), who probably lived during the twenty-eighth century BC, featured in myths that were important in Mesopotamian literature. Conversely, impious actions resulted in social chaos, famine and disease, barbarian invasion, and other catastrophes. Myth and poetry vilified impious kings like Naram-Sin in the twenty-third century BC, whose deeds affronted the gods and caused the collapse of order. The biblical version of this attitude, phrased as a covenant with God, placed the responsibility for right behaviour and ritual correctness on the people as much as on their leaders.

The Bible, classical literature and early Christian writings preserved in the west a memory of the Iron Age civilizations of western Asia. Sections of the Bible like Kings and Nehemiah chronicle the fortunes of Israel and Judea, and their relations with the Phoenician and Aramaean kingdoms to the north and with the Assyrian, Babylonian and Persian empires. Isaiah and other prophets left vivid descriptions, couched in moral terms, of the gathering threat of imperial conquest, the resistance to invasion, eventual defeat and deportation. In these writings the

Assyrians epitomized insatiable conquest and brutality, and Babylon represented evil, debauchery and political oppression, with Babylon's end standing as an object lesson to the impious and wicked:

> And Babylon, the glory of kingdoms … will be like Sodom and Gomorrah when God overthrew them. It will never be inhabited or dwelt in for all generations … But wild beasts will lie down there, and its houses will be full of howling creatures. (Isaiah xiii, 19–21)

Assyrian blood lust. In this relief of chariots and cavalry in battle, the defeated enemy are trampled beneath the horses' hooves while a vulture hovers above.

The classical world

Classical literature provided another view of the 'oriental', and particularly of the Persians. The Greek perspective on the Persians combined admiration of social and military virtues with contempt for political subservience and 'oriental despotism'. After the failed Persian invasions of Greece in the fifth century BC, the Greek attitude also carried a smug conviction of Hellenic superiority. Classical literature preserved a memory of eastern cities, civilizations and history. The historian Herodotus, an admirer of the Persians, left a description of Babylon that guided antiquarian research well into the nineteenth century:

A vast city in the form of a square with sides nearly 14 miles long and circuit of some 56 miles, and in addition to its enormous size it surpasses in splendour any city of the known world ... There are a hundred gates in the circuit of the wall, all of bronze with bronze uprights and lintels ... The temple [of Bel] is a square building, two furlongs each way, with bronze gates [and] a solid central tower, one furlong square, with a second erection on top of it and then a third, and so on up to eight ... On the summit of the topmost tower stands a great temple.

Other classical historians and geographers recorded details of places and cultures east of the Mediterranean as far away as India in the wake of Alexander the Great's conquests and later Roman sea trade. While the details are often fabulous, many of these descriptions are valuable sources. For example, *The Periplus of the Erythraean Sea*, an anonymous trading manual of the first century AD, lists the goods from East Africa and Malaysia available in the Roman ports of the Indian Ocean. Classical literature also contains information that was crucial to the early study of Mesopotamian political history. A Babylonian priest named Berossus even wrote, in Greek, a history of his country from the creation to Alexander the Great's invasion in the fourth century BC.

The emergence of Greece from the so-called Dark Ages in the eighth century BC led to a renewed interest in remains from the Bronze Age. The monumental 'bee-hive' tombs of the Mycenaean world in particular recalled groups who had gone before. As Greek states tried to establish their identity, such tombs came to be seen as the burial places of the community's forerunners. As a result many Mycenaean tombs attracted new offerings – veneration for heroes of an earlier age. One tomb where such Early Iron Age offerings were made was at Menidhi in Attica. The contents included pots decorated in the Geometric style showing a procession of chariots, an allusion to earlier periods reflected in heroic oral poems like Homer's *Iliad*.

Mycenaean tombs continued to be revered in still later periods. During building work in the Athenian agora, the market place of ancient Athens, a tomb was uncovered by accident during the fifth century BC, and propitiatory offerings in the form of oil containers were left. In the Hellenistic period (the final centuries BC) tombs seem again to have attracted offerings. Following the Persian Wars in the early fifth century BC, Kimon, an Athenian commander, decided to repatriate the bones of the dead Athenian hero, Theseus. During an expedition to Skyros, he uncovered Theseus' bones, brought them back to Athens and placed them in a special sanctuary, the Theseion. Presumably the bones had been recovered from some convenient Bronze Age tomb on the island.

Similarly, in a dispute between the city-states of Tegea and Sparta, the Spartans were told that they would never get the better of their opponents until they recovered the bones of Orestes, the son of Agamemnon, leader of the Greeks in Homer's *Iliad*. Herodotus records that Lichas, a Spartan, found the bones by chance. In a blacksmith's, the smith told him of a remarkable discovery:

Conquering hero. The victories of Alexander the Great in Asia Minor, Palestine, Egypt, Persia and Bactria in 334–325 BC were instrumental in spreading the language and culture of the Greeks across the Near East as far as the lower Indus. Legendary for his military prowess but ruthless above all, and the instigator of many murders – perhaps even that of his own father, Philip of Macedon – Alexander died of fever in Babylon in 323 BC after months of drinking and debauchery. In this heroic coin portrait he is shown wearing the ram's horns of Zeus Ammon, a symbol of divine descent.

I was making me a well in this courtyard, when in my digging I chanced upon a coffin seven cubits long. As I could not believe that there had ever been men taller than those of our time, I opened the coffin, and found within it the corpse as long as itself; I measured it, and buried it in earth again.

Believing the bones to be those of Orestes, Lichas returned to the smithy and dug them up. As a result the Spartans were said always to have beaten the men of Tegea.

As today, the construction of new towns and buildings sometimes brought to light the remains of former times. When Julius Caesar laid out the new town of Capua (*Casilinum*) near Naples, his biographer Suetonius records that 'a number of vases of ancient workmanship' were found in 'very old tombs'; while the geographer Strabo tells us that when Caesar founded a Roman colony on the site of ancient Corinth in Greece, his soldiers discovered numerous seventh- and sixth-century BC pots and bronzes of such quality that every tomb was rifled. The objects were sold for high prices in Rome as 'Necrocorinthia' (from the tombs of Corinth) – an early example of grave-looting and the trade in antiquities.

In Greece there was a continuing fascination with the past even after the region had been incorporated into the Roman Empire. In the second century AD the geographer and historian Pausanias wrote a travel guide to the monuments of Greece. Buildings and artifacts were sometimes described against a key event in Greek history: the defeat of the Persian invasions in the early fifth century. Pausanias came across ruined temples in the countryside, which in his view had been left derelict since their destruction by the Persian invader, and he noted that the paintings in the fifth-century BC sanctuary of Theseus at Athens had deteriorated through the ravages of time.

New building, the digging of wells and cellars, and everyday cultivation of the soil within ancient cities for vegetables and vines yielded relics of the past long before the Renaissance. According to the historian Livy, when disinterred in Rome in 181 BC, the tomb of the Sabine Numa Pompilius, semi-legendary second king of the city in the seventh century BC, was found to contain philosophical treatises written by Numa himself.

This recreation of the scene by Polidoro da Caravaggio dates to 1525, not long after the rediscovery in Rome in 1506 of the famous marble Laocoön sculpture of *c.* 200 BC, now in the Vatican, that so influenced the work of Michelangelo.

The statue of Zeus at Olympia

One of the seven wonders of the ancient world was the monumental chryselephantine (gold and ivory) statue of Zeus that nudged the roof of the main temple at Olympia. The masterwork of the Athenian craftsman Pheidias, it was erected in the late fifth century BC and survived until the late fifth century AD – a span of 900 years, the time that separates modern Britons from Domesday Book.

The detailed description left in the second century AD by the travel-writer Pausanias describes Zeus seated, holding a Victory in his right hand, a sceptre in his left.

The shoes of the god are of gold and so also is his robe. On the robe there are animate figures and also lily flowers represented. The throne is variegated with gold and stones, and still further with ebony and ivory. Upon it, moreover, there are painted figures and sculpted images.

Pausanias goes on to describe the decoration of the throne, which included the shooting of the children of Niobe by Artemis and Apollo. The statue stood 13 metres (43 feet) high, the height of a three-storey house.

The measurements of the Zeus at Olympia, both its height and breadth, have been written down and are known to me, but I will not bestow praise upon those who did the measuring, because the measurements that have been recorded by them are far less impressive than the effect that the statue makes on those who see it. For when the image had just been completed, Pheidias prayed to the god to send him a sign if the work was pleasing to him, and at that very moment, they say, a lightning bolt struck the floor at a spot which in my day was covered with a bronze water container.

The Roman geographer Strabo was more critical in the first century AD, feeling that the scale of the seated statue was not right, 'for although [Pheidias] represented the god as seated, [Zeus] almost touches the peak of the roof and thus gives the impression that, if he were to stand up straight, he would take the roof off the temple.'

A near-contemporary image of the statue appears on an Athenian red-figured *krater* (wine-mixing bowl) which was found at Baksy in Russia. The head also appears on coins issued by the nearby city of Elis during the reign of the emperor Hadrian. 'All the floor in front of the statue', concluded Pausanias, 'is paved with black marble, not white, edged in a semicircle by a raised rim of Parian marble, which acts as a basin for the olive oil that is poured over the statue.'

Pheidias' statue of Zeus reconstructed in 1721 by the Austrian architect, Johann Fischer von Erlach. Von Erlach was the first to devise a plausible reconstruction systematically incorporating all the details given by ancient writers.

The statue was erected around an intricately shaped scaffolding of timber overlaid with thin plates of ivory to represent the face, torso and other skin areas. Details like drapery were represented by beaten sheets of precious metal, fitted neatly together around the wooden armature so that the joins were almost invisible.

On the ivory finger of Zeus was reputedly scratched the graffito 'Pantarkes is beautiful', an allusion to the lover of Pheidias who, according to Pausanias, won the wrestling at the Olympic games of 436 BC and modelled for one of the sculptures between the legs of the throne, 'placing the ribbon of victory in his hair'.

For the Roman orator Cicero in the first century AD, Pheidias at Olympia 'had a vision of beauty in his mind so perfect that concentrating on it he could direct his artist's hand to produce a real likeness of the god'. A century later, less reverently, the satirist Lucian joked that the timber interior of the statue had become infested by mice.

Finally, in AD 391, through the growing influence of the Christian church, the temples at Olympia were closed and the Olympic games ceased. The statue of Zeus was dismantled, transported across the Aegean and re-erected in a palace in Constantinople. It was destroyed by fire in AD 475.

The past continued to be revered even after the fall of the western Roman empire. As Christianity became established in the lands of the Mediterranean, pagan cults faded, abandoning their statues and temples as well as their beliefs. Officials of the new church started to collect the ancient statuary. One Byzantine chronicler recorded an array of major statues from the classical world in the palace of Lausus at Constantinople, destroyed by fire in AD 475. These included Praxiteles' famous statue of Aphrodite from Knidos, the statue of Lindian Athena given to the sanctuary by Amasis the Egyptian, and Pheidias' huge cult-statue of Zeus from Olympia.

Classical survival. Popularly known as Kaadmau, the St Albans cameo was a fourth-century cameo portrait of a Roman emperor that survived into medieval times as an amulet to help mothers in childbirth. Of sardonyx, bound in silver and 'almost too big to be held in one hand', it was presented to St Albans Abbey by the Anglo-Saxon king, Aethelred II. Drawing by Matthew Paris, 1257.

Medieval Europe

In medieval Europe belief was a potent mixture of Christian conviction and popular mythology. Genesis placed the geographical origin of the human race in the Near East, both at the time of the Creation and after the Flood when Noah's sons repopulated the earth. Paganism was thought to have developed through degeneration as people moved away from the Near East and lost touch with the mainstream of Jewish and Christian belief. Pagan monuments were thus considered the work of degenerate peoples, and wherever possible were destroyed, neutralized or Christianized. Churches were built alongside major prehistoric ritual monuments such as the stone circle at Avebury in southern England, and all over Europe springs sacred to the old religion were rededicated to Christian saints.

Coupled with this was a general lack of historical awareness. The world was thought to have been created by God, literally in seven days, as part of a divine plan whose end was to be Christ's second coming and the Last Judgement. There was scant understanding of long-term change, natural or cultural, and the idea that technology and society had constantly altered over the centuries was but dimly perceived. In medieval manuscripts and stained glass biblical characters are represented in contemporary dress.

A third factor contributing to the miasma was the power of scholarly mythology. In the ninth century, the Welsh monk Nennius claimed that Brutus, a Trojan prince, had been the first to settle the British Isles after the ravages of the Flood. A powerful argument in favour of his hypothesis was the supposed derivation of 'Britain' from 'Brutus'. Two centuries later, the Welsh chronicler Geoffrey of Monmouth, in his fictitious *History of the Kings of Britain*, even put a precise date on Brutus' arrival: 1170 BC. Similar mythologies and speculative genealogies were developed on the European mainland, where the Goths, for example, were thought to descend from Gog, a grandson of Noah mentioned in the Bible.

Such mythologies were closely tied to the development of a nascent nationalism in western Europe. In the twelfth century, French-born rulers could govern a motley assemblage of territories stretching from the Pyrenees to the Scottish border. Italian clerics could be appointed to livings in France and England, and French was widely spoken as, literally, the *lingua franca* of European aristocracies. By the

Idolatry defeated

The standing stones, or menhirs, erected in western Europe by Neolithic and Bronze Age societies thousands of years before Christ were seen by early Christian clergy as intolerable pagan symbols. Legends and beliefs still attached to them during the Roman period, even if they were no longer the focus for religious ritual. Destruction was common. But it was not always necessary to destroy the stones: they could be rededicated as Christian monuments.

The best examples are the menhirs of Brittany that have tops recarved in the shape of a cross. In other cases, a cross was simply cut into the stone's surface. The *Life* of the sixth-century Welsh saint Samson tells how, landing one day in Cornwall, he saw people worshipping at a menhir. He hastened to denounce their idolatry and convert them to Christianity, setting his seal on the conversion by carving a cross on the menhir's uneven surface with his own hand.

Sixteenth-century painting of Saint Geneviève, patron saint of Paris, with a flock of sheep within a prehistoric stone circle, almost certainly a now destroyed monument at Nanterre.

This is one of the oldest pictures of a megalithic monument in Europe, and links Christianity with pagan religion. It was formerly housed in the church of St Merri, Paris.

Illustration from a fourteenth-century English manuscript depicting the magician Merlin building Stonehenge. This very rare medieval depiction of a prehistoric monument is the earliest known picture of Stonehenge.

The scene illustrates the colourful legend, first propagated in Geoffrey of Monmouth's *History of the Kings of Britain* (*c.* 1136), that Merlin – wizard, prophet and son of an incubus – re-erected on Salisbury Plain stones he had transported from Ireland by magic. Required, in the fifth century AD, to provide an everlasting memorial to a great British victory over the Saxons, Merlin sends for 'the Giants' Round which is on Mount Killaraus in Ireland. In that place there is a stone construction which no man of this period could ever erect, unless he combined great skill and artistry. The stones are enormous, and there is no one alive strong enough to move them. Many years ago the Giants transported them from the remotest confines of Africa and set them up in Ireland at a time when they inhabited that country. Their plan was that, whenever they felt ill, baths should be prepared at the foot of the stones; for they used to pour water over them and to run this water into baths in which their sick were cured.'

In reality, the sandstone of the Stonehenge trilithons is local to Wessex, and the great Neolithic circle that we see today was erected *c.* 2100 BC.

fifteenth century all this had changed. National identities and sentiments were well established, national churches had begun to develop, English was spoken at the English court, and foreign interference was fiercely resisted. In these conditions the appetite for nationalist myths grew apace. In Italy, links with the imperial Roman past were explored and reinforced through the rediscovery of classical literature and the revival of classical architecture (p. 59). In Tudor England, writers turned to Brutus and the Arthurian legends to shape the nation's past. The invention of printing provided the means to satisfy the growing demand for this popular mythology among the educated middle class. One version of the story of Brutus and Arthur, Caxton's *Chronicles of England* (1480), was among the first books printed in English.

There are also cases of early and unusual interest in antiquities in central and eastern Europe. Some were purely mercenary. Finds of ancient silver coinage directly enriched the state treasury, so Gustav Vasa, king of Sweden, following a 1547 find of ancient coins in the Åland Islands, publicly proclaimed his interest in more such finds. At other times, it was the way finds manifested themselves that provoked curiosity, as with the 'mysterious' appearance of pots. In his *Historia Polonica*, the fifteenth-century chronicler Jan Długosz reported extraordinary occurrences near the town of Śrem, where whole ceramic vessels emerged from the ground as if by magic. At Śrem and other localities in western Poland such events had become commonplace, and there was a long-standing folk tradition about 'magic crocks' that sprang from the earth. In 1416, on the orders, and in the presence, of Władysław II Jagiello, king of Poland, excavations took place at Nochowo which unearthed some of these vessels.

This event marked one of the first conscious efforts to investigate the remains of eastern Europe's prehistoric inhabitants. The 'magic crocks' were probably cremation urns from the Late Bronze Age (1200–700 BC), almost certainly from one of the large cemeteries that are distributed widely across east-central Europe. Erosion of the soil covering the shallow pits in which the ash-filled pots were placed created the impression that they were rising from the ground by themselves.

'Magic crocks'. Pots emerging from the ground through the attentions of burrowing animals as if by magic in an illustration from the fifteenth-century manuscript *Le Livre des propriétés des choses* by Barthélemy de Glanville.

Chroniclers like Długosz were common in eastern Europe and they frequently set down legends about the cultural origins and homelands of the local people. Burial mounds were usually ascribed to pagans. Długosz pondered the origins of two massive burial mounds near Kraków, speculating that they housed the remains of the legendary Krak, whom he identified as a Roman in an attempt to connect the early Poles with classical antiquity. Megaliths, the great prehistoric stone monuments of the Baltic coast, were similarly attributed to pagan tribes or antediluvian giants. The German term *Hünenbett*, used to denote megalithic tombs, is derived from the Old German for 'giant's bed'.

There are also accounts of what we would now call 'historical archaeology'. In 1390, for instance, Prince Louis of Brzeg in Silesia undertook excavations at the Slavic stronghold at Ryczyn on the Oder to determine whether it had been the seat of the bishops of Wrocław (Breslau) three centuries earlier. Even in that era, as early as 1091, excavations were being carried out in Kiev in an attempt to find the grave of Theodosius, founder of the first Russian monastery. Battlefields too were studied, chroniclers noting piles of half-buried human bones at some sites. Yet overall such excavations were rare: this was an era in which magic and mystery were still the main explanatory tools.

Traces of palaeolithic (Old Stone Age) people were encountered repeatedly in central and eastern Europe, but, as in western Europe, their significance remained unrecognized until the second half of the nineteenth century. In eastern Europe, early finds were almost invariably linked to the discovery of mammoth bones of the last Ice Age. In 1679 a Cossack troop engaged in the digging of a mill dam near Khar'kov uncovered a collection of mammoth bones which, like finds of human and animal bones from caves and other sites in western Europe, were attributed to a giant. When the Cossack leader publicly exhibited a mammoth tooth several years later, Tsar Fyodor Alekseevich ordered excavation and measurement of the site, but this failed to produce more finds.

The Tsar's action set a pattern of state involvement in Russian archaeology that has continued to the present day. In 1718, Peter the Great issued instructions to civilian and military authorities throughout Russia to collect and record finds of 'ancient things in the soil, namely unusual stones, bones of animals, fish, or birds, unlike those we have now'. Among the discoveries brought to his attention were mammoth bones from the Don river, collected from what later became known as the concentration of open-air palaeolithic sites near the village of Kostyonki (*kost* is 'bone' in Russian). The Tsar personally examined some of the mammoth bones from Kostyonki, which he judged to be the remains of war elephants from a wandering army of ancient Greeks. In fact the bones had been collected by Ice Age people over 20,000 years ago, many of them to construct dwellings in a cold and treeless landscape.

For centuries, European farmers had been turning up humanly-flaked flints and polished stone implements as they ploughed their fields. Popular belief had explained them away as elf-shot or thunderbolts (*ceraunia*, as the ancient Greeks had christened them). This theory was given pseudo-scientific elaboration by some writers. In the mid-seventeenth century, one authority described their origin as 'generated in the sky by a fulgurous exhalation conglobed in a cloud by the circumposed humour'. Such obfuscation did not help in discovering the true nature of these strange objects. The Etruscans and Romans used ancient arrowheads and polished stone axes as amulets and folk belief ascribed magical powers to such stones well into modern times. In southern France until the late nineteenth century shepherds would often put a polished stone axe in a bag around the neck of a

This Neolithic chambered long barrow of *c.* 3500 BC in Oxfordshire, southern England, has been known since Anglo-Saxon times as Wayland's Smithy. The smith, Volund, was a northern god. According to legend, if a traveller's horse lost a shoe, he only had to leave the animal by the tomb and place a coin on a stone. When he returned, the horse would be shod, the money gone.

The first barrow at Wayland's Smithy was an ovoid mound, 16 metres (54 feet) long, covering a wooden mortuary structure with a stone floor. It contained fourteen bodies and was enclosed in sandstone boulders and chalk. Some years later, this original barrow was subsumed by the present wedge-shaped mound, 55 metres (180 feet) long, edged by a kerb of sandstone blocks and provided with flanking ditches on either side. The facade is impressive, made up of four – originally six – sarsen boulders, 3 metres (10 feet) high.

When excavated, the tomb proved to contain eight people, including a child.

leading ram to protect the flock, hang one in the sheepstalls or bury one on the threshold of the barn to protect the ewes from disease. They might even carry one themselves as a charm.

Beyond Europe

Similar beliefs existed in other parts of the world. In central Africa polished axes were thought to be thunderbolts, and carefully passed down from one generation to the next, while in west Africa perforated stones were called thunderstones (*kwes, sokpe, nyame akuma*). Two bored stones from the western shore of Lake Tanganyika were given to E. C. Hore, a master mariner on the 1877 London Missionary Society expedition, by local people who regarded them as messages from ancestors, keeping them carefully in baskets or small huts. Such oral traditions throughout the dark continent indicate that an interest in ancestors and relics from the past existed long before the arrival of Europeans.

The first recorded finds of polished stone axes in India, from the 1840s to the 1860s, all came from beneath trees in villages: Mahadeo or Mahadeva is generally worshipped in Indian villages under a peepul tree, and any polished stone axes found are placed under these trees even today. In North America too, Iroquoian sites of the fifteenth and sixteenth centuries AD sometimes contain projectile points, stone pipes and native copper tools made thousands of years earlier – clearly objects discovered in later centuries and retained for veneration. Mammoth molars were found and kept in the prehistoric, multi-storey pueblo of Paquime, in Chihuahua, Mexico, which was abandoned *c.* AD 1400. An Olmec stone mask was found as an offering at the Aztec Great Temple of Tenochtitlán (p. 22), despite being two thousand years older than the temple itself. In Peru, it is said too that Inka emperors kept collections of centuries-old Moche pottery – for its pornographic interest.

While commoners may display curiosity about the past, it is the élites in any society who have a vested interest in establishing their origins. Information about ancestors and lineage helps bolster status and keep social inferiors at a distance. In 1692, Japan's first recorded excavation took place when a regional *daimyo* or feudal lord dug two tombs to investigate a stone inscription. In southeastern Korea a similar excavation was undertaken by the father of a local governor in 1748: he excavated six ancient tombs to see if they were lost tombs of his ancestors from the Koryo dynasty (AD 918–1392).

The earliest form of Far Eastern antiquarianism can be traced to the Song dynasty of China (AD 960–1279). Confucianism was at this time undergoing a revival after having been eclipsed by Buddhism for several centuries. A reverence for the golden age of the past – an attitude developed by Confucius in the fifth century BC – was reinstated in Song China through the study and imitation of ancient bronzes preserved in private and imperial collections. Some thirty actual catalogues of ancient collections, including descriptions and drawings of objects, have survived from a total of 119 catalogue titles known from literary references.

The Vikings in North America

Historical documents indicate that Viking mariners reached Iceland by the ninth century AD, and that in the late tenth and early eleventh centuries Leif Erikson and others landed on Greenland. More controversial has been the putative presence of Vikings in North America, especially their settlement of an unknown land, 'Vinland', tentatively identified with the coast of Maine. The mystery has created pseudo-archaeology of the worst kind as well as some first class research.

On the negative side, a Viking presence has been inferred from the most un-Viking remains, such as, for example, the stone windmill of the colonial period in Newport, Rhode Island, that has been interpreted by some as a Viking church (although carbon dioxide bubbles in its mortar have been radiocarbon dated to AD 1650). Equally bogus is the 'Kensington Stone', a set of forged runic inscriptions found in Kensington, Minnesota, in the nineteenth century and claimed in some quarters to be authentic even now.

The real archaeological evidence that the Vikings reached North America comes from the site of L'Anse aux Meadows, a Norse settlement in northern Newfoundland, founded c. AD 1000. This contains remains of eight turf structures, including Scandinavian-style houses and a smithy, as well as indisputably Norse artifacts.

More ambiguously, on Ellesmere Island in the Canadian High Arctic, archaeologists have recovered Viking objects including pieces of a wooden box and barrels, iron and copper pieces, boat rivets and, most intriguingly, a piece of chain mail. Vikings might have come this far north but such artifacts could equally be no more than trade goods.

This limited contact with the New World lasted only a few centuries as the area's deteriorating climate prevented significant European settlement. In AD 983–85 Icelander Erik the Red became the first Scandinavian 'archaeologist' when he 'found tools and weapons of stone' in Greenland that he later compared with similar objects seen by his son in Vinland. This exercise led him correctly to conclude that 'Skraelings' (a term applied by Norsemen to the Eskimo they met in the New World) had formerly lived in Greenland.

The discovery of the east coast of north America by the Norseman Leif Erikson c. AD 985 was for long an episode consigned to the borderland between history and legend. According to the Icelandic *Saga of the Greenlanders*, a tale that assumed written form no earlier than AD 1200, Leif was the first European to set foot in Vinland (Vine or Berry Land), a land of frost-free winters, wild grapes and self-sown wheat; here he erected winter accommodation, returning to Greenland with his crew the following spring. Only in the 1950s did the saga accounts receive independent corroboration from archaeology, through the excavations at L'Anse aux Meadows in northern Newfoundland.

In Christian Krohg's romantic portrayal of the Viking landfall – painted in 1893 barely a decade after the discovery of the Gokstad ship – Leif grasps the steering oar of the pitching ship and points excitedly towards the promised land.

Chinese connoisseur. This late sixth-century painting by Tu Chin depicts a rich collector of ancient bronzes relaxing in his terraced garden. His latest acquisitions, displayed on a low table, are being covetously examined by a friend who is evidently an equally passionate collector.

The earliest, written by Lu Dalin in 1092, documents 210 bronzes and 13 jades dating from from the Shang to Han dynasties (1700 BC–AD 220). Imitations of these ancient forms were used in court rituals to legitimize and strengthen the Song government's rule.

In Japan, the principles of Confucian analysis – rational explanation of the natural world and its contents, accompanied by measurement, description and illustration – led to the emergence in the Edo period (1603–1868) of naturalists interested in rocks, herbs, fossils and archaeological artifacts. In the absence of the court records available for élite objects like bronzes, everyday objects like arrowheads or stone axes were explained differently in Japan from in the west.

In England, the Phoenicians, the Lost Tribes of Israel or the Druids were regularly invoked to explain prehistoric remains. In Japan, artifacts were attributed either to peoples mentioned in the first formal histories of Japan, compiled in the early eighth century AD, or to the aboriginal Ainu of Hokkaido island, who only came to the attention of urban Japanese culture in the nineteenth century. Archaeological objects were thought to be 'primitive' rather than 'prehistoric', the work of ancient historical peoples. For example, the Confucian historian Hakuseki Arai attributed the stone arrowheads of Japan to the 'Shukushinjin' – ancient inhabitants of Manchuria mentioned in Chinese historical sources – not then knowing of the prehistoric Jomon peoples who in reality made them between the tenth and fourth centuries BC. It took half a century of unsettling research to sever the link with the historical texts; the fully prehistoric nature of artifacts like these was not acknowledged in Japan until 1936 (p. 259).

THE SEARCH FOR A TIMESCALE

Although the idea that humankind was tens of thousands of years old had existed among the Greeks, Egyptians, Assyrians and Babylonians, as well as in ancient Mesoamerica, there was at this time no conception of prehistory in the scholarship of either west or east. The only framework for human affairs and the origins of the world was thought to lie in written documents, especially, in the west, the Bible. In modern times the claim, published in 1650 by James Ussher, Archbishop of Armagh, that the world was created at noon on 23 October 4004 BC has often been ridiculed. Such attempts to develop a chronology for all of human history were, however, a major focus of seventeenth-century scholarship, and Ussher was by no means the first to venture such a date. The Venerable Bede, the eighth-century English historian, placed the Creation in 3952 BC, while the estimate of 3761 BC stands in the Jewish calendar even today.

For its time, Ussher's figure was perfectly conventional. Contrary to popular misconception, he did not produce it by adding up the ages and dates of all the lineages in the Old Testament – this would have been impossible. Instead he compared the six days of God's creation with the 6,000 years envisaged for the earth's duration ('one day is with the Lord as a thousand years'), a then widely accepted scheme which implied that the earth was created 4,000 years before the birth of Christ and would endure 2,000 years after it. The extra four years came from the fact that Herod died in 4 BC, making that, paradoxically, the year of Christ's birth. Scholars like Bede had envisaged the Creation taking place in the spring, the appropriate season for birth. Others were proponents of the autumn because the Jewish year began then and Hebrew scriptures were the basis of the whole scheme. Ussher chose the first Sunday after the autumnal equinox (October in the old Roman calendar), and arbitrarily began his chronology with the creation of light, which he assumed must have occurred at noon. Other scholars, like the seventeenth-century divine, John Lightfoot, equally arbitrarily preferred the

morning. 'Heaven and earth, centre and circumference', wrote Lightfoot, 'were created all together in the same moment and clouds full of water ... This took place and man was created by the Trinity on 23 October 4004 BC, at nine o'clock in the morning.'

Today the calculations of Ussher and Lightfoot appear naive in the extreme (though even now there are some who regard the date of the Creation as fixed by faith alone). Yet these were intelligent scholars, whose conclusions were widely accepted in educated circles. Their naivety is understandable for two reasons. First, it was a feature of the age in which they lived to regard the Bible as God's infallible word, a text of supreme and unquestioned authority; and second, Ussher and Lightfoot were living in a pre-scientific age, before techniques had been developed that would allow a chronology to be built up on the basis of natural science rather than hallowed text.

These were the first glimmerings of understanding of the ancient past and the earliest attempts to place the history of humankind within a firm chronological framework. Even then, other pioneers were becoming aware that the soil could speak about the past as clearly as – and perhaps more reliably than – written texts. Ancient relics made, moreover, a profound impression on the imagination, increasing respect for one's predecessors and precipitating enjoyably melancholic reflection on the nature of time, death and life itself. As the doctor and antiquary Sir Thomas Browne wrote in 1652, on his discovery of burial urns in Norfolk:

> Unto these of our Urnes none here can pretend relation, and can only behold the Reliques of these persons, who in their life giving the laws unto their prede-cessors, after long obscurity, now lye at their mercies. But remembering the early civility they brought upon these Countreys, and forgetting long passed mischiefs, we mercifully preserve their bones and pisse not upon their ashes.

Opposite. A masterpiece of *Sturm und Drang*, William Blake's prophetic *The Ancient of Days* or *God creating the Universe* of 1794 epitomizes the biblical concept of Creation that held universal sway until the mid-nineteenth century.

Blake's immediate source of inspiration was probably Milton's *Paradise Lost* (vii, 225–7):

He took the gold'n Compasses, prepar'd
In God's Eternal Store, to circumscribe
This Universe, and all created things ...

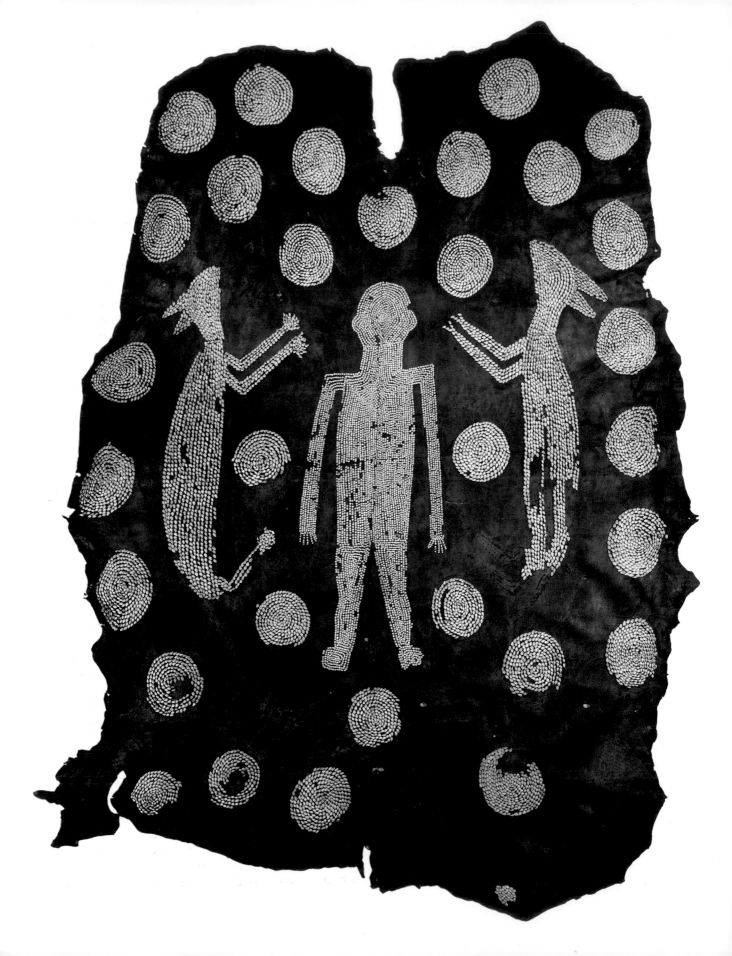

Old Worlds and New, *1500–1760*

CHAPTER 2

The era of European expansion overseas from the sixteenth to the eighteenth centuries saw the rise of antiquarianism – an increasing awareness of the remains of the past coupled with unprecedented revelations about far-off, exotic societies around the world. The peoples of the Americas in particular, in western terms so alien in looks, behaviour and way of life, soon came to be equated in culture and appearance with ancient peoples of the Old World known from classical sources.

ENCOUNTERS WITH OTHER CULTURES

By the end of the fifteenth century, European contact with the New World was increasing, with Italian explorers like John Cabot (Giovanni Caboto) and Christopher Columbus making landfalls, Cabot in the north on Cape Breton island in 1497, and Columbus in the Caribbean in 1492. When Columbus landed on the shores of the New World it caused an intellectual upheaval of, literally, biblical proportions. Nowhere in the Bible was there mention of the New World or its inhabitants, so debate immediately centred on whether or not the Native Americans (misnamed 'Indians') were human beings, and if so, how their existence could be explained. One popular theory – maintained even today by the Mormon church – was that they were descendants of the so-called Lost Tribes of Israel, whose expulsion by the Israelites from Canaan is described in the Book of Joshua.

Scarcely had the question of Indian humanity been addressed when Europeans received an even greater shock: the discovery in the New World of civilizations as advanced and as powerful as their own. In 1519 the Spaniard Hernán Cortés landed on the Yucatán peninsula, in what is today Mexico, to investigate tales of a major civilization many days travel into the interior of the country. Burning his ships behind him to inspire his men to pursue his objectives, he made alliances with local groups, people chafing under the yoke of the Mexica empire (popularly called the Aztecs – a name referring to a people under their domination – the rulers of this empire actually called themselves Mexica).

Cortés and his men were unprepared for what they encountered on reaching the heart of the empire: the great city of Tenochtitlán. After several attempts, Cortés captured the Mexica ruler, Moctezuma, and in 1521 successfully took control of the empire. However unwittingly, Cortés had come across a civilization as populous and complex as his own. Until then it had never occurred to the Europeans that there might exist civilizations of high splendour and wealth in what had been thought the territory of savages. The conquest of the Mexica inspired a generation of Spaniards to sail to the New World in search of great fortunes.

The same year that Cortés first encountered the Mexica, the Spanish established a ship-building settlement at Panama City, to facilitate exploration of the newly discovered Pacific Ocean. Soon they heard of another great civilization, to the south

Opposite. 'Powhatan's mantle'. Made from the hides of seven white-tailed deer, decorated with thousands of shells and measuring 2.35 metres (8 feet) by 1.6 metres (5 feet), this ceremonial mantle was the most renowned New World 'rarity' acquired in Britain in the early seventeenth century by the John Tradescants father and son, gardeners to King Charles I.

A visitor to the celebrated Musæum Tradescantianum at Lambeth in 1638 recorded seeing 'the robe of the King of Virginia', and the piece was later catalogued as 'Pohatan, King of Virginia's habit all embroidered with shells or Roanoke'.

Powhatan – properly Wahunsonacock, paramount chief of the Powhatan confederacy – was the father of Pocahontas, the Native American princess who embraced Christianity at Jamestown, married an Englishman and was brought to Britain in 1616; presented to James I and initially feted at court, she succumbed to smallpox the following year at the age of twenty-two.

With the rest of the Musæum Tradescantianum, 'Powhatan's mantle' passed in 1659 into the hands of the antiquary Elias Ashmole, and on his death in 1692 to the Ashmolean Museum, Oxford, as part of its founder's collection.

Tenochtitlán

When the Spanish conquistador Hernán Cortés reached the summit of the mountains on his journey toward the heart of the Mexica empire, he gazed down upon a vast plain, lying in the shadow of the great snow-capped volcanoes of Popocatépetl and Iztaccíhuatl, and surrounded by steep forested slopes. Five huge lakes filled the centre of the basin. The island city of Tenochtitlán, the Mexica capital, was a dazzling sight, adorned with dozens of towering pyramids, whitewashed and painted in brilliant colours, and provided with three great earthen causeways to link it to the mainland. Nothing the Spanish had been told had prepared them for this wondrous sight. Tenochtitlán, the living heir to over thirty centuries of Mesoamerican civilization, stood on the eve of its final destruction.

Founded in c. AD 1345, the city now lies almost completely hidden beneath the urban sprawl of modern Mexico City. Estimates of actual size are problematic but it is thought that, with its lake-shore suburbs, Tenochtitlán had a population of at least 200,000 people. Its territory was divided into four quadrants representing the division of the Mexica universe, each with its associated sign, colour and god. Like earlier Mesoamerican cities, it was also laid out on a grid that had symbolic, and possibly astronomical, meaning. At the centre of this symbolic universe, where the four quadrants intersected, was the most sacred precinct in the entire Mexica civilization, the heart of Tenochtitlán, where the most important religious buildings were located.

On the sacred central square stood the most impressive building in the entire city, a huge double pyramid, the Great Temple. Its remains were accidentally rediscovered by workers of the Mexico City Light and Power Company in 1978, and excavations were carried out over the next ten years progressively to expose the sacred precinct. The pyramid stood about five storeys tall, with two steep, parallel stairways up the front and two temple structures at the summit: one was devoted to Tlaloc, god of water and rain, the other to Huitzilopochtli, god of war. In front of each temple was a sacrificial stone over which human victims were stretched, their still-beating hearts torn from their chests by priests to be offered to the sun. It is said that after one remodelling of the Great Temple over eighty thousand people were sacrificed as part of the dedicatory ceremonies. It took four days to carry out the sacrifices and the temple was drenched in streams of human blood.

Other temples flanking the sacred square included those dedicated to Quetzalcoatl, the feathered serpent, god of the wind. Additional decoration was provided by great stone carvings, one a disc, nearly 10 feet (3 metres) in diameter, carved with a detailed representation of the Mexica calendar. One small temple represented a *tzompantli*, a skull rack with 240 human skulls carved in stone along its flanks. Such racks were used to display the severed skulls of sacrificial victims.

Also in the square was a ball court, the purpose-built venue for a ritual athletic contest of notable brutality played by two opposing teams with a large, solid rubber ball. Postgame ceremonies included the sacrifice of the losing team. Archaeological evidence indicates that the ball game – whose rules and purpose remain unknown – was played from the first millennium BC by cultures as distant in time and space as the Olmec, who lived along the Gulf coast 1200–400 BC, and the Maya, who occupied southern Mexico and Guatemala AD 300–900.

Surrounding Tenochtitlán along the shores of the lakes were *chinampas*, the 'floating gardens' of the Mexica. In the shallows, silt from the lake bottom was dug out and piled on reed mats to form long mounds that rose above the water level; both ends were anchored by trees, whose roots held both mats and soil in place. The waterways between the mounds provided access by canoe for the planting, fertilizing and harvesting of crops. Human excrement collected from the city was carried each morning by canoe to the chinampas where it was deposited, making the plots so fertile that they could be cropped continuously year after year.

Most common were the food plants that had sustained Mesoamerican culture for millennia: maize, beans, squash, tomatoes and chilli peppers.

along the west coast of South America, in a land called 'Biru'. As a result, in 1524 Francisco Pizarro embarked on the first of several expeditions that would result in the discovery and conquest of the Inka empire. The largest empire ever known in the New World, it included what are today Ecuador, Peru, Bolivia, northern Chile and northwestern Argentina.

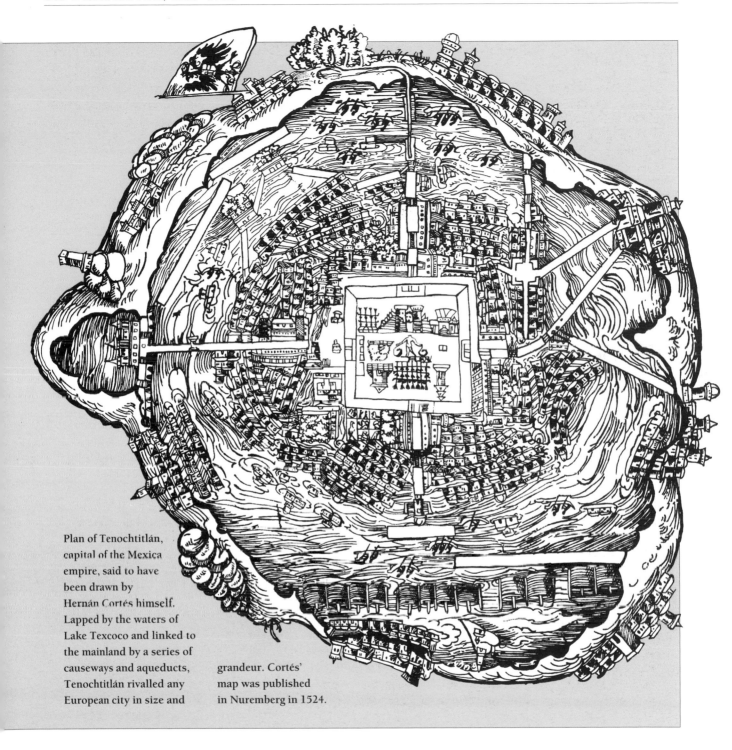

Plan of Tenochtitlán, capital of the Mexica empire, said to have been drawn by Hernán Cortés himself. Lapped by the waters of Lake Texcoco and linked to the mainland by a series of causeways and aqueducts, Tenochtitlán rivalled any European city in size and grandeur. Cortés' map was published in Nuremberg in 1524.

Before his successful third expedition Pizarro briefly returned to Spain, meeting Cortés, who encouraged him to persist with his efforts. So it was that on 16 November 1532, Pizarro came face to face with the Inka emperor, Atahuallpa, in the city of Cajamarca in northern Peru. Recently triumphant in a bloody civil war, Atahuallpa was surrounded by thousands of seasoned Inka soldiers, and saw little

Gold diggers of 1521. Contemporary drawing by Felipe Guaman Poma illustrating Spanish contact with the Inka. The Inka emperor (left) sits chatting with a Spaniard; behind them are Inka buildings, storehouses and a throne. In Quechua, the Inka is asking if the Spanish eat gold. The Spaniard is answering in the affirmative.

reason to fear the 150 strangers in his midst. It was a fatal error. Using the strategy that had worked so well for Cortés, Pizarro took the emperor prisoner at the first opportunity. Atahuallpa was held for a ransom of gold and silver that staggers the imagination: in modern currency the treasure would be worth over ten million pounds. As the precious metals poured into Cajamarca, the captive Inka emperor waited, whiling away the time playing chess, a game he learned, supposedly to excellent effect, from his friend Pizarro. Fearful of an Inka revolt, the Spanish in the end reneged on their agreement. Atahuallpa was strangled.

Other tales of great riches surfaced as the conquest of the Mexica and Inka gripped the Spanish imagination. Expeditions were sent out in search of great mythological civilizations such as El Dorado, in northern South America. Looking for Cibola, north of Mexico, the Spanish explorer Francisco Vázquez de Coronado in 1542 despatched an expedition to seek seven cities whose streets were held to be paved with gold. His men did encounter various pueblo groups in the American southwest, notably the Zuni of New Mexico who killed his agent, Esteban the Moor. But these were much simpler societies than the Mexica or the Inka; no golden cities were found, and the European search for fabulous riches began to fade.

The Catholic church had meanwhile established itself firmly in the Spanish possessions. A few priests wrestled with the philosophical issue of who the Indians were and where they came from, but others set about destroying all evidence of pagan idolatry. So many hundreds of written documents, both Mexica and Maya, were burned in Mesoamerica that today parts of only four major Maya codices survive. In Yucatán, however, bishop Diego de Landa took great interest in ancient Maya ruins, becoming the first European to appreciate the intricacies of the Maya calendar. This complex calendar was built on interlocking time cycles and astronomical observations, overlaid with a count of the number of days that had passed since the beginning of time. Maya dates were carved in hieroglyphic form on every major stone monument.

Another priest, Bartolomé de Las Casas, perceived that the living peoples around him were descended from the past cultures that had built the ancient ruins. He saw that complex societies could develop out of earlier, simpler ones; he was also a staunch defender of native rights, protecting the Indians from European abuses. In South America, Pedro de Cieza de León travelled through much of the former Inka empire, describing the places he visited en route. He noted major ruins like Wari and Tiahuanaco, capitals of pre-Inka empires, and was probably the first person to realize that other civilizations existed prior to the Inka. Records like these left by

Spanish priests and travellers constitute the earliest ethnographic accounts of the descendants of the great prehispanic civilizations of the Americas.

In North America early European contact took a different form. The major powers sought to exploit the continent for different reasons, using local tribes as mercenaries in war. The Spanish who arrived in large numbers during the sixteenth century – some travelling overland from Mexico into the Southwest, others by boat into Florida and adjacent parts of the Southeast – were primarily after gold. After Paul III's papal bull of 1537 decreed Native Americans to be human and therefore convertible, they sought also to win souls for Catholicism. The French, who despatched the explorer Jacques Cartier into the Gulf of St Lawrence during the

Cosmic conflict. In this detail from the Maya Codex Cospi, preserved today in Bologna, the planet Venus, Tlauixcalpantecuhtli, is shown attacking an ocelot warrior. Its spear has pierced the warrior's heart.

seven-year voyage he began in 1534, wanted to develop commercial resources such as fishing and the fur-trade – though their priests were not far behind. The English approach was essentially pragmatic and secular: they were interested in the lands of Canada for the fur trade and the eastern seaboard for land and settlement.

The attitudes of early Europeans towards the aboriginals they encountered varied. On the one hand, Native Americans were considered inhuman savages without the thinnest veneer of civilization, on the other as noble savages rich in the natural qualities that decadent Europeans had lost. Cotton Mather, an American clergyman remembered for writing 382 books and the arrogant piety with which he conducted the Salem witch trials of 1692, believed the Indians to be too inhuman even to be convertible to Christianity. In marked contrast, early nineteenth-century painters like George Catlin of Pennsylvania portrayed the Plains Indians of the middle Missouri as romantic warriors distinguished by their dignity and courage; he even took three parties of Indians on a tour of the courts of Europe to drum up public sympathy for their plight. Both attitudes were unrealistic, and either way the Native Americans were treated unfairly.

European impressions of the Indians were distorted through judging them by European rather than Indian values. The attitude of eighteenth-century fur-traders to Indian women provides a striking example. In the Europe of that time, a woman was seen as an ornament to a man; a woman who worked, especially manually, was considered inferior to one who did not. This judgement was transferred directly to Plains women, who worked but were independent and often physically strong, running the domestic side of village life, and tanning and preparing animal skins. Societies where women played such roles were, by extension, considered 'primitive and little evolved'.

CONTACT WITH THE EAST

First-hand European acquaintance with Asia was intimately tied to trade and politics. The Italian merchant-cities of Venice and Genoa at this time dominated European trade in the eastern Mediterranean. In exchange for military assistance to the Byzantine empire and the Crusader kingdoms in the twelfth and thirteenth centuries, the two cities had won special trading privileges with ports like Alexandria, Constantinople and Tripoli. Through these great centres of exchange Europe gained access to the overland and maritime commerce of Asia that brought silk and fine cotton textiles, pepper and spices, precious stones, porcelain and other luxury goods from China and India. By the end of the fourteenth century, Venice enjoyed a monopoly of trade in the eastern Mediterranean, while Genoa controlled access to overland routes through the Black Sea.

Over time, commercial, military and diplomatic contact sparked increased European interest in Asia. Travellers to China, like Marco Polo in the thirteenth century, brought home descriptions of Mesopotamia, Persia and India. Diplomatic missions, like the Papal embassies to the Mongols in the thirteenth and fourteenth centuries, also returned with detailed reports. Most accounts addressed contemporary conditions, but ancient places were mentioned even then. Benjamin of Tudela, a rabbi in Moslem Spain, undertook a world tour in the years 1160–73. In Mesopotamia, he identified and cursorily described Nineveh and Babylon: 'The ruins thereof are thirty miles in extent', he wrote. 'The ruins of the palace of Nebuchadnezzar are still to be seen there, but people are afraid to enter them on account of the serpents and scorpions.'

The pace of discovery accelerated after 1498, the year Vasco da Gama landed in Calicut on India's southwest coast, opening up the maritime route round Africa. In return, Portugal's European rivals intensified exploration of overland routes from the eastern Mediterranean to the Indian Ocean and Central Asia. Trade between Europe and Asia by way of the Persian Gulf and the Mediterranean continued throughout the sixteenth century. The Ottoman rulers, who had replaced the Byzantines as the dominant power in the eastern Mediterranean, granted special privileges to foreigners to stimulate commerce, and communities of foreign merchants sprang up in the main towns of the Levant at which caravans of

Opposite. Noble savages or brutal barbarians? 'How Outina's men treated the slain of the enemy', an engraving from Le Moyne's *America* (1591), revels in the perceived brutality of the North American Indians.

'In their skirmishes, any who fall are instantly dragged off by persons detailed for the purpose; who, with slips of reed sharper than any steel blade, cut off the skin of the head to the bone, from front to back, all the way round, and pull off with the hair, more than a foot and a half long, still adhering, done up in a knot on the crown ... Then ... they dig a hole in the ground, and make a fire ... and then dry these scalps to a state as hard as parchment. They also are accustomed, after a battle, to cut off with these reed knives the arms of the dead near the shoulders, and their legs near the hips, breaking the bones, when laid bare, with a club, and then to lay these fresh broken, and still running with blood, over the same fires to be dried. Then hanging them, and the scalps also, to the ends of their spears, they carry them off home in triumph'.

Biblical imagery. Early archaeological exploration of the Near East was fuelled largely by curiosity about biblical sites like Babylon, and its Tower of Babel. Painting by Pieter Brueghel the Elder (c. 1515–69).

eastern goods arrived. Some venturesome European merchants travelled into Mesopotamia and Persia, even to India, encountering ruined ancient cities in these distant regions.

Europeans were already familiar with biblical sites near the Mediterranean coast. Palestine in particular attracted pilgrimages and the curiosity of devout Christians. Observers such as Henry Maundrell, an English chaplain in Aleppo during the late seventeenth century, investigated ruins like Baalbek, the massive Roman temple in

the Biqa'a valley of Lebanon. Individual merchants even began acquiring coins, inscriptions and other antiquities – though the intensity of their efforts did not match the wholesale ransacking of western Turkey for Greek and Roman statuary destined to grace aristocratic gardens in England (p. 34).

Farther east, the problems of identifying Babylon and Persepolis were often raised in travellers' accounts, the first direct encounter between western culture and the ancient civilizations of the Near East. The Bible remained the main source of historical information for understanding the monuments of Mesopotamia and Persia, but the revival of classical learning in the Renaissance had made more available the Greek and Roman writings about these once great cities. Leonhart Rauwolff, a physician from Augsburg who travelled through Syria, Palestine and Mesopotamia in 1573–76, identified as the Tower of Babel Aqar Quf (the ancient Dur Kurigalzu, whose ruined ziggurat still rises 55 metres (180 feet) above the ground). Recalling the Bible, he saw the ruined 'Babylon' as a 'most terrible example to all impious and haughty tyrants'. A decade later, the English merchant John Eldred described the Tower of Babel as covering a quarter of a mile to a side and constructed of sun-dried bricks laid with a mat of reeds between courses; Eldred compared the ziggurat's height to that of the newly built St Paul's Cathedral in London. John Cartwright, another English merchant and cleric, spent several days at Babylon, which he found to be an extremely large but shapeless mound. Viewing Babylon led him (in *The Preacher's Travels*, 1611) to ponder the evanescence of life:

> now we may justly aske. what is become of this proud city, which once held the
> world in awe? Where are her conduits, the rarenesse of her bathes, the hugenesse
> of these towers, the greatnesse of her Temples, the beauty of her princely palaces,
> & a number of other monuments of her kings vanities? Alas! time hath worne
> them out: and we may say:
>> Why wonder we that men doe die?
>> Since monuments decay,
>> And towers fall, and founders names,
>> Doe perish cleane away.

Cartwright also visited Persepolis, which he knew from Greek descriptions. He encountered 'the ruines of many ancient monuments' across the Persepolis plain, among them 'the ruines of a goodly Pallace, built as they say by King Cyrus' and 'a mountaine, on which was erected a goodly Chappell, in which most of the Persian kings in anticke time were intombed.'

Several years later, in 1615, the great Italian traveller Pietro della Valle made a pilgrimage to the Holy Land and then toured widely through western Asia and lived a year in India. Returning to Rome after a decade, he brought with him inscribed bricks from Babylon and Ur, and copies of an inscription found at Persepolis. His inscriptions made Europe aware for the first time – if only as a curiosity – of cuneiform writing, the wedge-shaped script of ancient Mesopotamia.

Giant griffin at Persepolis. Founded by the Achaemenid king Darius *c.* 518 BC, captured and burnt by Alexander the Great in 330 BC, the ruins of Persepolis drew many seventeenth-century travellers to Persia.

Most influential of all was the description left by Thomas Herbert who in 1627 travelled the length of Shah Abbas' kingdom – a round trip of 2900 kilometres (1800 miles) – in the company of James I's new ambassador to Persia, Sir Dodmore Cotton. The ambassador died en route.

Herbert's vivid account of the landscape of southern Persia and of the ruins of Persepolis, with its maze of columned buildings standing on a massive stone terrace, was a revelation to English readers when published on his return.

The accumulation of information at this time was haphazard, resulting from the whims of individual travellers. Yet as early as the mid-seventeenth century the first stirrings of a more systematic antiquarian interest in the Near East appeared. Europe's earliest learned societies began to furnish travellers going east with lists of pressing questions, some of them concerning ancient places. The Royal Society in London, for instance, drew up questions about Persepolis in 1667 for a merchant who was going to Shiraz in Persia. Other merchants, seized with curiosity, took the initiative themselves. Two such men, on hearing rumours of a ruined city in the Syrian desert, attempted to travel there. Blocked in their first attempt (in 1678) by unsettled conditions, they eventually reached what proved to be the ancient caravan city of Palmyra in 1691. Their account of this journey, published by the Royal Society in 1695, describes the monuments they encountered; it can be considered the first specifically archaeological expedition in the Near East.

INDIA AND THE FAR EAST

Europeans encountered India and its past at the time the subcontinent was first colonized. Dissatisfied with their share of overland trade with Asia, first England and Holland (in 1600 and 1602), then France (1664), established East India companies to vie for shares in Portugal's maritime trade. These companies sought to break the Portuguese stranglehold over the Indian Ocean by combining commerce with military operations, and by the end of the seventeenth century all three were firmly established in India and southeast Asia. By the time rule over India was transferred from the East India Company to the British crown in 1858, the company had secured direct or indirect rule over almost the entire sub-continent, establishing British agents and residencies in surrounding regions such as Mesopotamia, where the British residency in Baghdad played a pivotal role in the archaeological exploration of the region during the nineteenth century.

The colonial presence of the Portuguese and other Europeans facilitated the investigation of the ancient monuments of South Asia. The temples of India, with their alien design, sculpture and rituals, attracted early attention – those cut into rock at Elephanta, Kanheri and Ellora in western India excited frequent comment, alternating admiration and disgust. Dom João de Castro, a sixteenth-century Portuguese viceroy in Goa, was so impressed by Kanheri that he judged it 'almost one of the seven wonders of the world'. In contrast, the Portuguese physician Garcia da Orta viewed the rock-cut temples near Bombay with revulsion in 1534, even while admitting their beauty: 'Certainly [Elephanta] is a sight well worth seeing, and it would appear that the devil has used all his powers and knowledge to deceive the gentiles into his worship.' This attitude towards ancient Indian monuments continued well into the eighteenth century. Moses' *Sketches of India* (1750) dismisses the temples as barbarous, 'once polluted by the exercise of a vile and debasing superstition, and crowded by a degraded multitude – who were even, we may conclude, little better than the people of Sodom, and like unto those of Gomorrah'.

Such reactions inevitably sprang from encounters with an exuberant cultural tradition for which the biblical and classical heritage of western Europe provided little preparation. Some suggested that the style of sculpture in the rock-cut temples was derived from Greek models after Alexander the Great's invasion of north India in the fourth century BC. Other writers thought the Indian monuments had been borrowed from China's little-known ancient civilization. In fact, the temples of western India had been built during the second half of the first millennium AD: they included Hindu and Jain constructions but most were Buddhist in origin. Yet this only became clear much later. European knowledge of Indian history and culture remained minimal for the next century and a half.

Portuguese voyages beyond the Indian Ocean in the seventeenth century also brought them into contact with early states in southeast Asia. Rather than destroying them, as the Spanish had done with the high cultures of the New World,

the Portuguese negotiated trading treaties with local courts, restricting their use of force to the takeover of existing ports. Yet, as in India, native art was greeted with incredulity. In the early 1600s, the earliest Portuguese visitors to encounter the remains of early Khmer monuments in Cambodia, for example at Angkor, had difficulty in crediting their indigenous nature: one author attributed them to Alexander the Great while another credited the Jews 'who settled in China'. Such conclusions reflected the general western reluctance to acknowledge that easterners too had the power and capacity to create high civilization and art.

The experience of encountering other cultures was not, however, limited to the fifteenth and sixteenth centuries nor to Europeans. Most of the great early Mediterranean empires – such as those of Alexander the Great and the Romans – brought about collisions between large bureaucratic states and cultures existing at lower levels of development. In Asia too, the imperial expansion of the Han dynasty (206 BC–AD 220) brought Chinese courtiers into contact with many unfamiliar cultures. Because emissaries were routinely sent to investigate these peoples and their customs, Han dynastic records contain long ethnographic descriptions. Among the Samhan of the southern Korean peninsula, it was recorded, for example, that 'young, healthy youths of Mahan put wood rods into holes made on their backs and bound them with straw rope, but felt no pain, even though they worked all day long with the rods on their backs.' This passage is interpreted as describing the wooden A-frame back-racks in which even today Korean farmers carry loads to and from the fields.

THE SURVIVAL OF THE CLASSICAL

Many of the medieval cities of Europe – London, York, Paris, Lyon, Mainz, Cologne – were built on the sites of early classical foundations. In Britain the anonymous *Life of Saint Cuthbert* of c. 700 tells how the saint visited the remains of Carlisle (ancient *Lugovalium*), marvelling 'at the city wall and the well formerly built in a wonderful manner by the Romans'. Some large buildings were turned into churches and, at Arezzo in modern Tuscany, Roman granaries were still being used as housing in the ninth century. In Rome itself the triumphal arches of Titus, Septimius Severus and Constantine were turned into fortresses, probably in the twelfth century. The debris from such later building and construction brought to light much of earlier Roman civilization, and as certain wealthy families started to display and collect, the habit was picked up by those visiting Italy from northern Europe.

The discovery of Greek and Roman sculpture also inspired contemporary artists to study and copy the classical form: schools of sculptors learnt to recreate classical carvings using elaborate measuring techniques. Such developments were, moreover, just part of a wider educational emphasis on the classics amongst the European aristocracy. By the late seventeenth century, a gentleman's education was based firmly on study of the art, language, literature and history of the classical world – a pattern that endured for more than two hundred years.

Opposite. Angkor Thom. These ornate bas-reliefs on the Terrace of the Leper King look much as they did when first seen by the earliest Portuguese visitors to Cambodia.

Capital of the Khmer state of Kambuja, occupying most of southern Indo-China between the ninth and fourteenth centuries AD, the Angkor region houses two ancient walled cities, the moats of the later nested within those of the earlier: Yasodharapura, built by the Khmer king Yasovarman I (r. 889–900), and Angkor Thom, whose central monument, the Bayon, was built by King Jayavarman VII (r. 1181–1219?).

The Bayon, described as a 'flower of stone', served as physical centre of the capital and philosophical centre of the world. The face of Jayavarman VII is inscribed onto all four sides of each of many of the monument's towers, keeping watch over the world, and his countenance appears on the Buddha sculpture lodged inside the monument, commemorating the King's divinity. All around the Bayon's exterior are galleries of sculptures and friezes illustrating great battles, lordly processions and festival scenes.

Like ancient Maya centres in Mesoamerica, Angkor consists of many temples but few secular structures: elites and commoners resident at the site probably lived in ephemeral buildings of wood and thatch among the great stone structures.

Thomas Howard, Earl of Arundel

The discovery in the ruins of Rome of marble statues, like the famous Laocoön recovered in 1506 that so excited Michelangelo, stimulated the formation of aristocratic collections of sculpture. The growing fashion for English gentlemen to travel in Italy was increasingly accompanied by a desire to 'discover' ancient works of art that could be shipped home to dignify house or garden.

One of the earliest collectors was Thomas Howard (1585–1646), son of Philip, Earl of Arundel. In 1612, Howard was advised by his doctors to travel abroad, and on this tour came to Rome. With permission from the papal authorities, he conducted 'excavations' in the course of which he 'discovered' a buried room containing Roman portrait sculptures. These sculptures, probably planted for his benefit, were thereafter supplemented by purchases, gifts from other collectors and new sculptures commissioned in the style of the antique. To house his growing collection, Howard, by now the second Earl of Arundel, added a long sculpture gallery to Arundel House in London.

In 1621 Howard commissioned Sir Thomas Roe, ambassador to the Sublime Porte (the Ottoman court at Constantinople), to collect sculpture on his behalf, and later sent his chaplain, William Petty, to Constantinople also. In an attempt to acquire fourth-century Theodosian reliefs from the Porta Aurea that had been built into the Turkish fortress of Yedikule, Howard's agents engaged an *imam* to condemn the reliefs as idolatrous – the hope being that they would be removed and dumped, and so retrieved for Arundel House. The plan failed. As a last resort Roe and Petty approached the Grand Treasurer, but a popular riot put an end to that design.

Petty then travelled along the western coast of Anatolia, only to be shipwrecked, losing his entire cargo of sculpture. However, at Izmir (Smyrna) his luck improved and he was able to purchase a substitute collection, originally intended for another connoisseur, de Peiresc. This was shipped back to England without mishap and published in 1628 as the *Marmora Arundeliana*.

The Arundel Marbles' 250 Greek inscriptions, the first to reach Britain, aroused particular interest. In addition, the collection included 37 statues, 28 busts, and miscellaneous antiquities like sarcophagi and altars. Among these were part of the hellenistic Gigantomachy relief from the Great Altar at Pergamon, a monumental depiction of the battle of the Gods against the Giants.

With Arundel's death in 1646 interest waned and the collection was damaged, one important Greek inscription even being turned into a hearthstone. After the Restoration,

in 1667, some of it was given at the instigation of the diarist John Evelyn to the University of Oxford to be displayed around the outside of the Sheldonian Theatre. Further damage prompted a transfer to the Ashmolean Museum, where the nucleus of the collection was reassembled in the eighteenth century after the demolition of Arundel House.

Thomas Howard, second earl of Arundel, painted by Daniel Mytens *c.* 1618 with part of the pioneering collection of sculptures and inscriptions assembled for him by agents in Italy, Greece and the eastern Aegean. The antiquities adorned Arundel House, just south of the Strand in London, where they made a profound impression on visitors. The philosopher Francis Bacon 'coming into the Earl of Arundel's garden, where were a great number of ancient statues of great men and women, made a stand, and as astonished, cried out "The Resurrection"'.

More surprisingly, the humbler aspects of classical archaeology were already receiving attention in western Europe at this time. In 1603 John Stow described pots he had acquired from a Roman cemetery at Spitalfields in London, and in 1677 John Conyers, a London apothecary and antiquary, made accurate drawings of Roman pottery kilns he saw during groundbreaking for the construction of new St Paul's Cathedral:

> The form of a killn in wich the olde Romans' lamps, urns and other earthen potts & vessels were burnt, & some left in the kiln; & that within a unstired loamy ground about 26 foote deep … the discovery made Anno 1677 at the digging the foundations of the north east cross part of St Paull's London … so many foote storeys or depths of coffins lay over this loamy killn, the lowest coffins made of chalk & thus supposed to be before or about Domitian ye emperor's tyme.

THE FIRST ANTIQUARIES

In Europe, the ever-growing interest in national origins did not long remain satisfied with legends and fanciful stories. Despite Francis Bacon's observation that 'the most ancient times (except what is preserved of them in scriptures) are buried in silence and oblivion', with the expansion of education, literacy and book-learning, people began to look for more solid grounds for historical belief.

A crucial change in northwest Europe came in the sixteenth century, when people first began to recognize that information about the prehistory and early history of their homelands could be derived from study of field monuments. This new interest led to the appointment of John Leland as King's Antiquary by Henry VIII in 1533. Leland had a scholarly upbringing, first at St Paul's school in London, then at the universities of Cambridge, Oxford and Paris. Upon his appointment, he first concentrated on seeking forgotten documents in monastic and college libraries, 'to the intente that the monuments of auncient writers … mighte be brought owte of deadely darkenes to lyvely light.' By 1540 he had embarked on a lengthy tour of England and Wales, visiting and describing monuments, 'and noted in so doing a whole world of things very memorable.'

This promising start was followed up by the Tudor antiquary and historian William Camden, who in 1586 published *Britannia*, the first general account of early British remains. Stonehenge was included, as was Hadrian's Wall, the stone and earth fortification built by the emperor Hadrian (AD 117–38) to form the northern boundary of Roman Britain. Camden refers to it as the 'Picts' Wall', commenting that it was already a notable monument in the eighth century when Bede wrote his *Ecclesiastical History*. His description is, however, based on personal observation:

> Verily have I seen the tract of it over the high pitches and steepe descent of hills, wonderfully rising and falling: and where the fields lye more plaine and open, a broad and deepe ditch without, just before it, which now in many places is

William Camden (1551–1623), painted by Gheeraerts in 1609.

Ole Worm's Cabinet of Curiosities, from *Musei Wormiani Historia*, 1655.

grounded up: and within a banke or military high-way, but in most places interrupted. It had many towres or fortresses, about a mile distant from another, which they call castle-steeds … also turrets standing between these, wherein souldiers being placed might discover the enemies, and be ready to set upon them.

Later investigations have borne out Camden's description. Milecastles are placed along the wall at intervals of a Roman mile, with smaller towers or turrets between them, and there is a military road and an earthwork (*vallum*) running parallel behind it, much as he describes. *Britannia* also includes engravings of a number of Roman inscriptions from sites on and around Hadrian's Wall and uses these to throw light on the origins and history of the fortification.

These first British antiquaries established a tradition that was to last over two hundred years. It was a development soon mirrored in other parts of northwest Europe. In Scandinavia, for example, national awareness was heightened by the political separation of Denmark and Sweden in 1503. By the following century both countries could boast distinguished antiquaries – Johan Bure in Sweden and Ole Worm in Denmark – who documented ancient remains (notably stones bearing runes) and assembled important collections of antiquities. Bure was tutor to the young Gustavus Adolphus, king of Sweden 1611–32, who encouraged the study of

Swedish antiquities and appointed Bure *Riksantikvariat* (Royal Antiquary). Worm, son of the mayor of Aarhus, trained as a doctor and became physician to King Christian IV of Denmark; a true polymath, he also taught as professor of humanities and later of Greek at the University of Copenhagen. Worm assembled a museum of natural and artificial curiosities, including ancient artifacts, and attempted to draw up a systematic inventory of Danish antiquities by means of a royal circular sent to all clergymen. Church authorities were asked to enquire in their parishes about reports of archaeological finds and to ask clergy to draw up local lists of ancient monuments. These appeals were renewed several times in the course of the next century. A royal proclamation of 1684 declared in addition that finds of ancient metal objects must be offered to the crown, thus perpetuating the laws of 'treasure trove' that can be traced back to the thirteenth century in Denmark, and to the twelfth in Britain.

In Germany, too, the sixteenth and early seventeenth centuries witnessed a new interest in national antiquities. Here antiquaries had the advantage of a helpful classical text: the *Germania*, a memorable account of the early Germans written in the first century AD by the Roman historian Tacitus. Though it took more than two centuries for the biblical chronology of the Creation to be superseded by a strictly archaeological approach, the foundations had been laid for a new understanding of the European past.

The seventeenth and eighteenth centuries saw more systematic interest in archaeological remains. In particular, the pioneering Swedish antiquarian Olof Rudbeck was one of the first people to treat excavation like anatomical dissection, not simply retrieving objects from the ground but noting their relationships to different layers of soil and publishing stratigraphic sections of the monuments he investigated.

Treasure trove. Fifteenth-century illuminated manuscript showing a peasant who has found a pot filled with gold coins while digging with a hoe; two more pots stand beside the hole.

Burying money and plate in the ground for safety was common practice in the days before banks, particularly in time of emergency. Recovering them could be more difficult. Scared by reports of Dutch ships on the Thames in June 1667, the diarist Samuel Pepys' wife and father buried bags of gold coins in his garden. Only four months later Pepys had endless trouble locating them.

'My father and I with a dark lantern, it being now night, went into the garden with my wife, and there went about our great work to dig up my gold. But Lord! what a tosse I was for some time in, that they could not justly tell me where it was; that I began heartily to sweat, and be angry, that they should not agree better on the place, and at last to fear that it was gone; but by and by, and by poking with a spit, we found it.'

The bags, though, had disintegrated. Even after sieving the soil, Pepys was unable to recover all his gold.

Opposite. American Indian chief, *c.* 1585, by the Elizabethan explorer and artist, John White. White was one of the first Europeans to draw Native Americans and his pictures directly shaped western perceptions of what their own prehistoric ancestors would have looked like. In particular, the tattooing and body painting White encountered in Virginia matched the accounts of Picts and ancient Britons left by classical authors. He was struck by 'the manner of their attire and painting themselues when they goe to their generall huntings or at theire Solemne feasts'.

In central and eastern Europe early antiquaries followed a pattern similar to that in western Europe, collecting relics and investigating obvious field monuments. The megalithic tombs and stone circles that attracted particular attention in Britain, France, Spain and Scandinavia were largely absent further east. Antiquaries therefore concentrated their attention on the burial mounds that abounded throughout the region, on Iron Age and Slavic strongholds with bank-and-ditch fortifications, and on the forts and camps of the *limes*, the Roman boundary with the barbarian world that ran from Holland along the Rhine and Danube to the Black Sea.

One extraordinary personality in the archaeology of the period in east-central Europe was Jan Johnston, a seventeenth-century physician of Scottish descent who was born in northwestern Poland. He was educated in Toruń and later travelled widely to England, Holland and Silesia. Johnston, in his 1632 volume *Thaumatographia Naturalis*, noted that 'the clay vessels found in the ground were burial urns, inside are the bones of the dead. In all … were ashes, and in some, rings. The ancients, we know, had the custom of burning the body and burying the cremated bones.' Thus, what for two centuries had been characterized as 'magic crocks' were now rationally explained as prehistoric urn burials.

Johnston is thought to have seen a number of excavated urns in the library in Toruń and to have read about ancient germanic burial customs in the works of earlier authors like the sixteenth-century German mineralogist Georg Agricola, eventually making connections between the two. In other works, he reflects on the development of human culture, advancing the idea of progress and cultural change over time. Though not fully realized, such ideas clearly presage the emergence of evolutionary thought in the nineteenth century.

PREHISTORY EMERGES

A further major advance in the study of prehistory came about with the construction of Louis XIV's great new palace at Versailles. The Sun King's grandiose ambitions led indirectly to one of the earliest recorded excavations in the history of European archaeology.

The year was 1685, the place Cocherel, in southern Normandy. By royal command, a local nobleman, Robert Le Prévôt, was seeking stone to repair a lock gate on the River Eure. This would normally have been an easy task: the stone would have come from a local quarry. However, in 1685 the project at Versailles, and the massive aqueduct it called for, was consuming every block of stone in the region. Fortunately, another source was to hand, on Le Prévôt's own land. Near the top of a slope, overlooking the river, two slabs of stone stood poking out of the soil. Assembling a band of workmen, Le Prévôt soon had these disinterred, only to find a third slab, previously hidden, alongside; this too was dug out, to reveal human bones six feet below the surface. At this point the stone-breaking operation was transformed into a careful archaeological excavation. Le Prévôt and his team, consumed by interest in their discovery, abandoned their original intention and began the painstaking recording and recovery of a prehistoric chambered tomb. By the end they had found the remains of twenty skeletons, together with stone axes, pottery vessels and a mass of ash.

Le Prévôt's discovery at Cocherel is memorable not just for what he found – a Late Neolithic collective tomb of megalithic slabs. What is truly remarkable is the way he performed the excavation, with painstaking care worthy of twentieth-century techniques, and the minute detail in which he recorded his discoveries. Unlike most of his contemporaries, he was not attracted by a lust for buried treasure, but by a genuine desire to understand the monument he had unearthed. It is this, above all, which makes his discovery a major landmark in the history of European archaeology.

Although the Sun King's Versailles aqueduct was never in fact completed, the significance of the Cocherel excavation lived on into the following century. In 1719 Le Prévôt's brother, Dom Bernard de Monfaucon, a Benedictine priest who wrote books on ancient monuments, used the stone axes from the site to ascribe all such tombs to 'some barbarous Nation, that knew not yet the Use either of Iron or of any metal'. This recognition of a pre-metal age formed the cornerstone on which the chronology of European pre-history was built.

Almost equally important was the discovery of the true nature of early stone tools. The clues had long been there, in the flaked and polished stone artifacts brought back by European explorers from the Americas, but only a few sixteenth-century scholars drew the logical conclusion that comparable stone tools found in Europe must be human artifacts. Among them were the mineralogist Georg Agricola, and Michel Mercati, physician to Pope Clement VII and superintendent of the Vatican Botanical Gardens. Mercati undertook an inventory of the Vatican's collections, which included *ceraunia* and flint arrowheads, and decided that they had been humanly made, in a time before iron. A plate in his *Metallotheca*, published posthumously in 1717, includes a typical Upper Palaeolithic blade (p. 52).

It was only towards the end of the seventeenth century that such ideas began to achieve general acceptance. Le Prévôt's discoveries at

Cocherel provided important confirmation that such flaked and polished stones were indeed early tools. Then, in 1720, the German antiquarian A. A. Rhode published an account of his own pioneering attempts to make flint objects and reconstruct the manufacturing techniques of the ancients. 'Thunderbolts' similar to the ones he replicated so successfully had been collected for centuries, ending up in cabinets of curiosities from the Renaissance onwards. The final leap came just a few years later, in 1723, when the Frenchman, Antoine de Jussieu, compared the 'thunderstones' in such cabinets with stone axes known to come from Canada and the Caribbean. Like Mercati and de Monfaucon before him, de Jussieu attributed the thunderbolts to a remote period when iron was unknown; unlike them, he was able to back up his idea of a Stone Age by applying ethnographic observation to prehistoric remains – a technique that has otherwise only been fully exploited in the last fifty years.

A rather different application of New World ethnography is that of the artist John White who, in 1585, went with Raleigh to Virginia, and drew not only Indians but also imaginary reconstructions of ancient Britons and Picts; his ancient and modern peoples show many features in common, the one directly modelled on the other. The Dutch artist Lucas de Heere also rendered American Indians as ancient Britons at about the same time. Native Americans thus came to be used as direct sources of analogy and information on the appearance and tools of ancient Europeans: in fact, concluded the antiquary John Aubrey in 1659, the ancient Britons of Wiltshire 'were 2 or 3 degrees, I suppose, less savage than the Americans.'

AUBREY AND STUKELEY

Aubrey was the leading figure of seventeenth-century antiquarianism in Britain. This 'colourful but rather sad figure' was a 'squire fallen on evil days' who spent much of his life in lawsuits or hiding from creditors. A gifted raconteur, he made many friends, immortalized in the short sketches he wrote of them in *Brief Lives*. He began his researches into prehistoric monuments while a gentleman of independent means, continuing until the 1670s when debts reduced him to such a condition of poverty that even his books were forfeit. Through the generosity of friends like Thomas Hobbes and the antiquary Elias Ashmole, Aubrey nonetheless managed to continue studying the monuments of his native Wiltshire and preparing impressive plans of the prehistoric stone circles of Stonehenge and Avebury. Though his greatest work, the *Monumenta Britannica*, lay unpublished until recently, Aubrey's observations were accurate, his conclusions influential. Where he went wrong was in interpreting stone circles as druid temples.

This theory, firmly fixed in the popular imagination until the present day, was further developed by Aubrey's distinguished successor, William Stukeley. Stukeley was first a doctor, then a clergyman, and one of the most colourful of early antiquarians. Like Aubrey, he was an acute observer. He appreciated the time-depth of the landscape, noting, for example, that Silbury Hill (an enormous prehistoric mound

The Wicker Image.

The entrance hall of the old British Museum, Montagu House, opened to the public on 15 January 1759. The present museum stands on the same seven acre site in Bloomsbury acquired from Ralph Montagu, along with his fine but decaying mansion, for £10,250 five years earlier.

Initially the collections were organized into three departments: Printed Books, Manuscripts, and Natural & Artificial Productions. Drawing on a fund of £95,194.8s.2d raised through a lottery, the Museum acquired at the outset – aside from the immense Sloane collection – two major groups of manuscripts: the Harleian collection, purchased for £10,000, and the Cotton collection, which included the Lindisfarne Gospels, the manuscript of *Beowulf* and two of the four surviving copies of Magna Carta.

King George II donated the Royal Library in 1757, a gift followed up in 1823 with 62,250 volumes and 19,000 unbound pamphlets that had belonged to George III.

In 1772 the Museum purchased Sir William Hamilton's collection of Greek vases for 8,000 guineas and in 1808 the Townley marbles for £20,000. In 1756 the first mummy arrived, part of a modest private bequest of Egyptian antiquities, and in 1802 George III presented to the Museum a mass of antiquities, including the Rosetta Stone, that had been seized in Egypt from Napoleon's scientific expedition (p. 67).

Visions of Stonehenge

Stonehenge, one of the world's most distinctive prehistoric monuments, has been the subject of wonder and speculation down the centuries. Its first mention is in a history of England written c. 1130 by Henry of Huntingdon, an archdeacon of Lincoln. 'Stones of wonderful size have been erected after the manner of doorways', he writes, 'and no one can conceive how such great stones have been so raised aloft, or why they were built there.' A few years later, Stonehenge won more prominent attention in Geoffrey of Monmouth's fanciful *History of the Kings of Britain* (1136). Here we find the first explanation for the building of the monument, transported by the magic of Merlin from a mountain in southern Ireland to Salisbury Plain as a memorial to noble Britons treacherously massacred by the Saxons. Later, insists Geoffrey, it became the burial place of Utherpendragon, father of King Arthur.

Medieval mythology gave way in the sixteenth century to more critical attitudes to the early history of Britain. When, in the early seventeenth century, the classical architect Inigo Jones visited Stonehenge, he sketched actively. So sophisticated a structure could not, he felt, be the work of barbarous Britons. By smoothing out irregularities and making allowances for the ravages of time, Jones produced a reconstruction of Stonehenge as he thought it must originally have appeared: this was a Roman Stonehenge, the outer ring a perfect circle with six symmetrically disposed trilithons (two uprights spanned by a lintel) at its centre. No matter that his drawing departed in major respects from the actual ruins and that no comparable Roman building had ever been found. A desire to tidy up the monument according to the rules of classical symmetry rather than accurate field observation lay behind Jones's vision of Stonehenge.

As field archaeology in southern Britain became more firmly established in the later seventeenth century, Stonehenge developed into a prime focus of interest. Aubrey studied and made a rough plan of the monument. It was he who first connected the stones with the druids, the pre-Roman priesthood of Britain mentioned by classical writers like Caesar and Tacitus. The druids were a spurious addition to the Stonehenge story – once established, the idea of a druid temple proved almost ineradicable – but Aubrey did at least recognize Stonehenge as a pre-Roman monument.

The druidic connection was taken further by Stukeley in the eighteenth century. The adoption of evocative names such as Altar Stone and Slaughter Stone for key parts of the monument also helped foster feverish images of dark druidic ceremonies involving human sacrifice. By this time Stonehenge was regularly sketched and painted, a romantic image

of the stones having now replaced the tidiness of Jones's classical reconstruction. Early in the nineteenth century, the artists Constable and Turner both painted views of Stonehenge against a backdrop of dramatic, stormy skies.

Romantic appreciation of Stonehenge gave way to a more scientific approach only at the end of the nineteenth century. The first disciplined excavations at the monument were carried out in 1901, with further campaigns in 1919–26 and in the 1950s. They revealed a monument of several phases, added to and modified over the centuries, beginning with an earthen bank and ditch around 2800 BC and culminating in the erection of the great sarsen trilithons at the centre of the circle towards the end of the third millennium BC – thousands

of years before the druids. Stonehenge was a major ritual monument for the surrounding area and may indeed have been aligned on sun and moon; but though burials have been found, there is no evidence for the sacrificing of maidens on the 'Altar Stone', in fact an upright that has fallen flat.

These findings have not dispelled popular belief in the druidic connection. Since 1905, modern-day druids – the so-called Ancient Order of Druids – have used Stonehenge as the setting for their annual ceremony at the midsummer solstice. Thus Stonehenge continues to the present day: not just a major prehistoric monument but a potent symbol for alternative beliefs.

'Stonehenge' by John Constable (1776–1837), shown at the Royal Academy in 1836. The artist's catalogue description read: 'The mysterious monument of Stonehenge, standing remote on a bare and boundless heath, as much unconnected with the events of past ages as it is with the uses of the present, carries you back beyond all historical records into the obscurity of a totally unknown period'.

The rugged stones offer a powerful counterpoint to the romantic skyscape, and the bounding hare, bottom left, acts as a neat reminder of the transience of life compared with the age of the stones.

in southern England) was of pre-Roman date since the Roman road from Milden-hall to Bath made a detour to avoid it. During his early life, Stukeley visited and surveyed many field monuments, including Stonehenge and Avebury, but in seeking to relate what he saw to historical accounts he could go no farther back in time than the writings of classical authors such as Julius Caesar, who wrote of the druids:

> As a nation the Gauls are extremely superstitious; and so persons suffering from serious diseases, as well as those who are exposed to the perils of battle, offer, or vow to offer, human sacrifices, for the performance of which they employ druids. They believe that the only way of saving a man's life is to propitiate the god's wrath by rendering another life in its place, and they have regular state sacrifices of the same kind. Some tribes have colossal images made of wickerwork, the limbs of which they fill with living men; they are then set on fire, and the victims burned to death.

Towards the end of his life, Stukeley came to see the hand of the druids in virtually all the prehistoric monuments he studied. He derived his interest in druidism from his own religious beliefs, and concocted a vast scheme of British prehistory, according to which the druids had come to England as part of a Phoenician colony soon after Noah's flood.

In the work of Aubrey and Stukeley we see the paradox of improving standards of fieldwork coupled with uncritical interpretation and an overwhelming desire to associate visible monuments with peoples mentioned in historical accounts. To this extent, they were still tied to the philosophy and outlook of the middle ages. But in the sketches, plans and descriptions which they made, Aubrey and Stukeley laid the foundations of modern understanding of British field monuments. They also showed how difficult it was to study the prehistory of Britain – or anywhere else – without an established chronology. For them, Neolithic, Bronze Age and Iron Age monuments were all mixed together in a hazy epoch sometime before the Romans; whether decades, centuries or millennia before, they had no means of telling.

When London's Society of Antiquaries was founded in 1707 by a small group of men interested in the study and publication of antiquities, Stukeley became its first president. Formally constituted in 1717, the Society began publication of an annual journal, *Archaeologia*, in 1770. Around this time too, the British Museum was created through the purchase – from the proceeds of a lottery – of the 80,000-item collection of coins, antiquities, paintings, books and manuscripts amassed by the physician and naturalist Sir Hans Sloane, who died in 1753. Originally located in Montagu House in semi-rural Bloomsbury, the Museum's contents were transferred over the next century to a purpose-built home on the same site, completed in 1847. This grandiose building on Great Russell Street, a true temple to the arts in Greek Revival style, has been steadily added to since as the museum's collections have grown.

FIRST INKLINGS OF A REMOTE PAST

Flint tools from the palaeolithic, the Old Stone Age, turned up sporadically in Britain and elsewhere, but their importance went unrecognized. One such was the big point of black flint found by John Conyers *c.* 1690 in a gravel pit at Gray's Inn Lane near London. We now know it was a handaxe several hundred thousand years old found with 'elephant' (perhaps mammoth) bones; at the time it was assumed, plausibly enough, to be a weapon used by a Briton to kill an elephant brought over by the Romans in the reign of Claudius.

The conception of human antiquity still did not extend beyond written memory. Objects devoid of classical symmetry and finish like handaxes and megalithic monuments were therefore attributed to Celts or pre-Roman Gauls. The Roman writer Lucretius did allude to a 'time before writing which escapes us' (p. 52), a notion that has been called a 'non-archaeological prehistory'. However, such perceptions only slowly became re-established. A firmer idea of prehistory is apparent by the mid-seventeenth century in the work of 'Pre-Adamites' and 'Antediluvians' like Isaac Lapeyrère, a Protestant polymath born in Bordeaux. In 1655 Lapeyrère published a book in Amsterdam and London called *A Theological System upon that pre-supposition that Men were before Adam,* which argued that 'thunderbolts' were artifacts of an ancient pre-Adamite race. The book was seized by the Inquisition and publicly burned in Paris, and the author was forced to recant before the Pope. However, the notion of pre-Adamites was based on no more than a literal interpretation of the Bible as an historic document. To Lapeyrère at least, it was clear that Adam could not be the first man, since his son married a woman who was not his sister, and built a town, which implies the presence of inhabitants! Other such works of the seventeenth century also used an historical approach, with the Bible as their main source. Thomas Browne's 'antediluvian epoch' of 1646, for instance, only evokes the antediluvian (pre-Flood) patriarchs of the Bible, nothing more.

The early antiquarians were, literally, 'Renaissance men' – polymaths, scholars with deep curiosity and profound knowledge of a wide range of subjects such as medicine or astronomy. But towards the end of this period, one can discern a transition towards something which, while not yet archaeology, was taking shape as a separate discipline: the construction of knowledge about the remote past through its material traces, and a means of explaining those traces as well as describing them. Scholars were edging towards the realization that the ground and the landscape could be interrogated and read like a document.

From the time before writing. The Lower Palaeolithic hand-axe found in Gray's Inn Lane, London, three centuries ago by Conyers. Length 16.5 centimetres (6 ½ inches).

CHAPTER 3

Antiquarians and Explorers, *1760–1820*

Goethe in the Roman countryside, by Johann Tischbein, 1787. Though he found the ruins of antiquity disappointing in scale after the engravings of Piranesi, the poet Goethe's passion for classical Italy was fired on his first long visit in 1786–8. In Rome he immediately felt more at home than in his native city of Frankfurt. 'Only now do I begin to live!', he exclaimed on entering the city, lamenting bleakly after his departure, 'I have not spent an entirely happy day since I crossed the Ponte Molle to come home'.

The true challenge of neo-classicism was to take from antiquity not just the measur-able and observable, but the unmeasurable spirit – *das Unmessbare*. For ultimately, insisted Goethe, 'Classicism is health, romanticism disease'.

The medieval view of the human past saw the story in essentially religious terms, based on humankind's dependence on God's plan. The source of human moral and physical well-being lay in obedience to the will of God. So intransigent was human nature that, unless perpetually replenished by contact with divine revelation or the

Christian church, there was an inevitable tendency to backsliding and degeneracy. No better illustration of this was to be found than the condition of the pagan peoples encountered by European explorers and colonists in Africa, the Americas and southeast Asia. Their technology was simple, their social and economic life apparently rudimentary compared with that of contemporary Christian Europe.

By the end of the eighteenth century this view of the human past had been turned entirely on its head. The progress of technology and learning, coupled with Europe's economic and military ascendancy, began to convince people that the present was not inferior to the past, that the past had not been some kind of lost golden age and that humans could fashion a better future for themselves. This new confidence led people to reassess the pattern of the past. Even at the beginning of the century, rational enquiry and the growing evidence of fieldwork was spawning a new scepticism, prompting antiquaries to question whether the Bible held all the answers. As the clergyman Henry Rowlands wrote in 1723, in his *Mona antiqua restaurata*:

> Antiquity recordeth … the sons of Japhet to have been the first planters of Europe. Our commonly received stories make out Britain to be peopled by these men, very soon after the flood. But it is not easy to imagine how so large and remote a territory should become thoroughly planted and peopled in so short a time.

ENLIGHTENMENT VIEWS OF THE HUMAN PAST

This new spirit of enquiry was but one part of the larger intellectual movement known as the European Enlightenment, associated with names such as Voltaire and Montesquieu in France and John Locke and David Hume in Scotland. The Enlightenment's principal impact on archaeological thought was its firm advocacy of human progress – the conviction that the human condition was becoming better, not worse, an improvement due largely to human endeavour and natural processes. It was in this climate that the seminal idea of evolution eventually took root.

Archaeology could have provided excellent support for the idea of human progress. Stone artifacts were now securely identified as the tools of early European societies from a period before the use of iron. However, the channel that Enlightenment thinkers generally adopted was much more speculative in nature. It was based not on stone tools and other evidence of technological advance but on knowledge of non-European societies, particularly hunters and gatherers; writers naturally speculated that the ways of life of such peoples might resemble early stages in the development of European society.

Insights into this way of thinking are provided by Sir Thomas Pownall, who in 1769 visited the prehistoric burial mound of Newgrange in Ireland. In his account of the monument published four years later, he endeavoured to place the tomb within a general scheme of human development:

The face of the earth being originally everywhere covered with wood, except where water prevailed, the first human beings of it were Woodland-Men living on the fruits, fish and game of the forest. To these the land-worker succeeded. He settled on the land, became a fixed inhabitant and increased and multiplied. Where-ever the land-worker came, he, as at this day, ate out the thinly scattered race of the Wood-Men.

The final sentence of this quotation suggests that Pownall had in mind the European colonization of North America and the replacement of North American Indians – who were hunter-gatherers or horticulturalists – by British and French farmers. He was using a known recent phenomenon to explain changes he thought had occurred in the distant past. This eighteenth-century approach – understanding past societies through the study of recent or contemporary societies in other parts of the world – remains invaluable to archaeologists even today.

The corbel-vaulted inner chamber of New Grange, in the Boyne river valley north of Dublin, dates to c. 3100 BC. At sunrise on 21 December, the winter solstice, the sun shines through a small opening above the entrance, along the slab-roofed passage and into the cross-shaped burial chamber for 17 minutes.

Sheathed with a layer of white quartz pebbles and retained by a kerb of decorated boulders, the burial mound itself stands 11 metres (36 feet) high and measures 85 metres (280 feet) in diameter. The pecked abstract ornament of the kerb, passage and chamber ranks among Europe's finest collections of prehistoric art.

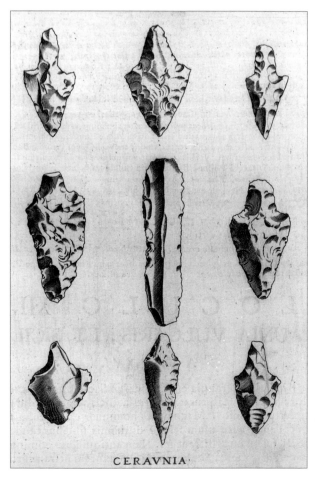

Michel Mercati (1541–93)

The idea of progress was soon applied to technology as well. Mercati (p. 39), an early proponent of the view that the stone objects popularly interpreted as elf-shot or thunderbolts were early human tools, drew on his knowledge of the classical literature to relate such tools to the writings of Lucretius, the Roman poet of the first century BC. In addition to interesting ideas about atoms, Lucretius' masterpiece, the poem *De Rerum Natura*, contains a passage on the likely sequence of human technologies, from stone to bronze and iron. Mercati's *Metallotheca* quotes Lucretius directly:

> The earliest tools were the hands, nails and teeth, as well as stones, pieces of wood, flames and fire as soon as they were known. Later the properties of iron and bronze were discovered, but bronze came first, the use of iron not being known until later.

Even before Lucretius, a similar scheme had been propounded in the Far East by a Chinese philosopher of the Eastern Zhou period (*c.* 770–221 BC), who quoted the following poem:

> In the age of Xuan Yuan, Shen Nong, and He Xu, weapons were made of stones, for cutting trees and building houses, and were buried with the dead … In the age of Huang Di, weapons were made of jade, for cutting trees, building houses, and digging the ground … and were buried with the dead. In the age of Yu, weapons were made of bronze, for building canals … and houses … At the present time, weapons are made of iron.

Mercati's sequence of stone, bronze and iron did not gain general acceptance in the sixteenth and seventeenth centuries because the *Metallotheca* lay in manuscript for well over a hundred years. It was printed and published only in 1717. By this time, other scholars had read Lucretius for themselves and were speculating independently about the idea of successive stone, bronze and iron ages. Even then the idea was slow to become established. It was only with Christian Jurgensen Thomsen's reorganization of the Danish National Museum in Copenhagen in the early nineteenth century that the Three Age System took its proper place as the cornerstone of prehistoric chronology (p. 89).

Central and eastern Europe were on the margins of development of western Enlightenment. It was not until late in the eighteenth century that the Age of Reason and a systematic interest in antiquities as sources of information about the human condition had much effect east of the Elbe. As a result, archaeology developed differently in different countries. In eighteenth-century Poland, for example, it took on an aristocratic character, with King Stanisław Augustus and Count Jan Potocki taking an avid interest in Polish and classical antiquity. In Bavaria, Bohemia and Moravia, the prime movers were local dignitaries, especially clerics like Josef Dobrovsky, a pattern repeated also in Scandinavia. Everywhere in Europe, the focus at this period was still on artifacts as the primary bearers of information about the past. Little attention was paid to context except where it could not be ignored, as in cave deposits in which extinct animals and artifacts were found in association.

ROMANTICISM

Although the eighteenth century fostered grandiose schemes of human progress, it did not wean people from the desire to recreate a romantic past peopled by bards and druids. Savage Celtic warriors and priests described in classical sources became transformed into national heroes and symbols of an idealized past. Already in the sixteenth century, classical texts were being used to foster nationalist myths in which pre-Roman Gauls and Germans were depicted as honoured forbears – ancestors who vigorously resisted aggression from outside. The testimony of writers such as Julius Caesar, who mention human sacrifice and other comparably gruesome druidic practices, seemed only to enhance the mystique of these pagan forbears.

Opposite below: *ceraunia*, from Mercati's posthumously published *Metallotheca* (1717). These were not thunderbolts, he insisted, but arrowheads and other implements chipped from flint by the hand of man.

Romantic rebellion. The German artist Johann Tischbein (1751–1829) was notably successful in reconciling the conflicting pulls of neo-classicism and romanticism. Attracted in youth to classical architecture and antiquities, he drew Greek vases in the collection of Sir William Hamilton and painted the most celebrated of all oil portraits of his friend Goethe (p. 48). Later in life, he turned to watercolours of prehistoric sites and even drew germanic antiquities for publication.

This romantically rendered megalithic tomb, apparently eaten away by barrow-digging, was painted towards the end of his life, in 1820.

By the end of the eighteenth century, in France as in Britain, it had become common practice to associate virtually every prehistoric monument with the druids. Some enthusiasts came to believe that the Celts were the oldest people in the world, guardians of a profound philosophy handed down by the bards to their successors; megalithic tombs were the altars where they offered human sacrifice. So great was the popularity of all things Celtic that in the 1760s the Scottish poet James Macpherson found it worthwhile to fabricate a whole series of 'translations' of poetic epics about the legendary hero Fingal, supposed to be the work of his son, a Gaelic bard named Ossian. His work was received initially with huge acclaim.

This Celtic enthusiasm in western Europe ran in parallel with a continuing interest in classical antiquities. In the end, however, classicism belonged to the Mediterranean world. It was the scarcity of upstanding classical remains in Britain and their total absence in northern Europe that seems to have helped stimulate the precocious development of prehistoric archaeology. Those who held classical antiquity in high esteem tended to regard the intervening period, the 'middle ages' between late antiquity and the Renaissance, as an episode of barbarism and degeneration. It was only with the rise of Romanticism in western Europe during the late eighteenth and early nineteenth centuries that medieval remains began once again to be fashionable. Yet interest in the middle ages was never wholly lost and the basic outlines of medieval history remained well known. The Society of Antiquaries of London included articles on medieval antiquities in its earliest publications. There were even excavations of medieval sites, such as those conducted in 1727 by Louis XIV's librarian and genealogist Pierre de Clérambault at the thirteenth-century graveyard of Châtenay-Malabry in France.

It was nonetheless in the nineteenth century that medieval ruins came into their own, with the Gothic Revival movement associated in England with Pugin and Ruskin and, in France, with the architect and archaeologist Viollet-le-Duc. Medieval archaeology thereafter focused for many years on works of art and on standing buildings like castles and abbeys. Only within the last thirty years has it taken its proper place within the fold of mainstream European archaeology.

MEN OF THE SPADE

While the aristocrats of northern Europe travelled to the Mediterranean to develop a refined appreciation of classical civilization, at home less exalted antiquarian interests continued to flourish. In particular, it was towards the end of the eighteenth century that the craze for barrow-digging began to take hold. A few of these early excavations were well conducted, many much less so. With hindsight, terrible damage was done to the prehistoric monuments of western Europe by people who thought nothing of digging half a dozen burial mounds before breakfast. In many cases, little record was kept, and the finds were subsequently lost.

Luckily, not all excavators were cavalier in their approach. One pioneering dig that deserves mention was conducted in Denmark by Crown Prince Frederik, later

Frederik V, and his court chaplain Erik Pontoppidan in June 1744. Beside a path in the royal park, they noticed a 'giant's chamber', an ancient burial mound, and decided to excavate it. Just below the surface they found two urns containing cremated bones and small metal fragments. Yet this by no means exhausted the potential of the mound. They continued digging down, their persistence eventually being rewarded by the discovery of a stone-built chamber containing four skeletons. These were accompanied by chipped stone tools, 'of the sort the peasants call thunderstones but which in fact formed the tip of an ancient spear or other weapon', but no metal. Pontoppidan's careful observations led him to conclude that the cremation urns were more recent than the chambered tomb, presumably burials cut into the still sanctified mound at a later date.

With Pontoppidan in Denmark and Le Prévôt in France (p. 38), we see the beginnings of excavations undertaken not so much to recover buried treasure as to understand the prehistoric past. In Britain, the principal forerunners of scientific excavation were William Cunnington and Richard Colt Hoare. Together they excavated hundreds of Wiltshire barrows, many of them near Stonehenge; in each one, they left a lead token to indicate to future archaeologists when, and by whom, it had first been opened.

Cunnington and Colt Hoare sought a pattern in the types of burial mound they encountered but they were surprised to discover that small barrows often contained richer graves than their larger neighbours. Their endeavours were successful: in one of the barrows nearest to Stonehenge, the so-called Bush Barrow, they found

Pioneers in Wessex. William Cunnington (1754–1810) and Richard Colt-Hoare (1758–1838) supervising the excavation of a group of barrows south of Stonehenge. Watercolour by Philip Crocker, 1807.

Hard facts were the goal for Cunnington and Colt-Hoare, not romantic conjecture. As Colt Hoare insists bluntly in the introduction to his *Ancient History of South Wiltshire* (1812), 'I shall describe to you what we have found; what we have seen; in short, I shall tell you a plain unvarnished tale, and draw from it such conclusions as shall appear not only reasonable, but even uncontradictable'.

British barrow-diggers

Earthen barrows and stone cairns were raised in antiquity to leave physical memorials to the dead in the landscape. Some mounds cover the central grave of a single individual, while others have a long and complex history of addition and enhancement. Most are prominently located, often on the brow of a hill so as to be clearly visible from below.

Though the use of barrows extended into Roman and Anglo-Saxon times, in Britain the great majority are prehistoric. Neolithic long barrows tend to occur singly, while Bronze Age round barrows usually form loose-knit groups or linear cemeteries. By the Iron Age, the square-ditched barrows typical of east Yorkshire and east-central Scotland are ranged in formal burial grounds.

Strong folklore links with fairies and the devil long protected most barrows from disturbance, but today, outside military training areas like Salisbury Plain, many have been flattened by agricultural development. The antiquarian J. R. Mortimer estimated that, even by 1843, 25 per cent of the barrows on the Yorkshire Wolds had been obliterated by agriculture and the enclosure of medieval open fields and commons over the previous half century.

By the early eighteenth century barrows were recognized as the burial places of Britain's ancient inhabitants. Digging barrows thus became a fashionable country sport for gentlemen, the results reported in the respected columns of *The Gentleman's Magazine* until late in the nineteenth century. Labourers did the pick and shovel work, sometimes opening several mounds in a day. Excavation often became little more than a Sunday afternoon's diversion to impress the house guests.

More serious practitioners tended to be doctors, lawyers, clerics – the educated middle classes rather than landowners. Eighteenth-century barrow-diggers with serious antiquarian interests include the clergymen Bryan Faussett in Kent and William Stukeley in Wessex (p. 40). It was for a site near Stonehenge that Stukeley in the 1720s left the first clear record of a barrow excavation. Wessex figured prominently in the activities of the 'barrow knights', Wiltshire being the particular stamping ground of wool merchant William Cunnington and London banker Sir Richard Colt Hoare.

In this team Cunnington was the practical excavator, Colt Hoare the financial backer, wealthy enough to sponsor an excavation programme that extended in the end to 465 barrows. Their techniques of excavation, approaches to recording, attempts at classification and synthesis, and publications were a major influence on all who followed, in Wiltshire and beyond. Their digging was always tied to the development of empirical scientific investigation, hence Colt Hoare's famous comment, 'We speak from facts, not theory'.

The nineteenth century saw a massive expansion in barrow digging among men who often became bitter rivals as they attempted to add more and more sites to their list of conquests, more and more objects to their collections. At the root of their passion lay a fascination with ancient sites and a genuine desire to record and order the distant past. Several major figures stand out. Particularly impressive is the work of the wealthy Derbyshire landowner Thomas Bateman and his associates in the Peak District and Yorkshire. Together they excavated over 360 sites, Bateman himself leaving detailed publications and a fine archive to record their discoveries. As was usual at the time, barrows were opened by driving a trench from the side of a mound towards the centre or by excavating in quadrants. In *Barrow Digging by a Barrow-Knight* (1845), the Rev S. Isaacson describes in excruciating rhyme how Bateman's

> … eyes upon the barrow bent are
> As if they'd pierce earth's very centre …
> Uprouse ye then, my barrow-digging men,
> It is our opening day!
> And all exclaimed, their grog whilst swigging,
> There's naught on earth like barrow-digging!

In contrast, William Greenwell was a canon of Durham Cathedral and librarian to the Dean and Chapter of Durham. He dug over 443 barrows in many parts of Britain and had wide interests and contacts, amassing a substantial collection of finds now housed in the British Museum. His techniques were similar to Bateman's: parallel trenches were dug into the barrow and often the whole mound was dug over. Greenwell was criticized by others – principally his rival Mortimer – for inadequately supervising his labourers and for the poor quality of some of his work. However, his published records are mostly of high quality and he is credited with giving one of archaeology's greatest figures – General Pitt-Rivers (p. 131) – his first taste of excavation.

Mortimer was an East Yorkshire corn merchant whose interest in archaeology and geology had been fired by the Great Exhibition of 1851. He and his brother Robert had such a passion for excavating archaeological sites and for collecting geological and archaeological specimens in Yorkshire that flint and stone objects became known locally as 'Mortimers'. In addition to the Iron Age cemetery at Danes Graves and Anglo-Saxon cemeteries near Garton-on-the-Wolds and Driffield, he excavated 304 barrows in east

Yorkshire, created a special museum for the finds and produced a detailed publication. The collection is now in Hull City Museum. Although Mortimer concentrated on the centre of barrows, his excavation techniques varied and in later years he re-excavated some sites at which he thought he might have missed some details. He excavated at Danes Graves with Greenwell and another East Yorkshire antiquarian (Boynton), although for most of their lives they were fierce rivals.

With the rise of systematic excavators such as Pitt-Rivers who worked on sites of all types and dates, the passions that barrow digging aroused faded. In this century the entire phenomenon died.

ANDREW FOXON

Above. Bateman's opening of the Derbyshire barrow known as Taylor's Low, Wetton, on 28 May 1845. Drawing by F. W. Lock, for the frontispiece to Isaacson's poem *Barrow Digging by a Barrow-Knight*.

Right. Canon William Greenwell (1820–1918), said to have been 'an admirable raconteur, with a keen sense of humour'. His favourite, much quoted dictum was 'Never mind theories, collect facts'.

exquisite decorative lozenges of sheet gold and a dagger hilt decorated with tiny gold nails. But in one important respect they had to admit defeat. Their aim had been to discover who had built these mounds, 'to which of the successive inhabitants of these islands they are to be ascribed'. Ten years and 465 barrows later, this was still a question Cunnington and Colt Hoare could not resolve. What crucially they lacked was a chronological yardstick – any means of organizing their finds into earlier and later. Only in the present century has it become clear that these burial mounds were those of an Early Bronze Age elite, and that the Bush Barrow gold belonged to one of their leaders who died around 4,000 years ago.

ARCHAEOLOGY AND THE GRAND TOUR

In an age when a gentleman's education consisted largely of studying the classics, it was natural that the antiquities of Greece and Rome should provide the aristocracy of eighteenth-century Europe with one of their principal cultural interests. This appetite for the classical was easily satisfied in Italy, where Roman monuments stood above ground for all to see: in Aquileia, Benevento, Cassino, Verona and, above all, in Rome itself. But the aristocracy of northern Europe, where standing monuments were scarce, needed to travel in search of the antique, by sea or by carriage overland across the Alps. Their mecca was Rome.

Most travellers were in their twenties, English gentlemen or German princelings completing their education in the company of tutors before entering into their inheritance at home. Occasionally entire families and their retainers decamped for Italy by carriage, but older collectors more often sent agents to purchase statues, gems and other antiquities for them. Such sculpture ultimately formed the basis of the great national collections like those of the British Museum in London, the Louvre in Paris, and the Altes Museum in Berlin.

The romantic dream of antiquity. Open to the sky, this loggia designed by C-L. Clérisseau in the 1760s was built near the top of the Spanish Steps in Rome, at the convent of St Trinità dei Monte. It still survives. The furniture was intended to look like antique fragments: the desk takes the form of a damaged sarcophagus; a slab of cornice acts as a table; an inverted capital forms a seat; and a classical niche provides a kennel for the dog.

The interest of the aristocracy in Greece and Rome was reflected too in the neo-classical architecture of their country houses: in England most famously in the work of Robert Adam at Syon House (1761) and Kedelston (1759–65), and in elysian landscape gardens – like those at Stourhead and Stowe – adorned with temples, grottoes and lakes. It is apparent also in the classical themes of many pictures of the period, and in the columned ruins which decorated so many idyllic landscape paintings from the time of Claude and Poussin onwards.

Cities buried by Vesuvius

Long before the eighteenth century, chance finds of ancient sculpture and masonry around the Bay of Naples pointed to the presence of ancient cities, buried by the eruption of Vesuvius in AD 79. Historically, the lost cities were known from the graphic account written in old age by the Younger Pliny:

> They debated whether to stay indoors or take their chance in the open, for the buildings were now shaking with violent shocks, and seemed to be swaying to and fro as if they were torn from their foundations. Outside, on the other hand, there was the danger of falling pumice-stones, even though these were light and porous; however, after comparing the risks, they chose the latter ... As a protection against falling objects, they put pillows on their heads tied down with cloths.

Systematic exploration of Herculaneum, begun in 1738 at the expense of the king of Naples, soon yielded sculpture, columns and wall paintings. But objects had to be recovered piecemeal as work proceeded by tunnelling through the volcanic mud which engulfed the city, often with the help of gunpowder. Two years after work started, the poet Thomas Gray, in Naples on the Grand Tour with his friend

Pompeii, by J. P. Hackert (1737–1809). When Goethe and Tischbein arrived in Naples in 1787, it was the landscape artist Hackert who made them welcome, effecting an introduction to Sir William Hamilton and encouraging them to visit Pompeii. Goethe initially found the 'mummified city left us with rather a disagreeable impression'. Yet he found himself haunted by the memory of the place, and returned two days later. 'Many a calamity has happened in the world', he reflected, 'but never one that has caused so much entertainment to posterity as this one'.

Horace Walpole, wrote home to describe what he had seen. 'The passage they have made with all their turnings and windings is now more than a mile long … As you walk you see parts of an amphitheatre, many houses adorned with marble columns encrusted with the same, the point of a temple, several arched vaults of a room painted in fresco.' Robert Adam, visiting much later, in 1755, recorded a descent to the underground amphitheatre by the light of torches. He saw 'earthen vases and marble pavements just discovered' as well as 'feet of tables in marble which were dug out the day before we were there'. Overall, he wrote, this town 'once filled with temples, columns, palaces, and other ornaments of good taste is now exactly like a coal-mine worked by galley slaves who fill in the waste rooms they leave behind'.

Work started at Pompeii ten years later. Here smothering ash had rained down on the city, preserving it in a different way from Herculaneum. Organic materials like wood and textiles had decayed and the bodies of the city's inhabitants were found encased in hardened ash, their forms only recoverable if the void that once contained tissue and bone was filled with plaster – a technique developed in the nineteenth century by the archaeologist Giuseppe Fiorelli. Both cities now became important stops on the Grand Tour, the more important visitors witnessing contrived excavations at which unusual finds would emerge from the volcanic debris at precisely the right moment.

From the eighteenth century onwards Pompeii and Herculaneum have provided us with invaluable insights into Roman town life in the first century AD. In part this is due to their being preserved like time capsules; most ancient cities decayed and were stripped of movable contents and reusable building materials before being abandoned. But in part it is the discovery of furniture, household objects – even carbonized food – that has allowed archaeologists to work out how buildings and individual rooms were used. Walls often survived to full height, so these buried cities also preserve unique wall-paintings, many of which were hacked off as a sheet of plaster early on and carried off to hang as works of art in the museum in Naples.

The definition of the classical

Johann Joachim Winckelmann, the father of classical archaeology, is an intriguing figure. Born in Prussia the son of a cobbler, he was a connoisseur who spent much of his adult life in Rome, becoming librarian to Cardinal Albani in 1755 and Prefect of Papal Antiquities in 1763. He published works on Greek painting and sculpture and investigated Paestum, Herculaneum and Pompeii – where he complained that with only eight men at work the town would take centuries to uncover.

Winckelmann's philhellenic aesthetic – based on the study of idealized statues of athletes and divinities and fuelled emotionally by his homosexuality – became hugely influential, reaching a wide public through guidebooks written for those on the Grand Tour. His monumental *History of Ancient Art* (1764), published first in German, then in French and English, ushered in the age of neo-classicism. He also introduced a wholly new approach to the study of antique sculpture. Instead of attempting to identify notable historical figures or cataloguing pieces according to their owner, he established a chronological framework that was permanently to influence the way such sculpture would be viewed, displayed and discussed.

The display of the classical

Those returning from the Grand Tour were keen to furnish their country and town houses with fine collections of ancient, and not so ancient, sculpture to convey an impression of learning and culture. Many resorted to bribing papal officials so that they could remove their acquisitions from Italy. For example, the Lansdowne Antinous – a portrait of the youthful lover of the emperor Hadrian who drowned in the Nile – was acquired for William, second earl of Shelburne, by the dealer

Charles Townley in his gallery, by Johann Zoffany (1733–1810).

Townley fell under the spell of the classical on visiting Italy in 1768. In Naples, he met the British envoy, Sir William Hamilton, an enthusiastic collector of five years standing, and soon afterwards acquired his first piece of antique sculpture: a statue of two youths fighting over a game of knucklebones.

As his collection grew over the next decade, Townley's London house at Park Street, Westminster, was adapted to accommodate it. The dining room was presided over by 'one of the chiefest glories of his gallery', a Venus, over life-size and in suitable déshabille, found at Ostia, near Rome, in the ruins of the baths of Claudius. Diana and Thalia stood in alcoves on either side of the fireplace, while busts of Athena and Zeus-Serapis graced the mantelpiece.

Fastened to the wall was a frieze ornamented 'with festoons of Ivy, and trophys composed of the instruments used in orgies'.

From the villa of the emperor Hadrian at Tivoli came a colossal head of Hercules and the 'Townley Discobolus', a life-size Roman copy of a Greek discus-thrower by the fifth-century sculptor Myron, a contemporary of Pheidias.

On Townley's death in 1805, the collection passed to the British Museum, where a new gallery built specifically to house it was opened in 1808.

Gavin Hamilton in 1769. The head, recovered from the ruins of Hadrian's villa at Tivoli just outside Rome, was not granted a papal licence for export, and it was said that Hamilton was only able to remove it by offering an 'additional present to the under antiquarian'. This was also a time when Italian sculptors were producing items such as portrait heads and relief panels from sarcophagi that could be sold as ancient. Today they might be considered fakes; then, they were objects of pride that enhanced the range of any newly formed classical collection.

Many of these great English collections were broken up when their owners subsequently fell on hard times, but some remain virtually intact. The sculpture at Newby Hall in Yorkshire was placed – and is still displayed – in a special wing of the house designed by Robert Adam in 1767. This collection was acquired in Rome by William Weddell in 1765. Another important collection still in its intended setting is the series of sculptures acquired for Thomas Coke, earl of Leicester to dignify Holkham Hall in Norfolk.

Travels in Greece

Many aristocratic collections were formed during visits to Italy. However, when the Napoleonic wars disrupted the established shape of the Grand Tour, attention switched to the east, especially the eastern Mediterranean. One notable early traveller, who designed a working model of the eruption of Vesuvius and acted in his twenties as tutor to a number of noble families, was Dr Edward Daniel Clarke. On his travels round the Aegean and the Black Sea, he formed an important collection of antique sculpture and inscriptions that in 1803 was put on display in the University Library in Cambridge, where he was also librarian.

It was at the Greek sanctuary of Eleusis in Attica that Clarke made one of his most important acquisitions: a colossal figure thought for many years to be the cult statue of Demeter, goddess of agriculture. He obtained a permit and made preparations to remove the figure. As he did so, an ox ran loose, butting the marble – an event that unnerved his superstitious local labourers, who took it as a sign that the fertility of their land would be lost if the statue were taken away. Their reluctance to be involved was only overcome when the local Orthodox priest donned his vestments and 'gave the first blow with a pickaxe for the removal of the soil, that the people might be convinced no calamity could befall the labourers'. After this, the ill-starred statue was nearly lost when the ship carrying it to Britain ran aground on the Goodwin Sands. Today, the 'goddess' is no more. Now in the Fitzwilliam Museum, Cambridge, the figure is recognized as being one of two Roman caryatids – columns in the form of standing women – that once flanked the entrance to the sanctuary of Demeter.

The most notorious collector who passed through Greece in the Napoleonic era was Thomas Bruce, seventh earl of Elgin, who in 1799 was appointed British Ambassador to the Sublime Porte at Constantinople. It was Elgin who, in circumstances of doubtful legality while Greece was under Turkish rule, acquired the superb architectural marbles of the mid-fifth century BC that adorned the Parthenon on the Athenian akropolis. The temple had been severely damaged in 1687 by a Venetian shell which detonated the gunpowder store of the Turkish garrison then manning it. As a result, Elgin's agents were able to obtain a firman to acquire 'any piece of stone with old inscriptions or figures', a phrase they took to cover the wholesale removal of the building's frieze, pedimental sculpture and metopes (square relief panels). Shipments to England started in December 1801, although it was January 1804 before most of the collection arrived. Elgin's efforts won him few

Sir William Hamilton

The fashion amongst English gentlemen for collecting the decorated pottery of Ancient Greece can be traced to Sir William Hamilton (1730–1803), British Envoy and Plenipotentiary at the court of Naples. Hamilton's collection was assembled over thirty-seven years in Naples. Yet even in 1764, just a year after his arrival, he already possessed a good sized collection. Throughout his stay he bought in bulk, often negotiating for complete collections like the Porcinari collection which he purchased in 1766. Such acquisitions he supplemented by material 'excavated' from the Campanian cemeteries around Naples. An engraving in Tischbein's *Collection of Engravings from Ancient Vases ... discovered in Sepulchres in the Kingdom of the Two Sicilies* (1791–5) shows Hamilton and his wife present at the opening of a tomb from which are emerging red-figured pots.

Publications like these were intended to sell the collection. Pierre d'Hancarville, in whose hands Hamilton placed an earlier sale, wrote that the vessels 'were equally proper for the compleating of well understood Collections of Prints and designs, or to furnish in a manner not only agreeable but useful and instructive, the Cabinet of a Man of Taste and letters'. The first of d'Hancarville's two volumes appeared in 1768 and 1770, but the third and fourth were delayed after he pawned the plates.

The first collection was sold to the British Museum in 1772 for 8,000 guineas. A second, formed between 1789 and 1790, was sent to England in 1798, but a third of it was lost when HMS *Colossus* was wrecked off the Scilly Isles. Most of the remaining pieces were purchased for 4,500 guineas in 1801 by Thomas Hope, the son of a wealthy Amsterdam merchant, to be displayed at his home in Duchess Street, London.

Often the iconography of these vases was interpreted in a very loose way. Nevertheless the images evoked for many the glories of the classical past. The noted English porcelain producer Josiah Wedgwood reproduced them on his 'Etruscan' wares, produced at 'Etruria' in Staffordshire.

Sir William and Lady Emma Hamilton at the opening of a tomb in a Campanian cemetery at Nola, 1790. The sixty-year-old Hamilton was besotted with his glamorous young wife, later the mistress of Nelson, encouraging her to loosen her hair and pose in flowing dresses in the manner of dancers in the Herculaneum frescoes – a performance, wrote the astonished Goethe, 'like nothing you have ever seen'. Frontispiece by C. H. Kniep to Tischbein's *Collection of Engravings from Ancient Vases ... in the Kingdom of the Two Sicilies* (1791–5).

The Elgin Room at the British Museum, the temporary gallery in which the Parthenon marbles were first displayed, by James Stephanoff.

Elgin always insisted that his intentions were honourable, 'wholly for the purpose of securing to Great Britain, and through it to Europe in general, the most effectual possible knowledge, and means of improving by the excellence of Grecian art in sculpture and architecture'.

If he had not rescued the marbles, he told a Select Committee of the British Parliament, they would not have survived.

friends. Lord Byron made veiled attacks on him, and few appreciated the beauty of the sculptures. Eventually Elgin offered his collection to the British Government, for £62,440 in 1811, and, more ambitiously, for £73,600 in 1815. In the end the marbles passed to the British Museum for just £35,000.

FIRST STIRRINGS OF FOSSIL MAN

The infant discipline of archaeology was an early beneficiary of the work of Niels Stensen (Nicolaus Steno), the Danish physician and naturalist, who in 1669 drew the first geological profile. It was Stensen who recognized that such profiles could be interpreted in developmental terms and who established the principles of sedimentation and stratigraphic superimposition: the idea that later layers must lie on top of older ones.

The first archaeological application of this maxim in western Europe came in 1797 when a British gentleman farmer, John Frere, found worked stone artifacts including Lower Palaeolithic handaxes in a brick quarry at Hoxne in Suffolk. They lay at a depth of 4 metres (13 feet) in an undisturbed deposit which also contained the bones of large extinct mammals. Frere's great insight was that he not only recognized his finds as artifacts but also that he attributed them to a very distant period. They were, he concluded '… weapons of war, fabricated and used by a people who had not the use of metals … (which) may tempt us to refer them to a very remote period indeed; even beyond that of the present world.' Frere drew the side of the brick pit, noting that the worked flints were distributed seven to eight per square metre in a thick gravel layer, and drew his finds to the attention of the Society of Antiquaries in London. Yet despite publication in the Society's journal, *Archaeologia*, the significance of Frere's discovery – like that of the 'Ancient British' handaxe found a century before by Conyers (p. 47) that eventually found a place in the second edition of Leland's *Collectanea* (1770) – went unrecognized in Britain and beyond for decades.

A generation earlier, in 1771, Johann Friedrich Esper, a Bavarian pastor, discovered human bones associated with the remains of cave bear and other extinct

Georges Cuvier (1769–1832). It was Cuvier who originated the natural system of animal classification, and through his studies of animal and fish fossils – notably the extinct giant vertebrates of the Paris basin – established the sciences of palaeontology and comparative anatomy. In 1789 he became professor of natural history at the Collège de France and, after the restoration of the monarchy, Chancellor of the University of Paris and a peer of France.

By 1808 Cuvier had established that the huge mammoth bones discovered across northern Europe since the Renaissance belonged not to drowned elephants carried north by the biblical flood, as had previously been supposed, but to cold-adapted, fossil elephants quite distinct from the modern forms existing in Africa and India.

animals in Gaillenreuth Cave, near Bayreuth in the German Jura. Esper speculated that the bones could have belonged to a druid, an Antediluvian or a mortal man of more recent times, but in the end he concluded that they must be intrusive to the deposits containing the fossil animal remains. 'I dare not presume without any sufficient reason these human members to be of the same age as the other animal petrifications', he wrote. 'They must have got there by chance.'

Elsewhere, however, scholars were beginning to challenge, albeit very tentatively, the account of the earth's formation given in Genesis. The stratigraphic principle was applied first to the study of fossils in geological layers ('stratigraphic palaeontology'), for example by William 'Strata' Smith, the canal engineer and father of English geology, in his *Geological Map of England* (1815). In France meanwhile, the great Georges Cuvier, the father of comparative anatomy, was extending the principle's range from shells to mammals; he could perceive differences between fossil animals and their modern equivalents, the differences increasing with the age of the layers – a perception that would eventually culminate in the notion of evolution (p. 117). Cuvier also used comparative anatomy to reconstruct whole animals from very incomplete skeletons, a technique archaeologists have only developed fully over the last fifty years.

Human history so far remained unaffected by these developments in the natural sciences: the discovery of fossil man would be needed to change the situation. Despite Esper's find and many other less well-founded claims, Cuvier doubted that fossil humans had coexisted with vanished species found in 'antediluvian' deposits predating the Flood. He went by the Bible, believing that man appeared *after* the animals, a view that seemed to correspond to geological findings made to date. Unlike his pupils and disciples, Cuvier did not, however, categorically deny the possibility that fossil humans once existed; he merely denied that their bones had ever been found.

ANCIENT AND DISTANT LANDS

'Concerning Egypt itself I shall extend my remarks to a great length because there is no country that possesses so many wonders.' Though writing as early as the fifth century BC, the Greek historian Herodotus typifies early European attitudes to Egypt – a strange land, full of remarkable monuments and bizarre people. This fascination endures to the present, particularly where the monuments of ancient Egypt are concerned. So compelling are the Pyramids of Giza that visitors have long felt them to be charged with mystic significance: built for demi-gods, designed by men steeped in arcane ritual, and constructed through the blood and toil of sweating multitudes slaving under the sting of the lash.

The interest of the Greeks and Romans in Egypt, and the ways this interest was manifested, in many respects parallel reawakened European interest in Egypt after the Renaissance. The thirteen hieroglyph-adorned obelisks transported from the Roman province of Egypt to dignify the city of Rome itself are early testimony to a civic urge to collect that is otherwise principally associated with the nineteenth century when similar monuments were shipped to London, Paris and New York as diplomatic gifts. Cleopatra's Needle, for instance, was erected on London's Embankment in 1878 after an eventful voyage from Alexandria on which it was almost lost in a storm in the Bay of Biscay. As so often, the urge to see and to own gave rise to a desire to understand – one important strand in the nascent discipline of archaeology.

At the time Europeans came into close contact with Egypt at the end of the eighteenth century, after a long period when the region had been difficult of access as part of the Ottoman Empire, there was already current a considerable body of knowledge about the ancient Near East. The two main sources were Herodotus – accessible because he wrote in Greek, a language known and studied in Europe – and the Bible. It was the Bible that provided the earliest impetus for archaeology in the Near East.

The origins of Near Eastern archaeology

Paradoxically, at the time archaeologists and geologists in western Europe were using the evidence of recent palaeolithic finds in a furious debate with biblical fundamentalists about the evolution and antiquity of humankind, those same fundamentalists were encouraging archaeological exploration in the Near East. They assumed that excavation, particularly in the Levant, would prove the literal veracity of the Bible by discovering evidence of the cities, individuals and events – such as the Flood – that were mentioned in the Old Testament.

Bible-based scholarship sought equally to explain cultural change and the rise of civilization in the ancient world. One early idea that was vigorously promoted was diffusionism: the view that society, culture and technology change in one part of the world primarily through the spread of ideas or peoples from another part. This theory ignores the possibility of the independent invention of similar ideas and technological innovations as part of the natural learning curve of different peoples, but it was a view of the past given power and sustenance by the Bible. Genesis itself espouses hyperdiffusionism in the shape of the expulsion from the Garden of Eden and the dispersion after the Flood of the families of the sons of Noah to become the ancestors of all humankind. Superficially attractive but crucially flawed, it was a view of cultural change given new respectability in the early twentieth century by the anatomist and Egyptologist Grafton Elliot Smith, who in books like *Migrations of early culture* (1915) propounded the view that all civilization worthy of the name originated in Egypt, spreading from there to other parts of the Near East and beyond.

Napoleon in Egypt

When Napoleon invaded Egypt in 1798 he took with him not just the formidable army that defeated the Mamluk forces at the Battle of the Pyramids, but a smaller

army consisting of 167 scholars. During the brief French occupation, these savants staffed a commission charged with examining Egypt in detail – its geography, its flora and fauna, the customs of its natives and, particularly, its ancient monuments.

Champollion and the Rosetta Stone

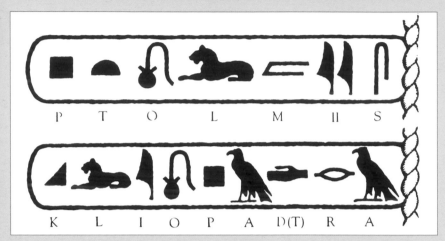

Jean-François Champollion, by Leon Cogniet (1794–1880).

Right. The cartouches of Ptolemy and Cleopatra on the Rosetta Stone that provided Champollion with the key to Egyptian hieroglyphic writing.

The centrepiece of the Egyptian collection seized from the French and presented by George III to the British Museum in 1802 was the Rosetta Stone – the key to unlocking the hitherto undeciphered hieroglyphs of ancient Egypt. This slab of black basalt, found in 1799 during the construction of Fort Saint-Julien, near the town of Rosetta on the north coast of Egypt, was inscribed with three copies of the same text (a decree of Ptolemy V datable to 196 BC), but in three different languages: Greek, Egyptian hieroglyphs and Egyptian demotic. Once it was realized that the content of the three inscriptions was identical, the fact that the Greek version could easily be read and understood revealed the Rosetta Stone as the key to the ancient Egyptian language.

The chief 'locksmith' was Jean-François Champollion (1790–1832), a precocious orientalist already on the academic staff of Grenoble University at nineteen, whose interest in Egypt was sparked and supported by his elder brother, his closest colleague in the long process of decipherment. Champollion's genius for ancient languages, particularly Coptic, was combined with a determined and systematic approach to the problem of the hieroglyphs. Building on studies by earlier scholars like the English physicist Thomas Young, his work culminated in 1822 with the famous *Letter to Monsieur Dacier* in which he described the remarkable progress he had made in identifying phonetic signs in the hieroglyphic script and in translating the 'words' they constituted.

Champollion's initial task was to translate the hieroglyphic versions of the royal names 'Ptolemy' and 'Cleopatra', already identified in the Greek version of the text. This job was made easier by the ancient Egyptian practice of surrounding the royal name with the oval device we now call a cartouche. It was then relatively simple to work out the phonetic value of the hieroglyphic signs that made up the two royal names, a first step to identifying all the phonetic hieroglyphic signs by working on other royal names announced by a cartouche. Other parts of the text could be approached by comparing known phonetic values with similar words in Coptic, the pre-Islamic Christian Egyptian tongue descended from Ancient Egyptian, in which Champollion was already expert.

This notable success was followed by two foreign adventures: first, a tour of the Egyptian collections in Italian museums in 1826 and then, in 1828–9, the first systematic survey of the hieroglyphic inscriptions on monuments in Egypt. Champollion's achievements were recognized in 1826 by his appointment as conservator of the soon-to-be-opened Egyptian collection in the Louvre, and in 1831 by the creation for him of a professorship in Egyptian history and archaeology at the Collège de France in Paris. He died the following year.

Of greatest note was Baron Vivant Denon, a diplomat, dilettante and minor nobleman whose early antiquarian endeavours included a commission from Louis XV to arrange a collection of gems and medals for his mistress, Madame de Pompadour. Through frequenting the salon of Joséphine de Beauharnais, Denon made the acquaintance of Napoleon and so became attached to the Egyptian commission. It is his portfolio of 150 plates produced for the multi-volume *Description of Egypt* that constitutes one of the most enduring records of the commission's work, illustrating the condition of some of the most important standing monuments and recording in detail many of the portable antiquities the commission recovered. Denon's written account of his work, *A Journey through Upper and Lower Egypt* (1802), had significant impact too, bringing Egypt to the attention of the wider international community in its English and German translations. It is to Denon that we owe the memorable story of how, on rounding a bend in the Nile and first seeing the stupendous temples of Karnak and Luxor, 'the whole army, suddenly and with one accord, stood in amazement … and clapped their hands with delight.'

The antiquities the commission collected were destined to be shipped back to France, but with the defeat of the French navy by Nelson at the Battle of the Nile and the precipitate departure of Napoleon's troops from Egypt, the accumulated booty was lost to the British, ending up not in the Louvre but in the British Museum in London.

In the shadow of the pyramids. The French invasion of Egypt in 1798 brought with it scholars as well as soldiers, outstanding amongst them Vivant Denon, here seen measuring the sphinx in an illustration from his *Journey through Upper and Lower Egypt*. Egyptology as we know it today flowed directly from Denon's work and the fundamental record of Ancient Egypt published between 1809 and 1830 in the volumes of the *Description of Egypt*.

With the discovery of the Rosetta Stone and the work of Champollion, it generated a surge of enthusiasm for things Egyptian in Europe: in interior decoration, furniture, tableware, even garden design.

Orientalism

The pace of European exploration in the Middle East also increased from the second half of the eighteenth century. Expeditions became lengthier and more methodical, a trend illustrated by the Danish five-man team that set off for Arabia in 1761. Only the

Rediscovering Babylon

Claudius James Rich (1787-1821) was the last, and most thorough, of the great antiquarian observers of the Mesopotamian past, his place in the pantheon of archaeology founded on his study of Babylon, which he described and mapped on two separate visits.

Although born in Dijon, Rich grew up in Bristol where he taught himself Turkish, Persian, Arabic, Hebrew, Syriac and some Chinese. His linguistic abilities earned him a military cadetship with the East India Company at seventeen and later a posting to Cairo as British Consul-General for the Mediterranean. After short stays in Cairo and Bombay, he was appointed British Resident in Baghdad in 1808, a post he occupied for the next dozen years.

Rich's period in office was marked by insufficient funding from the East India Company and political skirmishes with the Pasha. In 1821, relations with the Pasha broke down completely and his position became untenable. Quitting Mesopotamia, Rich and his wife Mary sailed for Bushire on the southern coast of Persia, where Claudius stayed to await orders while Mary went ahead to Bombay. Kicking his heels and driven as ever by curiosity, Rich travelled onward to Shiraz, partly to see Persepolis. It was here, caught in an outbreak of cholera, that he died.

Rich's first visit to Babylon was in 1811, when he made a ten day excursion in the company of Mary, her sister and an armed guard. He described and made detailed measurements of Babylon's main topographic features, covering nearly 4 kilometres (2.5 miles) along the left bank of the river Euphrates. In his *Memoir on the Ruins of Babylon* (1815), he described prominent aspects of the site such as Babil – Nebuchadnezzar's summer palace – in the north and, in the south, al Qasr – his southern palace and the Ishtar Gate area where Alexander the Great died. The fame and controversy that followed led to a second visit in 1817, on which Rich looked for further information to answer his critics.

Rich was an amateur antiquarian, not an archaeologist, and he worked before reliably excavated information about ancient Mesopotamian cities had been gathered or the cuneiform script deciphered. Despite this, his work at Babylon introduced a large measure of precision to the accumulation

Claudius Rich. Already at twenty-one, he had 'acquired such a mastery over the languages and manners of the East that he personated a Georgian Turk for several weeks at Damascus, amidst several thousand pilgrims on their way to Mecca, completely'.

of vague travellers' reports, mapping intervening ground as well as the obvious ruins of baked brick architecture. He also made acute observations about the position of inscriptions within walls and the architectural associations of finds like cylinder seals and exposed burials.

Although Koldewey's systematic excavations at Babylon a century later eventually superseded his conclusions, Rich laid the foundations for all later work, not least by stimulating a spirit of antiquarian curiosity about Mesopotamia.

Frieslander Carsten Niebuhr returned home six years later, his companions having died on the road. Yet his travels had taken him as far as Egypt, Yemen, Oman, India, Persia and Mesopotamia. In his *Description of Travels in Arabia* (1778), Niebuhr described the architecture and sculptures of the Persian royal site of Persepolis, and accurately transcribed many of its inscriptions. These transcriptions began the work of deciphering Middle Eastern cuneiform, Niebuhr himself identifying the existence of three distinct scripts, one of them alphabetic with forty-two signs. He also described and illustrated several Mesopotamian ruins, including those he correctly identified as Babylon and Nineveh.

In the 1780s, the French botanist André Michaux travelled to Persia, bringing back a *kudurru*, a Babylonian legal document on stone or clay, set up in a temple, its cuneiform inscription soon the subject of a totally erroneous translation. In the same decade, Joseph de Beauchamp, the French Vicar-General in Baghdad, examined a number of Mesopotamian ruins and in 1786 dug experimentally at Babylon – the first known excavation of a Middle Eastern site. He discovered glazed and moulded brickwork showing an animal and astral signs, similar to those later found to have been used for the great Ishtar gate (p. 156) The report of his discoveries caused a sensation in both France and England in 1790 by showing that cuneiform texts could easily be recovered by excavation.

More systematic exploration now began, often promoted by governments and commercial organizations. The East India Company even charged its Residents in Baghdad and Basra with the task of acquiring cuneiform inscriptions. The most successful of these Residents, Claudius Rich, undertook a famous topographic study of Babylon, the ancient capital of Nebuchadnezzar, that won as much information as could be gathered without systematic excavation. Like his predecessors, he came with the writings of classical authors like Herodotus, Strabo and Diodorus Siculus in hand and interpreted the site in line with their testimony. 'I have endeavoured to show', he wrote, 'that the ruins of Babylon in their present state may be perfectly reconciled with the best descriptions of the Grecian writers, without doing violence to either.'

Rich did a little digging at Babylon, finding a coffin, and toured other sites in northern Mesopotamia. His reports, published in 1812–18, stimulated academic discussion and considerable public excitement. Lord Byron even worked a passing reference to Rich into his poem *Don Juan*: 'Though Claudius Rich, Esquire, some bricks has got, and written lately two memoirs upon't'.

Others too made robust contributions to the growing fund of topographic knowledge of the ancient Middle East. For instance, James Morier, the writer now best remembered for his picaresque novel *The Adventures of Hajji Baba of Ispahan* (1824), conducted the first 'excavations' at Persepolis during the 1810s, in order to acquire carved reliefs to take away. He broke into several pieces those stones too large to transport before his depredations were halted by the local governor.

Babylon from the air. The ziggurat, the biblical Tower of Babel, stands in the foreground. 'What city is like unto this great city?', demands the Book of Revelation, 'clothed in fine linen and purple and scarlet and decked with gold and precious stones and pearls … Babylon, the Great, the Mother of Harlots and of the Abominations of the Earth'.

When Rich first visited the site in December 1811, it took two tedious days travel from Baghdad, accompanied by his wife on a mule-borne litter. To guarantee their safety, the party included 'my own troops of Hussars, with a galloper gun, a havildar, and twelve sepoys; about seventy baggage mules, a memmandar from the Pasha, and a man from the Sheikh of the Jirbar Arabs'.

Rich surveyed all the mounds now known to represent the temples and palaces of the inner city of Babylon and, with help from his assistant, Abraham Lockett, produced a plan that corresponds well to the modern one. Labourers were set to work on the mound of Babil to investigate underground cavities among the ruins of the Summer Palace. When they came across a burial, Rich watched as 'piece by piece they pulled out the coffin and the bones'.

From local Arabs salvaging baked bricks for building purposes he acquired a group of well preserved cuneiform inscriptions, the beginnings of what eventually became a substantial collection of antiquities, inherited in 1825 by the British Museum.

Travellers in Arabia and the Levant

Systematic exploration of the Levant began early in the nineteenth century, after Napoleon's failed invasion of Palestine as part of his Egyptian expedition. The Swiss traveller Johann Ludwig Burckhardt was perhaps the most widely travelled of these explorers. Disguised as a Muslim merchant from India, he lived for several years in Damascus and Aleppo, recording information about the antiquities of Syria; he was the first European to record a Hittite inscription, on a stone set in the wall of a building at Hama on the Orontes river. He later travelled up the Nile, discovering the temples of Ramesses II at Abu Simbel (p. 310), and in 1814 crossed the Red Sea to make the pilgrimage to Mecca. When he died, Burckhardt was buried in a Muslim cemetery in Cairo, bequeathing his collection of manuscripts and journals to Cambridge University.

Travelling south from Aleppo, Burckhardt visited and described the famous Nabataean site of Petra, dated to around the time of Christ. He spent little time there, however, as he feared lingering would offend the sensibilities of his local guides who would then rob him of his money and his precious journal:

Rose-red city. The entrance to Petra, by David Roberts (1796–1864). Following Burckhardt's visit in 1812, the ruined rock-cut tombs and temples of Petra, today in southern Jordan, drew many nineteenth-century travellers.

Surrounded by mountains and located on the principal trade route between the Red Sea and the Dead Sea, Petra was a major stronghold successively of the Edomite and Nabataean kingdoms of the first millennium BC. Apart from a Roman theatre and temple of the second century AD, most of its surviving buildings belong to the last two centuries BC. Little is known of the later history of the site even today.

I regret that I am not able to give a very complete account [of Petra]: but I know well the character of the people around me; I was without protection in the midst of a desert where no traveller had ever been seen; and a close examination of these works of the infidels, as they are called, would have excited suspicions that I was a magician in search of treasures.

Burckhardt's description of Petra, in his *Travels in Syria and the Holy Land in 1810–12* (1822), was nonetheless detailed enough to attract a steady stream of visitors in the years that followed. Just a generation later, the Greek-inspired architecture of the city, cut into the living rock, was to inspire the poet John Burgon's famous description of 1845: 'A rose-red city – "half as old as Time".'

The first European actually to excavate in Palestine seems to have been the colourful English traveller, Lady Hester Stanhope. A granddaughter of the British statesman, William Pitt the Elder, she lived in the Levant from 1810 until her death in 1839 – by which time her eccentricities had earned her the sobriquet 'the mad nun of Lebanon'. During her long residence in the Levant, Lady Hester travelled extensively to inaccessible places like Palmyra, deep in the Syrian desert, where she imagined herself the heir to Queen Zenobia, the third-century AD rebel against Roman rule. In 1815 she organized an excavation in search of gold at Ashkelon, a ruined Philistine city on the coast near Gaza. Her diggings unearthed Roman remains, including the statue of an emperor that, in a fit of pique at failing to discover treasure, Lady Hester had destroyed.

India and the Mediterranean

Appreciation of India's ancient history began with linguistic and philosophical research in the second half of the eighteenth century that opened up new historical worlds and provided information linking Alexander the Great's campaigns in

northern India with the subsequent Hellenistic king-doms of Central Asia. Sir William Jones, a judge of the Calcutta Supreme Court, did more than any other scholar to shape the field. As early as 1774, together with the famous lexicographer Samuel Johnson, he was urging the Governor-General of India, Warren Hastings, to 'survey the remains of [India's] edifices, and trace the vestiges of its ruined cities'. Exactly a decade later came the foundation of the Asiatic Society of Bengal, a meeting ground for all Europeans inter-ested in the arts and sciences of Asia, whose members read papers on archaeology, coins and inscriptions, as well as literature and manuscripts. A notable mem-ber was James Prinsep (1799–1840), the first person to decipher the Brahmi and Kharoshti scripts of ancient India.

The link between early India and the classical Mediterranean was reinforced by numismatic discov-eries, not just of Greek and Indo-Greek coins in the north, but also of Roman coinage in the south. Reports of Roman coins first appeared in the 1780s, with the discovery of a hoard near Madras, and speci-mens were thereafter regularly discovered through-out southern India. This evidence for trade with early imperial Rome served to recall Pliny's alarm at the great flood of Roman bullion flowing east during the first century AD.

Even Indian art seemed to reinforce the lessons of a classical nineteenth-century education. When the Gandharan style of sculpture – a hybrid of Greek and Buddhist elements – was identified in the mountain areas of the northwestern frontier in 1852, the links between early Indian history and the classical world encouraged European scholars to adopt the same fine arts approach to the Indian past that was already established in the Mediterranean world. Architectural and art history accordingly remained the staple interest of antiquarians in India throughout the nineteenth century.

DISCOVERING THE LIMITS: OCEANIA

European exploration of the Pacific was characteristic of the eighteenth century in the way that European expansion across the Atlantic was characteristic of the sixteenth. The Spanish, Portuguese and Dutch had long been active in the East Indies and as early as 1606 the Dutch ship *Duyfken* had sighted Australia. By the mid-seventeenth century Dutch East India Company vessels had visited and mapped Tasmania, New Zealand, New Guinea and the western and northern shores of Australia.

Although by 1760 the British and French were also taking an interest in the opportunities for trade and settlement that existed in Oceania, the motive force for pushing forward the boundaries of the known world was now a genuine thirst for knowledge as much as blunt self-interest. The great voyages of discovery of the late eighteenth century were undertaken in the context of the Enlightenment and the beginnings of empirical science, so the systematic collection of information was important for its own sake as well as for the light it might shed on the supposedly natural condition of humanity. As the contemporary French philosopher Joseph-Marie de Gérando wrote:

> The philosophical traveller who sails to the extremities of the earth, traverses in effect the sequence of the ages; he travels into the past; each step he takes leaps a century ... [He] retraces for us the state of our own ancestors and the earliest history of the world.

The three voyages of Captain James Cook established a tradition of systematic exploration and recording that soon became standard practice. Cook was the son of a Yorkshire farm labourer who rose through the ranks of the Royal Navy to become the foremost navigator of his time. During his first voyage in the *Endeavour*, from 1768 to 1771, he explored the Society Islands, charted New Zealand and mapped the east coast of Australia. On the second voyage (1772–75) he had two ships and explored the Pacific extensively, twice crossing the Antarctic Circle and even visiting remote Easter Island. The aim of the final voyage (1776–79) was to look for the northwest passage around America. Cook spent considerable time

Opposite. Richly carved Buddhist stupas like this were the first archaeological remains to attract western attention in India.

The most notable was at Amaravati in the Deccan, once 'the most magnificent Buddhist monument in all India'. Where a sculptured limestone dome rising 18 metres (60 feet) high and measuring 40 metres (130 feet) in diameter had stood in the second and third centuries AD, British visitors in 1797 found just 'a circular trench, about 10 feet wide, dug about 12 feet deep, into a mass of masonry, composed of bricks 16 inches square and 4 inches thick ... In this ditch a white slab lay broken, which still exhibited some figures in relievo ...' Digging in the 1840s yielded many sculptures, most of them eventually shipped to London, and further excavations in the 1870s almost 400 more, today in the museum in Madras.

exploring the Pacific islands as well as the northwest coast of America and the Bering Strait, but was killed on his return to Hawaii. Many later British voyages were led by men who sailed with Cook – notably the navigator George Vancouver and the naval officer William Bligh, captain of the *Bounty* and later governor of New South Wales.

French voyages to Oceania were also strongly motivated by scientific curiosity. Jean-François de La Pérouse was an experienced naval officer who was sent to the Pacific in 1785 with instructions to observe the activities of other European powers and to investigate the physical characteristics and customs of the peoples of the Pacific. In 1800, the newly formed *Société des Observateurs de l'Homme* provided detailed instructions about the investigation of human societies for the expedition led by Nicolas Baudin, also a naval officer. François Péron, the medical student who proposed that the expedition should include scientists charged specifically with carrying out research into anthropology – a term he coined – accompanied Baudin.

The eighteenth-century age of exploration filled in a map of the world which, by the end of the century, was much as we know it today. The practice on voyages of discovery of including scientific personnel and demanding systematic documen-

Captain Cook's ethnography

The three voyages undertaken by Captain James Cook (1728–79) to the Pacific had an enormous impact on eighteenth-century England, exciting the popular imagination to the point that the British Museum's Otaheite (Tahiti) and South Sea rooms at Montagu House became one of the sights of London. The wealth of information Cook's expeditions collected influenced the development of both the natural and human sciences. Ethnographic accounts of Pacific peoples and their artifacts stimulated the development of ideas about social evolution, and the Pacific became a forum for investigating the nature of primitive society.

The aims of Captain Cook's first voyage on the *Endeavour* were scientific, at least in part. The Admiralty instructed him to:

> Be careful to observe the nature of the soil and the products thereof, the beasts and fowls that inhabit or frequent it; the fishes that are to be found in the rivers or upon the coast, and in what plenty, and in case you find any mines, minerals or valuable stones, you are to bring home specimens of each, as also such specimens of the seeds of trees, fruits and grains as you may be able to collect, and transmit them to our Secretary that we may cause proper examination and experiments to be made of them. You are likewise to observe the genius, temper, disposition and number of the Natives.

The Royal Society appointed scientific observers and artists to the expedition under the leadership of the botanist Joseph Banks, a wealthy Lincolnshire landowner, who fitted out the *Endeavour* as a floating scientific institution. The result was a huge body of data – natural history specimens, artifacts, notes, drawings and paintings – from the Pacific islands, Australia, northeast Asia, northwest America and Tierra del Fuego. The ethnographic records provide an unparalleled account of the peoples of the Pacific at the time of their first encounter with Europeans. So meticulously planned was Cook's voyage that it set the standard not only for his second and third voyages, but for journeys of exploration for the rest of the century.

Most contemporary interest inevitably focused on natural history: ethnography did not yet exist as a discipline so ethnographic specimens were simply labelled 'curiosities'. The president of the Royal Society did, however, provide Cook and Banks with a list of headings under which to describe the native peoples they encountered; similar lists of topics were used to structure the records of later voyages also. Naturally, the expedition's most detailed and comprehensive records are for places like Tahiti where they spent substantial periods of time, established friendly relations with the local people and learned some of the language. For New Zealand, where they had relatively little time on shore and encounters were often strained, topics such as social relations and

tation guaranteed that incomparable records survive from the meeting of Oceanic and western European worlds. And the specimens, artifacts, drawings and written descriptions explorers brought back to Europe not only stimulated interest in the 'new worlds' for their own sake but did much to shape the emerging disciplines of botany, zoology and ethnology.

Exploring Australia

Scientific curiosity about both land and people characterized the beginnings of settlement in Australia. Governor Arthur Phillip, a naval officer, and Captain John Hunter, a keen naturalist who eventually replaced Phillip as governor of New South Wales, were the first to conduct excavations in Australia, opening burial mounds at Port Jackson in 1788 to investigate their contents. John Oxley, a naval officer and surveyor-general of New South Wales, also excavated a grave near the Lachlan river during his exploration west of the Blue Mountains in 1817. Before re-interring the human remains, he carefully described the finds and their surroundings, concluding from his observations that the Aborigines of the inland had different customs from those of the coast.

Divine offerings being presented to Captain Cook in the Pacific islands.

The 366-ton *Endeavour* sighted the southeastern corner of Australia on 20 April 1770. The first white colonists landed at Sydney in 1788, some eighteen years after Cook claimed New South Wales for the British crown.

religious customs are sparsely covered. The material aspects of life are invariably described in meticulous detail, the written account supplemented by the drawings and sketches of the expedition artists.

Cook's expeditions collected more than two thousand artifacts, ranging from domestic items such as bowls to elaborate Hawaiian feather cloaks and headdresses worn on ceremonial occasions. On the first voyage the most important ethnographic accounts and collections were those of Cook and Banks themselves, but on the second voyage, the naturalists George Forster and his father Reinhold, a Prussian of Scottish descent, kept detailed records of encounters with native peoples. In addition, many officers and crew on all three voyages collected artifacts as mementos or as gifts for patrons and collectors in Britain.

Profit too was a motive, with scientists, collectors, private museums and dealers all competing to acquire 'curiosities'. Natural history specimens such as plants, animals and shells were the most sought after, but ethnographic items or 'artificial curiosities' were much easier to obtain and did not require special preparation. As a result of this informal trade, artifacts from Cook's voyages are now spread around the world from London to St Petersburg and from Stockholm to Sydney.

Deserted Indian village in King George Sound, New Holland, by John Sykes, 1791.

Despite the legal fiction of *terra nullius* – that the country was empty of inhabitants – around three-quarters of a million Aborigines inhabited all parts of Australia at the time the first white colonists arrived – the deserts of the centre as well as the rich riverlands of the southeast.

Population densities were low, technology simple and possessions few, as their carefully regulated nomadic life dictated, but starvation and malnutrition were almost unknown and the demands of the food quest left ample time for social and religious ritual and a rich imaginative and artistic life.

Captain Cook considered the Aborigines a happy people, without the burdens of care carried by Europeans, but whites soon came to view them as 'primitive' on account of their nomadism, different social structure and disregard of material possessions.

Many early explorers also saw and described Aboriginal paintings and engravings. George Grey, for instance, a colonial official who in 1841 became governor of South Australia, New Zealand and the Cape Colony, made drawings of rock art he saw in the Kimberley region of Western Australia. Although he thought the paintings 'uncouth and savage' he described them in detail and was impressed by the way they seemed to stand out from the rock. 'I was certainly rather surprised', he wrote, 'at the moment I first saw this gigantic head and upper part of a body bending over and staring grimly down at me.' These paintings are now known to represent Wandjina spirit beings, especially important in this arid region because they are held to control the rain.

WHO LIVED IN THE AMERICAS?

The earliest European settlers of North America were little concerned with the origins of humans on the continent, describing the Indians as descendants of the Ten Lost Tribes of Israel, refugees from Atlantis, or wandering Norsemen or Scythians. Wild theories long held sway, although as early as 1648 the traveller Thomas Gage had drawn attention to the physical similarities between North American Indians and the peoples of Mongolia and concluded that the Indians must therefore have come from Asia by way of the Bering Straits.

The prevailing view of the Indians as 'primitive and little evolved' is clearly seen in the nineteenth-century controversy over who made the earthen mounds found throughout the American Midwest at sites like Cahokia. Ironically, the controversy could rapidly have been settled if early Euroamericans had simply read the chronicles of Hernando de Soto's expedition in 1539 through the southeastern part of the continent; de Soto clearly documents the use of such mounds as temple and palace sites by the Indians he met.

Among the organizations that became interested in the moundbuilders at the end of the eighteenth century and encouraged their study was the American Philosophical Society, based in Philadelphia, one of whose presidents, Thomas Jefferson, later became third President of the United States. However, the first society in America devoted exclusively to antiquities was the American Antiquarian Society founded in 1812 to collect and present antiquities for the education of society. In the first volume of its journal was a paper by Caleb Atwater on the mounds of the Midwest.

The first recorded excavation in North America was conducted by Jefferson himself in 1784. Although it had long been known that the earthen mounds scattered through the countryside had been used for human burial, Jefferson set out specifically to find out how the mounds on his Virginia estate were constructed: they proved to be composed of several layers and burials. Among academic archaeologists, his work is therefore regarded as an early example of scientific method: establishing a research goal, then devising a specific strategy to achieve it.

Across the world, then, this period brought overwhelming events: the revelation of the lands of Australia and the Pacific, and the equally staggering revelation of the wonders of ancient Egypt; a rising mania for collecting classical art and antiquities and a passion for digging into prehistoric tombs. Although the emphasis was still on artifacts, it would not be long before new questions came to be asked of these relics of the past. Slowly, steadily, increasing numbers of people were querying the validity of Genesis – daring, in other words, to believe that humankind was far more ancient than the Bible said. This was the major battle that was now about to be fought and decisively won.

View of the Mississippi Valley, by John Egan, 1850. This painting of the excavation of a Louisiana mound is often erroneously used to illustrate accounts of Jefferson's pioneering dig of 1784. Nevertheless, his influence in the depiction of the mound's strata is clear. The painter shows it is of Native American origin, and not by a special race of mound-builders. Notice the presence of Indians bottom left, and the use of black slaves as excavators.

CHAPTER 4

Science and Romanticism, 1820–1860

The mid-nineteenth century saw the final transition from an age of antiquarians to one of archaeologists. The key principle of stratigraphy was adopted from geology, and the period culminated in 1859 – arguably the most important year in archaeology's history – with the publication of Charles Darwin's *Origin of Species* and a general acceptance of human antiquity.

Pompeiian style. The elaborate atrium of Prince Napoleon's Pompeiian palace, the Villa Diomède, on the Avenue Montaigne in Paris. Designed by Alfred-Nicolas Normand and begun in 1857, the villa rapidly became 'the rendezvous of all Paris, both of the Court and the Arts'.

The furniture by Rossigneux and table silver by Christofle was all carefully copied from first-century Roman pieces. In this painting of 1860 by Gustave Boulanger, actors dressed in Roman costume are rehearsing a play.

The influence of Pompeii was felt on architecture and interior decoration across Europe from the 1820s. At Aschaffenburg in the 1840s, Ludwig I of Bavaria commissioned a complete copy of the House of Castor and Pollux, while in London Prince Albert came up with the idea of a Pompeiian Garden Pavilion for Buckingham Palace. It was eventually built in 1844, six years after Victoria and Albert visited Pompeii, and survived until 1928.

GENESIS AND GEOLOGY

In western Europe the first inklings in the late eighteenth century that humans might have coexisted with extinct animals became by the mid-nineteenth century a certainty. It was a turning point in the history of archaeology, the era in which human antiquity was established once and for all.

Since *c.* 1810 a few people in the Périgord, southwest France, had been collecting flint tools and visiting caves, and a commerce in worked flints had begun. The area's pioneer archaeologist was François Vatard de Jouannet, a teacher and librarian from Bordeaux, often known as the 'grandfather of prehistory'. In 1810 he discovered his first worked flints – axes and arrowheads, some polished, others flaked – at Ecorne-boeuf, near Périgueux, attributing them, in the manner of the times, to 'Gauls'.

A few years later, in 1815–16, he found and dug the palaeolithic cave-sites of Combe Grenal and Pech de l'Azé. Jouannet wandered the countryside, hammer in hand, talking to peasants and stimulating their interest in worked flints. He was both the first person to take a serious interest in caves and rock-shelters, and the first to be intrigued by the heaps of ash, burnt bones and flints found in them; rather than simply attributing such finds to 'diluvian currents' like most of his contemporaries, he had fossil bones chemically analysed.

Jouannet was among the first to make a technological study of worked flints and the successive processes of flaking and polishing them: in 1834 he identified the first blows on cave flints and later modifications by 'light percussions' – what we would now call secondary flaking to refine the shape or cutting edge. In trying to reconstruct the way flaked and polished axes were made, he also perceived the differences between palaeolithic and neolithic stone tools. Though he had no idea how far apart they stood chronologically, he was the first to suggest the existence of two periods, the cruder flaked tools (of the Palaeolithic) preceding the more advanced polished forms (of the Neolithic).

Although at this time all worked flints were attributed to 'Gauls', it was troubling that Latin authors never mentioned the tribes of Gaul using such things, and that in Jouannet's caves these flints were mixed with bones. The same association of flints and bones was also apparent across the Channel in Britain. In 1823 William Buckland, an Anglican priest and first professor of mineralogy and geology at Oxford, published a book called *Reliquiae Diluvianae: Observations on the Organic Remains contained in caves, fissures, and diluvial gravel, and on other geological phenomena attesting the action of an Universal Deluge*. Buckland had uncovered a male burial, stained with red ochre and dated – as we now know – to about 26,000 years ago, in the Goat's Hole Cave at Paviland on the southwest coast of Wales. He thought this 'Red Lady of Paviland' was Romano-British, despite the presence of elephant, rhinoceros and bear bones together with fragments of ivory bracelets and rods which, he acknowledged, had been made from the 'antediluvian' tusk remains discovered in the cave.

Buckland plainly did not believe in the contemporaneity of humans and fossil animals. However, in 1825 another cleric, the Catholic chaplain John MacEnery, began exploring Kent's Cavern at Torquay in southwestern England, where he too found flint tools mixed with the bones of extinct fauna. MacEnery's initial conclusion, in 1828, was that 'there is no longer any question of the actual presence of flint implements under the stratified unbroken floor of stalagmite in the Cavern', but on consulting Buckland he was assured that the flints must be intrusive, having fallen into the lower deposit through 'cooking holes' in the stalagmite floor. As the contemporary rhyme had it:

Some doubts were once expressed about the Flood,
Buckland arose and all was clear as mud.

'The skeleton cave', a characteristically eerie painting by Caspar David Friedrich (1774–1840). The symbolic implications of skeletons walled up in caves beneath dripping stalactites for millennia were not lost on the withdrawn and ascetic Friedrich, the greatest of all German early romantic painters. Though a friend of Goethe, he had as a young man significantly refused to make the art student's traditional pilgrimage to Rome.

MacEnery refrained from publishing, since orthodox views were so clearly against him, and his findings were not presented in full until 1869. This was despite the fact that as early as 1840 his observations had won support from the geologist Robert Godwin Austen, who likewise concluded that objects 'such as arrow-heads and knives, flint-fashioned, are deposited in many parts [of Kent's Cavern] … The bones of the cave-mammals and the works of man must have been introduced into the Cave before the floor of the stalagmite had been formed.'

Sites like this aside, much of the most striking evidence continued to come from continental Europe. The eminent Austrian geologist Ami Boué, co-founder of the French Geological Society, claimed to have found, c. 1823, half a fossil human skeleton associated with extinct animals in deposits at Lahr, on the right bank of the Rhine. In southeastern France, Paul Tournal, a pharmacist from Narbonne who dug in the cave of Bize (Aude) in 1826, discovered human bones and teeth with crude pottery and the bones of extinct and modern animals, and 'fragments of quartz with very sharp edges'. He discerned no layering of archaeological levels, but in 1828 he did raise the question of the existence of fossil man. By 1834 he was more certain, having noticed marks of cutting tools on bones 'of lost species' recovered from the caves in 1831.

Tournal's great importance, however, is that he emphasized geological evidence to the point that he broke the tradition of linking ancient cave deposits with the Flood. By 1833 he was already dividing the last geological period – that of humans – into the historic (going back 7,000 years) and the *antehistoric*, of unknown duration. This was not only the first use of such a term, but the first real linkage of geology and history. It was a crucial turning point at which the concept of an

Boucher de Perthes

The man responsible for providing the final proofs of human antiquity was Jacques Boucher de Perthes (1788–1868), a French customs officer and amateur archaeologist who worked on open-air sites in the Abbeville region of Picardy.

In 1830, a young physician from Abbeville, Casimir Picard, had studied the stratigraphy of the Somme valley's river terraces and noted that the deepest layers contained 'Gallic'

Taken in a quarry at St Acheul (above and inset enlargement) on 27 April 1859 in the presence of Prestwich and Evans, this photograph shows a flint hand axe (opposite) in place in an undisturbed layer at a depth of 3.4 metres (11 feet).

– that is, Iron Age or pre-Roman – antiquities, with Roman material above and 'French' on top of that. He also established that 'Celtic' axes found in peatbogs predated, at least in part, the formation of the peat and that they were associated with the bones of aurochs (prehistoric wild cattle) and beaver: one of the first known correlations of geological, palaeontological and archaeological evidence.

After Picard's early death, his friend Boucher de Perthes carried on his work. He had not become interested in archaeology until the age of 49 and at first did not believe in fossil man, but because one of his first discoveries, in 1842, was a flaked stone tool found with a mammoth jaw in the 'diluvial' layers of Menchecourt-lès-Abbeville, he soon came to see that crudely worked flints associated with great antediluvial animals proved the existence of man 'as surely as would a whole Louvre'.

Boucher de Perthes' three-volume *Celtic and Antediluvian Antiquities* of 1847–64 was a decisive point in the history of archaeology. In it he drew a chronological distinction between two types of stone tools, corresponding to two successive stages of humanity: the most ancient flaked industries belonged to 'antediluvian' (fossil) man and the most recent, polished industries to modern, 'Celtic' humanity. Later, in 1865, the English naturalist and politician Sir John Lubbock would coin the words 'palaeolithic' and 'neolithic' (from the Greek for Old Stone and New Stone) to designate these two stages of human culture (p. 120).

The third book was illustrated in geological style with cross-sections that described the position and contents of each layer to demonstrate the truth of his arguments, but it took him many years to get his ideas on fossil man admitted by the scientific establishment. The difficulties were due in part to the important ideological and religious issues that were at stake in the recognition of human antiquity, but Boucher de Perthes' naivety – which sometimes led him to accept fakes as genuinely ancient human remains or tools – and poor drawings of the stone tools compounded the problem.

The orthodox view was still that human bones and tools all came from geological levels no older than Celtic and Gallo-Roman times. Thus the first pieces of portable art from the last Ice Age (between c. 30,000 and 10,000 years ago) were found around this time at Veyrier (Haute Savoie) c.. 1833 and at Chaffaud (Vienne) in 1852. The engraving of hinds on a reindeer bone from the latter site was catalogued as 'Celtic' in a museum, until recognized as palaeolithic by the notable French archaeologist Edouard Lartet a few years later (p. 118).

Yet slowly the climate was changing. In 1853 stone tools were found at St Acheul, near Amiens, in the same gravel layer as the bones of mammoth and woolly rhinoceros. Then, in October 1858, the English palaeontologist Hugh Falconer visited Abbeville as part of the scientific committee monitoring work at Brixham in southwestern England, a site at which stone tools had been found with the bones of extinct animals earlier the same year, sealed beneath a layer of stalagmite. These discoveries, albeit in a cave, were the result of extremely careful excavations run by the British Geological Society, and the scientific committee had accepted the contemporaneity of the finds. Falconer was equally convinced by what he found at Abbeville. In April the following year, the

eminent British archaeologist John Evans and the geologists Joseph Prestwich and Charles Lyell visited the site. Boucher de Perthes' claims were at last officially recognized.

The 'annus mirabilis' of 1859, a milestone in the establishment of human antiquity, also saw the publication of Charles Darwin's *On the Origin of Species*. In Darwin's conception of the history of the living world, man appeared not as the special object of divine creation, but as the product of an evolution rooted firmly among animals. Despite the opposition of the church, most scholars now accepted the obvious. In what has been called a 'great and sudden revolution', within the space of about eighteen months a long-standing but doubtful idea was transformed into a widespread consensus among scholars. Charles Lyell's work *The Antiquity of Man* (1863) put together the researches of one generation, and was the founding book for two new disciplines – prehistoric archaeology and palaeoanthropology.

CLAUDINE COHEN

historical antediluvian period was transformed into the idea of prehistory. As the meaning of antediluvian changed, so the defenders of 'antediluvian man' inevitably became the 'enemies' of the Bible and religion.

However, the debate should not be seen in simple 'Bible versus Science' terms. Some clerics, like MacEnery, recognized the archaeological evidence, while many geologists still believed in the universal floods described by classical authors. It was Tournal who came to see the disappearance of extinct animals as being due not to catastrophes but to the same gradual processes of change that can be observed today. In explaining the past by today's laws he anticipated the more famous work of the British geologist Charles Lyell.

Lyell, a pupil of Buckland's at Oxford, proposed in his *Principles of Geology* (1830–33) that all past geological processes were the same as those of the present, spanning an immensely long period, and that there was no need to believe in supernatural catastrophes like Noah's Flood to explain the fossil and stratigraphic record. So powerfully argued were his views that they transformed the intellectual climate. Traditional 'catastrophism' gave way to the doctrine of 'uniformitarianism' – the idea that if the geological processes operating past and present are uniform, the surface of the earth must have been shaped by sedimentation and erosion over aeons. Archbishop Ussher's date of 4004 BC for the creation of the world (p. 17) was rendered nonsensical and Buckland himself changed his mind about the contemporaneity of humans and fossil animals. Most important of all, Lyell's work had a huge influence on the work of British biologists like Charles Darwin, Alfred Wallace and Thomas Huxley, and on the development of the concept of evolution. As with geology, biology turned from an understanding constrained by a biblical seven day creation to the vista of an immensely long past. As far as human history was concerned, identifying crude stone tools as the work of humans became not simply plausible but absolutely crucial to the new understanding.

The breakthrough came in Belgium. Sporadic reports of fossilized human bones found in caves in Italy, France and Germany emerged in the eighteenth century, but they made no impact. In 1833, Philippe-Charles Schmerling, a Dutch doctor of Austrian origin, published his work in caves around Liège, where in deep layers he had found flint and bone tools with the remains of woolly rhinoceros, hyena and bear. Also present were human bones with archaic features – probably Neandertal burials. Schmerling was surprised to find that the human and animal bones were of the same colour and condition, and in the same deposits. From the cave of Engis, for example, he recovered the remains of three humans with flint tools – 'arrows or knives' – and the bones of elephant, rhinoceros and carnivores. Schmerling is important for being the first archaeologist to discover, save, and investigate the potential age of such bones and their link to modern humans, and for recognizing their contemporaneity with extinct fauna. The relatively complete human cranium unfortunately crumbled to bits when moved from the cave floor, but he was left with another partial cranium as well as some postcranial fragments.

Charles Lyell (1797–1875). Lyell denied the antiquity of humankind for thirty years, but revised his views dramatically in 1859 after visiting Boucher de Perthes' excavations at Abbeville. A tour of archaeological sites in England and France two years later only served to confirm his belief that stone tools regularly occurred deeply stratified alongside the bones of extinct animals. Lyell's *Geological Evidence of the Antiquity of Man* appeared in 1863. Darwin was delighted. 'It is great. What a fine long pedigree you have given the human race.'

Not all discoveries were so well investigated. The fairly complete adult skull – now known, like Engis, to be Neandertal – found fifteen years later, in 1848, in Forbes' Quarry, Gibraltar, remained forgotten until it was 'rediscovered' in a cupboard in 1862 and sent to England. By that time, 'Neandertal man' himself had made his appearance. In August 1856, limestone quarrying of a cave near Düsseldorf in Germany, the Feldhofer Grotto in the Neander valley – the apt name, Greek for 'new man', comes from a hymn-writer called Neumann – led to the discovery of a skull cap and some skeletal fragments. The skull cap had prominent brow-ridges, even bigger than those of the find from Engis.

The remains were handed to Carl Fuhlrott, a local schoolmaster and keen natural historian, who realized that they were not from a modern human and sent a plaster cast of the skull to Hermann Schaaffhausen, professor of anatomy at Bonn University. They published the skull jointly the next year, claiming that it represented a form of human now 'not known to exist, even in the most barbarous races' and concluding that it might be a local inhabitant of the region from a time before the Celts and Germans arrived. The sceptical academic community, however, dismissed the find as 'undoubtedly a Celt', an 'ancient Dutchman', a 'poor hydrocephalic idiot who had lived like an animal in the forest', a 'hermit', a 'wild cannibal', and a Cossack of 1814 whose horse-riding had caused curvature of the legbone (a feature now known to be a Neandertal characteristic). Fuhlrott and Schaaffhausen's most vigorous opponent, the pathologist Rudolf Virchow, attributed the curved legs to childhood rickets, which had led to pain, puckering of the brows and permanently ossified brow ridges. The world was not yet ready to accept the physical appearance of fossil man.

Despite abundant finds and serious claims from a wide array of scholars and naturalists around western Europe, the scientific establishment remained unmoved. Cuvier, until his death, dismissed all such finds as burials or redeposited bones dug down from later levels, while his followers denied categorically that man could have lived at the same time as extinct animals of the 'antediluvian epoch'. Lyell, the apostle of geological uniformitarianism, in 1832 still held that man had been created by the 'special and independent attention' of God – a belief he maintained for another twenty years. Moreover, like Buckland before him, he refused to admit geological proofs from excavations made in caves, where the stratigraphy was invariably complex and could easily have been disturbed. An indisputable open-air association of human bones and extinct fauna – like Frere's by now forgotten discovery of 1797 – was required (p. 64).

THE THREE AGES OF PREHISTORY

On the night of 4 May 1802 a thief broke into the antiquities room of the Danish royal collection, at Christiansborg palace in Copenhagen. Using a duplicate key, he made his way in darkness across the exhibition room, halting before the display case which held the priceless gold drinking horns from Gallehus in southern

The Gallehus horns. Discovered in 1639 and 1734 in the village of Gallehus in Jutland and dating to the fifth century AD, these two great ceremonial horns of solid gold passed into the royal collection in Copenhagen where they survived until being stolen and melted down in 1802. The thief was unmasked when he began selling clasps, Indian coins and other fakes made from the bullion.

The craftsmanship and symbolism of the horns, both evidently made in northern Europe, stimulated a steady stream of books and articles throughout the eighteenth century, and their loss generated bitter public recrimination. Both were decorated with human and animal figures cut from gold foil and attached with solder. The larger even carried a runic inscription giving the name of its maker: 'I, Hlewagast, son of Holt, made the horn'.

The modern replicas illustrated were reconstructed from detailed engravings made in the eighteenth century.

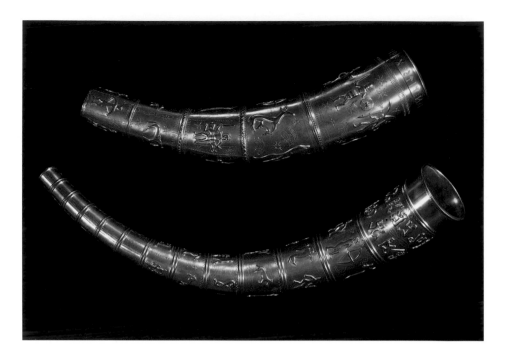

Jutland. Smashing the glass, he seized the two enormous prehistoric horns and made off. Only much later were the police able to catch the thief, when he began to sell fake gold coins and jewellery in suspiciously large quantities. By then it was too late to save the horns, which had been melted down for bullion.

The public outcry that followed this spectacular theft – one of archaeology's great losses – was one of the reasons behind the creation of a new museum in Copenhagen a few years later. Still more important was the fact that the evidence of Denmark's past was fast vanishing in the early years of the nineteenth century. Farmers were dismantling megalithic tombs and ploughing out ancient burial mounds to gain more land and new finds of prehistoric antiquities were being reported briefly in newspapers, only to disappear into the hands of private landowners soon afterwards. There was a feeling that something had to be done.

The government turned for advice to Frederik Münter, Bishop of Zealand and professor of theology at the University, who insisted that the most important field monuments should be protected by government decree against further depredations. He also recommended the setting up of a national museum to hold all archaeological finds made on Danish soil and a special commission to oversee the new measures.

The direct result was the establishment in 1807 of the Royal Committee for the Preservation and Collection of National Antiquities. The Committee at once established a collection of Danish antiquities, but within a decade its size had grown to the point where a professional curator was needed to look after it. Christian Jurgensen Thomsen, the man selected, was an inspired choice whose work was to transform the study of prehistoric archaeology in Europe.

Thomsen set about the reorganization of the collections with energy and enthusiasm in 1816. Within a few years he had adopted a wholly new way of ordering the remains of Danish prehistory, using the eighteenth-century concept of a three-age system in which tools of stone were replaced by tools of bronze, and

The Danish National Museum

Christian Jurgensen Thomsen (1788–1865), originator of the Three Age system of prehistoric chronology that still endures today, was the genial and wealthy son of a Copenhagen merchant.

Charged in 1816 with bringing order to the collections of the Danish National Museum, Thomsen's most pressing need was to organize the material for public display. He found there were two logical stages. First, he classified groups of finds according to the material used for their cutting tools: thus the earliest stage was represented by tools of stone, the second by tools of bronze and the third, and most recent, by tools of iron.

This in itself was hardly a revelation: the concept of three successive ages of stone, bronze and iron went back to classical times and it had gradually been winning acceptance in Britain, France and Scandinavia throughout the eighteenth century. What was new about Thomsen's scheme was the concept of association. He considered artifacts not on their own, but in relation to what was found with them. Working from this angle he discovered, for instance, that pottery vessels were made in all three ages, but glass vessels only in the Iron Age. This principle made it possible to organize not only the cutting tools but *all* the finds in his collections into Stone Age, Bronze Age and Iron Age.

Thomsen presented these individual phases of Danish prehistory in their own separate displays. He also extended the logic of his scheme far beyond the walls of the museum, to the field monuments of the Danish countryside, discovering, for example, that inhumations in stone-built chamber tombs were a feature of the Stone Age, whereas cremation burials were found only in the Bronze Age and Iron Age.

The rearrangement of the Danish National Museum's collections commenced in 1817, and by the following year the Three Age system had already begun to take shape. Thomsen was a cautious man, however, and though personally committed to his new chronology and the principle of association on which it was based, he did not rush into print. Indeed, he waited until 1836 before publishing an account of his work. This was the *Guide to Northern Archaeology*, which had wide influence and was rapidly translated into German, English and other European languages.

Thomsen demonstrating the collections, 1846. Drawing by Magnus Pedersen.

By that time the Museum had long been a popular success. Already in 1819, the demand was such that it was decided to open it to the public one day every week, on Thursday mornings between 11 am and 1 pm. Visitors were shown round by Thomsen in person. His enthusiasm and the straightforward welcome he extended to visitors won many adherents. He paid particular attention to farm workers 'because it is by them that we shall have our collections enlarged.'

By 1832 the museum had outgrown its original home in the loft of Holy Trinity church and new quarters were found for it in a wing of the Christiansborg palace. Later, in 1853, it moved again, to still larger quarters in the Prince's Palace opposite. By the time of Thomsen's death in 1865, the Royal Museum for Nordic Antiquities (as it had then become) had been built up into an impressive collection of 27,000 numbered items, providing an unrivalled overview of Denmark's past from earliest times.

Jens Worsaae (1821–85). The precocious Worsaae carried out excavations at the Danish megalithic tomb of Grønhøj, near Horsens, while still a boy and published his first scholarly article at seventeen. From 1844 he devoted himself entirely to archaeology.

tools of bronze were replaced in turn by tools of iron. Classical writers like Lucretius had envisaged the remote past in this way (p. 52). Thomsen's crucial additional step was to arrange all the rest of the material in his collection according to whether it had been found with tools of stone, bronze or iron.

Thus was born the Three Age system, the basis of European prehistoric chronology to this day. At last it was possible to bring order to chaos: to place objects in sequence, grouped according to the period to which they belonged: Stone Age, Bronze Age or Iron Age. The new system had its limitations: in particular, it did not allow precise dates to be attached to prehistoric sites or finds – that only became possible in the present century with the development of radiometric dating methods such as Carbon 14. Yet Thomsen's Three Age system offered immense new possibilities for the archaeologist, providing for the first time some means of unravelling the prehistoric past by giving it a chronological dimension. Before long the scheme had been adopted in museums across Europe and it had become clear that the three ages could themselves be subdivided internally to achieve finer chronological gradations. Thomsen had initiated a quiet revolution.

Discovering the Mesolithic

The Three Age system proved so successful a means of organizing artifacts and thinking about the prehistoric past that even within Thomsen's lifetime the original scheme had been outgrown. New problems stimulated major refinements. In particular, in 1851 there erupted the so-called 'kitchen midden' controversy. The middens were enormous rubbish heaps of shells on the coast of Denmark, apparently the remains of innumerable meals deposited at some distant period in the past. But how old were they?

The man who was to both pose the question and answer it was Jens Jacob Worsaae, a law student in Copenhagen who began helping Thomsen in the National Museum as a volunteer in the late 1830s. The two did not hit it off and, after the collapse of the family finances following the death of his father, Worsaae left to pursue his archaeological career by other means. Through natural ability and good fortune he gained the support of the Danish king, and by this means was able to write, in 1843, the first discursive account of Danish prehistory, *Primeval Antiquities of Denmark*. With this book, Worsaae won his place in the archaeological pantheon as the first professional archaeologist, the first real comparative archaeologist, and the true father of modern archaeology.

It was the controversy of the kitchen middens a few years later that prompted Worsaae to revise Thomsen's Three Age scheme. Japetus Steenstrup, a distinguished zoologist who had been working on these mounds since 1827, claimed that they had been formed naturally, through wave action. Worsaae took the opposing view, that the shells had been discarded by human groups who had relied on shellfish as part of their regular diet. While excavating one of these mounds at Mejlgaard in east Jutland in 1851, Worsaae came to realize that Thomsen's Stone

Skeletons in a megalithic tomb, from Worsaae's *Primeval Antiquities of Denmark* (1843). Worsaae developed Thomsen's Three Age system and used it to study not only museum collections but also the field monuments of Denmark. By excavating shell middens, burial mounds and other sites, he was able to demonstrate the potential of this approach. He even had King Frederik VII of Denmark as colleague on some of his excavations.

Age could be subdivided and that he could distinguish between an early and late Stone Age in Denmark. The early sites, such as the shell middens, had roughly-shaped chipped stone tools; the later Stone Age sites had more neatly formed stone tools, often ground smooth and polished. Furthermore, Worsaae found that it was only in the later of these two phases that pottery had been in use.

What Worsaae had lighted upon was the distinction we now draw between the Mesolithic (Middle Stone Age) and the Neolithic (New Stone Age). These terms were not used by Worsaae himself. The word 'neolithic', coined in 1865 by the British archaeologist Sir John Lubbock, became the standard term for those early societies who manufactured pottery, raised crops and livestock, and used polished stone tools. Before it in Lubbock's scheme stood the Palaeolithic, the 'Old Stone Age', the period of the ice ages, the 'cave dwellers', and the flaked flint tools found by Boucher de Perthes and others in the river gravels of western Europe. Worsaae's shell middens clearly belonged to an intervening phase, the Mesolithic or 'Middle Stone Age'.

As new discoveries accumulated and knowledge increased, further subdivisions of the Stone, Bronze and Iron Ages were proposed, some to be accepted, some hotly debated, others quietly abandoned. As the century wore on the concept of typology – the classification of artifacts into different types – was introduced as a means to provide ever more detailed chronological refinements. The resulting schemes were inevitably far more complex than the original Three Age system, the concern of professional archaeologists rather than the museum visitor. But none would have been possible without Thomsen's pioneering achievement in creating the first workable prehistoric chronology.

Daniel Wilson and prehistory

Great Lakes Indians. Wilson undertook pioneering studies of Native American groups around the Great Lakes in the 1850s. This Ojibwa camp near Sault-Ste-Marie on the northern shore of Lake Superior was painted by Paul Kane a few years earlier. The largest lodge, covered with sheets of birch-bark at the top and matting near the bottom, suggests a temporary camp. Notice the baby's cradle with headbar.

Daniel Wilson (1816–92), a poor but clever Edinburgh engraver and antiquary who could not afford a university degree, was the man who catapulted the term 'prehistoric' into the English language. The word *préhistorique* was already in use in France in the 1840s – having been coined by Gustave d'Eichthal in 1843 – but it was Wilson who first popularized the concept of prehistory in Britain and America with his two books, *The Archaeology and Prehistoric Annals of Scotland* (1851) and *Prehistoric Man: Researches into the Origin of Civilization in the Old and New World* (1862).

In the first book, Wilson drew upon the collections of the Society of Antiquaries of Scotland to distinguish Stone and Bronze Ages from the Roman and Christian epochs in Scotland; in the second, 'unexpectedly transplanted among the colonists' in Toronto, he developed the comparative method for illuminating prehistoric periods through analogy with contemporary 'primitive races'. With characteristic High Victorian confidence, Wilson believed evolution was the Creator's means of realizing his design and that Britain epitomized the highest degree of progress; but unlike many of his compatriots, he recognized civilizations among non-western races and insisted that all humans can become civilized. He stressed the universality of evolution and its impact on the rise of civilizations, as well as the value of prehistoric archaeology for studying long-term social change.

In Canada, teaching English and history at University College in Toronto, Wilson used the summers of 1855 and 1856 to explore the antiquities and observe the Indians of the Great Lakes region, where 'a long obliterated past of Britain's and Europe's infancy was reproduced in living reality before his eyes', an experience that gave scope and substance to *Prehistoric Man*.

Wilson wrote the magisterial article on archaeology in the ninth edition of the *Encyclopedia Britannica* (1878), but his pre-eminence was contested by the aristocrats of London science, members of the Royal Society and contributors to Darwin's enterprise. One of Darwin's protégés, the banker Sir John Lubbock, was invited by a publisher to collate his already printed articles and add a new comparative section to produce a book to compete with Wilson's *Prehistoric Man*. Lubbock's *Pre-Historic Times* of 1865 is invariably cited as the first book in English on prehistoric archaeology and the basis of the discipline we know today – a claim that testifies more to the power of a wealthy and politically influential metropolitan clique than the true passage of events. The lower middle class Daniel Wilson, who emigrated to Canada because he could not obtain suitable employment in Britain, found himself in exile, unable to challenge Lubbock's move to take over leadership of the discipline he had been the first to describe.

Though ignored by the Royal Society in London, Daniel Wilson was influential in Canada. He became president of the Royal Society of Canada (1885–86) and first president of the University of Toronto (1887), and he was knighted in 1888. The honours course in anthropology he inaugurated at University College, Toronto, in 1857 seems, moreover, to have been the first formal university course in the subject anywhere in the world.   ALICE KEHOE

THE ARCHAEOLOGY OF NATIONS

At the time when modern nation-states were being established in western Europe, eastern Europe remained firmly in the grip of the Prussian monarchy and the great empires of the past: Austro-Hungarian, Russian and Ottoman. Yet within this region many peoples with aspirations to nationhood were discovering their own archaeological past.

One prerequisite for the emergence of nationalism in archaeology was a sense of time and sequence – a dimension established in the early nineteenth century through Thomsen and Worsaae's work identifying and classifying archaeological finds. The second was the emergence in the mid-nineteenth century of the idea of evolution, a concept that soon came to be extended from biology to archaeology, stimulating archaeologists to trace the origins of particular categories of artifacts to ancestral types.

In particular, efforts were made to identify archaeological remains as being those of either ancient Slavs or Germans. The historian and linguist Wawrzniec

Romantic decay. Tintern Abbey, by Joseph Mallord William Turner (1775–1851).

The fascination of the romantic movement with the primitive and the picturesque, with wild scenery and decay, helped stimulate nineteenth-century interest in national origins, both in remote pre-history and in the millennium that followed the fall of the Roman empire in the west.

The ruins of Gothic abbeys and castles, dismissed since the Renaissance as barbarous and ugly, became in the later eighteenth century a focus for sentimental and romantic study. At Tintern in the Wye valley the abbey church was cleared of debris and the ground levelled and turfed, but the ivy that clothed the ruins – a key part of the site's attraction – was allowed to remain. Some visitors wanted even more decay. 'Though the parts are beautiful', wrote one, 'a number of gable-ends hurt the eye with their regularity; and disgust it by the vulgarity of their shape. A mallet judiciously used might be of service in fracturing some of them ...'

By the early nineteenth century, Tintern had become a popular tourist attraction. Some visitors complained that the abbey was 'encumbered on every side with unpicturesque cottages and pigsties, rudely built with the consecrated stones of the violated ruin', but all were overcome by 'its indescribable grandeur and beauty'. Some even made moonlight visits to experience the full romantic impact of the ruins by torchlight.

Surowiecki identified the ancient Slavs with the Veneti mentioned in Tacitus' *Germania*, while German scholars of the 1820s and 1830s tried to connect the ancestral Germans with northern peoples, particularly those responsible for the rich archaeological remains then beginning to be found in large quantities in southern Scandinavia. Seen in these terms, the problem region was that in which Slav and German settlement had historically overlapped: the area between the lower Elbe and Vistula rivers.

While the nationalist movement had a profound effect on early nineteenth-century archaeology, its cousin, romanticism, also influenced how people thought about the past. In some respects, the romantic movement stimulated a gentle and civilized fascination with the past – with nature, with classical authors, with fairy tales and with beauty. This optimistic strand reflected a benign faith in the goodness of humanity and the closeness to nature of the past. Yet romanticism

The Swiss lake dwellings

Was prehistoric life pastoral idyll or bloodthirsty struggle? Because nineteenth-century archaeologists projected their own preoccupations onto the remains of the past – just as we do today – discoveries like the Swiss lake settlements are fascinating today as mirrors of the age, as revealing of patterns of thought at the time they were discovered in the 1850s as of prehistoric life itself.

During the cold, dry winter of 1853–54, the water levels of many lakes in the Zürich area fell markedly. At Obermeilen, on Lake Constance, this revealed a layer on the lake bottom, 30–60 centimetres (1–2 feet) thick, containing the stumps of many wooden posts, innumerable animal bones and antlers, and artifacts made from stone, clay and wood, as well as bone and antler. A local schoolteacher who collected antiquities saw the site and contacted Dr Ferdinand Keller, president of the Zürich Antiquarian Society.

Obermeilen, and sites like it, soon came to be known collectively as the 'Swiss lake dwellings'. From the moment of Keller's first newspaper report in 1854, ascribing the settlements to 'Celts', they excited the public imagination and triggered an intense debate about their construction and purpose. Now known to date from the neolithic period (c. 3000 BC), the settlements above all offered an extraordinary glimpse into the lives of the early farmers in the foothills of the Alps, owing to the preservation through waterlogging of organic materials like wood, hides, textiles and food remains that perish in normal conditions.

Keller's story was picked up by other papers and went out to the world. By now he was advancing two alternative explanations for the Obermeilen finds: either the post

dwellings stood on the sandy lake edge or the posts supported houses on platforms in the shallows. He eventually came down firmly in favour of the second option, which he illustrated with a drawing of houses several metres offshore on a platform reached by a succession of gangplanks. In Keller's mind these were not houses with structural posts driven down into the lake bottom. He imagined the posts as the piles for timber platforms upon which houses were then built – in effect wooden islands.

This romantic idea was probably borrowed ultimately from travellers' accounts of the lake-villages of Malaya and the East Indies that were at this time filtering into the consciousness of Europe. Keller also compared the Swiss sites with the lake crannogs of Ireland, artificial islands of the first millennium AD mentioned in historical sources like the Irish annals. Another possible inspiration may have been the writings of the Greek historian and geographer Herodotus, who describes a lake-dwelling of the fifth century BC on Lake Prasias in Macedonia.

Whatever Keller's source, the idea of prehistoric houses on platforms over the water fast passed into popular myth. Keller's drawing, embellished and amplified in ever more fanciful reconstructions – like the painting commissioned in 1867 from Rodolphe Auguste Bachelin by the Zürich Antiquarian Society (right) – became accepted as the archetypal reconstruction of the many waterlogged settlements found in the shallows of Alpine lakes in the years that followed. Since Keller's reconstruction had established the nature of the dwellings, most new sites were simply mined for their abundant, well-preserved artifacts.

had its darker side too, elevating *Sturm und Drang* – the emotional, the imaginative and the violent – in febrile opposition to the supposedly bloodless rationalism of the Enlightenment.

It was this passionate, avowedly primitive, strand in romanticism that fuelled interest in the study of the past. The morbid fascination with graves and death that emerges in the music and painting of the period led to the excavation of many burial sites, while the Dark Ages and Middle Ages – the barbarous millennium from AD 500 to 1500 – received serious scholarly attention for the first time.

THE DEVELOPMENT OF FIELD ARCHAEOLOGY

By no means all prehistory in Europe was coloured by incipient nationalism or yearning for an idyllic, pre-industrial past. Above all, the nineteenth century was a period in which archaeology developed as a serious scholarly activity in which the

In reality, the idea that water flowed constantly beneath the houses was by no means securely established. After Keller's time, prehistorians suggested that the buildings were erected in areas that were subject to seasonal inundation but at other times stood on dry land, or that they stood originally on the lake shore and had only later been inundated. Today, conventional wisdom differentiates between bog settlements (*Moorsiedlungen* in German) and lake-shore settlements (*Ufersiedlungen*), firmly rejecting Keller's idea of wooden islands in the open water. Both types of settlement were made up of small groups of rectangular houses, sometimes with animal stalls and storehouses of the type found recently at the bog settlement of Thayngen-Weier.

Even so, Keller's imaginative reconstruction, perpetuated in innumerable pictures and museum dioramas, shows no signs of disappearing from public view. His idyllic view of prehistoric life continues to appeal to our romantic impulse, and its impact appears to be indelible.

Bachelin's reconstruction of the Obermeilen 'lake village', 1867, now in the Swiss National Museum in Zürich.

accurate collection of data was paramount. In Britain, for instance, a new society devoted to field archaeology, the British Archaeological Association, was founded in 1844, its proclaimed aims to visit – and sometimes excavate – sites and to look at private collections and museums outside London (the capital being by precedent the territory of the Society of Antiquaries, established more than a century earlier).

Ramsauer's excavations at the early Iron Age site of Hallstatt in the Austrian Alps between 1846 and 1863 were meticulously recorded, the graves invariably with striking watercolours. Many of the thousand burials were richly furnished with weapons, jewellery, ceramics, trade goods like amber and ivory, and even bronze vessels from Italy that help date the site to the seventh and sixth centuries BC.

Hallstatt's prosperity, derived from mining the local rock salt, came to an end in the fifth century when more easily won sources were found elsewhere. Up the valley from the cemetery, excavation of the mine galleries themselves located tools, clothing, even the body of a prehistoric miner perfectly preserved by the salt like a side of bacon.

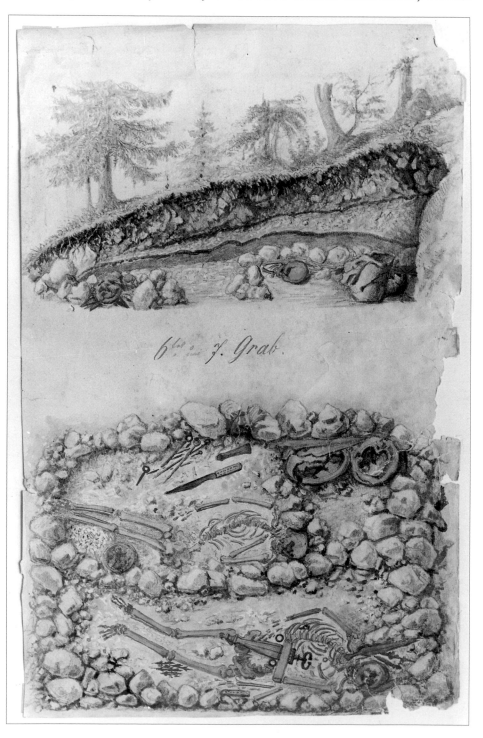

Excavation was becoming steadily more methodical and extensive. Near Salzburg in Austria, the mining engineer Johann Georg Ramsauer embarked in the 1850s on excavations of the Early Iron Age cemetery at Hallstatt (*c.* 1200– 600 BC). High on a mountain above the lakeside town, using miners as labourers, he excavated about a thousand graves over the course of nineteen years. About 55 per cent were skeletal burials, and 45 per cent cremations; together they yielded thousands of artifacts, including lavish grave goods of bronze and iron. Each grave was cleaned, sketched and described in writing. Only when it came to publication did Ramsauer's meticulousness fail him; the master record of his excavations disappeared after his death, only to resurface in a second-hand bookshop in Vienna in 1932.

Like the Swiss lake sites, Hallstatt provided scholars of the late nineteenth century with a revelatory glimpse of life in prehistoric Europe. Visitors to the marvellous collection of artifacts displayed today in the Natural History Museum in Vienna can easily imagine the impact Ramsauer's finds made. Above all, his excavations revealed the sophistication of the prehistoric community that existed on the northern fringe of the Alps during the first half of the first millennium BC. Some of the objects found in the graves were made from exotic materials like amber and ivory, commodities traded over long distances in exchange for the locally mined salt that lay at the root of Hallstatt's prosperity; others were imports from Etruscan Italy.

THE DISCOVERY OF THE ETRUSCANS

The plentiful existence of antiquities in Etruria, the area to the north of Rome, had long been known. As early as 1558, numerous rock-cut tombs bearing Etruscan writing had been discovered during digging near the church of the Madonna delle Piaggi di Campo in Perugia. For years afterwards the area continued to produce large numbers of pots, so much so that by 1768 the industrial potter Josiah Wedgwood was turning out imitative red on-black 'Etruscan' wares from his workshop at 'Etruria' in the English Potteries. In fact, the pots Wedgwood was copying were not Etruscan at all; they were Greek vessels shipped in quantity from Attica on a flourishing trade network.

Renewed British interest in the Etruscans in the nineteenth century is reflected in particular in the traveller George Dennis' *Cities and Cemeteries of Etruria* (1848). Though much of his interpretation was outdated, Dennis knew Tuscany well and he provided his readers with an impressive amount of descriptive detail about many sites and monuments.

At the same time, Italian artists such as Carlo Ruspi were also touring the cemeteries of Etruria, making careful coloured drawings of the painted tomb chambers they encountered. Such records are invaluable to today's archaeologists, recording the state of the tombs when they were first opened and allowing subsequent damage and deterioration to be gauged and restoration undertaken.

Antiquaries at work in an Etruscan cemetery, by Giovanni Battista Passeri, 1767. Frontispiece from *Picturae Etruscorum in Vasculis.*

PIONEER WORK IN THE NEAR EAST

The Napoleonic *Description of Egypt* (p. 69) established a trend central to early Egyptology that came to be echoed in both Etruscan Italy and the classical world: the recording of standing monuments. The vast archaeological treasure-house of the Nile valley contained information and monuments in abundance, and excavation to produce large buildings was not necessary. What was needed was the recording of this information and its publication for an eager European public. Champollion's work too spurred the publication of monuments, in particular

View under the Grand Portico, Philae, from *Egypt and Nubia* by David Roberts (1796–1864).

Roberts was the greatest nineteenth-century painter of Egyptian antiquities, his work both atmospheric and archaeologically accurate. Born into a poor family in Edinburgh, he initially worked fifteen-hour days as a house painter before graduating to painting theatre scenery, first in Scotland, then at the Old Vic and Covent Garden in London.

In 1838, Roberts set out for Egypt, travelling the length of the Nile in time-honoured fashion from Cairo south to Abu Simbel. So vermin-ridden was the small boat he hired that he had it submerged in the Nile for twenty-four hours before he would embark.

Ultimately, Roberts made over a hundred detailed sketches on a journey that took three months, 'struck with amazement at the beautiful preservation and endless labour spent upon the carving' of the monuments he recorded. A wealth of finished watercolours and oil paintings followed on his return to London, and in 1842 a series of some 284 lithographs, so precise in their detail that they are referred to by Egyptologists even today.

transcriptions of the hieroglyphic texts with which the walls of temples and tombs were liberally decorated. Cracking the hieroglyphic code was fundamental to understanding ancient Egypt: as with the classical world, it was thought that the direct testimony of the Egyptians through their writing was the best way to understand historical events, religious ritual and myth, even everyday life.

The copying of texts and recording of standing monuments was thus the major preoccupation of Egyptologists in the first half of the nineteenth century. Especially notable figures were the German philologist Karl Richard Lepsius and epigraphers like the Englishman John Gardner Wilkinson, whose three-volume *Manners and Customs of the Ancient Egyptians*, a magisterial account of twelve years single-handed and self-funded recording, was published in 1837–41. Lepsius was, after Champollion, the most important Egyptologist of the period, his major achievement the continuation of his predecessor's work recording monuments in Egypt and the Sudan. Between 1842 and 1845 he led an expedition under the patronage of the king of Prussia that drew monuments and inscriptions as far south as Meroe in the Sudan, and conducted excavations at 'The Labyrinth', the mortuary temple attached to the pyramid of King Amenemhat III (*c.* 1844–1797 BC) at Hawara. The masterly result of this work, *Monuments of Egypt and Ethiopia* (1849–60), is one of the largest archaeological publications ever produced, its twelve huge volumes containing 894 plates measuring a memorable 77 by 61 centimetres (30 by 24 inches).

Mariette. Order out of chaos
In 1878 a flood in Cairo brought about one of Egyptology's great losses: the destruction of the archaeological records of Auguste Mariette (1821–81), the man who for a quarter of a century had been the dominant figure in Egyptology.

Born in Boulogne, Mariette's interest in Egypt was sparked in 1842 when his family acquired the papers of a relative, Nestor L'Hôte, who had been a draughtsman on Champollion's 1828 expedition. Mariette taught himself hieroglyphs and Coptic, and in 1849 joined the staff of the Louvre. The following year he was despatched to Egypt to acquire Coptic, Ethiopic and Syriac manuscripts; instead, he undertook the excavation of the Serapeum at Saqqara, a subterranean cemetery-gallery sacred to the bull god Apis. His sensational discoveries in 1851 provided the springboard for a career further enhanced by Mariette's connections with Ferdinand de Lesseps, probably the most influential foreigner in Egypt at the time, who obtained the concession for building the Suez Canal between 1859–69. Through his connections at the court of the Khedive, Mariette was appointed Director of Egyptian Monuments in 1858.

By 1850 the major problems of reading hieroglyphic texts had been solved and a descriptive account of ancient Egyptian history had begun to be written, its narrative based primarily on the large-scale copying of monumental inscriptions in standing temples and tombs. European museums had begun to fill with antiquities

Giovanni Belzoni

Giovanni Belzoni (1778–1823)

The Napoleonic invasion of 1798 brought Europe into direct contact with the civilization of ancient Egypt and triggered a scramble for Egyptian antiquities. The flavour of the period is well reflected in the careers of a few colourful but unprincipled adventurers whose ambition was little less than the wholesale acquisition of ancient Egypt for their patrons.

One of the most successful was Bernardino Drovetti, a colonel in Napoleon's army of invasion who became, sporadically, French consul in Egypt until 1829. So enterprising and energetic was Drovetti and so numerous were his agents that the antiquities that passed through their hands eventually came to form the core of three of the world's greatest Egyptian collections, in Berlin, Paris and Turin.

Other European officials were just as active. The British consul-general in Cairo, an ex-portrait-painter called Henry Salt, employed from 1816 a quite literally larger-than-life character to collect antiquities on his behalf. This was Giovanni Belzoni, a 6'7" circus strongman – reputedly capable of

lifting an iron frame containing twelve people – who had originally come to Egypt to sell waterwheels to the Egyptian government. When this venture failed, he entered Salt's employ. Among his achievements was the transport from Thebes in the hottest season of the year of the colossal, 'quite perfect and very beautiful' granite head of Ramesses II known as the 'Younger Memnon', now in the British Museum, with equipment that consisted of fourteen poles, four ropes of palm leaves and four rollers; and the removal from the Valley of the Kings of the sarcophagus of Ramesses III, now – except for its lid, which was presented to the Fitzwilliam Museum, Cambridge – in the Louvre.

It is for his work in the Valley of the Kings that Belzoni is best known, his most notable achievement being the discovery in October 1817 of the tomb of Seti I (c. 1306–1290 BC), the most richly decorated and, at over 100 metres (330 feet), the longest of all Egyptian royal tombs. Belzoni's account of his work for Salt is contained in a book he published in 1820, the most memorable passage of which contains his description of exploring tombs on the West Bank at Thebes:

> After the exertion of entering into such a place, through a passage of ... perhaps six hundred yards, nearly overcome, I sought a resting-place, found one and contrived to sit; but when my weight bore down on the body of an Egyptian, it crushed it like a band-box. I naturally had recourse to my hands to sustain my weight, but they found no better support; so that I sank altogether among the broken mummies, with a crash of bones, rags, and wooden cases, which raised such a dust as kept me motionless for a quarter of an hour, waiting till it subsided again. I could not remove from the place, however, without increasing it, and every step I took crushed a mummy in some part or other.

Though productive, Belzoni's time in Egypt was short. He left in 1819, returning to England where he was lionized by London society and embarked on an ambitious project to reconstruct the tomb of Seti I in the Egyptian Hall in Piccadilly. Unable to find backers to continue his work in Egypt, Belzoni's restlessness overcame him. He died of dysentery in Benin in west Africa in 1823 on an expedition to find the source of the river Niger.

Right. Illustration from *The Tombs of the Kings of Thebes*, *discovered by G. Belzoni* (1820).

imported from Egypt, which were still being collected in a more or less uncontrolled manner. What was now required, Mariette realized, was regulation of the activities of people digging archaeological sites and carrying off loot, and the encouragement of competent excavators to carry out digs of a quite different character.

The core of Mariette's achievement was the founding of the first national antiquities service and the first national museum in the Islamic world – the Cairo Museum which opened at Bulaq in 1863. He fostered real concern for the proper maintenance of Egypt's archaeological heritage and his antiquities service initiated a vast, albeit poorly supervised, programme of excavations at most of the major sites in Egypt. Monuments such as the New Kingdom temple at Luxor, and the Graeco-Roman temple at Edfu, built between 257– 237 BC, were cleared wholesale. To celebrate the completion of the Suez canal in 1869, Mariette even devised the plot for Verdi's *Aida*, an Egyptian opera which ends with hero and heroine perishing entombed in a real building, the Temple of Ptah at Memphis.

The civilization of ancient Mesopotamia

The topographic work of Claudius Rich was essentially historical geography, identifying ancient sites and their principal monuments from evidence embedded in the Bible and in the writings of classical authors like Herodotus (p. 3). Ancient Mesopotamian civilization itself remained hidden from view. The limited digging that Rich and others carried out at Babylon and elsewhere yielded curios but no systematic archaeological knowledge, and cuneiform remained unreadable, rendering Assyrian and Babylonian accounts of their own civilization meaningless. Yet this gloomy situation was about to change. In several hectic decades of archaeological discovery and epigraphic decipherment, a few soldiers and diplomats, of scholarly as much as martial disposition, invented Assyriology.

The years between Napoleon's fall at Waterloo (1815) and the Crimean War (1854–56) witnessed a collision of imperial ambitions across western Asia. The decaying Ottoman empire lost control of Greece and Egypt; Russia expanded its empire, seizing Ottoman territories to the south and moving toward central Asia; the French and British, united only in their fear of Russia, competed for influence in the Mediterranean and western Asia; and Britain sought to protect the passage to India by propping up the Ottoman government as a hedge against Russian ambition. This geopolitical struggle directly concerned Mesopotamia. Because the region carried the overland trade routes that linked the eastern Mediterranean to India, it was of strategic importance to France as well as Britain. Persia sat astride these routes, in the eyes of the Europeans a bulwark against possible Russian expansion into central Asia.

Strategic and commercial interest in Mesopotamia helped stimulate antiquarian research. When in 1839 the French sent a mission to report on the inscriptions, architecture and sculpture of Persia and Mesopotamia, its diplomatic context was quite clear: the published account goes under the explicit title *Travels in Persia, undertaken by order of the Minister of Foreign Affairs and according to the instructions of the Institute of France*. It is not therefore surprising that the first large-scale excavations in western Asia were the work of two men in government service, the Frenchman Paul Emile Botta and the Englishman Austen Henry Layard. It was they who drew the world's attention to the archaeological wealth of Mesopotamia.

Assyrian palaces

Botta, the French consul in Mosul in northeastern Iraq, began his excavations at Nineveh (Kuyunjik) late in 1842, but soon abandoned them because of meagre results. The following year his luck changed. Hearing of impressive ruins at Dur Sharrukin (Khorsabad), just 20 kilometres (12 miles) to the north, he shifted his operations there, uncovering almost at once the palace of the Assyrian king Sargon II (721–705 BC). The building was richly ornamented with alabaster wall reliefs depicting the military and ritual accomplishments of the king. Guarding the entrances were enormous winged bulls with human heads measuring 4 metres (13 feet) high. The one difficulty Botta encountered – a problem that was to bedevil many later excavations on Assyrian sites – was that the palace had burned down, leaving some of the reliefs and sculptures calcinated. As he reports in his *Essays on the Remains of Nineveh* (1850), as soon as they were uncovered, they began to crumble:

> The walls yield to the swelling of the ground, the action of the sun reduces the surface to powder, and even now a considerable portion has disappeared. This is truly grievous, but I can devise no remedy, unless the whole, as I draw it, should be again filled up, and thus preserved for future investigation; this is my present purpose, since ... it will always be possible to make a fresh clearing, whilst, by leaving the walls uncovered, in three months not a vestige of them would remain.

Botta's reports generated enormous excitement, provoking the French interior minister to arrange financial subsidies and transportation of the finds to Paris. Except for the finest bull colossus, which was burnt for gypsum by local farmers after being abandoned on the road to Mosul when its trolley collapsed, the best pieces were floated down the Tigris to Basra in 1846 and shipped to Paris for display in the Louvre. The Minister of the Interior and the Institut de France even supported Botta's massive five volume report, *Monuments of Nineveh* (1849–50).

With the Paris revolution of 1848, French archaeological work in Mesopotamia was interrupted. Botta was dismissed in 1851 and disappeared from sight, politically disgraced. The initiative now passed to the British in the shape of Botta's friend, Austen Henry Layard. Inspired by the discoveries at Khorsabad, the spirited and energetic Layard induced Stratford Canning, the British ambassador to Constantinople, to secure him a permit and funds to excavate to provide a British response to recent French successes.

Layard at Nineveh

Mesopotamian archaeology effectively began with Austen Henry Layard (1817–94) and his excavation of Nineveh. He was not the first to uncover the magnificence of the Assyrian palaces – that honour belongs to Botta – but it was Layard who, in just half a decade of intense work, revealed the civilization itself and presented it to the mid-nineteenth-century public.

Born in Paris, Layard grew up in Switzerland and Italy. At sixteen he went to London to study law, a pursuit he kept up for six years until, disenchanted, he secured a job in Ceylon (Sri Lanka). He embarked for Ceylon in 1839 but never reached his destination. Sidetracked by the lure of exotic travel and adventure, he decided to take the overland route to India by way of Palestine and Syria, eventually arriving in Mosul in northern Mesopotamia, where he visited Nineveh, Nimrud and Ashur.

Layard then travelled through the perilous mountains of western Persia, where he spent time with the nomadic Bakhtiyari tribes. When he reached Baghdad in 1842, he agreed to travel on to Constantinople to brief the British ambassador, Stratford Canning, on border conditions between Ottoman Turkey and Persia; on the way, he visited Nineveh where Botta had begun to dig – his first taste of Mesopotamian archaeology.

Layard's abilities impressed Canning. He was offered a post in the British Embassy and worked in Constantinople for two years, a period in which Botta's successes at Khorsabad were both firing Canning's antiquarian interests and in-flaming his diplomatic instincts. A wish to compete with the French for influence in the region played no small part in Canning's decision to sponsor Layard's first excavations at Nimrud in 1845.

By twentieth-century standards, the excavations were primitive in the extreme. For both Layard and Botta the aim was to recover monumental statuary and stone wall reliefs that could be displayed in their national museums. Large gangs of workmen trenched or tunnelled along the palace walls as quickly as possible; anything more fragile – limestone and metal objects and murals on plaster – disintegrated as soon as they were exposed.

In 1847 Layard began shipping his finds to England, endeavouring to transport the monumental sculpture intact, avoiding Botta's stratagem of cutting large objects into more manageable pieces that needed to be reassembled for exhibition. There were problems even so. While the crates were in transit, inquisitive British visitors to the Bombay customs house opened many of them, breaking some of the carefully packed artifacts. It was October 1848 before the precious cargo arrived in London and went on display in the British Museum.

The aggressive assurance of Assyrian art struck a chord in Victoria's England and aroused enormous interest. At the request of the Foreign Secretary, Viscount Palmerston, and backed by British Museum funds, Layard returned the following year to excavate further in Mesopotamia, continuing work at various sites until 1851.

By this time, the decipherment of cuneiform script had made great progress, shifting the emphasis from recovering works of art to finding texts and inscriptions. Layard excavated extensively in Sennacherib's palace at Nineveh, where he located a large portion of the royal library as well as nearly 3 kilometres (2 miles) of wall reliefs in 71 rooms and hallways. The library contained innumerable clay tablets, not fully intelligible immediately but in time the source of a mass of detailed information about Assyrian religion, literature and politics.

Layard also continued to dig at Nimrud and other sites in the Mosul area; in 1850, he made a tour of southern Mesopotamia, cutting trenches at sites like Babylon and Nippur, though with meagre results. On completing this second round of excavations, Layard wound up his archaeo-logical career, supervising the packing of 120 more cases of Assyrian finds and returning to England, where he published *Discoveries in the Ruins of Nineveh and Babylon* (1853) and *The Monuments of Nineveh* (1853).

Layard's work in Mesopotamia between 1845 and 1851 capped the adventurous first half of his life. Still only in his mid-thirties when he abandoned archaeology for politics, he spent the remaining four decades of his life in public service: as Liberal Member of Parliament for Aylesbury, and later as Chief Commissioner of Works, and British ambassador to Madrid and Constantinople.

His archaeological reputation followed him everywhere: as the humorous magazine *Punch* sceptically observed, 'the public in England look upon [Layard] as an oracle on all political questions in Asia, because he was an energetic excavator of antiquities at Nineveh.'

Layard's activities in Mesopotamia left two legacies to his archaeological descendants. Most obviously, his excavations at Nimrud, Nineveh and other cities revealed the grandeur of Assyrian palaces and art, providing the first direct contact with a dimly remembered Biblical empire, and filling museum

displays with their artifacts. His other legacy consists of vividly written books, part archaeological reports, part adventure stories, part ethnographic descriptions of the peoples of the Near East. Enormously popular in the 1850s, they stimulated mid-nineteenth-century enthusiasm for ancient civilizations as surely as did the British Museum.

In less than a decade, Botta and Layard had revealed three Assyrian capital cities – Khorsabad, Nimrud and Nineveh – manifesting as museum displays an ancient culture previously known only from the Bible. Even after both men had retired from the field, the French and the British continued to vie with each other for antiquities. Victor Place, Botta's successor as French consul to Mosul, dug at Khorsabad in 1851–55, establishing the ground-plan of the palace, and later at the Assyrian capital of Ashur on the Tigris river.

On the British side, Rassam continued Layard's work in Mesopotamia for a generation. At Nineveh he worked on the palace of Assurbanipal (668–627 BC), uncovering further wall reliefs and the remains of the library, before moving on himself to Ashur and later to southern Mesopotamia – to Babylonia.

Above. This 2800-year-old Assyrian relief was excavated by Layard from the palace of Ashurnasirpal II at Nimrud in 1845–51. Measuring 1.83 metres (72 inches) by 1.17 metres (46 inches), it shows a winged genie anointing a royal eunuch carrying a bow and quiver. Layard presented the stone to his benefactor and patron Sir John Guest, a distant relative and wealthy Welsh ironmaster. Guest's home, Canford Manor in Dorset, became an independent school in 1923 and the relief was rediscovered there recently, white-washed, set in the walls of the tuckshop. At Christie's in 1994 it was sold at auction for £7.7 million to a Japanese religious sect that believes it gains spiritual inspiration from fine works of art.

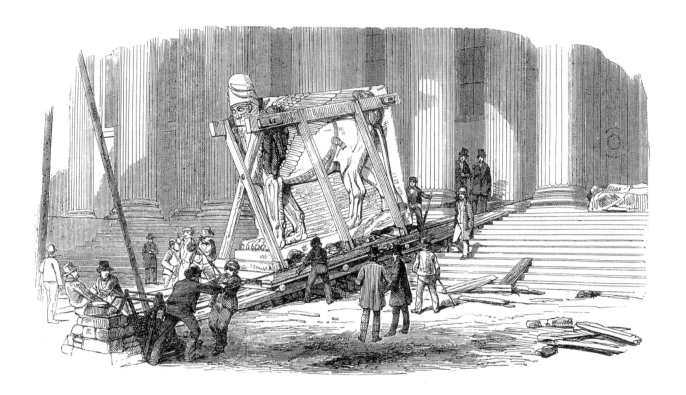

The reception of the Nineveh sculptures at the British Museum, 1852. Weighing more than 10 tonnes and standing 3.5 metres (11 feet) high, this human-headed winged lion from Ashurnasirpal II's palace at Nimrud was transported from the London docks on a truck drawn by eleven horses. Bearing horned headdresses to symbolize divinity, these massive figures guarded the palace gates at Nimrud. 'They had awed and instructed races which flourished 3,000 years ago', wrote Layard. 'Through the portals which they guarded, kings, priests, and warriors had borne sacrifices to their altars'.

Assisted by Hormuzd Rassam, a Nestorian Christian who was brother of the British vice-consul in Mosul, Layard began digging at Nimrud, the ancient city of Kalhu, late in 1845. By the evening of the first day, on widely separated parts of the site, his workmen had already uncovered two alabaster-lined chambers adorned with cuneiform inscriptions; on the second day they found fragments of gilded ivories. The digging team was expanded to thirty, and more successes, including winged bulls and sculptured reliefs of chariots and hunting scenes, followed; soundings were made also at Nineveh (Kuyunjik) and Ashur (the traditional capital city of Assyria). Nimrud, where Layard's activity was concentrated, was a royal city – the Calah of Genesis – founded by the Assyrian king Ashurnasirpal II (883–859 BC) and focused on the enormous and richly appointed palaces of Ashurnasirpal and his successors. Nineveh was older, comprising two distinct mounds, Kuyunjik and Nebi Yunus; though Assyrian kings also built palaces and temples here, most such activity is dated to the period after Sennacherib (704–681 BC) made the city his capital.

Layard's success attracted the financial support of the British Museum, but their funds proved inadequate, leaving him 'to obtain the largest possible number of well-preserved objects of art at the least possible outlay of time and money'. In 1847 the massive figures of human-headed bulls that once protected the entrances to the palaces of Nimrud were shipped to England – by raft down the Tigris to Baghdad, by boat to Basra, and by ship to Bombay and then London. Layard returned to England and the British Museum opened its Assyrian hall in the same year. Helped by his bestseller *Nineveh and its Remains* (1849), so popular in railway station book-shops that year, boasted its author, that it outsold everything except *Mrs Rundell's Cookery*, Layard became a celebrity. After a second expedition to Mesopotamia in 1849–51, he abandoned archaeology for good and entered Parliament.

Excavations in Babylonia

Layard's exploration of Babylonia in 1850 was but a shadow of his work in Assyria; far more successful was the work of his British contemporary, the geologist and traveller William Loftus. Between 1850 and 1854, Loftus twice investigated the huge site of Warka on the Euphrates (also called Uruk, the biblical Erech), before shifting his attention to Senkhere (ancient Larsa, biblical Ellasar), where he excavated the temple of Shamash, the god of light and justice, recovering inscriptions of the Old Babylonian and Kassite periods dating to the second millennium BC. At the same period, J. E. Taylor, the British vice-consul in Basra, also excavated in Babylonia on behalf of the British Museum, in 1854 driving a tunnel into the centre of a mound of brick at Tell-Mugayyar (Arabic for 'Mound of Pitch'). This he was able to identify from inscriptions found at the top as the ziggurat, or temple-tower, of Ur of the Chaldees, the biblical home of Abraham.

Babylonian sites in general presented difficulties for early excavators. Large teams of unskilled local labour brought results when excavating stone-faced palace walls in Assyria or fired brickwork at Babylon itself: distinguishing the walls of a building from the rubble and debris that had engulfed them was straightforward. However, most Babylonian cities were built of unfired mud-brick that rain, the passage of time and successive rebuildings on the same site had turned into

The ziggurat at Ur. Constructed of sun-dried mudbrick with a 2.4 metre (8 feet) thick outer sheath of fired bricks set in bitumen, this is the best preserved temple-tower in Mesopotamia, restored now for visitors as it was at the end of the third millennium BC. The brick stairway is one of three, each of one hundred steps, giving access to the gate tower and the first of the structure's three terraces.

The ziggurat of Ur-Nammu formed the core of a sacred precinct dedicated to the moon-god, its outer enclosure containing a temple store-house, a priestesses' house and a royal palace for use on ceremonial occasions. On the northwestern side stood the moon-god's kitchen, where his meals were prepared.

Until systematically excavated in 1919–24, using a light railway and innumerable labourers with baskets, the mound remained much as Taylor found it in 1854. When British troops in Mesopotamia reached the site during the First World War, recorded Leonard Woolley, 'only a few ragged bricks could be seen protruding from the top of a huge mound of undisturbed sand and rubble up whose gently sloping sides a man could ride on horseback'.

amorphous and extremely thick deposits which lacked the riches of easily re-trievable art that made the Assyrian palaces so attractive. Experience in Assyria provided poor training for digging in Babylonia. Even an authority like Layard 'on the whole [was] much inclined to question whether extensive excavations … would produce any very important or interesting results.' Only the next generation of work in Babylonia would reverse this pessimistic evaluation.

The hard-won ability to read Akkadian opened a world hitherto only vaguely glimpsed through the eyes of the Biblical chroniclers and prophets. Victorian scholars could now study the diplomatic and military affairs of Assyrian kings and the administration of their empire. The libraries of Sen-nacherib and Ashurbanipal contained clay tablets that related the history of Assyria and Babylonia, the myths and cults of ancient Mesopotamian religion, and bilin-

Sir Henry Creswicke Raw-linson (1810–95). Less scholarly in youth than he appears here, as a Grenadier lieutenant Rawlinson once boasted he would 'compete with any rival for a stake of £100, in running, jumping, quoits, racquets, billiards, pigeon-shooting, pig-sticking, steeple-chasing, chess and games of skill at cards'. A noted horseman, in Persia he once rode 750 miles in 150 con-secutive hours.

During the seventeenth and eighteenth centuries, European travellers to the Near East regularly brought home tablets of clay bearing cuneiform inscriptions, the wedge-shaped writing of ancient Mesopotamia. Stamped using sharpened reeds, the symbols were clearly a code – used, as we now know, to represent many different languages over millennia. Without a key the inscriptions remained unintelligible curiosities; with one, a whole new world of understanding opened up.

Cuneiform deciphered

Cracking the cuneiform code was the work not of one scholar but of a dozen, persevering patiently over more than half a century. Their success rested on two particular inscriptions, from Naqsh-i Rustam, the burial place of the Persian kings near Persepolis, and from Behistun in western Persia. Both repeated the same text in two or three different languages – Old Persian, Neo-Elamite and Akkadian – and in three different cuneiform scripts. The Naqsh-i Rustam texts were too short to sustain a full decipherment, but the Behistun text, a defence by the Achaemenid king Darius I (521–486 BC) of his usurpation of the throne, was much longer. The problem was that it was almost impossible to copy: located in a mountain pass near Kermanshah, it covered in all more than 300 square metres and was carved on the face of a high cliff 122 metres (390 feet) from the ground.

Early work on cuneiform inevitably concentrated on the more accessible, but shorter, Naqsh-i Rustam texts, accurate copies of which first arrived in Europe as a result of Carsten Niebuhr's work at Persepolis at the end of the eighteenth century. Niebuhr himself identified the language on one set of inscriptions as Old Persian, written in an alphabetic version of cuneiform with 42 signs. It soon became clear that the inscriptions contained many formulaic repetitions of royal titles of the form 'Xerxes, great king, king of kings, son of Darius, great king, king of kings' – a formula very similar to one used in the third to seventh centuries AD by later Sas-sanian kings of Persia whose script European scholars could already read.

The first breakthrough came in 1802 when Georg Grotefend, a German high-school teacher of Greek with an

gual vocabularies that translated other ancient languages like Sumerian. In the same way, the endeavours of Botta and Layard brought the Assyrians alive through their art.

In *Nineveh and its Remains*, Henry Layard, standing on top of Tell Afar in the Sinjar area of northern Mesopotamia, wrote:

> From the walls I had an uninterrupted view over a vast plain, stretching westward toward the Euphrates, and losing itself in the hazy distance. The ruins of ancient towns and villages rose on all sides; and, as the sun went down, I counted above one hundred mounds, throwing their dark and lengthening shadows across the plain.

The future of Assyriology, founded during the few years between 1842 and 1857, lay buried in those mounds.

enthusiasm for secret codes, realized that certain repeated phrases in the Persepolis inscriptions followed the later Sassanian formula. Using the genealogy of Achaemenid kings recorded by Herodotus, Grotefend succeeded in identifying the names of Darius and Xerxes, the word for king, and thus the phonetic value of many letters. Other scholars added to, and emended, Grotefend's partial results over the decades that followed but the brevity of the Persepolis inscriptions frustrated full understanding even of the Old Persian script.

From the 1830s progress became more marked as a result of the work of the great British Assyriologist Sir Henry Creswicke Rawlinson. A classicist by training, Rawlinson won a cadetship in the East India Company and after learning Persian and several Indian languages was seconded to Tehran in 1835 as part of a mission to train the Persian army. While there, he managed to copy half of the Old Persian text of the Behistun inscription. Applying the same logic as Grotefend though ignorant of his work, Rawlinson succeeded in deciphering many proper names and place names; by 1839, with knowledge of Grotefend and other existing work on cuneiform, he had made a complete translation of the Old Persian text he had copied. Returning to Behistun in 1844, Rawlinson finished copying the Old Persian inscription and, at no small risk to himself on the steep cliff, began transcribing the Neo-Elamite text, itself now easier to decipher because of the progress made with the parallel Old Persian.

The more sedate labours of the Irishman Edward Hincks and the Frenchman Jules Oppert, in the late 1840s, confirmed and elaborated Rawlinson's work. Hincks even took the first steps towards deciphering Akkadian, showing that Akkadian cuneiform contained both syllabic signs and signs for entire words (logograms).

Rawlinson himself returned to Behistun in 1847, this time employing a 'wild Kurdish boy' to climb down the overhanging cliff-face to make a papier-mâché cast of the inaccessible Akkadian inscription. Driving wooden pegs into clefts in the rock, he secured 'a swinging seat, like a painter's cradle, and, fixed upon this seat, he took under my direction the paper cast'; the cast itself, after giving up its secrets, was reputedly eaten by mice in the vaults of the British Museum.

By comparing Akkadian with the translated Old Persian, Rawlinson determined the values of over 100 signs and deciphered 200 words, with Hincks and Oppert, he was then able rapidly to expand the known vocabulary and grammar of Akkadian.

The seeming chaos of Akkadian cuneiform, in which the same sign could represent several different syllables and several different words, aroused considerable scepticism and challenge. The validity of Rawlinson's work was only finally settled in 1857 when William Fox Talbot, the Victorian polymath and pioneer of photography, sent the Royal Asiatic Society a transcription and his own translation of a text newly discovered during Hormuzd Rassam's excavations at the Assyrian capital of Ashur.

The Society in turn sent copies of the original text to Rawlinson, Hincks and Oppert, requesting that they independently translate the text. When the Society opened the translations, the four versions were found to be identical in all their basic points.

EXPLORING ANCIENT AMERICA

By the beginning of the nineteenth century, Spain's hold on her American colonies was weakening and the new Latin American nations were establishing independent contact with Europe and its scientific community. And as increasing numbers of scientists and travellers journeyed through the region, word began to spread of the fabulous ruins of ancient civilizations, especially in central America and Peru.

The first true scientist to travel through the area was the Prussian nobleman, Baron Alexander von Humboldt. Leaving Europe on a botanical expedition to South America in 1799, he provided the first scientific observations of the remains

Alexander von Humboldt (1769–1859), by Friedrich Georg Weitsch, 1806.

Physically tough and intellectually omnivorous, Humboldt was feted in his lifetime as no explorer before or since for his five years of river and overland travel through South America in 1799–1804.

Anthropology, geography, zoology and medicine fascinated him equally. It was his *Personal Narrative* of the journey, running to seven volumes and 3,754 pages, that prompted Darwin to undertake his own *Beagle* voyage a generation later.

Humboldt nearly lost his life more than once, in swamped canoes in alligator-infested rivers and in trying to climb Chimborazo, in the Ecuadorian Andes near Quito, believing it to be the highest mountain in the world. He experimented with curare, swallowing it to show it was only lethal when injected into the bloodstream and, with his companion, the French botanist Aimé Bonpland, seized an electric eel, enduring shocks of up to 600 volts.

of the Inka empire in Ecuador and the Chimú civilization that for centuries controlled the north coast of Peru. He was also the first to measure the climatic changes that occur with altitude and changing latitude – factors that shaped millennia of prehistoric cultural evolution. The magnificent ruins of Chanchan, the Chimú capital of AD 1000–1450 on the north coast of Peru, puzzled Humboldt: why was it that no rain had ever apparently fallen on the ancient adobe walls? The solution presented itself when he measured the temperature of the Pacific Ocean nearby, identifying a current of very cold water that flows northward along the west coast of South America, the current that bears his name today.

Humboldt introduced to Europe the use of bird guano, long used as a fertilizer by the ancient peoples of the coast of Peru, and in so doing shaped the economy of the emerging Peruvian nation. After leaving South America he journeyed on to Mexico where, in addition to pursuing his botanical studies, he continued to record major archaeological sites. Years later Charles Darwin was to call him 'the greatest scientific traveller who ever lived'.

Stephens and Catherwood in Yucatán

In 1799, the same year that Humboldt set sail for the Americas, Frederick Catherwood was born in England. Serious and melancholic by temperament, he trained as an architectural draughtsman and at the age of twenty-five embarked upon a journey through the Mediterranean and Near East that lasted nearly ten years. He took a great interest in archaeology and returned home with a large portfolio of drawings of spectacular sites in Egypt and Palestine, including Thebes, Philae, the Dome of the Rock, Jerash and Baalbek. While exhibiting some of his work in London in 1836 he met an outgoing and exuberant American lawyer, John Lloyd Stephens, just returned from a two-year journey through Egypt and the Holy Land. The two men immediately recognized their shared interest in archaeology and agreed to travel together in the future when the opportunity arose.

On his return to New York, Stephens published two volumes about his travels, *Incidents of Travel in Egypt, Arabia Petraea and the Holy Land* (1837) and *Incidents of Travel in Greece, Turkey, Russia, and Poland* (1838), establishing himself as a popular writer of travel books. At this time reports were emerging from central America of the existence of lost cities and pyramids belonging to an ancient Mexican civilization. Most people dismissed such reports as fanciful, but Stephens took them seriously: he knew the great Humboldt had himself described such ruins in central Mexico.

In 1839 Stephens and Catherwood therefore set off on a journey of exploration through the jungle of central America and the Yucatán peninsula. On this first expedition, they visited Copán, Palenque and Uxmal, some of the greatest monuments of the Classic Maya period (AD 300–900); Stephens actually purchased the entire site of Copán for fifty American dollars. On their second expedition, in 1841–42, they visited numerous smaller sites as well as the great Post-Classic Maya

Stela D and its altar at Copán, Honduras, drawn by Frederick Catherwood (1799–1856). His companion, John Lloyd Stephens, wrote: 'Working our way through the thick woods, we came upon a square stone column ... The front was the figure of a man curiously and richly dressed, and the face, evidently a portrait, solemn, stern and well fitted to excite terror. The back ... and the sides were covered with hieroglyphics.' From the glyphs we now know to the day when this Maya monument was erected: 26 July AD 736.

centre of Chichén Itzá in central Yucatán (AD 850–1200). Catherwood recorded the Maya art he saw in magnificent and incredibly accurate drawings. When published with Stephens' account of their travels in two volumes, *Incidents of Travel in Central America, Chiapas, and Yucatán* (1841) and *Incidents of Travel in Yucatán* (1843) they captured the imagination of American and European readers and engendered an excitement and interest in the ancient ruins of the Americas that carried over into literary and scientific circles.

Another adventurous man prompted to do more than just dream about the splendours of the ancient world was the newspaper editor and diplomat Ephraim George Squier. In his fifties, Squier undertook a journey through the Andes of southern Peru and Bolivia, during which he observed and photographed the astonishing remains of Inka and pre-Inka civilizations. Etchings made from his photographs were published with a written account of his travels, *Peru: Travel and Explorations in the Land of the Incas*, in 1877: the first published account of such towns and religious centres as Ollantaytambo, the Temple of Viracocha and Sacsayhuaman, the Inka gate cut through the Wari wall at Pikillaqta, and the pre-Inka city of Tiahuanaco. He also described and illustrated the most famous of all the Inka suspension bridges: the bridge over the Apurimac. The artist who accompanied Squier's team would not attempt the crossing of this terrifying rope bridge, preferring to cross the river at some fordable point. Squier never saw him again. Apparently the artist had found a place to cross the river and had removed his clothes to bathe. The wind carried off his clothes and shoes, and he was forced to seek shelter with the local natives; horrified at this naked apparition, they drove him off with stones, causing such injuries that it was several months before he recovered.

Like the works of Stephens and Catherwood, Squier's *Peru* was a bestseller. Its accuracy is more questionable. Ever the newspaperman in search of a good story, Squier's published etchings exaggerate the size and magnificence of some of the ruins. Most notably, his published etching of the Gate of the Sun at Tiahuanaco in Bolivia shows the gate as enormous: tall enough for a mounted rider to pass through. In reality, the opening is barely the height of an adult.

The Moundbuilders

Nowhere did North America have cities or monumental architecture on the scale of Tiahuanaco to entice artists and travellers; it did, however, have monuments that were just as mysterious. Scattered throughout the American Midwest are the remains of thousands of earthen mounds. The smaller, conical mounds are burials belonging to the Adena and Hopewell cultures, now known to date to the period 1000 BC–AD 500; the larger, flat-topped mounds are bases for large buildings such as temples and chiefs' palaces and belong to the later Mississippian tradition (AD 700–1700).

Apart from well-preserved ruins like Chaco Canyon in the American Southwest (p. 340), Great Serpent Mound in Ohio and the 35 metres (115 feet) high Monk's Mound at Cahokia in Missouri are visually the most impressive archaeological sites on the continent. But who built them? Early on the earthen mounds of the Midwest attracted the attention of European settlers, generating the so-called Moundbuilder controversy: an object lesson in how archaeology cannot escape wider social issues and debate.

What surpassed the credulity of nineteenth-century European Americans was that Native Americans could have built the mounds. If Indians were savages, their ancestors would not have had the necessary engineering skills. If such skills were

Great Serpent Mound, Ohio, from the air. This uncoiling snake, 390 metres (1280 feet) long, 6 metres (20 feet) wide and 1.5 metres (5 feet) high, holds an egg or frog in its jaw.

conceded, the moral and intellectual superiority that European settlers took to be their justification for seizing Native American land would be manifestly undermined.

From late in the eighteenth century to late in the nineteenth the controversy raged. On one side were those who believed Native Americans intellectually incapable of erecting such monuments; they attributed them instead to Toltecs from Mexico, Hindus on their way to Mexico, Welshmen, Vikings – even refugees from the lost island of Atlantis. On the other side was a small group of antiquarians certain that the mounds could only have been constructed by Native Americans. To prove their point, they turned to the developing techniques of archaeology.

The first to record the mounds effectively, in 1820, was the Ohio antiquary Caleb Atwater. Atwater's drawings were accurate, but he came down against the idea of an indigenous origin. More innovative was the work of Samuel Morton, a pioneer of American physical anthropology, who in 1839 initiated a study of human skulls recovered from the mounds. After taking ten measurements from each skull, Morton concluded that the moundbuilders and contemporary Native Americans belonged to the same race. To explain the difference between the civilizations of Mexico and the less spectacular cultures of North America, he proposed that the American Indian race comprised two families: Toltecan – which included the moundbuilders – and Barbarous.

A few years later the newly founded Smithsonian Institution in Washington DC entered the controversy, awarding funds to two Midwestern antiquarians, Ephraim George Squier (p. 112) and Edwin Hamilton Davis to publish the results of a comprehensive survey of the mounds in the Ohio and Mississippi valleys. The result, *Ancient Monuments of the Mississippi Valley* (1848), is a pioneering work of American archaeology. Yet even though its authors meticulously described and classified the sites they visited and carefully weighed up ideas about their origins, their conclusion was much the same as Atwater's: the moundbuilders could not have been Native Americans.

The opposing camp was slower to become established. As early as 1813 J. H. McCulloh was attributing the mounds to ancestors of the Mississippi Indians and pouring scorn on the idea of an external origin. His views were endorsed by Henry R. Schoolcraft, an early and influential expert on Native American culture, in his *Indian Tribes of the United States* (1851–57); but, like McCulloh, he was too far ahead of his time to overturn conventional wisdom. Samuel Haven agreed that the mounds could be the work of Native Americans but only because he judged them unspectacular enough as monuments to match his idea of Indian capabilities.

It was another generation before the truth was established by Cyrus Thomas, an archaeologist hired in 1881 to investigate the mounds for the American Bureau of Ethnology. Making intensive use of survey and excavation, Thomas slowly built up an unassailable case for a Native American origin over a decade; and in 1894 his final report at last laid the myth of the moundbuilders to rest.

Buffalo Bull's Back Fat, Chief of the Blood Tribe, by George Catlin (1796–1872). Between the 1830s and 1850s, a handful of artists like Catlin and the Swiss painter Karl Bodmer sympathetically recorded many aspects of Native American life before it was irrevocably disrupted by the white man.

Born in Pennsylvania, Catlin studied law before turning to painting. Some of his Indian pictures belonging to 1832 to 1840, exceptionally productive years in which he painted some 470 full length portraits, were published in *Manners of the North American Indians* (2 vols, 1841) and *The North American Portfolio* (1844). Many others survive in the Smithsonian Institution's National Museum of American Art in Washington DC.

By the later nineteenth century archaeology as we understand it today was therefore starting to take shape. Major excavations were taking place in several parts of the world; the Three Age system was injecting order and a sense of time-depth for the first time; and increasing quantities of material – monumental statuary as well as small objects discovered by chance – were being found and displayed in national museums. The following sixty years were to see the consolidation of these gains, an increasing quality of excavation and the development of new means of classifying finds to provide a detailed chronology of the prehistoric past. There were to be setbacks too: the First World War, the first political event to have a radical impact on the practice of archaeology.

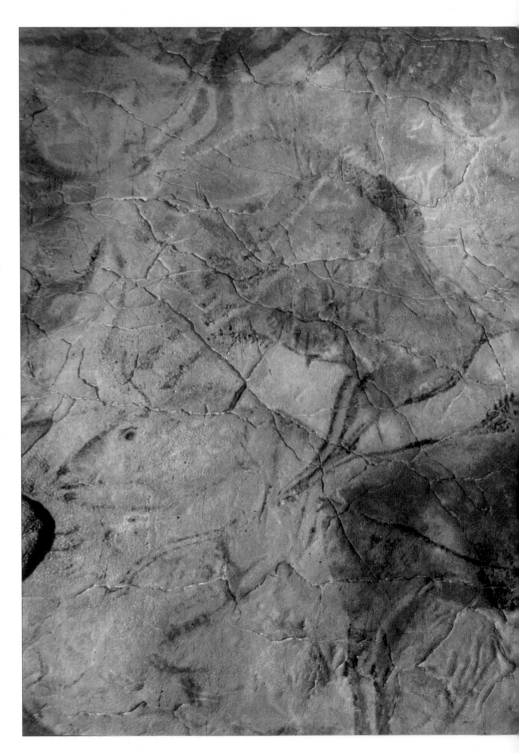

CHAPTER 5 — *The Search for Human Origins, 1860–1920*

Part of the 14,000-year-old painted ceiling in the cave of Altamira, northern Spain, the first Ice Age paintings ever discovered. The curled-up bison are 1.5 metres (5 feet) to 1.8 metres (6 feet) long.

The Altamira ceiling was brought to light in 1879 by a local landowner, Marcelino Sanz de Sautuola, whose small daughter was, she wrote later, 'running about in the cavern and playing about here and there', while her father dug the cave-floor. Suddenly she made out forms and figures on the roof. 'Look, Papa, oxen!', she called. At first de Sautuola laughed, but finding the figures were executed in some sort of fatty paste rather than paint, soon became 'so enthusiastic that he could hardly speak'.

Though de Sautuola published a booklet about his discoveries the following year, for twenty years Europe's archaeological establishment dismissed the paintings as too good to be ancient, 'a dauber's vulgar joke'. His discovery rejected and his honour impugned, de Sautuola died in 1888.

The publication of Darwin's *Origin of Species* had immense impact on nineteenth-century society and the practice of science. The impact was no less in archaeology and anthropology, where Darwin's concept of the survival of the fittest soon came to be used to explain the shaping of human culture. Late in the century anthropologists such as Lewis Henry Morgan in North America and Edward B. Tylor in

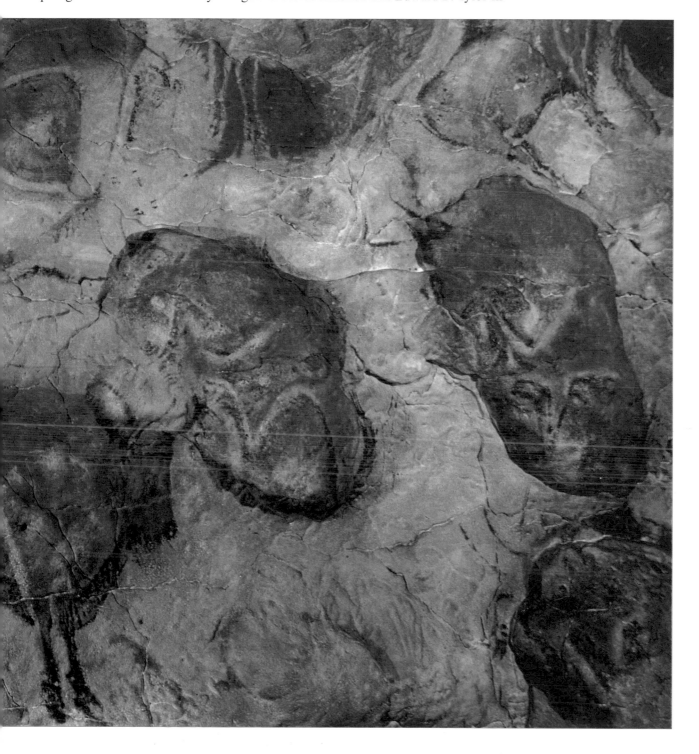

Britain developed explicitly evolutionary theories of cultural change, Morgan, for instance, arguing that all societies went through successive stages of savagery, barbarism and civilization. In the same way, Sir John Lubbock's influential *Prehistoric Times* (1865) argued that natural selection had created the differences between human societies, technological simplicity equating directly with intellectual simplicity.

Archaeology has shown definitively in the last half century that such ideas are incorrect: social change is far more complicated and unpredictable. If the evolutionary error had never penetrated beyond scholarly circles, the damage might have been limited. Unfortunately it did. A century ago archaeology and anthropology had in practice become pillars of imperialism: disciplines held to show that it was a law of nature for primitive societies to be taken over by the civilized. In both Britain and North America concepts such as 'the white man's burden' and 'manifest destiny' were given spurious intellectual respectability through the study of the past.

Charles Darwin (1809–82) dressed for his daily constitutional on the verandah of his home, Down House in Kent, about 1880.

THE EARLIEST EUROPEANS

Until the watershed of 1859, the investigation of the remote past had been a pastime for amateurs and country gentlemen; it now began to become a science, with specialist practitioners and established procedures and terminology.

The man most responsible for this transformation was the French scholar Edouard Lartet, founder of human palaeontology and prehistoric archaeology. A lawyer by training, Lartet was first drawn to palaeontology in 1834 when a peasant gave him a mastodon tooth. Just three years later he discovered a fossil ape's jaw (*Pliopithecus*) at Sansan in southern France – a find of crucial significance since Cuvier had denied the existence of both fossil primates and humans, and had therefore linked the appearance of the one with the other. In 1856 Lartet received a letter from Alfred Fontan, a civil servant, telling of his discovery of bone tools mixed with flints and fossil fauna in the cave of Massat in the French Pyrenees, and by 1859 he was corresponding with Boucher de Perthes (p. 84) and was convinced of the geological antiquity of the human species. Like Tournal, he was impressed by the apparently human cut-marks found on some fossil animal bones. By way of experiment, Lartet cut modern bones with a metal saw to see how the results compared with the marks on ancient bones. Metal produced a totally different effect; flint knives matched precisely.

The autumn of 1860 saw particularly important developments. In September, Lartet dug at Massat to check Fontan's earlier observations. He found the same kinds of tools and fauna, and also a bone with a bear's head engraved on it, the first piece of palaeolithic art ever recovered from an archaeologically observed context. On his way home, in October, he also stopped and dug at the rock-shelter of Aurignac in the Pyrenees, a site where human skeletons had been uncovered a few years before. Publication of the two sites followed only months later, with Lartet proposing the first ever classification of prehistoric times based on animal palaeontology: the cave-bear age, mammoth/rhinoceros age, reindeer age and bison/aurochs age.

Shortly after, in 1862, a Paris antiquary showed Lartet some bone-filled breccia (cemented cave deposits) and worked flints from the area of Les Eyzies in the Dordogne. Recognizing reindeer bones in the mass, Lartet set out for a five-month campaign of excavation in the area in August 1863, aided and financed by his friend, the English banker, ethnologist and philanthropist Henry Christy. It was decided that half the finds, including all exceptional pieces, would remain in France, and the rest would go to the British Museum. The result, published in *Reliquiae Aquitanicae* (1865–75), was the discovery of a series of Ice Age rock-shelters of enormous importance, including Le Moustier (which gave its name to the 'Mousterian' or Middle Palaeolithic period, *c*. 180,000–30,000 BC) and La Madeleine (which gave its name to the 'Magdalenian', a west European palaeolithic culture of *c*. 16,000–10,000 BC).

Also at Les Eyzies in 1863 was the Marquis Paul de Vibraye, an agronomist and owner of the Château de Cheverny, who had been won over to Boucher de Perthes' ideas in 1858 and had been seeking proof of the contemporaneity of man and extinct fauna ever since. He began work himself at Laugerie-Basse, another Magdalenian rock-shelter, probably before Lartet, and they simultaneously produced decisive proof of human antiquity. De Vibraye found the ivory 'Vénus impudique' (shameless Venus), an ivory figurine of a naked female from Laugerie-Basse, while Lartet and Christy, in May 1864, discovered at La Madeleine an engraving of a mammoth on a piece of mammoth ivory. This depiction of an extinct animal was the final clinching piece of evidence.

Lartet's work in the Dordogne was at once the culmination of a search and a new beginning. It triggered an uncontrolled 'gold-rush' as people began to pillage rock-shelters with pickaxes looking for stone and bone tools and especially portable Ice Age art: there was no conception yet of noting the position or context of finds, and fine objects, dug up like potatoes, were of supreme importance. The better diggers established a crude sequence of animal and tool types, but even the best relied heavily on untrained labourers, whose ignorance and wiliness led to theft and fakery as well as a neglect of recording. Lartet and Christy alone brought a modicum of scientific method and palaeontological skill to their excavations, but their partnership was short-lived. Christy died in 1865 after catching a severe cold in caves he was visiting in Belgium.

Mammoth engraving on a piece of mammoth ivory. Discovered during Edouard Lartet's excavations in the rock shelter of La Madeleine, near Les Eyzies, in 1864, it was this engraving that proved humans once co-existed with mammoths.

About 400 other palaeolithic depictions of mammoths are now known, ranging from paintings and engravings on cave walls in Spain, France and Russia to engravings and three-dimensional carvings in bone, stone, antler and ivory.

In Britain the same year William Pengelly, tutor to the children of several European royal families, began fifteen years of work in Kent's Cavern. His pioneering and very systematic excavation involved laying out an elaborate grid, echoing that of Pouech (p. xii), which enabled him to record the position in three dimensions of each bone and artifact, and to write find-numbers on individual specimens.

Yet it was France above all that showed the way forward in the 1860s. The château of St Germain-en-Laye, just west of Paris, was opened as a 'Gallo-Roman Museum' by Napoleon III in 1862 and six months later extended to embrace all national antiquities. The emperor himself, probably at Lartet's suggestion, encouraged Boucher de Perthes to place his finds there and in 1863 conferred on him the Légion d'Honneur. The Musée des Antiquités Nationales that endures today was finally inaugurated in 1867, the year of the Paris Universal Exhibition at which palaeolithic portable art was prominently displayed for the first time.

Communicating new discoveries, not just to the public but to other archaeologists, became an increasing priority. It was at the first Congress of Prehistoric Anthropology and Archaeology in 1865 that the word 'palaeoethnology' was coined to describe the comparative study of ancient cultures; the same year Sir John Lubbock's *Prehistoric Times* replaced the terms 'flaked stone' and 'polished stone' with 'palaeolithic' and 'neolithic'. The first journal devoted to prehistoric research, the *Matériaux pour l'histoire positive et philosophique de l'homme*, was founded in 1864, at first written almost single-handed by Gabriel de Mortillet, a man who fast became prehistory's chief editor and publicist; it was followed by Germany's *Archiv für Anthropologie* in 1865.

Discoveries were now coming thick and fast. In 1868, Louis Lartet, Edouard's son, took charge of the accidental discovery (by railway-quarrying) of the skeletons of three men, a woman and a child buried in the Upper Palaeolithic layers of the Cro-Magnon rock-shelter in Les Eyzies – the site which would give its name to modern humans as a whole.

Caves and rock-shelters continued to act as the greatest draw, though with one notable exception. In 1866, the historian Adrien Arcelin and geologist Henry de Ferry started excavations at the open-air site of Solutré in central France, a complex palaeolithic occupation covering several hectares at the foot of a great cliff; its archaeological levels, up to 10 metres (33 feet) thick in places, proved to be rich in

Rock of ages. Hand-tinted photograph of Otto Hauser's crude excavations at the Upper Palaeolithic rock-shelter of Laugerie, Les Eyzies, Dordogne, in 1911. Hauser was a German-Swiss antiquary who worked in the area from 1898 onwards, but fled – under suspicion of being a spy – in 1914.

The Musée des Antiquités Nationales, St Germain-en-Laye, inaugurated in 1867. The notice over the door reads 'Quaternary deposits. Worked flints found with animal bones belonging to extinct species'.

material from almost every phase of the Upper Palaeolithic (*c.* 30,000–10,000 BC). The most spectacular find, a layer containing thousands of horse bones, brought Lartet, de Mortillet and even Lubbock to visit the site; the prehistoric occupants of Solutré specialized in the exploitation of horse herds, rounding them up for slaughter against the foot of the cliff.

With human antiquity now firmly established, some scholars' minds were turning to the reconstruction of daily life in the Palaeolithic, using archaeological evidence mixed with the early ethnography of 'savage' peoples. To bring Solutré's occupants to life for the general public Arcelin therefore produced the very first prehistoric novel, *Solutré ou les chasseurs de rennes de la France centrale* (Solutré or the reindeer hunters of central France, 1872). It was a worthy effort but had the unfortunate consequence of creating in only two pages one of prehistory's most enduring myths – that Solutré's hunters used to drive horses to their death from the top of the precipice. Arcelin never put this idea forward in his scientific articles on Solutré since the location of the horse bones meant they would have had to fly 100 metres (330 feet) from cliff-top to site.

In 1869–72 de Mortillet proposed the first classification of palaeolithic sites based on their stone tools rather than on their fauna. He chose Le Moustier and Aurignac to typify the Mousterian (*c.* 180,000–30,000 BC) and Aurignacian (*c.* 40,000–28,000 BC) periods, and Solutré and La Madeleine for the Solutrean (*c.*19,000–16,000 BC) and Magdalenian (*c.* 16,000–10,000 BC), the two phases into which he divided Lartet's reindeer age. These epochs de Mortillet imagined evolving one from the other in a single, unbroken linear sequence: a conclusion based of necessity at this date on logic rather than detailed stratigraphic evidence.

The 1860s and 1870s saw cave-excavation and increasingly imaginative follow-up studies proliferating all over Europe. In Belgium, for example, the geologist Edouard Dupont began to investigate the differences between damage done to bones by carnivores and the butchery marks and fractures made by humans. In Switzerland, the first discovery of portable palaeolithic art in central Europe occurred in 1874 when a young teacher, Konrad Merk, discovered the famous engraving of a reindeer in the Magdalenian cave of Kesslerloch bei Thayngen. In Spain and Portugal, new interest in prehistoric antiquities resulted in the foundation of anthropological and prehistoric societies. Here, as elsewhere in Europe, more and more amateurs were beginning to dig in caves.

Among the few established scholars to accept Altamira (p. 124) from the start was the great French prehistorian Edouard Piette, a magistrate and geologist whose pioneering series of excavations along the Pyrenees, at sites like Brassempouy, Gourdan, Lortet and Le Mas d'Azil, not only amassed an unrivalled collection of palaeolithic portable art and tools, but also led him to important conclusions about the succession of archaeological cultures in the late Ice Age. Although financially ruined by his researches, Piette donated his collections to the Musée des Antiquités Nationales at St Germain; ahead of his time, he had kept large quantities of animal bones and had problems making the museum accept them as part of the whole. He was admirably open-minded, proposing an array of radical ideas about the Upper Palaeolithic, from the semi-domestication of animals – that is, close control by humans that falls short of full husbandry – to plant cultivation and rudimentary writing.

However, Piette's most durable contribution to prehistory was to fill the apparent empty 'hiatus' that existed between the end of the Upper Palaeolithic and the Neolithic. In 1866 the Irish archaeologist Hodder Westropp had proposed a 'Meso-lithic' or Middle Stone Age phase, but this included the Upper Palaeolithic – the age of cave art – as well as the Danish kitchen middens (p. 90). It was Piette who, in his excavations at the huge Upper Palaeolithic tunnel-cave of Le Mas d'Azil in the 1880s and 1890s, established the existence of truly transitional phases such as the 'Azilian' (c. 9,000–8,000 BC), characterized by its painted pebbles and small har-poons. Other later industries would eventually be given their own names.

Posterity also owes Piette a lasting debt for, in 1897, initiating a young French priest, Henri Breuil, into the study of palaeolithic art. Breuil's talent for drawing Piette's finds soon brought him to the attention of Cartailhac, with whom he began to study the newly validated cave art of La Mouthe and Altamira. By his own reckoning, Breuil spent over 700 days underground, copying cave-drawings. From then until the end of his long life he dominated, by the power of his personality as much as his scholarship, not only the field of palaeolithic art but the whole of prehistory – indeed, he was sometimes known as the 'Pope of Prehistory'.

Breuil owed his eminence to palaeolithic art and also to the classification of stone-tools: in 1912 he emerged victorious from the so-called 'Bataille aurign-acienne', a struggle to establish the correct succession of Upper Palaeolithic cultures, and especially to prove that the Solutrean should be placed after the Aur-ignacian and before the Magdalenian. Although his opponents even had recourse to fraud to bolster their position, Dupont's work in Belgium had demonstrated the correct order thirty years before, so Breuil was eventually able to publish a great synthesis, improving and amplifying de Mortillet's scheme, which set out the characteristic tool types of each stage of the palaeolithic in western Europe. This remains broadly valid today.

By 1900 European prehistory was becoming more rigorous by the decade. In his last years de Mortillet himself continued to inflict damage through fixed ideas and a vehement anticlericalism caused by miserable years as a child in a Jesuit school: having held back cave-art studies for twenty years through his rejection of Altamira, he also dismissed all claims for palaeolithic burial, proclaiming that religion – and hence burial – was an invention of the Neolithic. Yet his influence was waning. Emile Cartailhac, the leading prehistorian of the next generation, initially echoed de Mortillet's prejudices, but by 1902 he had changed his mind about both burials and cave art, becoming for the next twenty years one of cave art's most fervent champions. In 1890 Cartailhac initiated the teaching of prehistoric archaeology at

Henri Breuil (1877–1961). A talented artist, excelling in animal figures, Breuil was becoming active in prehistory at just the time the first cave art was authenticated in 1902. He copied figures at Altamira the same year, in the sputter-ing light of candles, lying flat on his back for hours on sacks filled with ferns, the wax drip-ping on his clothes. Soon after he moved on to the caves and rock-shelters of the Dordogne.

Working methods remained primitive by modern stand-ards, but with time Breuil's determination and patience achieved remarkable results.

Stamina was the first requirement. Tracing paper was held directly against the cave-wall by boy assistants so the lines beneath could be directly traced with a crayon or pencil. Light was provided by carbide lamps, often held at arm's length for long periods, by further assistants.

Utterly absorbed, hardly speaking for hours on end, the quick-tempered Breuil might administer a sharp slap if a boy's cramp or fatigue caused the light to waver or the paper slip. He simply adjusted the arms of his 'human cande-labras' when necessary.

Toulouse and by 1906 he was offering an official course for students. At Munich University meanwhile, a generation after Daniel Wilson in Canada, Johannes Ranke had in 1886 been made Germany's first professor of anthropology.

Although the French prehistorian Gustave Chauvet suggested as early as 1887 that prehistoric art had a magical motivation – injury to the engraved image bringing injury to the real animal – portable palaeolithic art was dismissed initially as mere decoration: 'art for art's sake'. However, with the acceptance of the authenticity of cave art in Europe and increasing ethnographic knowledge of Australian

Altamira and the discovery of cave art

Don Marcelino Sanz de Sautuola (1831–88) was a gentleman landowner in the province of Santander, northern Spain, who in middle age became a well-known collector of antiquities. At the Paris Universal Exhibition of 1878 he was deeply impressed by the palaeolithic portable art on show and, on his return to Spain, started digging himself at sites such as El Pendo.

In 1879 he returned to the cave of Altamira where a few years earlier he had noticed black painted signs on a wall. That November, while he was digging in the cave-floor searching for prehistoric tools and portable art, his little daughter, Maria, was playing in the cavern. Suddenly she spotted the great cluster of coloured bison paintings on the ceiling.

Incredulous at first, her father became more interested when he found that the figures seemed to be painted with a fatty paste. He also noticed the close similarity in style between these huge figures and the small portable depictions he had seen in Paris, deducing therefore that the cave-art must be of similar age. In this de Sautuola was correct: we now know that the Altamira paintings belong to the period c. 17,000–12,000 BC. Unfortunately, his attempts to communicate the discovery to the academic establishment met with rejection and accusations of naivety or even fraud: at the 1880 International Congress of Anthropology and Prehistoric Archaeology in Lisbon, his claims were contemptuously dismissed by Emile Cartailhac, a

leading French prehistorian who had been warned by the virulently anticlerical de Mortillet that anti-evolutionist Spanish Jesuits were going to try to make prehistorians look silly. De Sautuola died early, in 1888, a sad and disillusioned man.

Figures had also been noticed on the walls of some French caves in the 1860s and 1870s, but their date and significance remained unknown. True understanding of cave art only came in 1895 when the removal of sediments containing palaeolithic material at the cave of La Mouthe, Dordogne, exposed a previously unknown gallery with figures that were clearly very ancient engraved on its walls. Discoveries in other French caves followed rapidly, culminating in those of Les Combarelles and Font de Gaume in 1901. At Les Combarelles, the art – horses, bison, bear, reindeer and mammoths – is engraved, at Font de Gaume mostly painted. All these caves are now known to belong to the last Ice Age, c. 16,000–10,000 BC.

By 1902 Europe's prehistoric establishment had officially accepted the existence and authenticity of palaeolithic cave art. Cartailhac published a famous article 'Mea culpa d'un sceptique', in which he openly, if somewhat grudgingly, admitted his earlier mistake; de Sautuola was vindicated.

Once again scholarly endorsement triggered a 'gold-rush', and a great many more decorated caves were discovered.

Right. Altamira bison, c. **12,000 BC.**

aboriginal art (p. 78), more complex explanations began to emerge. Particularly influential was the view that prehistoric art represented sympathetic hunting magic, an idea espoused in 1903 by Salomon Reinach, director of the Musée des Antiquités Nationales; through Breuil's influence, it was to dominate studies of prehistoric art for decades.

Once cave art was accepted, finds in southern France snowballed, with new discoveries at Niaux (1906), the Tuc d'Audoubert (1912) and Les Trois Frères (1914). The same was true in northern Spain, where Hermilio Alcalde del Rio, a

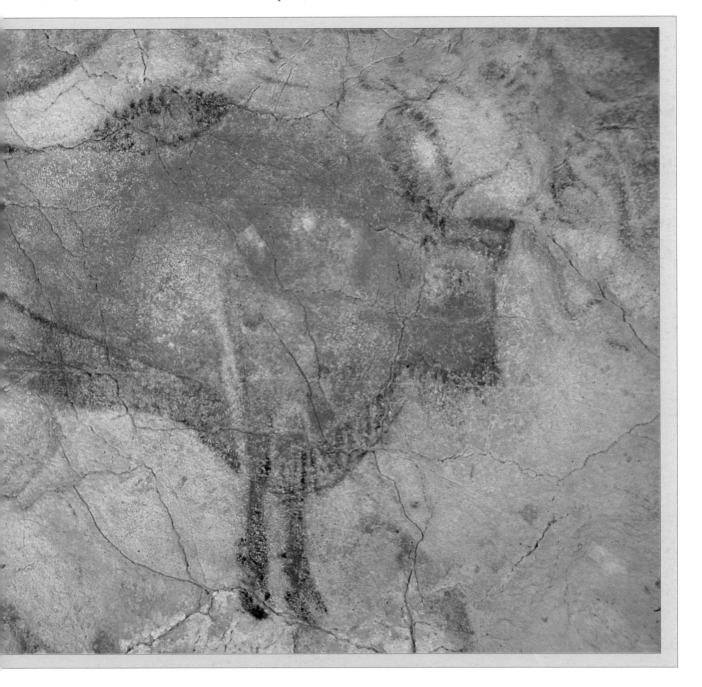

prehistorian who had worked with Cartailhac and Breuil at Altamira, discovered art in a whole series of caves, such as El Castillo, Covalanas and Pindal. He excavated at both Altamira and El Castillo, applying de Mortillet's French artifact-based subdivisions to Cantabria for the first time.

Prince Albert I of Monaco visited the Cantabrian caves in 1909 along with Breuil and Hugo Obermaier, an expatriate German cleric who later became the first professor of prehistory in Madrid, and was so impressed that he offered the money to establish an Institute of Human Palaeontology in Paris. The Institute opened the following year with Marcellin Boule as its first director, and promptly embarked on a major excavation at the mouth of El Castillo cave. An immense sequence of archaeological levels up to 18 metres (59 feet) deep was revealed, spanning all periods from the Acheulian to the end of the last Ice Age, a sequence that greatly assisted Breuil in constructing his influential classification of palaeolithic stone tools. The dig, run by Obermaier, was brought to an end by the First World War.

In Europe as a whole, the explanatory power of evolution became ever more apparent throughout this period. Darwinism had been explicitly extended to man, primarily by Thomas Huxley in his *Man's Place in Nature* (1863) and by Darwin himself in *The Descent of Man* (1871), and early human remains continued to come to light. In 1885–86 Marcel De Puydt, a lawyer, uncovered Neandertal burials in the Belgian cave of Spy, near Liège. And in southwestern France a Neandertal skeleton

The Neandertal man from La Chapelle-aux-Saints by Kupka, 1909. 'It is not the artist's intention to depict merely a type of prehistoric man, but the actual man whose skull was found recently', read the caption.

This was the first reconstruction of an entire Neandertal based on the scientific analysis of anatomical remains. Its depiction of a primitive, stooping, brutish figure reminiscent of a gorilla powerfully conveys Boule's view of Neandertal inferiority.

The bleached skull lying in the left foreground carries the implication of cannibalism.

was unearthed in 1908 in the cave of La Chapelle-aux-Saints by three clerics, who, keen to avoid the anticlerical school of de Mortillet, sent it to Boule for study. Boule, who did not believe that Neandertals could be ancestral to modern humans, identified features caused by the deforming effects of osteoarthritis on an old man as characteristic of all Neanderthals – a view that became entrenched for decades.

The Piltdown hoax

Among many notorious fakes in the history of archaeology, the name of Piltdown Man remains pre-eminent. The finds, made in 1912–15 in surface gravel workings at Piltdown in southern England, supposedly constituted a perfect 'missing link' – a 'Dawn Man' that fulfilled Darwin's prediction of fossil finds intermediate between humans and apes.

The essential features of the Piltdown finds were a human cranium and an ape-like jaw. Charles Dawson, a Sussex solicitor, geologist and antiquarian, claimed that two workmen gave him a first piece of the skull in 1908, part of a 'coconut' they had smashed while digging gravel. In 1911 he found more fragments, together with flint implements and prehistoric animal remains, and alerted the British Museum. The Museum's excavations in June 1912 brought to light a jaw that appeared to go with the skull. A canine tooth was found the following year by a young Jesuit priest, Teilhard de Chardin, and fragments of a second skull turned up in 1915. Dawson himself died in 1916.

Piltdown Man was only proved to be a fake in 1953 after chemical analysis of the bones revealed that the skull and jawbone were of different ages. The skull proved to be human, but only about 600 years old, while close examination of the jaw showed it to be that of a modern female orang-utan. The teeth had been crudely filed down to make them look more human, and the bones had been subjected to chemical staining; the canine had been painted.

The hoax was frighteningly effective – reconstruction drawings abounded and the skull was cited in the palaeontological literature for a generation – but it was probably not the work of an expert in anatomy. The clumsiness of the fakery points to an amateur. The fact that it was successful for so long was due mostly to scientific wishful thinking. In a jingoistic era, this seemed to be England's long-awaited contribution to the roster of 'fossil men', until then an entirely and frustratingly continental phenomenon, most recently in Germany where the archaic Mauer (or Heidelberg) jaw had been found in 1908. When presenting the first finds, Dawson cried 'How's that for Heidelberg!'

It is possible that the faker – or someone else with doubts about Piltdown – aimed to mock the barrage of triumphant

'The Piltdown Men', by John Cooke. Charles Dawson, the likely forger, is standing second from the right. Arthur Keith, wearing the white coat, is measuring the skull under the direction of the anatomist Grafton Elliot Smith, who stands behind him. Charles Darwin surveys the scene from the picture on the wall.

declarations that greeted this 'earliest Englishman' by subsequently salting the site with a bone implement shaped by a steel knife into the rough form of a cricket bat! But even this did not cause suspicion.

Debate still rages endlessly over the identity of the hoaxer or hoaxers – anyone remotely involved with the site from Teilhard de Chardin to Sherlock Holmes' creator Sir Arthur Conan Doyle has been implicated, most recently the anatomist Sir Arthur Keith. However, the simplest explanation is that Charles Dawson was the faker. He repeatedly sought the limelight through finding extraordinary objects, and in 1909 even wrote in a letter that he was 'waiting for the big discovery that never seems to come.' Among his other Sussex 'finds' were some stamped Roman tiles commemorating the late fourth-century AD refurbishment of the sea defences of the Saxon Shore fort of Pevensey; analysis has proved these to be modern forgeries too. It is therefore quite likely that Dawson, the fantasist and forger, acted alone.

Pioneering excavations in southwestern France were also being undertaken at this time by the naturalist and anatomist Dr Henri Martin. Working at the Mousterian site of La Quina in the Charente between 1906 and 1936 he paid particular attention to the bones he found, identifying different species and analysing fragments in detail. Instead of tossing out animal bones like most of his contemporaries, he sought to distinguish the different marks left by animals and humans, and studied the way limbs were cut and broken by prehistoric hunters when their prey was dismembered. It was work that heralded a new, more rigorous, phase in prehistory.

Human antiquity in eastern Europe

While ideas about life in the Ice Age in central and eastern Europe continued to be derived essentially from the west, especially France, prehistoric archaeology in these areas developed early on some unique characteristics. These were due in good part to the different social and economic climate. The countries of central and eastern Europe lagged behind the west in the decline of feudalism and absolute monarchy, and in the rise of nationalism and an educated middle class – social trends that were fundamental to the development of modern archaeology. Moreover, they never embarked on a programme of global exploration and colonization that would bring them into contact with tribal peoples and stimulate ideas about the nature of primitive society.

The development of palaeolithic archaeology in central and eastern Europe was also influenced by landscape. On the vast east European plain, the lack of caves deprived investigators of readily identifiable places to search for early remains in deep, stratified deposits. Archaeologists encountered palaeolithic sites in the open – often recognizing them by large accumulation of mammoth bones – but deep occupation layers offering a long chronological sequence were generally lacking.

Palaeolithic open-air sites were also found in many parts of central Europe, although numerous cave sites exist here as well. Such caves inevitably acted as a draw for early archaeologists. As early as 1867, palaeolithic artifacts were reported by Jindrich Wankel from Byci Skála, near Brno in the Moravian karst region, and in 1873 Count Jan Zawisza began excavations at Mamutowa cave on the banks of the Kluczwoda river near Kraków in southern Poland. It was 1880 before Wankel and others began work at Předmostí in northeastern Moravia, the first open-air site to be explored. Buried in massive deposits of wind-blown silt, or loess, Předmostí is typical of open-air sites in central and eastern Europe; it proved to be a large encampment with dwellings, hearths and pits, its archaeological levels yielding huge quantities of stone tools as well as portable art that included a fine mammoth carved in ivory. A spectacular multiple burial covered by mammoth bones that proved to contain the skeletons of eighteen Stone Age people was found in 1894.

Recognition of open-air sites occurred marginally more quickly in Russia where caves are largely confined to the eastern Carpathians and Crimea. The first discovery came in 1871, during construction of a military hospital in the remote city of Irkutsk in Siberia, when stone tools were found with artifacts cut from mammoth tusks, and the remains of Ice Age animals; Ivan Dement'evich Cherskii, who reported the finds, was also the first Russian archaeologist to identify the cut-marks of stone tools on a fossil bone.

In European Russia too, mammoth bones signalled the first open-air sites to be uncovered: in 1873 the village of Gontsy on a tributary of the Dnepr yielded hearths and flint debris, and four years later stone tools were recovered from Karacharovo on the Oka river. Karacharovo was investigated by Count Aleksei Sergeevich Uvarov, a leading figure in Russian archaeology who had, with his wife, founded an Imperial Russian Archaeological Society in Moscow in 1869 to rival the Imperial Archaeological Commission in St Petersburg established by government decree a decade earlier. Much of the history of Russian archaeology – during the Soviet as well as the Tsarist period – may be told in terms of the often bitter contest between the two cities; on this occasion the Moscow archaeologists scored an early victory when Countess Uvarova exploited her friendship with the Tsar to retain control over the issuing of excavation permits.

Between 1879 and the outbreak of the First World War, numerous other sites were investigated. Stone tools were recovered from Kostyonki on the Don river in European Russia in 1879 and from Willendorf on the Danube in northeastern Austria during 1884, both in this century to become famous open-air sites of the Stone Age. At Willendorf, occupied when the last glaciation was at its most severe, a long sequence of stone tools has been excavated together with the bones of rein-deer and woolly mammoth; among the finds of portable art was a famously obese limestone figurine coloured with red ochre discovered in 1908, the so-called Venus of Willendorf. Cave excavations were undertaken in the Bükk mountains of north-eastern Hungary, but the results were dwarfed by developments in western Europe in this period.

The first large-scale palaeolithic excavation was conducted by a Czech brewer and amateur archaeologist named Vikenti Vyacheslavich Khvoika between 1893 and 1902 at Kirillovskaya, an open-air site on a bluff overlooking the Dnepr in the city of Kiev. Khvoika dug some 7,500 square metres (1.8 acres), encountering the remains of perhaps four mammoth bone huts, but excavation techniques were so primitive that he did not recognize them as such.

Catching the imagination of the public
During the late nineteenth century major archaeological museums sprang up across Europe, in the east as well as the west, among them the Römisch-Germanisches Zentralmuseum in Mainz (1852), the archaeological section of the Naturhistorisches Museum in Vienna (1882), and the Museum für Völkerkunde in

Opposite. Schematic female figure engraved on a mammoth tusk from Předmosti, Czech Republic. The bones of over one thousand woolly mam-moths were found, and the site, known from as early as the sixteenth century, proved to be rich in bone and ivory tools, pendants, and portable art.

Berlin (1886). In Russia parallel institutions were established in cities like Moscow and St Petersburg, and, rather later, in outposts of the empire such as Warsaw and Lódz. Stimulated by national pride and the development of public education generally, such growth had been made possible in archaeology by the more systematic ways of presenting artifacts developed initially in Denmark by Thomsen and Worsaae (p. 89)

In Scandinavia itself, with increasing public awareness of archaeology's potential for revealing life in the past, discoveries of spectacularly well-preserved prehistoric remains were now being made. Excavation standards were also far in advance of those elsewhere. In 1871–75, the Bronze Age burial mound of Borum Eshøj in eastern Jutland yielded two large tree-trunk coffins of the fourteenth century BC, containing the bodies of a young man and an elderly woman, and accompanied by items of male and female clothing, including skirts, hair nets and shirts. The man's coffin was opened, the excavator told Worsaae, 'before a large crowd of people. Inside lay the best preserved skeleton I have seen, clothed in a tunic which had been held together by a (corroded) leather belt with a well-preserved wooden button. In the left arm, which was crooked, rested a finely-ornamented wooden scabbard'. Exceptionally preserved by waterlogging, these finds can still be seen in the Danish National Museum.

In Norway an equally dramatic find came to light a few years later at Lower Gokstad Farm, near Oseberg on the Oslofjord. Legend held that a king had been buried here in a large mound accompanied by great quantities of treasure. In 1880 local people began to dig in the mound in the hope of recovering this grave-wealth. What they found was of no great commercial value, but priceless in its archaeological importance: a complete Viking ship of the ninth-century AD, over 23 metres (75 feet) long, lying almost perfectly preserved on a bed of blue clay; the moisture retained by the clay had prevented the decay of the timbers for a millennium. At the centre of the vessel stood a timber burial chamber in which rested the skeleton of a Viking chieftain, laid out on a bed and arrayed in his finest attire. All the Gokstad ship's tackle survived, including mast, spars, ropes, blocks, gangplank, and sixteen pairs of oars – sufficient to build an accurate replica that was sailed across the Atlantic in 1893 to commemorate the four hundredth anniversary of Columbus' discovery of America.

In Britain, too, wetlands were attracting the attention of archaeologists. Particularly notable for their impact on the public imagination were the first-century BC lake villages of Glastonbury and Meare in the Somerset Levels of south-western England. These were excavated by Arthur Bulleid, a local doctor, from 1892 to 1938, and became the basis for many popular perceptions of life in Britain during the Iron Age.

A new sense of method

The professionalization of archaeology in the last quarter of the nineteenth century and the first quarter of the twentieth was marked by a growing appreciation of *context* as important archaeological information. Though careful by the standards of the age, Bulleid's excavations fell well short of the new standards of professionalism established by his older contemporary, Augustus Henry Lane Fox Pitt-Rivers.

Pitt-Rivers spent his early career as an officer in the British army, seeing active service in the Crimean War and rising to the rank of Major-General. His interest in archaeology began in the 1860s, while he was stationed in Ireland, but he had no opportunity to excavate until he inherited the vast Pitt-Rivers estates on Cranborne Chase in Dorset in 1880. Freed by wealth from the demands of a military career, he devoted the last twenty years of his life to archaeology, investigating prehistoric and Roman sites on his estates and devising fastidious new techniques of excavation and recording. Pitt-Rivers applied military discipline to everything he did, placing particular emphasis on the importance of 'common objects' and 'trivial details' for the dating and interpretation of archaeological sites. His results were privately printed in four handsome volumes, *Excavations in Cranborne Chase*, published between 1887 and 1898.

Exceptional though his fieldwork was, Pitt-Rivers' impact on others was limited by his eccentricity and reputation as a martinet. He remained unheard of outside Britain, though in Europe too there was a growing sense that careful recording of

Opposite. Replica of the ninth-century Gokstad ship at the Chicago World Fair, 1893.

To the delight of the Norwegian community in the United States, the *Viking*, a full-size oak replica of the Gokstad ship, was sailed across the Atlantic to Chicago to prove that the Norse could have reached America in an open sailing boat long before Columbus.

Captained by Magnus Andersen, the *Viking* left Bergen at noon on 30 April 1893, with a crew of twelve and a thousand bottles of beer. The passage was often stormy, but aided by its shallow draught and the astonishing flexibility of its hull, the boat regularly logged speeds of ten knots or more.

Anderson recorded 'The bottom together with the keel, gave with every movement of the ship, and in a strong head-sea the keel could move up and down as much as three-quarters of an inch. But strangely enough the ship stayed completely watertight. The ship's remarkable elasticity was also apparent in other ways; in heavy seas, for instance, the gunwhales would twist out of true by as much as six inches.'

Newfoundland was reached after an epic twenty-eight days at sea, on 27 May, and the ship became the triumph of the 1893 World Fair. After the Fair, the crew returned to Norway by more conventional means. The *Viking* itself was put on display at Chicago Zoo.

General Pitt Rivers (1827–1900) on his newly acquired estate at Cranborne Chase, 1882, by Frank Holl. Notice the notebook and pickaxe, and the Bronze Age shield and spearhead at the General's feet.

Physically imposing, Pitt-Rivers was a man of energy and fierce temper who dominated the lives of both his family and his archaeological assistants. In the judgement of his own great-grandson, he was a 'powerful personality; cold, impersonal and serious, but never very human. He evidently inspired respect rather than affection; loyalty but not love'.

Unlike most earlier antiquaries, Pitt-Rivers' interests were not in the classics and history so much as in anthropology, anatomy and geology. Though very much the eminent Victorian in his opinion of other races, he was notably active in promoting the links between archaeology and anthropology.

He wrote in 1887, 'Whilst geology was to carry us back to periods that had not before been thought of in the history of man, anthropology was to teach us how to estimate the stature and physical peculiarities of the skeletons found in the graves, and ethnology was to enable us to appreciate the social and material condition of the aborigines of our country by a comparison of their relics with the arts of modern savages. All these branches have now become indispensable to the prehistorian'.

the context and associations of finds was needed if a reliable prehistoric chronology was to be constructed. In Serbia, for instance, Miloje Vasić excavated the neolithic tell at Vinča, near Belgrade, between 1908 and 1912, separating the finds from each layer of rubbish and demolished buildings that made up the mound. The Vinča sequence soon became established as a chronological yardstick for the Balkans as a whole, into which could be linked both the better-known cultures of the southern Balkans and Greece on one hand, and central Europe on the other. Vasić also emphasized Vinča's links with the Aegean Bronze Age, going so far as to see Vinča as a northern outpost of Aegean civilization.

Burials, often treated in the past as no more than mines for museum objects, came to be recorded in more detail as it was realized that grave goods could contribute to building up a regional chronology; unlike settlement deposits which are haphazard, cumulative and often disturbed, burials provided instantaneous 'snapshots' of the artifacts in use at a particular time. Equally clearly, some graves were more spectacularly furnished than others, suggesting the presence of royalty or other exalted individuals.

In eastern Europe the archaeological potential of grave finds was dramatically underscored in 1897 when Nikolai Vesselovskii, professor of archaeology in St Petersburg, opened the *kurgan* or burial mound at Maikop in the foothills of the northern Caucasus. Inside was a three-section wooden mortuary house surrounded by a stone pavement, each section containing a single burial. In the large, richly furnished central chamber lay a man, in the smaller chambers on either side two women, all three skeletons crouched on their sides accompanied by ritual red ochre. The finds in the male grave were extraordinary. Four silver and gold posts supported a canopy bearing 135 figures of bulls and lions as frontal ornaments. With the burial itself was a gold diadem with rosettes; carnelian, turquoise, and gold beads and earrings; six rings of gold and silver; seventeen vessels of gold, silver and stone; copper tools; and a mass of elaborately decorated textiles. These objects established a clear link between the Russian Caucasus and the Bronze Age cultures of the Near East in the period *c.* 2500–2200 BC.

Building a chronology

The flow of new discoveries from sites like Vinca and Maikop during the late nineteenth century helped establish a whole raft of chronological schemes built on the work of Thomsen and Worsaae. Relative chronologies were refined as more and more artifacts were collected and 'typology' became a key pursuit. The archaeologist would take all the available examples of a class of object like bronze axes and arrange them in a series, usually with the simplest at one end and the most complex at the other; this was assumed to correspond to the order in which the objects were made, so each item could be dated relative to others in the sequence. Along the way, comparisons could also be made with corresponding categories of objects used in other regions: thus the development of Danish bronze axes might be compared with those of northern Germany, enabling connections and the occasional borrowing of ideas to be detected. The creation of these typologies was a hazardous enterprise, a house of cards based on a number of critical assumptions. Treated cautiously, however, they could be used to construct valuable chronological schemes, extending over vast distances in time and space.

Oskar Montelius (1843–1921), on the right, being shown the Oseberg Viking ship by the excavation's director Gabriel Gustafson, 1904.

A synthesizer rather than an excavator, Montelius was nonetheless a central figure in the development of European archaeology, fascinated by the chronological problems of the Neolithic, Bronze and Iron Ages across Europe and the Mediterranean world.

His essential aim, he proclaimed, was to give 'individual consideration to each of the main series of weapons, tools, ornaments, and pottery, together with their ornamentation, so as to determine the course of their evolution and to find out in what order the types – judged according to their own criteria – succeed each other'.

The most famous of all nineteenth-century typologists was the Swedish archaeologist Oskar Montelius. He had travelled widely in Europe and the Mediterranean, and his wide experience led him to perceive subtle changes in artifact types. As he examined finds from closed deposits like burials, he noticed that particular forms always occurred together and could therefore be placed in chronological order. He famously illustrated his use of the typological method by showing how the railway carriage had developed from the horse-drawn carriage, shedding over time all traces of its horse-drawn origin. By the 1880s, he was able to propose a division of the northern Bronze Age into a series of six consecutive phases, his most lasting contribution to European prehistory; the Neolithic he subsequently divided into four periods.

Montelius laid the groundwork for the typological approach that still dominates archaeological research in much of Europe. Others devoted their attention to the Iron Age, dividing it into two separate stages named after the cemetery of Hallstatt in Austria (c. 700–500 BC; p. 97) and the settlement of La Tène on the shores of Lake Neuchâtel in Switzerland (500 BC to the Roman conquest), a votive site at which brooches, tools and weapons – including over 150 swords, many with decorated bronze scabbards – had been cast into the waters as offerings to the gods. For the most part, divisions like these have stood the test of time and remain in use today, eloquent testimony to the painstaking work of these ardent typologists.

Montelius recognized the possibilities of cross-dating similar objects found in different places, and repeatedly attempted to link his northern European sequences to dated finds from the Aegean and Egypt. By this means he placed the end of the European Bronze Age in the fifth century BC and assigned it a duration of 1,000 years, thus dating the Neolithic–Bronze Age transition to approximately 1500 BC and the beginning of the Neolithic to 3000 BC. This 'short chronology' was accepted

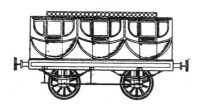

Montelius used the development of the railway carriage to illustrate the principle of typology. Top left: England 1825. Bottom left: Austria 1840. Right: Sweden/Germany 1850.

by most archaeologists until the development of radiocarbon dating after the Second World War. By assigning chronological priority to the Aegean and Egypt, Montelius also became an early proponent of *Ex oriente lux*, the thesis – subsequently to dominate prehistory until the late 1960s – that civilization in all its aspects spread to northern Europe from the eastern Mediterranean.

Later, Montelius' rival, the Danish prehistorian Sophus Müller, extended the typological method to characterize whole complexes of finds, including artifact types and their associated architecture. It is in Müller's writings also that one finds the roots of the notion of archaeological 'cultures', a term later used by Kossinna and Childe to describe archaeological finds that are uniform over large areas or occur repeatedly together. Although the concept was only weakly developed in his *Prehistory of Europe* (1905), Müller was even then using 'culture' to describe related complexes of finds.

The typological approach of Montelius and Müller thus provided the crucial bridge between the Three Age system developed in the early nineteenth century by Thomsen and Worsaae and the regional sequences on which the broad syntheses of Schuchhardt and Childe were built in the early twentieth. Their work was scholarly and detached, without the romantic or nationalist overtones of their predecessors and contemporaries; and their typologies were 'anonymous', with a primary focus on museum artifacts. Such tidy-minded detachment made it easy to invoke an abstract concept such as diffusion – the spread of artifact types through contact between peoples – to explain cultural change in prehistoric Europe. The disadvantage, increasingly apparent in the years that followed, was that prehistory was now in danger of becoming an arid pigeon-holing exercise, neatly ordering sites and artifacts in relation to each other but losing sight of the people who made them.

Nationalist archaeology

During the first half of the twentieth century, the nationalism that had characterized much of archaeology a hundred years earlier reappeared, this time in an extreme form used to support claims of racial and ethnic superiority and territorial title.

Central to the rebirth of this nationalist archaeology was Gustaf Kossinna (1858–1931), a comparative linguist who transferred his allegiance to prehistory, becoming professor of German archaeology at the University of Berlin in 1902. Kossinna was no excavator, drawing his data instead from museum collections and

Excavation of the Roman cemetery of Praunheim, near Frankfurt, 1901–2. Painting by F. Gumsheimer.

the publications of others. His method, which he called 'settlement archaeology', relied on mapping characteristic finds to establish the boundaries of their distribution; if a clear geographical distribution emerged, the spread of finds was taken as a straightforward expression of an ethnic entity. From 1895 Kossinna studied particularly the area between the Oder and the Vistula rivers, the traditional border zone between the empires of central Europe, in an attempt to trace the course of germanic settlement. The importance of non-germanic peoples such as the Celts and Romans was dismissed out of hand.

By the 1920s, Kossinna's views were causing alarm outside Germany. The creation of new nations in eastern Europe after 1918 meant a loss of territory to Germany, and Kossinna's nationalism was becoming steadily more chauvinistic. The presence of 'germanic' artifacts, no matter how distant from Germany itself, was viewed as legitimizing territorial rights, and he began to articulate a difference between innovating cultures and passive, recipient cultures. This ideology was viewed with alarm by the Poles and Czechs, who had gained territory at the expense of the Germans and who could see only too clearly the justification Kossinna's writings offered for the military reclamation of lost lands.

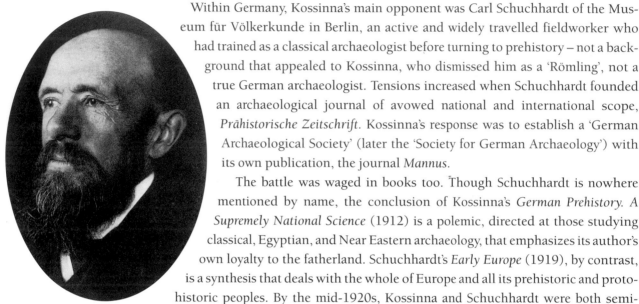

Carl Schuchhardt (1859–1943)

Within Germany, Kossinna's main opponent was Carl Schuchhardt of the Museum für Völkerkunde in Berlin, an active and widely travelled fieldworker who had trained as a classical archaeologist before turning to prehistory – not a background that appealed to Kossinna, who dismissed him as a 'Römling', not a true German archaeologist. Tensions increased when Schuchhardt founded an archaeological journal of avowed national and international scope, *Prähistorische Zeitschrift*. Kossinna's response was to establish a 'German Archaeological Society' (later the 'Society for German Archaeology') with its own publication, the journal *Mannus*.

The battle was waged in books too. Though Schuchhardt is nowhere mentioned by name, the conclusion of Kossinna's *German Prehistory. A Supremely National Science* (1912) is a polemic, directed at those studying classical, Egyptian, and Near Eastern archaeology, that emphasizes its author's own loyalty to the fatherland. Schuchhardt's *Early Europe* (1919), by contrast, is a synthesis that deals with the whole of Europe and all its prehistoric and proto-historic peoples. By the mid-1920s, Kossinna and Schuchhardt were both semi-retired, but in 1928 each produced a major book. Kossinna's *Origins and Expansion of the Germans in Prehistoric and Early Historic Times* (1928), the culmination of his obsession with Germanic territoriality, ends with a tribute to Field Marshall von Hindenburg, who is shown in the photographic frontispiece visiting excavations in East Prussia. Schuchhardt in the same year published a *Prehistory of Germany* in which he depicted prehistoric German society as a mosaic of many peoples, including Germans, Celts, Slavs and eventually Romans.

Kossinna died in 1931, before his nationalist ideology could find expression in the Nazi regime and its attempts to enlist prehistory and archaeology in the service of the state. His disciples, including Hans Reinerth who followed him as professor in Berlin from 1934 to 1945, took on prominent positions in the Nazi regime, and Kossinna's view of prehistory became the official one taught in schools during the Third Reich. Schuchhardt lived on, a respected elder statesman of German archaeology despite his decidedly un-nationalistic view of the past. His last months, however, were tragic. In 1943 his home in Berlin-Lichterfelde was destroyed by allied bombing, and with it his library; heartbroken, he left Berlin for Kassel, where he died a few months later at the age of eighty-five.

Prehistory in southern Europe

Given archaeology's long history in northern Europe, it is surprising to find that serious interest in the prehistory of the western Mediterranean began only at the end of the nineteenth century. The key figures were Henri and Louis Siret in Spain and Themistocles Zammit on Malta.

Henri Siret and his younger brother Louis were educated and trained in Belgium as engineers, and found employment in 1880 with a Spanish mining company in the Almeria region of southeastern Spain. Here they began to excavate prehistoric sites, bringing to light a whole series of discoveries, including the Copper Age settlement and cemetery of Los Millares, where they worked from 1891. Los Millares remains one of the key sites in European prehistory, a promontory settlement in arid Almeria high above the Andarax river. The dry-stone fortification wall is strengthened by the use of solid semicircular towers at regular intervals, giving an impression of a much more recent construction than one would expect from its third millennium BC date. The cemetery lies outside the walls, a series of 80 stone vaulted tomb chambers, each containing the remains of several individuals in what were perhaps family vaults. It was here that the copper axes and daggers and ivory objects that so surprised the Siret brothers were found.

They went on to excavate other sites in the region, including El Argar, a fortified village with some 950 burials in stone cists or pots below the house floors, some of the dead wearing gold or silver diadems around their skulls. The Sirets were uncertain how to explain their discoveries. Lacking any means of accurate dating, they thought initially they must have alighted on colonies of Phoenicians, the famous trading people who roamed the shores of the western Mediterranean in the first millennium BC. Later, however, they abandoned this idea, concluding, correctly, that such sites were the achievement of Spain's own prehistoric farming communities.

A few years later it was Malta's turn to be the location of unexpected archaeological discoveries. During the nineteenth century there had been reports of ruined temples on the islands. The British archaeologist Sir Richard Colt Hoare, more famous for his work on the barrows of Wessex (p. 55), visited Malta in 1791 and explored the Ggantija temple on Gozo. Ggantija, Hagar Qim and Mnajdra were excavated in the 1820s and 1830s, but all those who wrote about them thought they were the remains of the Phoenician colonization of the islands. An accidental discovery during house building in 1902 was to change all this. The Maltese islands have a dry climate, and to offset the effects of summer drought traditional houses have cisterns cut into the rock below them. It was while cutting such a cistern on the outskirts of Valletta that workmen broke into an underground chamber that proved to be part of a vast underground burial complex, the Hal Saflieni hypogeum – a veritable maze of rock-cut chambers and corridors on three levels, the lowest 10 metres (33 feet) below ground. Excavation showed that at least 7,000 defleshed bodies had been placed there over centuries. Whoever had dug the complex had

Hal Saflieni hypogeum, Malta. Settled from the early fifth millennium BC, the Maltese islands spawned in the fourth and third millennia a distinctive series of neolithic temples like Tarxien, Hagar Qim and Mnajdra – ceremonial stone buildings with internal courts and facades sometimes two storeys high. The limestone-cut chambers of the Hal Saflieni hypogeum may have paralleled the rooms of an above-ground megalithic temple that once stood over the hypogeum itself.

lavished careful attention on the visible surfaces, which were carved with decorative doorways and spirals, and – in the case of ceilings – covered with intricate designs. From 1907 work at the hypogeum was entrusted to Themistocles Zammit, director of the Malta Museum; it was he, by his excavations at Hal Saflieni and at the above-ground temples of Tarxien nearby, who placed the prehistory of Malta on a firm footing. Zammit showed above all that these monuments were much more ancient than had been thought, belonging to the neolithic period: the third millennium BC.

Such excavations, together with new work in Italy and Sicily, stimulated interest in the prehistoric archaeology of southern Europe. No longer was it just Roman remains which drew the attention of archaeologists; slowly but surely, as the twentieth century wore on, the prehistory of the area became integrated with that of the rest of Europe, filling yet another gap in the complex pattern of the European past.

THE CLASSICAL WORLD

Opposite. Column drums of the temple of Zeus at Olympia, toppled by an earthquake sometime after the removal of Pheidias' cult statue of Zeus in the fourth century AD. A thick flood-deposit of silt and sand blanketed the site, which was as a consequence lost and little robbed of its architectural components and marble sculptures when rediscovered by German archaeologists in the 1870s.

The largest temple erected in Greece before the Parthenon, the building was of the Doric order, constructed from local limestone to the design of Libon of Elis, *c.* 470–450 BC.

The liberation of Greece from Turkish rule in 1828 gave archaeologists from northern Europe access to the major sites known from classical literature. Important sanctuaries, such as Olympia and Delphi, which served as centres for athletic competitions in the Greek world, as well as major cities like Athens and Corinth, immediately became the focus of attention. These sites were the setting of known historical events and – in the case of Athens – Greek drama, and they also figured in the Itinerary of the geographer and historian Pausanias, an important text which provided an *Itinerary* of Greece in the second century AD; thanks to Pausanias, excavators were able to look for, and uncover, buildings mentioned in classical texts. Given the interests of ancient Greek writers, it was natural that the emphasis in the early years of exploration was on sanctuaries that were also important

depositories for religious dedications; their athletic sites were, moreover, panhellenic, drawing people from all over the Greek world.

Olympia in the western Peloponnese attracted early interest from German excavators, who began work in the 1870s. This cult centre dedicated to Zeus, the chief deity of the Greeks, had as its focus a huge colonnaded temple measuring 28 by 64 metres (92 by 210 feet) which from the fifth century BC contained Pheidias' monumental statue of the god (p. 6). Digging through a layer of silt left by medieval flooding, the team discovered the substructure of the temple complete, its columns toppled by earthquakes. Amidst the debris lay the pedimental sculptures described by Pausanias: vivid depictions of the mythological foundation of the Olympic Games and the famous battle, known from the verse of Ovid, between drunken Centaurs and the Lapiths, a primitive mountain tribe from Thessaly. Relief sculptures in the metopes depicted the labours of Herakles. Further excavations have since revealed the temple of Hera, the consort of Zeus, the treasuries for individual Greek states, and the classical Olympic stadium – a linear running track one *stadion* (192.28 metres or 630 feet) long, set between parallel earthen banks that provided seating for spectators.

The long tradition of excavating at Olympia has brought more recent finds too. Pausanias mentions the workshop in which the huge gold and ivory statue of Zeus was created by the sculptor Pheidias, a building constructed so as to have the same dimensions as the inner room of the temple itself. Excavations have discovered both the workshop and debris that includes a mug with the supposedly ancient inscription, 'I belong to Pheidias'. Elsewhere on the site, votive deposits have yielded a range of dedications made in the sanctuary including armour and bronze tripods (three-legged cauldrons, sometimes with relief decoration on the legs). One carried an inscription which revealed that it had been dedicated by Miltiades, the Athenian general at the battle of Marathon in 490 BC.

German archaeologists were also active in Athens, where, as early as 1835, Ludwig Ross had proposed the existence of an earlier Parthenon. In large-scale excavations on the akropolis from 1885 to 1891, they explored the foundations around the Parthenon and discovered the massive base of an earlier temple belonging to the sixth century BC. Exploration of fill between the foundations of the two temples and the outer wall of the sanctuary also brought to light caches of buried marble sculpture, notably *korai* – statues of young women – that once stood within the sanctuary of the patron goddess of the city. Some still bore traces of paint on the drapery; the colour of the hair on one male statue, or *kouros*, led to the piece being dubbed the 'Blond Boy'. As they were hardly weathered, it was thought the statues had probably been toppled during the Persian sack of the city in 480 BC and buried by the returning Athenians.

The French chose to excavate the sanctuary of Apollo at Delphi, home of the oracle described in the Homeric *Hymn to Apollo* and numerous later ancient authors, including Pausanias who vividly recounts how an attack by invading Gauls was

Opposite. Every inch the businessman. Heinrich Schliemann (1822–90) aged about forty, during his period as an indigo merchant in St Petersburg. He made another fortune in the California gold rush, buying gold-dust from prospectors.

Energetic, self-advertising and a master of hyperbole, Schliemann himself conceded that his 'biggest fault, being a braggart and a bluffer ... yielded countless advantages' in life.

However, about his archaeological instincts there can be no doubt. Rather later, Arthur Evans described Schliemann as a 'spare, slightly built man of sallow complexion and somewhat darkly clad, wearing spectacles of foreign make, and through which – so the fancy took me – he had looked deep into the ground'.

routed in 279 BC by supernatural intervention that included rock falls sent by Apollo himself. The oracle attracted visitors from across the Greek world, and rulers and states were eager to provide buildings within the sacred space or set up monuments. In the mid-sixth century BC the Lydian king, Croesus, consulted the oracle about whether to go to war to check the rising power of Cyrus the Great of Persia; reassured when told that 'a great kingdom would be destroyed' if he did, he dedicated costly offerings of solid gold to the sanctuary that made his name a by-word for wealth and piety. When he did invade Persia, the kingdom destroyed proved to be his own.

Many of the buildings at Delphi described by Pausanias and others have been found. These include the Athenian treasury, decorated with reliefs showing the Attic hero Theseus, said to have been built with booty 'taken from the army that landed with Datis at Marathon' in 490 BC. With seating for seven thousand, the running track is the best preserved in Greece; one of Delphi's most stunning finds was a bronze charioteer dedicated by Polyzalos, tyrant of Gela in Sicily, to commemorate a victory in the games. Near the temple of Apollo was found the base of the great bronze snake dedicated by the Greek cities who fought against the Persians at Plataia in 479 BC. Made up of three scaly serpents twisted together to form a column surmounted originally by a golden tripod, it was carried off to Constantinople in the fourth century AD and placed in the city's hippodrome; the stump of the snake survives and one of its gaping-jawed heads has been found during excavation.

The discovery of Bronze Age Greece

> Mycenae certainly was a small place, and many of the towns of that period do not seem to us today to be particularly imposing. Yet that is not good evidence for rejecting what the poets and what general tradition have to say about the size of the expedition ... there is no reason why we should not believe that the Trojan expedition was the greatest that had ever taken place

For Thucydides, who wrote his *History of the Peloponnesian War* in the fifth century BC, the events described by Homer in the *Iliad* and the *Odyssey* lay in the remote past, since it was reckoned that the Trojan War had been fought *c.* 1200 BC. Yet the Greeks accepted the Homeric epics as historical, not least because their heroic ancestors had left a tangible legacy. In the Argolid, for instance, Pausanias saw at Mycenae:

> parts of the ring-wall left, including the gate with lions standing on it. They say this is the work of Cyclopes, who built the wall of Tiryns ... In the ruins of Mycenae is a water-source called Perseia, and the underground chambers of Atreus and his sons where they kept the treasure-houses of their wealth. There is the grave of Atreus and the graves of those who came home from Troy to be cut

Schliemann and Troy

Heinrich Schliemann (1822–90) was born at Neubuckow in Germany, his father a pastor who supposedly kindled his son's passion for Homer when he was just eight. Family circumstances did not allow him to pursue an academic career despite his extraordinary aptitude for languages (he was to speak twenty-two and could write eleven perfectly),

so he settled in St Petersburg where he became a wealthy businessman, dealing first in indigo, the blue dye that came from Java and India, and then increasing his fortune in the California gold rush. At 46, he was able to retire. Inspired by philhellenism, Schliemann resumed his classical education in Paris and visited Greece and Turkey for the first time. It is clear from the account written on his return, *Ithaca, the Peloponnese*

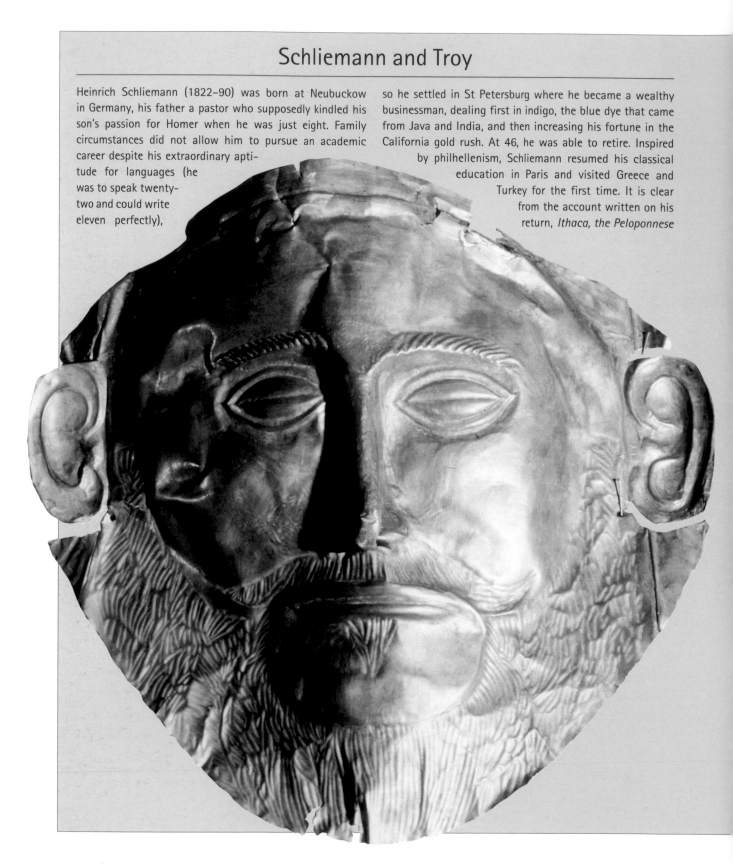

and Troy (1869), that his faith in Homer as a historical source had been confirmed.

To convince the sceptics, Schliemann in 1870 undertook preliminary excavations at Hisarlik, a tiny mound – no more than two hectares in area – overlooking the Dardanelles in northeastern Anatolia, that the English antiquarian Frank Calvert had dug five years before and identified as Troy. Impressed by the results, he returned in 1871–73 with a team of 150 workmen to drive vast trenches through the mound. The sheer scale of the excavations and the complex stratigraphy, up to 15 metres (49 feet) deep, at first baffled Schliemann but he eventually identified four successive Bronze Age 'cities', the second of which had been destroyed by fire. His conclusion that this was the Troy the Greeks had besieged and sacked seemed to be confirmed at the end of his final season, in May 1873, when he discovered a spectacular collection of gold and silver vessels and jewellery, the so-called Treasure of Priam, which he promptly smuggled out of Turkey.

Because of the fury of the Turkish authorities, Schliemann could not continue his excavations at Troy. In 1876 he therefore turned his attention to Mycenae, across the Aegean in the Greek Peloponnese. Pausanias had said that Agamemnon and his companions were buried inside the citadel at Mycenae, and Schliemann followed his directions literally. The fame he craved was the reward. With his discovery of the royal shaft graves of the sixteenth century BC – now known to be too old by several centuries to have belonged to Agamemnon – and their sensational face masks of beaten gold and wealth of other golden objects, Schliemann rediscovered a civilization and judged his faith in Homer vindicated. One skull in particular, he wrote:

> was wonderfully preserved under its ponderous gold mask ... both eyes perfectly visible, also the mouth, which owing to the enormous weight that had pressed upon it was wide open and showed thirty-two beautiful teeth ... the man must have died at the early age of thirty-five ... The news that the tolerably well-preserved body of a man of the mythic heroic age had been found ... spread like wildfire through the Argolid, and people came by thousands from Argos, Nauplia, and the villages to see the wonder.

In 1884 Schliemann was in the Peloponnese once more. The massive cyclopean fortifications of Tiryns, on the coast 15 kilometres (9 miles) south of Mycenae, had been praised by Pausanias and drawn by early travellers like Edward Dodwell, but the site had not been excavated. Schliemann, with his assistant, the capable Wilhelm Dörpfeld, made good this omission, revealing 'the great palace of the legendary kings of Tiryns' on the citadel. 'From now until the end of time', Schliemann wrote, 'it will be impossible ever to publish a book on ancient art that does not contain my plan of the palace of Tiryns.'

There were failures. He did not find the palace of Menelaos and Helen at Sparta and his search for the palace of Nestor at Pylos, revealed in this century by the American Carl Blegen (p. 230), was also fruitless. Schliemann particularly regretted that he could not purchase the site of Knossos where he 'hoped to discover the original home of the Mycenaean civilization'. Throughout it all, the lure of Troy remained irresistible. He returned in 1878–79 and again in 1882, accompanied by Dörpfeld who clarified the stratigraphy of the site and demonstrated that there were in fact seven 'cities', spanning, as we now know, most of the third and second millennia BC. Even then, Schliemann was perplexed because he failed to find the close links he expected between Mycenaean Greece and Troy II, the fortified town then identified as the Troy of the *Iliad*. He resumed his excavations in 1889–90, at last finding Mycenaean pottery in Troy VI, and would undoubtedly have discovered the impressive and more plausibly Homeric fortifications of this sixth settlement, but for his last illness and death in December 1890, in Naples.

Schliemann had an exceptional eye for sites, but his crude, pre-Dörpfeld excavation techniques, particularly in the early seasons at Troy, destroyed more than they found and he was not above fabrication; a comparison of his books, diaries, notebooks and letters reveals significant discrepancies of which he must have been aware. Tactless and quarrelsome though he was, his drive, flair for publicity and prompt publication gave Aegean archaeology an impetus it has never lost. As his collaborator, Rudolf Virchow wrote, '[Troy] would still have lain hidden in the earth had not imagination guided his spade'.

Opposite. The gold 'Mask of Agamemnon' discovered by Schliemann in the fifth shaft grave at Mycenae. The individuality of the face implies portraiture rather than a merely conventionalized representation. Height 26 centimetres (10¼ inches).

down by Aigisthos … Klytaimnestra and Aigisthos were buried a little further from the wall. They were not fit to lie inside, where Agamemnon and the men murdered with him are lying.

The Bronze Age ruins of Mycenae and Tiryns were visited by many early travellers in Greece, and Elgin removed sculpture from the facade of the fourteenth-century BC Treasury of Atreus, largest of the beehive-shaped *tholos* tombs in which Mycenae's rulers were buried. But eighteenth- and nineteenth-century scholars were principally interested in classical sites and antiquities. Although it was evident that 'cyclopean' architecture – walls so impressive that later Greeks attributed them to Homer's race of one-eyed giants, the Cyclopes – must be prehistoric, the heroic age itself was regarded as myth. That the Homeric epics had an historical basis appeared unlikely to all but the determined Heinrich Schliemann.

Minoan Crete

Feted throughout Europe, Schliemann's discoveries stimulated the search for further prehistoric sites in the Aegean. Particularly active was Christos Tsountas, often known as the father of Greek prehistory, who dug both in Thessaly and at Mycenae, where between 1877 and 1902 he excavated the palace at the summit of the citadel. Even better known is the Mycenaean tomb at Vapheio in Laconia, investigated in 1889; the chamber had been plundered, but cut into the floor was an intact princely burial of the fifteenth century BC with offerings that included bronze weapons, jewellery and two richly decorated gold cups. Tsountas is remembered too as the pioneer of archaeology in the Cyclades. The cemeteries he systematically explored as the nineteenth century drew to a close produced splendid grave goods, notably the distinctive marble figurines dating from the third millennium BC that have been so extensively looted by tomb robbers in this century.

Crete was archaeologically long neglected as the island remained an Ottoman possession until 1898, outside the western sphere of influence. Schliemann was aware of the potential of the palace site of Knossos, near Heraklion, but failed to buy the land, and it was left to the British archaeologist Arthur Evans to reveal the site in excavations between 1900 and 1935. Oxford-educated, the wealthy son of the prehistorian John Evans, Arthur Evans made his name initially as a journalist, serving in his twenties as the *Manchester Guardian*'s special correspondent in Bosnia and Croatia. He studied the antiquities of the Balkans, and on his return to Britain became keeper of the Ashmolean Museum, Oxford, a post he held from 1884 until 1908.

Arthur Evans (1851–1941), by Sir William Richmond, 1907. If Schliemann could be derided as a nouveau riche upstart, Arthur Evans' academic credentials were impeccable. Surrounded by antiquities from childhood, he had accompanied his wealthy father, Sir John Evans, on his famous visit to Boucher de Perthes' excavations at Abbeville in 1859 and found a flint implement there at the age of eight.

As dogged as Schliemann, Evans too enjoyed submitting himself to the rigours of travel by foot or on horseback across rugged terrain.

Excited by an exhibition of finds from Troy, Evans made the acquaintance of Schliemann in Athens in 1883. On his return to buy antiquities a decade later, he became convinced from seals seen in the Athens flea market that the Mycenaeans had their own system of hieroglyphic writing; this prompted him to visit Crete, from where the seals had purportedly come. He set eyes on Knossos for the first time in the spring of 1894, confiding his impressions to his diary:

> Here at a place called *ta pitharia* are the remains of Mykenaean walls and passages (where the great pots, pithoi, were found) noted by Stillman and others. They are very complex as far as one can judge from what is visible to the eye but were hardly as Stillman supposes the Labyrinth itself. (Later: No, on further examination I think it must be so).

Decisive and determined, Evans at once enquired about the cost of the land, keeping up protracted negotiations until 1900 when Knossos at last became his.

Wall painting of female dancers, Knossos. Evans' approach to conservation was thoroughgoing. Passionate about conveying the grandeur of the site to posterity and believing his excavations to be definitive, in the last years of his life he supervised a wholesale reconstruction of the Minoan palace and oversaw the 'completion' of the fragmentary wall paintings. The result excites heated feelings even today.

Flinders Petrie in the Near East

William Matthew Flinders Petrie (1853–1942) was the first true 'archaeologist' to excavate in the Near East. Energetic and precise, by temperament drawn to the mathematical sciences, he was also self-taught, with little in the way of formal education. His long career brought an innovatory approach to excavation and the analysis of finds, particularly pottery, which originated in an early interest in metrology and surveying standing monuments.

Innumerable anecdotes are recounted about Petrie, an eccentric with uncompromising views on every subject from archaeological technique to the correct way of brushing one's teeth and the amount of water required for a bath (no more than five inches). Most such stories concern the frugal and spartan domestic arrangements of his excavation camps in Egypt. While digging for four seasons at Abydos between 1900–04, his habit was to bury uneaten tins of food until the next season, then to test the tins – still unpredictable in the early days of canning – by throwing them against a wall. Tins that exploded were clearly not up to standard.

Petrie's camp would 'cheerfully eat out of week-opened tins after scraping off the green crust inside', the young T. E. Lawrence reported while working with Petrie at Carchemesh in 1911. Even so, 'the Professor is the great man of the camp – he's about 5' 11" high, white-haired, grey-bearded, broad and active, with a voice that splits when excited and a constant feverish speed of speech.'

Petrie's introduction to Egyptology came at the age of thirteen through a book by a family friend, the Astronomer Royal, Charles Piazzi Smyth, called *Our Inheritance in the Great Pyramid*. Piazzi Smyth was a 'British Israelite', who believed that the British were one of the ten lost tribes mentioned in Genesis and that the Great Pyramid at Giza was built not by idolatrous Egyptians, but under divine supervision; using the 'pyramid inch' he had devised, the proportions of its passages and chambers could predict future events in world history.

Petrie initially had some sympathy with this view, but he saw that verification of the 'pyramid inch' and Piazzi Smyth's other measurements required a more accurate survey of the pyramid than any that had so far been undertaken. After a youth spent surveying British monuments like Stonehenge to a high degree of accuracy, often using techniques of his own devising, Petrie finally left for Egypt in November 1880 to carry out his pyramid survey. For two years, 1881–83, he lived frugally, sleeping in an ancient rock-cut tomb on the Giza plateau, oblivious to vermin, fleas and the night-time howling of dogs and jackals. The result of his work, the first accurate survey of the three pyramids of the Fourth Dynasty (c. 2575–2465 BC), was to discredit both the pyramid inch and Piazzi Smyth's conclusions. More important, it established wholly new standards in the recording of ancient monuments, in Egypt and elsewhere.

Petrie's competence and energy were recognized by General Pitt-Rivers, who visited him at Giza in 1881, but more especially by the Egypt Exploration Fund and Amelia Edwards, whose protégé he became. Between 1884–86 he excavated at a number of Nile delta sites, notably Tanis (the capital of Dynasties 21 and 22, c. 1070–712 BC) and Naucratis (home of a Greek colony during Dynasty 26, 664–525 BC).

For the Fund and for other fund-raising bodies he founded himself Petrie then dug successfully for more than forty years on the foremost sites in Egypt, publishing as ceaselessly as he excavated; major projects included the royal cemeteries of Dynasties 1 and 2 at Abydos (c. 3050–2686 BC), the Middle Kingdom town of el-Lahun (c. 2023–1633 BC), and the pharaoh Akhenaten's short-lived capital city at el-Amarna (1350–1334 BC). Yet Petrie's contribution to archaeology was much greater than this: his innovations in technique and method and his training of a whole generation of Near Eastern archaeologists were central to his achievement.

Petrie was at his strongest devising original solutions to immediate problems, and virtually invented what we would now call seriation – he called it sequence dating – a key technique for giving chronological order to a mass of excavated finds. Discovering unfamiliar pottery and other objects at the southern Egyptian sites of Naqada, Abadiya and Hu (Diospolis Parva) in 1895–99, Petrie at first interpreted them as evidence of a new race of invaders who entered Egypt in the First Intermediate Period (2181–2040 BC). However, it soon became clear that the finds were neolithic, from cultural groups already present in Egypt during what is now called the Predynastic Period (before 3150 BC). Once Petrie had accepted this new interpretation – something he was never enthusiastic to do – his lively mind began to work on the problem of how best to give chronological order to this unfamiliar material.

His solution was to select 900 tombs with a good variety of pottery from the three sites, rather less than a quarter of the total. Each was represented by a cardboard strip divided into nine sections, each section representing one of the major groups of pottery. Petrie then took the 900 strips and, by hand and eye, started to arrange them so that tombs with similar

pottery types were kept together – the assumption behind this system being that each pottery type had a 'life' during which it was used before evolving into a different type or falling out of use. Next the whole range of sorted types was divided into fifty equal groups, to which Petrie assigned 'sequence dates' numbered from thirty to eighty (starting at thirty to leave room for earlier types at the beginning). He was thus able to establish the chronological sequence of his tombs, if not their absolute dates.

Petrie's attempts to use raw archaeological evidence to construct a working chronology established a basic framework for discussing the Predynastic Period in Egypt and put an

invaluable analytical tool in the hands of archaeologists working with similar classes of material. Today it is a computer that does the sorting rather than an enthusiast with 900 strips of cardboard. But it is Petrie who deserves the credit for first introducing statistics to archaeology.

Above. Flinders Petrie excavating the Ramesseum, one of several temples he dug on the west bank at Thebes, December 1895. Painting by Henry Wallis.

Evans was not an experienced excavator, and he was assisted by the Scottish archaeologist Duncan Mackenzie, a member of the British team at Phylakopi on Melos in 1896–99. Between 50 and 180 labourers were employed and preparations were thorough: Evans' half-sister, Joan, commented that 'the scale may be measured by the purchase of a gross of bottles of Eno's Fruit Salts and a gross of nail-brushes'. Evans knew enough of Knossos to be optimistic, but even he could not have predicted how soon his expectations would be fulfilled. Within a week of starting to dig on 23 March, he had found 'a kind of baked clay bar, rather like a stone chisel in shape, though broken at one end, with script on it and what appear to be numerals' that proved this was a literate society. He was already sure that this was a palace 'of the prae-Mycenaean period', home to a distinctive early Cretan civilization for which he had already devised a name: 'Minoan', after the legendary king Minos, beneath whose palace in a labyrinth roamed the Minotaur slain by Theseus.

By 1905 the excavations were more or less complete, and Evans' systematic study of the finds, including superb coloured frescoes, elegant stone vases and richly decorated pottery, had begun. The result, published between 1921–36, was *The Palace of Minos* in which Evans brilliantly expounded his perception of Minoan civilization. More controversially, between 1922 and 1930 he also undertook the gaily painted reconstruction of the palace, with its central courtyard, throne room, royal apartments and pillared Hall of the Double Axes, that visitors see today. Originally constructed *c*. 1900 BC and completely rebuilt after an earthquake *c*. 1700, the palace continued in use until its final destruction *c*. 1370 BC.

BRITISH EGYPTOLOGY: DESPERATELY SEEKING MOSES

Although by the end of the 1870s Mariette's Antiquities Service had brought some order to archaeology in Egypt, the subject remained primarily historical: the job of the archaeologist was to provide documents for the philologist to study. This historical bias was still further reinforced in the 1880s by a series of excavations which drew their inspiration from Genesis and Exodus. In March 1882 the Delta Exploration Fund (later the Egypt Exploration Society) was established, bringing scholars together with other interested parties such as the writer Amelia Edwards, whose *A Thousand Miles up the Nile* had been a best seller in the 1870s. The Fund's aim was to conduct fieldwork in the salty marshland of the Nile delta, where 'undoubtedly lie concealed the documents of a lost period of Biblical History', specifically the 'Land of Goshen', the area of the Hebrew sojourn in Egypt according to Genesis, and Pithom and Raamses, the Cities of the Oppression.

The Fund's first, rough and ready dig was conducted at Tell el-Maskhuta in 1883 by the Swiss archaeologist Edouard Naville, work later published as *The Store-City of Pithom and the Route of the Exodus* – a title that at least makes clear Naville's determination to find what he had been sent to look for. Fortunately, a more rigorous and specifically archaeological emphasis was given to the Fund's work soon after by a landmark figure in Egyptology, the Englishman Flinders Petrie.

Cultural enterprise and enterprise culture

The emphasis on digging large royal monuments and cemetery sites in Egypt was fuelled by a number of factors. The desire of men like Naville to recover objects bearing ancient texts was one. Another was the better preservation of buildings and finds at dry desert-edge sites in Upper Egypt compared with settlement sites in the Nile valley or the Delta that were subject to annual flooding. Yet another was the lure of the spectacular finds associated with temples and tombs: rich cemeteries were inevitably attractive to archaeological missions sponsored by museums or private individuals who needed to show a return on their 'investment' beyond an advance in scholarly knowledge.

Flinders Petrie at Giza in 1880, standing outside the rock-cut tomb in which he lived for two winters.

A good example of this approach to excavating in Egypt can be seen in the career of John Garstang. He first dug in Egypt at Abydos for Petrie's Egyptian Research Account in 1899, but soon became an independent excavator, working in Egypt until the First World War under the aegis of Liverpool University's Institute of Archaeology. At that time, the dictates of Victorian philanthropy encouraged self-made men such as Sir Robert Mond and Sir John Brunner, the British chemists who founded ICI, to devote some of their wealth to archaeological research in Egypt and the funding of university posts to teach Egyptology. Each of Garstang's excavations was treated rather like a limited company, his backers being 'shareholders' who contributed a given amount to each project. The profits of the excavation, in the form of objects recovered and not retained by the Egyptian Museum in Cairo, were distributed as a 'dividend'.

A major limiting factor on the development of archaeological technique in Egypt was the sheer size of some sites. The wholesale clearance of masses of accumulated sand and rubble from enormous stone monuments placed an emphasis on the bulk movement of debris, and a major concern for excavators as different as Petrie and Naville was the organization and control of large numbers – sometimes many hundreds – of local labourers. Detailed investigation of the potential of urban sites has only been a major feature of fieldwork in Egypt in the last three decades, brought about partly by necessity – smaller archaeological budgets and the higher cost of local workmen – and partly by a genuine desire to explore sites other than tombs and temples.

Americans in the Near East

After 1900 there was a marked decline in the hitherto substantial membership of the Egypt Exploration Society in the United States, in large part caused by the increasing direct involvement of American archaeologists in the Near East. Thanks to the appearance of trained archaeologists – and American money – they soon became as active in the field as their British, French and German counterparts. American fieldwork in Egypt was supported by Phoebe Hearst, wife of the newspaper magnate William Randolph Hearst, and benefactions to archaeological institutions in the United States at this time included $50,000 given to the Univer-

Fresco showing two of Akhenaten's daughters, Neferure and Neferneferuaten, discovered at the royal palace at el-Amarna by Petrie in 1892. About 1350 BC.

sity of Chicago in 1903 by the oil magnate and philanthropist John D. Rockefeller for the founding of an Oriental Exploration Society.

Foremost among American Egyptologists was George Andrew Reisner, a Harvard law graduate who became one of the most prolific and skilled archaeologists of his generation. His excavations, particularly among the Old Kingdom monuments of Giza, including the richly furnished tomb of Hetepheres, mother of Khufu (c. 2551–2528 BC) and the valley temple and pyramid of Menkaure (c. 2490–2472 BC), are among the most important of this century. He also directed for the Egyptian government the important campaign to survey Nubian monuments threatened by the raising of the first Aswan dam (1907–09), returning in 1916–23 to explore the pyramids of Meroe and Napata. His emphasis on a systematic approach to excavation and recording extended equally to Palestine through his work between 1908 and 1910 at Samaria, the capital of the northern kingdom of Israel founded by King Omri (c. 882–871 BC).

DISCOVERING THE SUMERIANS

The half-century before the First World War saw an explosion of archaeological discovery in the Near East. Botta and Layard had laid bare the great palaces of the Assyrian kings in the 1840s, revealing the life of the great Assyrian empire contemporary with the kings of Judah and Israel during the first millennium BC. But in 1860, except for occasional mentions in cuneiform documents, the other ancient cultures of Mesopotamia remained unknown. Exploration now discovered

Sumerian silver. Vessel decorated with lion-headed eagles recovered during de Sarzec's excavations at Tello, between 1877 and 1900. The dedicatory inscription around the neck alluding to king Entemena of Lagash who reigned during the late 25th century BC, allows the piece to be closely dated.

the Sumerians, the inhabitants of Babylonia in the third millennium BC, while excavations at Babylon itself revealed the grandeur of Nebuchadnezzar's capital. Complementary work in what is now northern Syria and Turkey also revealed the Hittite empire of the second millennium and the Aramaean kingdoms of the first millennium BC.

European politics played a major, if discreditable, role in this further exploration. In the aftermath of the Crimean War, Britain and France guaranteed the integrity of the Ottoman empire to counter Russian pressure southward, further strengthening the European presence in Mesopotamia, and Germany's unification in 1871 brought an important new player into the region. Political intrigue continued directly to influence archaeological research: the British and French remained in competition, with the Germans and then the Americans arriving as the century progressed.

Although the retrieval of inscriptions, architecture, and 'museum quality' art continued to be the main object of Near Eastern excavation, greater emphasis was now placed on small objects and the stratigraphic context of finds. Excavation technique was established on a firmer footing after 1900, borrowing particularly from Petrie's work in Egypt; and, as in Europe, the period saw the emergence of professional archaeologists – the establishment of permanent archaeological missions, learned societies, specialized journals and university chairs, some devoted to Near Eastern archaeology specifically.

The greatest accolade goes to the French and then American excavators who revealed the Sumerians, the inhabitants of Babylonia two thousand years before the great Assyrian and Babylonian kings. It was Ernest de Sarzec, bored with life as French vice-consul in Basra, who first chose to excavate at Tello in southern Babylonia, a site from which finds had recently been trickling onto the antiquities market. Dealing with the local, semi-autonomous rulers rather than Ottoman officials and using his own money, de Sarzec began work in 1877. Success was publicly announced in 1881 with an exhibition at the Louvre and a vote of funds in the French national assembly to purchase his finds.

The site of Tello proved to be the ruins of the ancient Girsu, one of the main towns of Lagash, a Sumerian city-state, during the mid-third millennium BC, an unstable period of wars and shifting alliances. De Sarzec concentrated on the temple of Ningirsu, the chief god of the city. He encountered the same difficulty interpreting mud-brick buildings as his predecessors, but was able to distinguish the main levels within the temple. Among the more recent finds were six statues of Gudea, ruler of Lagash during the twenty-second century BC, portraying him as the architect and scribe who directed the reconstruction of the temple. The lower levels, four centuries older, yielded a wealth of artistic masterpieces, of which the Stela of the Vultures is the most famous: one side of this carved stone slab depicts the god Ningirsu holding the dead enemies of Lagash in a net; the other shows gruesome scenes of the Lagashite army marching into battle, vultures feeding on the dead after battle, and the preparation of a burial mound for the fallen enemy. Other key finds included a silver vessel decorated with cattle and lion-headed eagles dedicated to Ningirsu by the king Entemena, and a series of votive plaques dedicated to the god by various kings of Lagash.

De Sarzec also found tens of thousands of cuneiform tablets of the third millennium BC, written materials that, together with the inscriptions on art-objects, rapidly established an understanding of Sumerian political history and economic organization. The royal Assyrian libraries that Layard had discovered at Nineveh contained Akkadian–Sumerian dictionaries, so Sumerian itself was relatively easily intelligible. Tello's records now revealed that it was the Sumerians who originally invented the cuneiform writing system to record the economic affairs of their temples. The script was later adapted by the Akkadians and others, and Sumerian became a liturgical language – like Latin in Christianity – preserving ancient myths like the epic of Gilgamesh at the heart of the Mesopotamian literary tradition.

American archaeologists entered the field for the first time in the 1880s. After the newly inaugurated American Oriental Society called for a Mesopotamian expedition at its 1884 meeting, the American Institute of Archaeology sponsored a privately funded tour. A Babylonian Exploration Fund was established in Philadelphia and, in 1889, a University of Pennsylvania expedition under John Peters left for Nippur. Peters was inexperienced and had no Arabic to control a team of up to 250 local workmen, and relations among the Americans themselves were acrimonious. Everyone was anxious and conditions were perilous: one man died and the first season ended in chaos with an Arab assault in which 'half the horses perished in the flames, firearms and saddlebags and $1000 in gold fell into the hands of the marauders, but all the antiquities were saved. Under the war-dance and yells of the frantic Arabs the expedition finally withdrew ...'

Conditions improved in later years and the Pennsylvania expedition managed to endure four seasons of work between 1889 and 1900. Its most notable achievement was the recovery of 30,000 cuneiform tablets, many of them texts written in the scribal school at Nippur that contain Sumerian myths and other religious writings and together give us a systematic view of Sumerian belief. Important documents of later periods were also recovered. Even today, the administrative records of the Kassite dynasty provide our most detailed information about this period of Babylonian history (1595–1157 BC), while the business records of the Murashu banking firm of the fifth century BC open a window on the Achaemenid administration of Babylonia – a state in which even land-rich Persians had to borrow money to pay their taxes.

Koldewey at Babylon

Although latecomers to southern Mesopotamia, German archaeologists quickly exerted a strong and lasting influence. In 1887 the Royal Prussian Museum in Berlin sponsored excavations at two Babylonian sites by Robert Koldewey, a patient

and austere architect who was to pioneer systematic excavation in the Near East. At first unfamiliar with the problems of digging mud brick, Koldewey learned fast and was soon appointed by the newly founded German Oriental Society to explore Babylon itself. His excavations continued from 1899 until 1917, when they were halted by the First World War, and his team continued to dominate German Mesopotamian archaeology throughout the inter-war period.

Koldewey s particular achievement was to elucidate the layout and architecture of Babylon during the reign of Nebuchadnezzar (604—562 BC). The city s outer walls, studded with towers at regular intervals, enclosed some 850 hectares and were broad enough, as Herodotus observed, for a four-horsed chariot to turn. Inside lay a walled inner city, the sacred and royal centre of the Babylonian empire, entered by a processional avenue through the Ishtar Gate, a high arched gatehouse of glazed brick decorated with the moulded figures of dragons and bulls. Just inside the gate stood Nebuchadnezzar's southern palace, its hundreds of rooms ranged around large courtyards, its royal apartments decorated like the gate with colourful reliefs of glazed, moulded brickwork. Koldewey believed that a subterranean complex of vaulted rooms and wells, with traces of hydraulic lifting gear, in the northeast corner of the palace was the remains of the Hanging Gardens of Babylon, one of the seven wonders of the ancient world.

Koldewey's skill at excavating mud brick enabled him to distinguish building periods and methodically tease apart the complex succession of buildings on the site. Working in this way in the Merkes quarter of the city, he uncovered the remnants of earlier settlements dating back to the time of the law-giver Hammurabi, founder of the Old Babylonian empire in the eighteenth century BC. Between 1902 and 1914 the same techniques were applied with equal success by Walter Andrae at Ashur, revealing a wealth of public buildings of the second and first millennium BC. Each building was traced, cleared, photographed and planned in turn; its ruins were then cleared away so the excavators could turn their attention to the predecessor that lay beneath. Deep investigations in the temple of Ishtar and the Anu-Adad ziggurat complex identified a succession of older cities beginning in the first part of the third millennium BC, contemporary with the city at Tello that the French were still uncovering. The architectural arrangement of the early Ishtar temples, and the style of many artifacts found in these levels, gave early insights into the antecedents of the great Assyrian monuments that Botta and Layard had uncovered.

The French at Susa

Lying on the Khuzistan plain in southwestern Iran and occupied from 4000 BC to medieval times, Susa is one of the most important archaeological sites in the Near East, central to any understanding of early Mesopotamian and Elamite civilization. William Loftus explored the site in the 1850s. He was followed in 1884–86 by the French civil engineer Marcel Dieulafoy, who excavated the Apadana, the pillared hall of the Achaemenid kings, recovering the 'Frieze of the Archers' and other notable pieces of Achaemenid art.

The French at this time had a monopoly of archaeology in Persia and retained ownership of all the antiquities they excavated. They explored widely in western Persia, but their work concentrated on Susa, where they continued to work until the Iranian revolution of 1979. While the first dig-house took the shape of a château perched on the top of the mound, excavation techniques were crude. Around 1,200 labourers worked in squads whose principal goal was the rapid removal of arbitrary 'levels' five metres thick, experience reputedly having shown that 'if the workmen threw the earth into the wagons from a height of five metres, the materials would not suffer'. Susa's prehistoric levels and a long sequence of occupation from the fifth millennium BC to the Early Islamic period were identified in spite of these shortcomings and many pieces of Mesopotamian art looted from conquered Babylonian cities by the ancient inhabitants of Susa were recovered – the most famous

Opposite. Bull in glazed brick from the latest phase of Nebuchadnezzar's Ishtar Gate at Babylon, sixth century BC. The entire surface of this vivid blue gate, originally standing c. 23 metres (75 feet) high, is decorated with rows of bulls and dragons rendered alternately in yellow and white. According to Babylonian records, the Gate was guarded in addition by 'mighty bronze colossi of bulls and dragons'.

Dismantled brick by brick after Koldewey's excavations, the Ishtar Gate today stands reconstructed in the Museum of the Near East, Berlin.

a stela bearing the law code of Hammurabi, king of Babylonia in the eighteenth century BC. Surmounted by a scene showing the king praying before the sun-god, Shamash, god of justice, it proclaims Babylonia's dependence on the principle of an eye for an eye, so 'that the strong may not oppress the weak, to give justice to the orphan and the widow'.

British Museum expeditions

Although British research in Mesopotamia after 1860 was overshadowed by the efforts of the Germans and French, the 1870s saw three notable expeditions to Kuyunjik conducted by George Smith, a self-taught Assyriologist who identified part of the epic of Gilgamesh, the semi-legendary king of Uruk in the mid-third millenium BC, while classifying cuneiform texts in the British Museum. In part of the story that obviously parallels the account in Genesis of Noah and the flood, the god Ea instructs Utanapishtim to build a boat in which his family and pairs of all the animals can survive the flood the god Enlil is about to unleash on the world. 'On looking down the third column', Smith wrote:

> my eye caught the statement that the ship rested on the mountains of Nizir, followed by the account of the sending forth of the dove, and its finding no resting-place and returning. I saw at once that I had here discovered a portion at least of the Chaldean account of the Deluge.

A lecture to the Society of Biblical Archaeology in December 1872 stirred up so much public excitement that the *Daily Telegraph* offered Smith £1000 to undertake an expedition to recover the remaining sections of the Gilgamesh legend. Smith accepted, travelled to Kuyunjik and recovered the necessary cuneiform texts within a week. When the *Telegraph* refused to extend its funding, he turned to the British Museum to pay for two further expeditions, employing up to 600 workmen to sift a large number of fragmentary texts from the debris of earlier excavations. Only then did his luck run out; crossing the desert from Mosul in the summer heat of 1876, he died of cholera in Aleppo.

British work in Mesopotamia was thereafter in the hands of Hormuzd Rassam, Layard's assistant of the 1840s who excavated on his own in the 1850s before being 'exiled' as the British consul in Aden (p. 106). Remembered as much for his brutal tactics as his discoveries, Rassam worked throughout Mesopotamia and eastern Turkey between 1879 and 1882, often excavating several sites simultaneously. He acquired an impressive number of objects for the British Museum, most famously the great palace doors of the Assyrian king Shalmaneser III (858–824 BC) found at Balawat, near Nimrud. The copper sheathing of these doors Rassam found to be 'embossed with a variety of subjects, such as battle scenes, triumphal processions and religious performances'. In southern Mesopotamia, Rassam's most enduring contribution came from his work in the Shamash temple in the ancient city of Sippar, near Babylon, where he excavated nearly 200 rooms in the buildings around the ziggurat and recovered tens of thousands of cuneiform tablets containing the temple's administrative and legal records. Though of unbaked clay and very fragile, they greatly illuminate the economic life of Babylonia in the mid-first millennium BC.

Rassam left Mesopotamia for the last time in 1882, his crude techniques already outmoded. It marked the end of an era; with his departure, the Turks began to regulate archaeology within the Ottoman empire, establishing an Imperial Museum to house new finds and granting foreigners permission to excavate no more than one site at a time.

The Hittites

The European exploration of Anatolia began early in the nineteenth century with antiquarian travellers like the Frenchman, Charles Texier, who in 1834 located an enormous ruin at Boghazköy in central Anatolia, which he identified initially as Pteria, site of Cyrus the Great's defeat of Croesus in the sixth century BC. In addition to a massive stone wall enclosing 180 hectares (445 acres) pierced by a gate decorated with lions, Texier also observed a cult site nearby at Yazilikaya, where the cliff face was decorated with strange hieroglyphs and processions of figures. Reports of similar monuments in central and eastern Anatolia filtered through to Europe over the next few decades and the existence of a previously unsuspected ancient culture gradually became apparent.

In the late 1870s, the British orientalist Archibald Sayce and William Wright, an Irish missionary, proposed independently that the new Anatolian script should be

The rock-cut shrine of Yazilikaya, near Boghazköy, thirteenth century BC. The frieze of sculptured figures, some of them identified by inscriptions, is thought to belong to the reign of the Hittite king, Tudhaliyas IV. In all, more than 60 such figures can be seen.

attributed to the people called Hittites who were mentioned in the Bible and in Assyrian and ancient Egyptian sources; Sayce even envisaged the existence of a Hittite empire. His arguments seemed wildly implausible to cautious scholars, and controversy only receded with the discovery at el-Amarna in Egypt in the 1880s of an archive of diplomatic letters of the fourteenth century BC that explicitly mentioned a Hittite empire. The Amarna letters – clay tablets in Akkadian cuneiform script – were sent by rulers of Egyptian vassal kingdoms in Palestine and Syria, some vigorously professing their continued loyalty to Egypt despite Hittite attempts to lure them away. Others referred to Hittite aggression as the excuse for inaction:

> The king of Khatti (the Hittites) is staying in Nuhkashshe, and I am afraid of him. Heaven forbid that he come into Amurru. If he attacks Tunip, then it is only two day-marches to where he is staying. So I am afraid of him and for this reason I have been staying on until he departs.

Some correspondence between Egypt and the Hittites even uses the salutation 'brother' and seeks to arrange diplomatic marriage alliances.

The Amarna letters put the Hittite empire squarely on the map of the ancient Near East but they also posed a new problem. Many of the hieroglyphic texts and archaic-looking sculptures from sites in southeastern Turkey and northern Syria belonged to Iron Age kingdoms of the twelfth to eighth centuries BC: the Hittites of the Bible. The Hittites of the Amarna letters belonged, however, to the Late Bronze Age, centuries earlier. Even then their empire extended well into Syria from its home in central Anatolia, leaving monuments, art and inscriptions at many sites later occupied by the Hittites of the Iron Age – the Neo-Hittites, as they soon came to be called. The archaeological imperative was therefore to find out, through excavation, how Hittite Bronze and Iron Age cultures differed.

The challenge was taken up equally by German, British and French archaeologists. Felix von Luschan began digging at Zinjirli in the hill country of southeastern Turkey in 1888. Assisted by Robert Koldewey, later the excavator of Babylon, he uncovered an Iron Age citadel of fortified palaces and sampled enough of the town around it to establish the basic layout. The site's palaces and monumental gateways documented for the first time the characteristics of 'Neo-Hittite' art, and Aramaic inscriptions offered insights into the international politics of the time, particularly the Syrian resistance to Assyrian expansion in the ninth and eighth centuries BC.

The British worked at Carchemish, a Hittite city standing above a crossing of the Euphrates that from the beginning of the second millennium BC passed into Syrian control. First investigated by a British Museum expedition in 1878, it was more fully excavated by David Hogarth, assisted by Leonard Woolley and T. E. Lawrence, between 1908 and 1914; the young Lawrence, eager and hard-working, wore a blazer and football shorts as his regular digging gear. Their work focused on the

Opposite. Leonard Woolley (right) and T. E. Lawrence with a sculptured relief at Carchemish, 1912.

The ultimate fate of the Carchemish sculptures makes a sorry tale. The British expedition left them on site when they departed from Turkey in 1914. But when the newly drawn Turkish–Syrian border divided the site in two in 1920, Woolley lamented, 'a Turkish army officer stationed at Jerablus decided to move the stones ... Many were smashed, the rest put on railway trucks but pitched off on to the embankment, where they remained until 1921 or later. Some pieces were stolen and sold; one lion's head ultimately came to the British Museum by purchase (much to my disgust) and other bits to the Louvre'.

citadel and inner and outer town of the Syro-Hittite city, particularly its sculpture and inscriptions. In the citadel, on a broad terrace approached by a monumental stairway, stood row upon row of relief sculptures of gods, priests, warriors and kings, alternated with explanatory hieroglyphic inscriptions. In his book *Dead Towns and Living Men*, 'written … in a Turkish prison camp to amuse other prisoners of war' during the First World War, Woolley described the site:

> You stand there on flagged pavement or cobbled court whose polished stones have not known the tread of man's feet since Carchemish went down in smoke two thousand five hundred years ago, and about you and above are the long rows of sculptured figures, gods and beasts and fighting men, and inscriptions in honour of forgotten kings; statues of old deities; wide stairways and gates, where the ashes of the doors still lie in the corners of the threshold; column-bases whose shafts were of cedar and their capitals of bronze wrought in patterns of nets and pomegranates – and the scarlet anemones push up between the stones, and the lizards sun themselves on the walls of the palace or temple, and the spring wind drives the dust over the ruins of the imperial city.

Opposite. The Dome of the Rock and the Old City of Jerusalem. Among the earliest underground explorations were those conducted in the rock-cut passages beneath the city by Charles Warren in 1867–9.

The 520 metre (1700 foot) tunnel carrying spring water between the Fountain of the Virgin and the Pool of Siloam was particularly disagreeable and perilous, reported the *Illustrated London News*.

'The height of the passage diminishes in going up from Siloam till in some places it is not more than 16 inches or 20 inches high; so that Lieutenant Warren, Sergeant Birtles [his assistant], and a fellah, or Arab labourer, with them, were obliged to lie flat on their backs, and crawl along, with the measuring instruments, pencil and note-book, carried in one hand and a lighted candle held in the mouth, through a foul stream of water, sometimes 12 inches deep; they were four hours in making the passage, and might have been drowned by a sudden rising of the water'.

Deeper investigation of the site defined a succession of older settlements dating back another four thousand years. Although Carchemesh remains a key place for the archaeology of northern Syria, the modern Turkish-Syrian frontier runs across the site and it has not been excavated since the 1920s.

Bronze Age Hittite culture became better known after 1906 through systematic excavations conducted by Hugo Winkler at Boghazköy, the Hittite capital (ancient Hattusha). Here the sprawling 6 kilometre (3.7 mile) circuit of the walls enclosed an area of 180 hectares (445 acres), within which stood a separately walled inner town covering 80 hectares (198 acres). Working initially in the inner citadel, Winkler soon revealed temples and palaces and recovered 10,000 tablets, written both in cuneiform versions of Hittite languages and in Akkadian. He did not, however, have the technical expertise to understand the development of Boghazköy as an archaeological site initially occupied two thousand years before the Hittite empire of the Late Bronze Age (*c.* 1500–1200 BC). This task was accomplished only in 1931 when Kurt Bittel resumed the German excavations at Boghazköy, a highly successful, long-term programme that continues today.

The Hittite cuneiform tablets from Boghazköy again posed the problem of decipherment. On this occasion, the credit for breaking the code went to the Czech linguist, Friedrich Hrozny. Using proper names, ideograms (cuneiform signs representing an object or idea) and cognates (similar-sounding words with the same meaning in different languages), Hrozny recognized that Hittite belonged to the Indo-European family of languages. By 1915 his basic analysis was complete. The Boghazköy tablets went far beyond the information contained in external sources such as the Amarna archives and Egyptian inscriptions, establishing the outlines of Hittite history and filling out the picture of the Hittite empire. Only the Hittite hieroglyphic script remained an enigma – a code that would not be cracked until an Aramaic-Hittite bilingual inscription was found at Karatepe, in southeastern Turkey, in 1947.

SOLDIERS AND SCHOLARS IN THE HOLY LAND

It was above all the Crimean War of 1854–56 that drew the attention of Europeans to the deplorable condition of the holy places of Palestine. The monuments of the Levant were less impressive than those of Egypt and Assyria and there were no ancient languages to decipher, so earlier neglect was understandable. Yet a latent consciousness of ancient Palestine remained in the minds of a Bible-reading public, an awareness stimulated from time to time by events like Burckhardt's discovery of the city of Petra. The Old Testament's potential as a guidebook encouraged biblical scholars like the American Edward Robinson to become historical topographers; Robinson worked on the ground in the Holy Land from 1838, correctly identifying over a hundred ancient sites.

Excavation began late. Early work focused on Jerusalem, where Louis-Félicien de Saulcy in 1851 cleared rock-cut tombs that he fancifully assigned to the time of

King David (they are now placed in the period of King Herod, a thousand years later). A decade later, Napoleon III – aping his namesake's earlier adventure in Egypt – sponsored an archaeological expedition to Phoenicia led by the theologian Ernest Renan and de Saulcy. Renan explored Lebanon's Mediterranean coast, digging at Byblos, Sidon, Tyre and Arwad, and reaping an abundant harvest for the Louvre, but gaining little comprehension of the sites. In 1863 de Saulcy returned to Jerusalem, clearing further tombs and digging at the wall of the Haram ash-Sharif, the sacred precinct in which Herod erected his temple at the time of Christ and the Umayyid calif Abd al Malik (AD 685–705) built the Dome of the Rock. De Saulcy's work at this spot, sacred to two religions, excited local Jewish opposition and scandal in Europe.

England entered the scene through the establishment in London in 1865 of the Palestine Exploration Fund. Using skilled engineers and military surveyors, the Fund successfully mapped the Holy Land to a high degree of accuracy. Its attempts to investigate the topography of Jerusalem, its other main aim, were less auspicious. The initial excavations in 1867 were conducted by Lieutenant Charles Warren, a Royal Engineer – later to win renown as the police commissioner who hunted Jack the Ripper – who adopted the normal techniques of military mining. Tunnelling below the Haram wall, Warren established that Herod's temple and the Haram ash-Sharif were built over thick archaeological deposits filling a deep ravine; he also found masonry possibly attributable to Jerusalem's first temple, built by Solomon in the tenth century BC.

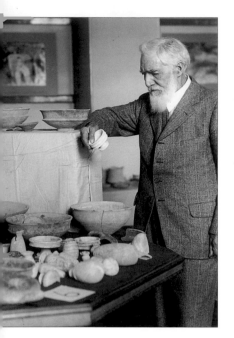

Flinders Petrie at his first Palestinian exhibition at University College, London, 1930. The pottery is from Tell el-Fara, a Late Bronze– Early Iron Age settlement he had excavated eighteen months previously.

Royal Engineers were also employed on the Fund's mapping expeditions. In 1864, Captain Charles Wilson explored the system of tunnels and cisterns created by Hezekiah (c. 715–686 BC) in the bedrock beneath Jerusalem to combat an Assyrian siege. In 1868, Wilson began a survey of Sinai ahead of the opening of the French-built Suez Canal, and in 1871–77 a team led by two more Engineers – Horatio (later Lord) Kitchener, then in his twenties, and Claude Conder – systematically mapped western Palestine. American cartographers worked east of the Jordan in the same period, leaving maps that were eventually completed by a German team in 1901. Finally, in 1913, Leonard Woolley and T. E. Lawrence, Hogarth's assistants at Carchemish, mapped the Negev. Important though they were archae-ologically, these maps also helped Allenby's army in the Palestine campaign against the Turks in the First World War. Their northern and eastern limits distinguished Palestine from Syria along lines later formalized by the foundation of Israel in 1948.

The archaeological potential of Palestinian sites was more fully realized after 1890, when the Palestine Exploration Fund induced Flinders Petrie to excavate outside Jerusalem, applying the stringent excavation standards and sequence-dating techniques he had developed in Egypt to create a chronological framework for Palestinian archaeology. The site chosen, Tell el-Hesy, is a classic Near Eastern tell, over 30 metres (100 feet) high, composed of layer upon layer of occupation debris. In just six weeks, Petrie recognized eleven superimposed settlements, which he dated to the period 1670–450 BC by comparing it to the established Egyptian pottery sequence.

At el-Hesy, Petrie became one of the first Near Eastern archaeologists to draw sections through the stratigraphy of a site and relate his finds to individual layers recorded in the drawing; grouping artifacts, particularly pottery, on this basis brought a chronological dimension to Palestinian archaeology for the first time and laid the foundation of all future work.

Although Petrie's season at el-Hesy was so successful, he was not to return to Palestine until 1926. It was not the discomfort that discouraged him: the tarantula he found in his tent, the scorpions or the well water brought 9.5 kilometres (6 miles) to the site, so stagnant even when boiled that 'it is three courses in one, soup, fish and greens'; far more intractable was the local hostility that culminated in a violent mugging by brigands at the end of the season.

Returning to Egypt did not encourage Petrie to refine stratigraphic excavation. Most of his work was at single period sites, and when he did tackle a multi-period site, the complex stratigraphy went largely unrecorded – a failing that was to become marked in his work in Palestine between the wars. Petrie's appreciation of archaeological context nonetheless places him in marked contrast to contemporaries like Naville, whose taste was for monumental architecture and whose excavations were notorious for the paucity of pottery and small objects they recovered. Recording the position of individual objects was a waste of time, Naville famously insisted: 'you might as well make a plan of the position of raisins in a plum pudding.'

Despite el-Hesy, most multi-layered Palestinian sites needing rigorous control and recording continued to be crudely dug. The Irish archaeologist Robert Macalister excavated the important Philistine city of Gezer between 1902–08, supervising 200 workmen with the lone help of an Egyptian foreman. A trench 12 metres (40 feet) wide was cut to bedrock along the eastern side of the site; a similar trench was then dug to the west, the spoil from the second trench being dumped in the first. In this way Macalister worked his way across the mound, eventually excavating three-fifths of it. His attitude to recording the context of small finds, like Naville's, was that 'the exact spot in the mound where any ordinary object chanced to lie is not generally of great importance.' Little wonder that the Englishman Mortimer Wheeler, who did so much to improve excavation standards between the wars, should have referred to Palestine as the place 'where more sins have probably been committed in the name of archaeology than on any commensurate portion of the earth's surface.'

The American archaeologist Frederick Bliss took over Petrie's work at el-Hesy in 1891, refining his conclusions and recovering the first cuneiform tablet ever found in Palestine: a record of an Egyptian garrison belonging to the Late Bronze Age, the period of the Amarna tablets. In 1894, Bliss turned to Jerusalem itself, revealing by tunnelling the remains of a stone fortification also probably of the Late Bronze Age, the period just before David seized the city c. 996 BC.

The first decade of the twentieth century brought more excavations and greater European and American involvement. Between 1900 and 1902, Bliss and Macalister dug four sites of different periods, Bronze Age to Roman, after which Macalister began work at Gezer. The Austrian Ernst Sellin and the German Gottlieb Schu-

American archaeologist George Reisner (1867–1942) in the dig-house at Samaria in Palestine, c. 1910. From left to right: Reisner; his daughter, Mary; an unidentified woman; expedition architect, Clarence S. Fisher; and Mrs Mary Reisner.

A meticulous excavator whose reputation was established in his thirties when he led the University of California's expedition to the burial ground of Koptos (1899–1905), from 1907 to 1910 Reisner worked for the Egyptian government in Lower Nubia on monuments threatened by the raising of the first Aswan dam.

So successful was his Nubian Archaeological Survey that Reisner has been called 'the greatest archaeologist that the United States has ever produced in any field'. In 1914 he became professor of archaeology at Harvard, a post he held until his death.

macher excavated at Tell Ta'anach, uncovering Bronze Age fortifications, a temple, and an archive of some 40 cuneiform tablets. In 1903, with substantial funds from the German Palestine Union, Schumacher moved to the Bronze Age town of Megiddo, and in 1907 Sellin started digging at Jericho on behalf of the Viennese Academy of Sciences. The following year, 1908, the Americans arrived in the shape of the Egyptologist George Reisner, who initiated excavations at Samaria, the capital of Israel during the ninth century BC. Reisner, even more than Petrie, brought impressive new standards of excavation to stratigraphically complex Palestinian sites – standards rarely matched even by his own assistants.

The First World War barely interrupted the momentum of archaeological discovery in the Near East, but the archaeologists themselves met with very different fates: T. E. Lawrence worked with other British archaeologists in intelligence and found everlasting fame as Lawrence of Arabia; Hogarth headed the Arab Bureau in Cairo; Woolley spent time as a prisoner of war; and Koldewey persevered at Babylon until 1917 when he fled, one step ahead of General Maude's army. When peace dawned on a much-changed political landscape in 1918, many archaeologists returned, seeking to solve problems that remained from before the war and posing new questions.

THE ARCHAEOLOGICAL SURVEY OF INDIA

Excavation in India began hesitantly, relatively late in the history of archaeology. The megalithic monuments of the south first attracted attention in 1819, when J. Babington opened graves in Malabar, finding iron objects, pottery and beads. Although he was unable to identify their occupants, other excavations followed. The linguist and administrator Colonel Philip Meadows Taylor, who dug megalithic burials in Hyderabad and elsewhere in central and southern India in the 1850s, was particularly careful by the standards of the day, observing the stratification of objects within the graves, and concluding speculatively that he had found works of 'the great Aryan nomadic tribes of the Eastern Celts or Scythians'. However, most megalithic tomb excavations were inevitably carried out in the robust spirit of the time. One judge in Madras used convicts to open a grave in 1821, discovering 'an old rusty sword, and an earthen jar, said to contain nothing', while others plainly excavated as a diversion from boredom. Such efforts, like barrow-digging in contemporary England, did little more than encourage the collection of antiquarian curios.

In northern India, early excavators concentrated their attention on Buddhist stupas, monuments of solid brick that enclosed a chamber housing sacred relics or texts. In 1830, a general in the army of the independent Sikh king Ranjit Singh, M. le Chevalier Ventura, dug into a stupa in the Punjab, penetrating as far as the central platform, where he found coins dating to the first centuries AD and several gold and copper boxes. Others soon followed in his footsteps, taking up stupa-digging as far north as Afghanistan. Once again, the motive was antiquarian: a desire to acquire artifacts, particularly coins of the last centuries BC or first century AD, rather than a wish to study early Buddhist architecture.

Increasing numbers of haphazard excavations and the perceptible decay of monuments eventually led to demands for government measures to preserve antiquities and encourage systematic research into India's past. One notable advocate of such action was General Alexander Cunningham, a military surveyor and chief engineer of the Northwest Provinces, who petitioned the Indian government to sponsor a systematic survey of sites and monuments, on the grounds that 'the discovery and publication of all the existing remains of architecture and sculpture, with coins and inscriptions, would throw more light on the ancient history of India, both public and domestic, than the printing of all the rubbish contained in the eighteen Puranas' [Sanskrit historical poems]. It was this plea that ultimately led to the creation of the Archaeological Survey of India.

From the mid-nineteenth century until independence in 1947, archaeology in India was strongly tied to British government policy. Lord Canning, first Viceroy of India and cousin of Henry Layard's patron Stratford Canning, established an Archaeological Department in 1860, with northern India as its area of responsibility. Cunningham was appointed temporary Archaeological Surveyor the next year, charged with making 'an accurate description of such remains as most deserve notice, with the history of them so far as it may be traceable, and a record of the traditions that are retained regarding them'. The position was abolished in 1866, but recreated more grandly in 1870 as Director General of the Archaeological Survey of India; aided by several assistants, Cunningham served in this capacity until his retirement in 1885.

The minutes of the council that appointed Cunningham, published in the *Journal of the Asiatic Society of Bengal* for 1862, make British government motives clear:

> It will not be to our credit, as an enlightened ruling power, if we continue to allow such fields of investigation, as the remains of the old Buddhist capital in Behar, the plains round Delhi, studded with ruins more thickly than even the Campagna of Rome, and many others, to remain without more examination than they have hitherto received. Everything that has hitherto been done in this way, has been done by private persons, imperfectly and without system. It is impossible not to feel that there are European Governments, which, if they had held our rule in India, would not have allowed this to be said.

Cunningham had a longstanding and passionate interest in Indian antiquities. Giving his qualifications for writing *The Ancient Geography of India* (1871), a book dedicated to the Assyriologist Henry Rawlinson, he wrote:

> My own travels have also been very extensive through the length and breadth of northern India ... Of southern India I have seen nothing, and of western India I have seen only Bombay, with the celebrated caves of Elephanta and Kanhari. But

during a long service of more than thirty years in India, its early history and geography have formed the chief study of my leisure hours.

Yet Cunningham had done more than travel. He had dug Buddhist stupas in Uttar Pradesh, in the 1830s at Sarnath – where the Buddha delivered his first sermon – and in the 1840s at Sanchi (also called Bhilsa). He also collected the Roman coins that demonstrated ancient India's trading connections with the Mediterranean world.

During Cunningham's tenure, the Archaeological Survey conducted annual programmes of mapping and excavation along the lines of army surveys or the cartography sponsored by the Palestine Exploration Fund in the Levant. Inventories of archaeological sites and standing buildings were drawn up with the aim of identifying places mentioned in ancient written sources such as the Indian epics, accounts of India by Greek and Roman authors, and Chinese records of Buddhist pilgrimages; in the last category were accounts of India by the Chinese pilgrims Fa-Hian and Hiuen-Tsang who in the fourth and seventh centuries AD visited all the famous sites of Buddhist history. Limited excavation at key sites added a measure of precision to this essentially topographical study, exposing architecture, sculpture and inscriptions, and providing coins for dating. Although the responsibilities of the Archaeological Survey were extended to western and southern India in 1874, Cunningham himself worked steadily on northern Indian problems, until his retirement at 71. In this way, he identified the locations of many important places, notably Taxila, the Gandharan capital and trade centre, nestled in the Himalayan foothills near the headwaters of the Indus.

Central to Cunningham's achievement was the way he systematized the knowledge of ancient India won by the Survey and developed a chronological framework into which to fit new discoveries. Indian antiquities were grouped into three basic periods, named Brahminical (before c. 500 BC), Buddhist (500 BC–AD 1200) and Mohammedan (after AD 1200). Recognizing that this simple classification could not adequately cope with the enormous variation of architectural styles evident in India's ancient monuments, Cunningham also devised a second, more complicated, scheme for identifying and dating Hindu and Muslim architecture. The oldest Hindu style, which he called Archaic and dated to 1000–250 BC, contained the various types of 'rude monuments' and localities associated with the Buddha and with Alexander the Great. His view that the earliest Indian monuments were no older than 1000 BC endured until the early 1920s.

Cunningham worked before the principles of stratigraphic excavation had been developed, and before archaeology had any means of dating except through documentary sources, inscriptions, coins, and styles of architecture and art. Even with these disadvantages, he was remarkably perceptive about India's ancient monuments. Digging into the brick terrace of one Sanchi stupa, he was struck by artifacts he found deliberately placed in small chambers as foundation deposits, among them 'various specimens of red and black pottery, especially those which are covered with a dark metallic glaze'. This black-glazed pottery, today called Northern Black Polished Ware and dated to the period after 500 BC, confirms Cunningham's original dating of the stupa to the third century BC.

Cunningham did not establish the foundations of Indian archaeology single-handed – others came before him, and his assistants in the Archaeological Survey also achieved significant results. James Fergusson and James Burgess drew up many detailed architectural surveys, particularly of Buddhist sites. But Cunningham was

Opposite. The domed Buddhist stupa at Sanchi, northern India, the most famous of the 84,000 such tombs reputed to have been built by the Mauryan emperor Asoka (c. 270–232 BC). Originally built in brick, the shrine was later encased in stone and surrounded by a stone balustrade. It stands 18 metres (60 feet) high and measures 40 metres (130 feet) in diameter.

the dominant spirit through much of the nineteenth century, first petitioning the government for an archaeological survey, then lending his energy and enthusiasm to guarantee its success. He might have written an appreciation of his entire archaeological career with these lines of poetry from *The Bhilsa Topes* (1854):

> Nought but the Topes themselves remain to mock
> Time's ceaseless efforts; yet they proudly stand
> Silent and lasting upon their parent rock,
> And still as cities under magic's wand;
> Till curious Saxons, from a distant land,
> Unlocked the treasures of two thousand years.

James Burgess, Cunningham's successor as Director General, continued the Survey for three years until his own retirement (1886–9). It fell thereafter into a period of stagnation that endured until the appointment of the young John Marshall in 1902.

The Marshall years

It was in the mid-nineteenth century that India's remote past was discovered for the first time. As early as 1842, Meadows Taylor had reported a polished stone axe from Lingsugar that he compared with prehistoric axes from Europe, and he continued to collect stone artifacts while excavating the cairns on the Deccan plateau that he published, complete with plans and sections, in 1862. In 1860, H. P. LeMesurier, a chief engineer on the East Indian Railway, found scores of neolithic polished stone axes under trees in villages (p. 13). Finally, on 30 May 1863, Robert Bruce Foote of the Geological Survey of India, the 'Father of Indian prehistory', discovered a palaeolithic handaxe in a gravel pit at Pallavaram near Madras; he returned later that year, and again in 1864, to find many more palaeolithic tools, some of them still *in situ*. Foote communicated his finds to John Evans, barely five years after the idea of fossil man became accepted in Europe; his natural assumption was that the palaeolithic implement-makers of Europe and India were contemporary.

Archibald Carlyle, a naturalist and geologist who had gone out to India as tutor to a rajah's son, became First Assistant to the Archaeological Survey soon after. Despite the general concentration on historical antiquities at this time, Carlyle began collecting stone tools such as arrowheads and microliths as early as 1867. Subsequently, in rock-shelters at Morhana Pahar, above the Ganga valley, he discovered paintings in a stiff and archaic style that represented 'scenes in the life of the ancient stone chippers'. He identified animals and hunting scenes featuring men with bows, arrows, spears and hatchets, concluding that the paintings were of various periods, including that of the makers of the thousands of small stone tools, or microliths, he had been finding. Although he published nothing on these discoveries until 1883, Carlyle's recognition that some of the Morhana Pahar paintings must be prehistoric predated the discovery of prehistoric rock art in Europe (p. 124).

It was in 1902 that the fortunes of the Archaeological Survey of India recovered with the appointment of John Marshall (1876–1958) to the revived post of Director General. Marshall had read classics at Cambridge and was already a seasoned field-worker, having dug in Greece, Crete and Turkey. Over his long tenure (1902–28) he reinvigorated the Survey, working to conserve the subcontinent's ancient monuments and excavating to provide new information. The nineteenth-century practice of clearing monumental architecture was abandoned in favour of the controlled excavation of more ordinary, residential sites, and the methodical evaluation of pottery and other finds. Reporting his work at Charsada, near Taxila in the Himalayan foothills, Marshall provided a special section on the classification of pottery, hoping that it 'would be of particular value to explorers among the innumerable *dheris* [mounds] of Northern India, where the ever constant presence of pottery fragments on the surface of the mounds makes them the most serviceable index to the date of the remains buried beneath'. This move towards using pottery as a dating device, inspired by early experience of the developing standards of archaeology in the eastern Mediterranean, was characteristic of his systematic approach.

Like Cunningham, Marshall's personal interests lay in the north of India, with its strong connections with the classical world. He began by investigating early Buddhist sites, working methodically backwards to earlier periods as time passed. At Bhita, near Allahabad in Uttar Pradesh, Marshall exposed 'for the first time in India, well-preserved remains of houses, shops and streets, dating as far back as the Mauryan epoch', and recovered 'numerous minor antiquities … which help us materially to visualize the everyday life of the towns-peoples of those early days'. Equally importantly, the Bhita excavations detected a succession of settlements through time, from before the Mauryan period (third century BC) through to Gupta

Sir John Marshall with his wife and daughter, and staff of the Indian Archaeological Survey, at Taxila, *c.* 1920. From 1902, Marshall reorganized the Survey, recruiting Indians for the first time. He also established an ambitious programme for the listing and preservation of monuments, expanded museum services, and excavated widely on early historic sites like Taxila, Sanchi and Sarnath, the holy place near Benares where the Buddha delivered his first sermon.

times (mid-first millennium AD). Marshall's early work, assiduously published and matching in quality anything being done elsewhere in Asia and the Mediterranean, in this way made good his intention of refocusing Indian archaeology.

Marshall later excavated for many years at the great city of Taxila itself (1912–36), continuing even after retiring from his duties as Director General. Now in northwestern Pakistan, the site has multiple mounds, some representing Buddhist stupas and monasteries, others repeatedly occupied settlements. Marshall exposed large areas of the city defences, town streets and houses, Buddhist monasteries and schools, and other features of a regional capital occupied for a thousand years between the fifth century BC and the fifth century AD. The Taxila excavations made a fundamental contribution to understanding the history of northern India, and stand as a monument to Marshall's archaeological career.

EXPLORING THE FAR EAST

European expeditions to the Far East long took central Asia and China as their destination, museums and sponsors often competing with each other to acquire works of art for their galleries. The British Museum, the Hermitage, the Tokyo

The Last Explorer

Aurel Stein (1862–1943) was the greatest explorer in the history of Asian archaeology, a restless traveller from early in life. Born in Budapest, he was educated in oriental languages and classical archaeology at universities in Germany and England, moving then to India where he became principal of the Oriental College in Lahore in 1887. While in Lahore, he studied and published the Sanskrit chronicles of the kings of Kashmir, and began touring Kashmir and other parts of India.

Stein's archaeological reputation rests on three lengthy trips he made between 1900 and 1920 to Chinese Turkestan, a remote region that he revealed for the first time. The Takla Makan desert in Turkestan, ringed by high mountains on three sides and the Gobi desert on the fourth, once provided a route through Inner Asia between China and northern India and onward to Iran and ultimately the eastern Mediterranean. Commercial traffic along this route was particularly active two thousand years ago, at the time Buddhism spread through Inner Asia towards China, and again 1300 years ago at the time of high Tang culture in China.

Travelling on horseback and on foot, Stein recorded sites and undertook test excavations, enduring desert heat and mountain cold, even losing his toes to frostbite. The results were remarkable. He discovered an early version of the Great Wall of China built by the Han dynasty in the second century BC to protect traders from incursions by nomads. The remains of trading towns like Niya and Dandan-uilik betrayed strong Indian influence. Stein found Buddhist shrines adorned with sculpture and representational art derived from Gandharan examples, as well as documents written on wooden tablets, birch bark, sheep skin, palm leaves, paper and silk. He also visited the Caves of the Thousand Buddhas on the eastern edge of the Takla Makan desert, where he acquired, by dubious means, innumerable early Chinese translations of sacred Buddhist writings and large painted silks of the ninth century AD. As the door of the concealed shrine swung open, he wrote:

> The sight disclosed in the dim light of the priest's little oil lamp made my eyes open wide. Heaped up in layers, but without any order, there appeared a solid mass of manuscript bundles rising to ten feet from the floor and filling, as subsequent measurement showed, close to five hundred cubic feet. Within the small room measuring about nine feet square there was left barely space for two people to stand on ... I could not feel surprise at such relics of ancient cult and learning having escaped all effects of time while walled up in a rock-cut chamber in these terribly barren hills. They were hermetically shut off from what moisture, if any, the atmosphere of this desert valley ever contained.

National Museum and Berlin's Museum of Indian Art all benefited from the plundering of sites by international adventurers such as Sven Hedin, Albert von Le Coq and Aurel Stein. A prime target was the Tarim basin in northwestern China, an area dotted with extinct trading towns, in which the Silk Road that linked China and Europe during the first seven centuries AD wound around the Takla Makan desert.

The Swede Sven Hedin mounted the first archaeological expedition to the region in 1895. Seven other campaigns followed between 1902 and the First World War: four German, two Japanese and one French. Funded by the Swedish crown, Hedin in 1899 discovered the Han-dynasty garrison of Loulan, from which he removed scores of manuscripts. Such discoveries brought him many honours, though his pro-German sympathies in wartime earned the memorable denunciation: 'What does it interest us whether you have discovered both Tibet and China?' Von Le Coq, a Frenchman working for German sponsors, was equally ruthless at the Buddhist cave-temple of Bezeklik, hacking from the walls magnificent frescoes revealed to him during a landslide: 'Suddenly, as if by magic, I saw on the walls bared in this way, to my right and left, splendid paintings in colours as fresh as if the artist had

Aurel Stein's convoy of treasures about to leave Abdal for Kashgar.

Stein also made significant, if rather less spectacular, contributions to archaeology further west. After joining the Archaeological Survey of India in 1910, he undertook exploratory trips through Baluchistan into southern Iran during the 1920s and 1930s, recording and sampling by excavation numerous prehistoric sites. Like Alexander Cunningham and others before him, he also retraced Alexander the Great's route through northwestern India.

His travels eventually took him through western Iran and into Mesopotamia and Palestine, where he followed the ancient route from Dura Europos to Palmyra in the Syrian desert, reporting many important sites that would later host major excavations. When he died, in Kabul, at the age of eighty, he was in the midst of preparations for yet another tour, this time of Afghanistan.

only just finished them'. The Bezeklik frescoes ended up in Berlin's Ethnological Museum, only to be destroyed by bombing in the Second World War.

The British orientalist Aurel Stein led his first Silk Road expedition in 1901, excavating around Khotan at abandoned town sites like eighth-century Dandan-uilik. On his second expedition, Stein discovered huge quantities of Buddhist statuary and frescoes and, in 1907, a manuscript library in the Caves of the Thousand Buddhas at Dunhuang in northwestern China that had been walled up since *c.* AD 1000. Many of his spoils, including 20,000 Dunhuang manuscripts, were transported to the British Museum, where they took half a century to catalogue. Some, such as the ninety-one Buddhist statues of Rawak at Khotan, he had to leave behind; reburying them in the hope of returning later to establish a purpose-built museum, Stein lamented sadly how much it cost him 'to watch the images I had brought to light vanishing again, one after another, under the pall of sand which had hidden them for so many centuries.'

A second, less romantic, type of exploration accompanied European settlement in the Far East. Usually under church, business or governmental sponsorship, the resident British were quick to establish branches of the Royal Asiatic Society, a key forum for the international exchange of knowledge about the orient that began publishing its transactions in Hong Kong (1847), followed by Shanghai (1859), then Singapore (1878) and Korea (1900). European descriptions of local anti-quities appeared in other publications too, though the frame of reference within which they interpreted their discoveries was not always the right one. In Japan, for instance, W. Gowland published a series of mounded tombs he investigated during the time he was adviser to the Imperial Japanese Mint. Because these earth-mounded tombs of the late fifth and sixth centuries AD contain huge stone chambers, with ceiling blocks of up to 70 tonnes, Gowland drew, quite inappropriately, on Euro-pean analogies and referred to them as 'dolmens'. 'In the mound-covered dolmens', he wrote, 'a relationship is also seen between those of Brittany and Scandinavia, in the passageway generally opening toward the south or east and never to the north.' Of all resident foreigners, only the American zoologist Edward Morse in Japan and the Swede Johan Gunnar Andersson in China were to have a profound influence on the development of archaeology in the Far East.

Japan was the first Far Eastern country to adopt western-style archaeology. Anti-quarianism was established on a national footing in 1876 by the promulgation of the first cultural properties protection law, and the following year saw Japan's first excavation, conducted by the American Edward Morse, then teaching at the Imperial University (now Tokyo University). It was Morse's work at the prehistoric Omori shell mound near Tokyo that first identified Jomon or 'cord-marked' pottery, the characteristic artifact of Japan's postglacial hunting and gathering Jomon cul-ture (*c.* 10,000–300 BC). As Charles Darwin commented loftily in 1880, 'several Japanese gentlemen have already formed large collections of the shells of the Archi-pelago, and have zealously aided [Morse] in the investigation of the prehistoric mounds. This is a most encouraging omen of the future progress of science in Japan'. In line with the thinking of the time, however, Morse attributed Jomon pottery and artifacts to the aboriginal Ainu of Hokkaido island; their true age was not established until 1936. Today, over 10,000 Jomon sites are known, most of them in areas forested in prehistoric times, rich in edible nuts and game and close to coastal resources of fish and shellfish.

Archaeology was first taught at Kyoto University in 1907, and in 1913 a department of archaeology opened under Hamada Kosaku. After studying with Flinders Petrie in London, Hamada returned to Japan to inaugurate European-style stratigraphic excavation at the Jomon–Yayoi site of Ko in Osaka in 1917 and to write the first archaeological textbook in Japanese.

In Southeast Asia – Indo-China as it was then called – French colonization led to the extensive exploration of ancient ruins, especially those at Angkor, and established archaeology in the region. The French School in the Far East was founded in 1889 on the model of other such schools in Athens, Rome and Cairo, and with it the Musée Louis Finot, named after its founding director but now the national museum of Viet Nam in Ha Noi. The museum eventually came to house the greatest repository of bronzes and monumental art in Southeast Asia. In 1900 the first comprehensive survey of Cham (southern Victnamese) and Khmer (Cambodian) standing monuments was undertaken by Henri Parmentier, the outstanding pioneer of archaeology in the region. Parmentier amassed a vast collection of drawings, photographs and maps, and later dug at the great Cham religious centre of Dong Duong, established in the ninth century AD.

The south gate of the outer wall of Angkor Thom, from Louis Delaporte's *Voyage au Cambodge. L'architecture Khmère* (1880).

In 1432 Angkor was abandoned to the jungle, to be 'discovered' by uncomprehending Europeans in the sixteenth and seventeenth centuries. Angkor became the subject of monumental art studies with the beginning of French archaeological work in Indo-China in the nineteenth century, but systematic survey and excavation have been added only recently.

Great Zimbabwe

For more than a century the impressive stone walls of Great Zimbabwe have stood as political symbol as much as archaeological monument. Although Zimbabwe Hill, today in south-eastern Zimbabwe, was first occupied c. AD 500–900 in the Early Iron Age, we now know that its earliest walls belong to the years around AD 1000 when black Shona-speaking farmers moved into the area. Thereafter, between c. 1270 and 1450, Great Zimbabwe became the capital of a vast Shona empire that extended west into Botswana and stretched from the Zambezi river to the Northern Transvaal. Unusually for southern Africa at this time, social organization was class-based, with a clear distinction between the ruling class and commoners; kings of Zimbabwe were thus able to accumulate great wealth and prestige by controlling the trade in gold and ivory with the East African coast.

Great Zimbabwe was made known to the western world by Karl Mauch, a young German geologist with a taste for adventure who had already made the first discovery of gold in southern Africa, at Tati in Botswana in 1866. Romantically attracted to the area by the Biblical account of King Solomon's mines (I Kings ix, 26–8), Mauch was nonetheless a seasoned traveller; he dressed for protection in a loose leather suit and cap, nail-studded boots and thick flannel underwear, and carried an umbrella to protect him from the sun as well as a revolver.

Reaching Zimbabwe Hill on 5 September 1871, he found to his amazement mortarless enclosure walls that stood 6 metres (20 feet) high and a conical tower that rose half as high again. Cutting wood from the collapsed lintel of a doorway, Mauch thought it matched that of his pencil:

It can be taken as a fact that the wood which we obtained actually is cedar-wood and from this that it cannot have come from anywhere else but from the Libanon. Furthermore only the Phoenicians could have brought it here; further Salomo used a lot of cedar-wood for the building of the temple and of his palaces; further: including here the visit of the Queen of Seba and, considering Zimbabwe or Zimbaoe or Simbaoe written in Arabic (of Hebrew I understand nothing), one gets as a result that the great woman who built the *rondeau* [enclosure] could have been none other than the Queen of Seba.

Though the wood was, in fact, a local hardwood and he could only guess at the age of the site, Mauch's highly coloured account of overgrown ruins built by the Queen of Sheba generated huge popular interest in Europe in the years that followed, fuelling myths linking the origins of the ruins with early Portuguese travellers that persist even today.

The European 'rush for Africa' was under way and rumours of fabulous treasure were readily believed. The ruins caught the imagination of Cecil Rhodes, the astute British-born politician and financier who co-founded the De Beers mining company and in 1890 became prime minister of the Cape colony. Rhodes' British South Africa Company occupied the region in which Great Zimbabwe was located, and he became convinced that the ruins were Phoenician and symbolized the need for a superior colonizing power to help the indigenous people of 'darkest Africa' rise above barbarism.

In 1891, the company sponsored J. Theodore Bent, an antiquarian who had travelled widely in the Middle East, to investigate further. Although Bent believed from the outset that the origins of Great Zimbabwe lay outside Africa, he otherwise attempted to keep an open mind, confessing that 'the names of King Solomon and the Queen of Sheba were on everybody's lips, and have become so distasteful to us that we never expect to hear them again without an involuntary shudder'. While characterizing finds from the site as 'native', he eventually decided that the ruins were not connected to any known African people.

A decade later, in 1902–04, the journalist Richard Nicklin Hall was instructed to make the site presentable for tourists. He cleared trees and undergrowth, and also many of the archaeological deposits without record of their stratigraphy or contents. Hall's identification of the builders of Zimbabwe as Sabaeans or Phoenicians and his vandalism of the site finally prompted two more rigorous investigations sponsored by the British Association for the Advancement of Science in London.

The first, by David Randall MacIver, a pupil of Flinders Petrie, in 1906, resolved that the site was of medieval date and African origin, but failed to come up with conclusive evidence. Only with the second expedition, undertaken by Gertrude Caton-Thompson in 1929, were datable artifacts recovered from a stratified context. 'Every detail', Caton-Thompson wrote, 'appears to me to be typical African Bantu ... You have here a mature civilization ... showing national organization of a high kind, originality and amazing industry'.

So began a long-running clash between colonial ideology and archaeologists, whose standards were those of the international community but who carried the burden of being white interpreters of a black past.

The idea of black civilization was anathema to white people living in a region dependent on cheap black labour for mining and agriculture. Even established scholars were not immune. One well-publicized outburst against Caton-Thompson came in 1929 from the palaeoanthropologist Raymond Dart, who four years before had won international fame as discoverer of the 'missing link', the first australo-pithecine (p. 260). *The Cape Times* reported that Dart 'delivered remarks in a tone of awe-inspiring violence ... He spoke in an outburst of curiously unscientific indignation and charged the startled chairman ... with having called upon none but the supporters of Miss Caton-Thompson's theory'. This violent reaction so upset the refined Caton-Thompson that she refused to undertake further work in southern Africa, writing even thirty years later that 'on the Zimbabwe experience, I preferred passionless archaeology'.

In the period of white Rhodesian independence between 1965 and 1980 archaeologists found that Great Zimbabwe became an explicitly political issue. In 1969, one Member of Parliament, Colonel Hartley, attacked the way the site was presented to visitors, and the idea that 'these ruins were originally erected by the indigenous people of Rhodesia. This may be a very popular notion for adherents to the Zimbabwe African Peoples' Union ... but [it] is nothing but sheer conjecture ... This trend among people, particularly among members of the staff of the National Historical Monuments Commission ... should be corrected'. Some archaeologists felt that more than their jobs were at risk, and left the country.

In Zimbabwe today, many hold that the ruins are the preserve of black Zimbabweans alone: even the president of Zimbabwe has been quoted as saying that it would be 'a mockery of our culture to ask a white man to interpret Great Zimbabwe'. The still unfolding story of Great Zimbabwe shows how completely the political and economic climate determines ownership of the past.

Aerial view of the ruins of Great Zimbabwe, capital of a huge Shona kingdom in the fourteenth century AD and home at its peak to 18,000 people.

The site falls into three parts: stone-walled enclosures (shown here) on the steep granite hillside that seem to include the residence of the king, members of his family and key officials; a central area that includes the 'great enclosure' and solid-stone conical tower; and surrounding town, originally covered with pole-and-mud houses with thatched roofs.

Exploration also took place under the auspices of the Geological Service of the Indochinese Union. In 1902 Henri Mansuy established the existence of a Southeast Asian Bronze Age through excavations at Samrong Sen in central Cambodia. A mound standing 6 metres (20 feet) high, some 150 kilometres (93 miles) southeast of Angkor, Samrong Sen yielded pottery, shells, polished stone tools, shell and stone jewellery, and bronze objects and casting moulds that proved to span the Neolithic and early Bronze Age (c. 3000–1000 BC). It was the region's first serious excavation.

Colonial archaeology in Asia was not, however, solely the preserve of Europeans: the restored Imperial government of Japan also looked upon itself as the saviour of the Far East. After annexing the Korean peninsula in 1910, it set out deliberately to 'enlighten the "backward" Koreans', attempting – as the French did in Southeast Asia – to turn the local inhabitants into citizens of the colonizing power through language teaching, 'moral' education and the rewriting of history. Ethnographic and archaeological research followed naturally from this agenda.

Riding everywhere by donkey, Torii Ryuzo, an anthropologist from Tokyo University, led numerous expeditions to the continent and Taiwan in this period, and undertook more than twenty field-trips to Korea. Such efforts inevitably focused principally on standing monuments: temples in the case of Southeast Asia, and dolmens, mounded tombs, earthworks, and inscribed stone slabs on the Korean peninsula. Torii was the first to divide Korean dolmens into two types: boulders supported by small stones in the south, and table stones supported on high stone slabs in the north. He was also commendably alert to local beliefs, recording of one menhir he encountered in southwest Korea that it was 'a monument contemporary with the dolmens, which the present-day surrounding population look on as a god and worship, commending themselves to it in times of sickness and troubles.'

EXPLORATION AND ETHNOLOGY IN AFRICA

The Swedish naturalist Anders Sparrman was probably the first to excavate in sub-Saharan Africa. Plant-hunting in the Eastern Cape with his compatriot Carl Thunberg, he swam rivers – clad in nothing but his wig – slid down precipitous slopes in pursuit of rare specimens and, out of curiosity but without result, in 1776 dug a stone mound near Cookhouse on the Great Fish river. From Sparrman's time, rock art too was sporadically recorded by travellers, colonial administrators, soldiers, traders and missionaries. Inevitably, however, the images were evaluated in European terms and dismissed as a quaint record of primitive life – hunts and fights with neighbours painted for amusement or to chronicle events. Local people were not asked what the art meant.

A century passed before African archaeology began in earnest. At least a year before Boucher de Perthes' claims for the antiquity of prehistoric stone tools found in France won scientific endorsement in 1859, Colonel Thomas Holden Bowker had, apparently independently, recognized such tools as ancient in southern Africa.

Thereafter, the acceptance of the antiquity of humankind in Europe led to a surge of interest in stone tools in the African colonies, most of it from amateur collectors.

One of the best known early collectors was Louis Peringuey, an entomologist who left France in 1879 to study the diseases of South African vineyards, developed an interest in archaeology, and in 1906 became director of the South African Museum in Cape Town. Peringuey delighted in retaining striking specimens on his desk, unlabelled, flourishing them dramatically as an inspiration to visitors. His *Stone Ages of South Africa* (1911) records the range of stone tools known, comparing them with finds from Europe on the – erroneous but then natural – assumption that African and European tools shared the same cultural origins. Such comparisons were rendered still weaker by the absence of any dating evidence or archaeological context. Unlike Europe, sub-Saharan Africa had no Neolithic or Bronze Age: in many places the Stone Age lasted until the introduction of iron tools in the nineteenth or even twentieth century.

Nigerian art

If perceptions of stone tools and substantial ruins could be distorted by blinkered European interpretation, African art stood no chance at all. Nigeria, with its rich heritage of finely crafted heads, statues and decorative plaques in wood, terracotta and bronze, some of them dating from the first millennium BC, was particularly vulnerable.

Benin City, 1897. Members of Admiral Rawson's British punitive expedition with their booty of ivory and bronzes, shipped to England within weeks to defray the costs of the expedition, and soon scattered.

Pitt-Rivers acquired many of the best bronzes, while noting tartly that 'as the expedition was as usual unaccompanied by any scientific explorer charged with the duty of making inquiries upon matters of historic and antiquarian interest, no reliable information about them could be obtained'.

For the British, moral justification for their actions came from the appalling slaughter they discovered at the abandoned 'city of blood' – some of it at least precipitated by their approach.

'It is a misnomer to call it a city: it is a charnel house', wrote one member of the expedition. 'All about the houses and streets are dead natives, some crucified, some sacrificed on trees, others on stage erections … In front of the king's compound stakes have been driven into the ground, and cross-pieces of wood lashed to them. On this framework live human beings are tied, to die of thirst and heat, to be dried up by the sun and eaten by the carrion birds.'

For another member of the expedition the explanation for what they found seemed only too clear: 'the custom of human crucifixions, as practised by the natives, was derived from the representations of the Crucifixion of our Saviour'.

The African art that first had an impact in Europe was a vast haul of West African bronzes and ivory carvings seized by the British navy's 1500-strong Benin punitive expedition in 1897. Benin's bronze-casting tradition of near life-size human heads and plaques flourished from before the arrival of Europeans in the late fifteenth century AD until the nineteenth century, and the British found an abandoned city that contained works of art and human sacrifices in equally astonishing quantities. Some 2,000 bronzes, including 160 heads, were taken, as well as hundreds of carved tusks and animal figures. The bronzes were dispersed to museums all over the world to defray the costs of the expedition.

Around the turn of the century, the German Leo Frobenius, one of the first anthropologists to study Africa, began his 'Inner Africa expeditions', in effect plundering the artistic heritage of the continent for the benefit of European collectors in a way that continues even today. Some of Africa's most famous works of art, such as the distinctive Nok terracotta figures of the period c. 500 BC–AD 500, were discovered by chance at this time during mining operations on the slopes of the Jos plateau in central Nigeria. The figures would have been destroyed had they not been collected, but the lack of documentation about the context of the finds frustrates our understanding of them; fragmentary limbs and torsos suggest that some of the heads originally belonged to life-sized figures. At the time, most Nigerians were more interested in acquiring European culture than conserving the 'uncivilized' art of their ancestors. Only in the late twentieth century has this attitude changed.

Visionary for a dark continent

Wilhelm Bleek (1827–75), an enlightened German philologist who in 1861 became curator of the Sir George Grey Library in Cape Town, stands as a beacon against the stark background of the expropriation of Africa's past in the late nineteenth century.

In 1870, Bleek learned that a group of /Xam Bushman convicts from the Northern Cape were working on a new breakwater in Table Bay and realized he had an opportunity to record the fast disappearing /Xam language (the symbol '/' indicates one of the clicks that characterize Bushman languages). He persuaded the governor of the Cape Colony to allow some of them to live at his home, and devoted the remaining years of his life to investigating Bushman culture. In all, Bleek and his sister-in-law, Lucy Lloyd, recorded verbatim some 12,000 pages of Bushman life, rituals and beliefs. He was awarded a state pension to continue his work following a petition from some of the world's leading scientists, including Darwin, Huxley and Lyell.

In the 1950s, the growth of interest in Bushman ethnography as a means of interpreting the African past led to the rediscovery of the Bleek records after decades of neglect.

They have had an enormous impact, particularly on studies of Bushman rock art, lending support to the idea that much of the art was essentially religious, and related to the trance experiences of shamans.

THE STONE AGE IN OCEANIA

Anthropological interest in Australia in the nineteenth century centred on the survival, especially in Tasmania, of so-called 'relic savages' who were taken to represent early stages in cultural evolution. The biologist and anthropologist, Sir Baldwin Spencer, made the point explicitly:

> Australia is the present home and refuge of creatures, often crude and quaint, that have elsewhere passed away and given place to higher forms. This applies equally to the Aboriginal as to the platypus and kangaroo. Just as the platypus, laying its eggs and feebly suckling its young, reveals a mammal in the making, so does the Aboriginal show us, at least in broad outline, what early man must have been like before he learned to read and write, domesticate animals, cultivate crops and use a metal tool. It has been possible to study in Australia human beings that still remain on the culture level of men of the Stone Age.

'What early man must have been like.' A late nineteenth-century studio portrait of Australian Aborigines.

The half century before the First World War in which anthropologists studied Aborigines as 'relic savages' coincided with the increased repression of many Aboriginal groups previously allowed to live in relative seclusion.

Farmers wanting to prevent the Aboriginal population increasing and taking over the land occupied by their reserves sought to expel the existing occupants. Town-dwellers too demanded that Aboriginal families who tried to settle on their margins were moved on.

The result, in Western Australia particularly, was the humiliation of forced relocations to a small number of large, highly regulated Aboriginal reserves. The notorious Moore River Settlement, founded in 1916, at times held over 1,300 people.

This view of Aboriginal people meant that they were valued more as scientific specimens than human beings well into the twentieth century; so valuable were they to science that the scientific institutions of the western world competed to acquire their skeletal remains. With Aborigines regarded as primitive life made flesh, there was understandably little interest in investigating the realities of Australian prehistory. Yet from the time of the first European settlement in Australia, there had been speculation about Aboriginal origins. The differences between Australian and Tasmanian Aborigines were recognized early on: mainland Aborigines were assigned to the 'neolithic' stage of development because they had the domesticated dog and ground stone tools; the Tasmanians lacked both, and were assigned to the 'palaeolithic'.

As the Tasmanians lacked sea-going watercraft and could only have reached Tasmania across a land-bridge during a period of low sea level, this two-stage model implied that the human occupation of Australia was of great antiquity. Greater precision was impossible, however, as there was no means of dating Aboriginal remains and no way of building up a cultural sequence on the basis of a succession of different artifact types. Variation in the shape of Aboriginal stone tools was thought to be due to raw material rather than style or function; and because drought and floods meant that large quantities of sediment could accumulate quickly in Australia, causing rapid alterations to the landscape, there was no confidence that artifacts found at great depths were necessarily very old. It was known that there were several extinct species of large marsupial which had once occupied Australia, including *Thylacoleo*, the marsupial lion, *Diprotodon*, a rhino-sized wombat, and *Sthenurus*, a giant kangaroo. Yet whenever sites were dug with the aim of demonstrating that Aborigines and megafauna had co-existed at some time in the past, proof remained elusive.

The most notable excavations conducted in Australia during the second half of the nineteenth century sought to establish the age and function of a group of low mounds in western Victoria, now known to date to the last 2,500 years. In 1884, Peter MacPherson, a Presbyterian minister, published the results of twenty years work on these mounds, comparing them with modern ash-heaps and suggesting that they could have formed very quickly and need not be more than a few hundred years old. In 1869, however, James Dawson, a farmer and amateur taxidermist concerned with the welfare of Victoria's Aborigines, dug one mound to establish its function, arguing on the basis of the stratigraphy he encountered that such earthworks could not be ovens, as was often thought, and must – as the testimony of elderly Aborigines suggested – be the sites of dwellings.

The moa-hunters

In New Zealand speculation about the origins of the Maori was similarly rife. A surveyor called Walter Mantell is credited with the first excavation: a dig at the Awamoa site in North Otago in 1852. First found in 1843, the remains of the extinct flightless birds known as moa had since been excavated at several sites, but Mantell was the first to show that people had hunted moas, even experimenting with one of the ancient ovens at his site to cook pork and eels. 'We all noticed an exquisite moa flavour', he wrote.

By the 1870s, six New Zealand sites had produced evidence of moa hunting and it seemed that the bird – the largest, *Dinornis giganteus*, up to 4 metres (13 feet) high – had been extinct at least since the sixteenth century. This raised questions about the antiquity of the sites and the identity of the hunters, and a lively debate ensued, largely stimulated by Julius von Haast, a German geologist who arrived in New Zealand in 1858 and became the first director of the Canterbury Museum. Haast himself investigated several sites with evidence for two distinct periods of occupation: for instance at a large camp-site at the mouth of the Rakaia river, near Canterbury, he distinguished an earlier occupation characterized by moa bones, ovens and flaked stone tools, and a later period with polished stone tools. Influenced by European discoveries of extinct animals associated with flaked stone tools, Haast proposed that the Maori occupation of New Zealand, which he equated with the 'neolithic', had been preceded by a 'palaeolithic' people who lacked polished stone tools and domesticated dogs. It was these more primitive people who had hunted the moa.

Amateur fossil-hunters indulging in the popular pastime of unearthing moa bones on Riverton beach, New Zealand, in 1895.

Easter Island

A tiny speck in the Pacific that is one of the most renowned archaeological sites in the world, Easter Island is the eastern-most inhabited island of Polynesia, lying 3,700 kilometres (2,300 miles) from the coast of South America. First visited by the Dutch mariner Jacob Roggeveen on Easter Sunday 1722, the island is one huge Stone Age site dotted with hundreds of

the great stone statues (*moai*) for which it is famous. Early visitors, including Captain Cook in 1774, wondered about the origin and construction techniques of the statues, and left

valuable information about the islanders. The first known excavations were carried out in 1882 by men from a German gunboat, the *Hyäne*, who were collecting material for Berlin's Kaiserliches Museum, but the earliest archaeological work worthy of the name was undertaken by an American team. Arriving on the *USS Mohican*, in eleven days in 1886 they recorded 555 statues and 113 platforms, as well as numerous caves, villages and rock-art sites.

A pioneering and courageous Englishwoman, Katherine Routledge, spent seventeen months on Easter Island during the First World War. She was the first person to make a detailed study of the quarry from which the statues were cut, and undertook extensive surveys of the 171-square-kilometre (66-square-mile) island, in addition to numerous excavations. So determined was she to gather as much information as possible that she even ventured into the leper settlement to interview elderly islanders about their memories and customs.

In 1955–56, a much-publicized Norwegian expedition led by the adventurer Thor Heyerdahl conducted fresh surveys and excavations. Heyerdahl obtained the first radiocarbon dates from the island, suggesting human arrival in the early centuries AD, and took the first pollen samples in an effort to reconstruct the past environment. He also undertook interesting experiments in quarrying, transporting and raising statues in an attempt to assess how these things had been done by the prehistoric islanders. Already in 1947, Heyerdahl had made a courageous experimental voyage on a balsa raft, the *Kon-Tiki*, to test his theory – now discredited – that Polynesia could have been settled from South America rather than from island Southeast Asia.

One of Heyerdahl's most enduring contributions to Easter Island archaeology was to make the American prehistorian William Mulloy part of his expedition. Mulloy devoted the rest of his life to the island, becoming the leading authority on its archaeology and the first person to restore its sites, re-erecting several statues on their platforms (*ahu*) and reconstructing the ceremonial drystone village of Orongo.

Captivated like so many by the atmosphere of the island, his sentiments matched those of Katherine Routledge: 'In Easter Island ... the shadows of the departed builders still possess the land ... the whole air vibrates with a vast purpose and energy which has been and is no more.'

Easter Island monuments by William Hodges (1744–97), artist during Captain Cook's expedition. Notice the skeletal remains scattered at the foot of the statues.

The picture Haast drew of a moa-hunter period of great antiquity was controversial. His critics soon came up with evidence of the survival of the moa into recent times and moa-hunter sites with polished stone tools, and Haast finally modified his views as a result of excavations at Moa-bone Point Cave, near Christchurch, where polished stone tools were found in moa-hunter layers dating back at least 600 years.

This early interest in excavation as a means of finding out about the past was not followed up, and by the end of the century had given way to interest in Maori oral traditions. The Polynesian Society was founded in 1892 to record what were thought to be the remnants of a dying and disappearing culture and the Maori scholar Peter Buck (Te Rangi Hiroa) took the lead in developing a new synthesis of New Zealand prehistory, based on a doubtful body of Maori tradition. In his view, the first inhabitants of New Zealand were primitive Maruiwi of Melanesian origin, a group who were displaced by the coming of the Maori 'Great Fleet' about the fourteenth century AD, the Maruiwi themselves living on as the Moriori of the Chatham Islands. Buck's account was so widely accepted by the 1920s that archaeology shrivelled to little more than an antiquarian study. Only the spectacular Maori fortified sites or *pa*, ditched and banked enclosures that are a prominent feature of the New Zealand landscape, especially in the north, excited much interest; many detailed plans were made of them in this period.

In the Pacific islands, isolated archaeological discoveries were made from the beginning of this century: on Watom Island in 1909, for instance, a German Catholic missionary, Father Otto Meyer, became the first to find sherds of the distinctive stamped pottery known as Lapita ware, later found to be distributed as far east as Fiji and Samoa. The Bishop Museum in Hawaii was the base for most such work in the region.

THE AMERICAS

North American archaeology by the late nineteenth century was already largely in the hands of organizations like the Smithsonian Institution in Washington DC, which in 1879 secured an unprecedented $20,000 grant from Congress to establish a Bureau of American Ethnology. Behind this success stood a larger than life figure who was to become the Bureau's first director: Major John Wesley Powell, a Civil War hero who lost an arm at the battle of Shiloh and in 1869 became nationally famous when he led a team of explorers down the Colorado river and through 'the best geological section on the continent', the Grand Canyon.

Powell was a geology professor who ended his career as Director of the United States Geological Survey, but his interests extended well beyond rocks. He had a longstanding interest in ethnography and archaeology and had studied Indian customs, languages and beliefs, particularly those of the Paiutes north of the Grand Canyon. On taking charge of the Bureau of American Ethnology, two of his first acts were to initiate – at the request of Congress – a study of the Moundbuilders of the

Midwest (p. 113), and to send the twenty-two year old Frank Hamilton Cushing to New Mexico to study the Zuni Indians. Though not a formally trained ethnologist, Cushing stayed for four and a half years during which he forcibly demonstrated the potential of anthropological research in the American Southwest, in 1886–89 excavating prehistoric sites along the middle Gila river in Arizona and making the then radical suggestion that variations in burials and architectural styles pointed to a class-based society.

Established slightly earlier than the Bureau, in 1866, the Peabody Museum of Harvard University nonetheless found its feet around the same time, in 1875 appointing as curator a young zoologist, Frederic Ward Putnam. Widely regarded as a founding father of American archaeology, Putnam was both an administrator and an energetic excavator, directing pioneer expeditions to the mounds of the Ohio river valley, and to the American Southwest, Mexico and South America. Author of more than 400 articles and organizer of the ethnological exhibit at the 1893 Chicago World Fair, he also helped found the Field Museum of Natural History in Chicago and, in 1903, establish west coast teaching in archaeology at the University of California at Berkeley.

The American Southwest was a particular concern of the Archaeological Institute of America, which in 1880 sent the Swiss born archaeologist Adolf Bandelier to explore the Indian pueblos of Arizona and New Mexico. Using a mixture of documentary research, ethnography and field survey, Bandelier worked particularly around Santa Fe, travelling on foot and horseback with a group of Cochiti Indians across the Pajarito plateau to the north, across deep, lava-strewn canyons and sharp volcanic mesas to the Rio Grande and then into Frijoles canyon, wooded with pines, oaks and cottonwoods, and with four pueblos of the fourteenth and fifteenth centuries AD at the bottom. Bandelier's reports on these and other sites he visited, like Pecos (p. 190), called attention to the fragility of the ruins and drew specific comparisons between the archaeology of the Southwest and that of Mesoamerica. In 1916, his work won permanent recognition when, after years of dogged opposition from lumbermen and stockmen, Frijoles became the centrepiece of an archaeological preserve named Bandelier National Monument.

The earliest Americans

When did the first humans reach the Americas? It is an issue that has excited passionate partisanship for more than a century now, and shows no signs of going away. With final acceptance of the antiquity of humankind in Europe in 1859, American patriots interested in archaeology were faced with a challenge: to find matching evidence in their own continent. Among the first to pick up the gauntlet was the physician Charles Abbott, who excavated gravels on his ancestral farm at Trenton, New Jersey, in the 1870s – though with negligible results. Both Abbott and his sponsor, Frederic Putnam of Harvard, believed that humans had arrived in North America before the end of the last Ice Age. But they were in a minority. It was

Mesa Verde

Indelibly imprinted on the memory of every visitor, the dramatic Anasazi ruins of Mesa Verde ('The green table') lie in southwest Colorado on a vast, flat-topped mesa of volcanic origin, scarred by gulches and canyons and thick with juniper and pines, in places rising some 300 metres (1000 feet) above the surrounding desert.

The first Mesa Verde site to be found by Europeans was the huge 'Cliff Palace', discovered on 18 December 1888 when Richard Wetherill, a cowboy interested in Indian ruins, was searching on horseback for stray cattle with his brother-in-law, Charlie Mason. The two men climbed on steadily, amid flurries of snow in failing light, until they reached a vantage

point at the top of the mesa. It was then, looking ahead up the canyon, that they saw an astonishing sight: clinging to the precipitous walls of the canyon opposite, protected from the snow by a huge rock overhang, stood a mass of houses and towers of fine masonry, stacked on top of each other in terraces, and giving the appearance of a city that had been abandoned no more than a day before.

Riding round the head of the canyon, they made their way down to the buildings, passing on foot from room to room. Timbers hung from the roofs, plaster still clung to the walls, and human bones lay on the floors amid corn cobs and scraps of pottery. 'It appeared', wrote Wetherill later, 'as though the inhabitants had left everything they possessed right where they had used it last.'

Today Mesa Verde is a national park famous for its Anasazi sites, the most visited archaeological site in the entire United States. The four-storey, 200-room Cliff Palace, now dated to the thirteenth century AD, remains its centrepiece but the 21,000 hectare (80 square mile) park contains in all some 4,000 prehistoric sites, ranging from Basketmaker pithouses (semi-subterranean structures of the early first millennium AD) to large pueblos or villages of AD 1150–1300, most of them built beneath overhangs in the numerous deep canyons that cut the mesa.

'Anasazi', from the Navajo meaning 'enemy ancestors', is the broad term used to describe the prehistoric Indian inhabitants of the arid 'Four Corners' area of the Southwest, where Arizona, New Mexico, Colorado and Utah meet The Anasazi way of life, largely based on the farming of corn, beans and squashes, is exceptionally well documented because of the dry desert soils. Thanks to the aridity, not only plant remains like corn cobs survive, but also clothing, sandals made from yucca plants, feathers, fibre rope – even naturally mummified human burials. This high level of organic preservation attracted archaeologists and explorers in considerable numbers after Wetherill's find became more widely known through his sale, to the Denver Historical Society, of $3000 worth of 'Cliff Dweller' artifacts dug from the ruins.

Over time, the Anasazi developed increasingly sophisticated pottery, architecture and agricultural techniques: buildings became larger and more substantial, made with walls of dressed stone around a wooden frame covered with wattle and daub. The most magnificent ruins, like Cliff Palace and Chaco Canyon, are true towns that belong to the final, Pueblo III stage (c. AD 1100–1300), after which the Anasazi seem to have abandoned the Four Corners area, probably as a result of the droughts that made farming extremely uncertain.

Largely because of the loss of Anasazi antiquities through illicit digging, Mesa Verde in 1906 became the first national park in America dedicated to archaeological conservation. Ironically, it was spectacular finds made in the Southwest by amateurs like Richard Wetherill around the turn of the century that sparked public interest and generated institutional support for archaeology in the first place. Wetherill was typical of early archaeologists in that he began as a cowboy with a shovel, digging up finds to sell, but became in time a committed prehistorian: excavating stratigraphically, publishing, and drawing comparisons between contemporary Indian groups and their Anasazi ancestors. The commitment is clear from his letters of later life:

In these [Basketmaker] caches are found the bodies of all ages and sexes – sandals upon the feet – human hair, gee string, cedar bark breech cloth. Beads around their necks. All wrapped in a blanket of rabbit fur – of a weave similar to the feather cloth. Then they are [also found] in a mummy cloth or a sack cloth such as the Peruvians used. This is made from yucca fiber and good cloth it is. Over the head is a small basket – flat – about 20 inches in diameter, usually found in good condition; Apaches make a similar one today …

Better educated men like the explorer and scientist Baron Gustaf Nordenskiöld, the son of a prominent Swedish family who arrived in the Southwest in 1891 as a twenty-two year old student, often worked with amateurs like Wetherill to help record their excavations. Ironically, it was Nordenskiöld's attempt to return to his native Sweden with antiquities from Mesa Verde – including fine painted pottery and probably at least one mummy – that provided the final impetus for the Antiquities Act of 1906 and the creation that year of the Mesa Verde national park. By then Wetherill himself had moved to Chaco Canyon, where he established a trading post and excavated for four seasons at Pueblo Bonito (p. 341).

In spite of mounting opposition from government and state officials and deteriorating relations with the local Indians, he continued to dig until 1910, the year he was shot dead by an aggrieved Navajo in a dispute about money.

Opposite. Cliff Palace, Mesa Verde. With over 200 rooms, and twenty-three circular kivas, it could house over 400 people. Originally roofed over, the kivas – accessed by ladder through a hatch – would have contributed to the flat open space in front of the buildings. Thirteenth century AD.

not until 1926 that flaked stone tools were finally found with the bones of extinct animals of the late Ice Age (p. 270). Until then, influential scholars like the archaeologist William Henry Holmes, from 1902 director of the Bureau of American Ethnology, and the Czech-born physical anthropologist Ales Hrdlicka were properly sceptical, vigorously debunking the often wild claims that were made.

By the end of the nineteenth century professional archaeologists were increasingly turning to more sober studies like the systematic excavation of the shell mounds left by prehistoric hunter-gathers. It was, above all, this type of site that encouraged the adoption in America of stratigraphic methods imported from Europe. Dug layer by layer in the manner being pioneered by Pitt-Rivers in Britain and by Flinders Petrie in Egypt, it was assumed that the range of finds in each level of a mound would correlate with changes in the prehistoric culture of the surrounding area over time; the sequence would provide a yardstick against which to judge other, simpler sites and would in time allow a regional chronology to be built up.

Particularly influential in introducing stratigraphic techniques were the excavations of William Dall, who worked on shell-mounds in the Aleutian Islands during the 1870s, and Max Uhle, a German-born archaeologist known in later life as the 'father of Peruvian archaeology', who in 1903 published his stratigraphic excavation of a shell-mound at Emeryville in San Francisco bay. The battle was not, however, won overnight. Initial opposition came in particular from the anthropologist Alfred Kroeber, who strenuously rejected the idea that every stratigraphic change Uhle identified was indicative of real cultural change. Only after the First World War did stratigraphic excavation really catch on, following the demonstrable success of work by Manuel Gamio at Atzcapotzalco near Mexico City in 1911, and in the pueblo ruins of the Galisteo basin, New Mexico, in 1913–15, by a pupil of Kroeber's, Nels Nelson, who had worked with Uhle in California. Opposition then faded away and the technique was developed actively for chronological purposes, in the Southwest most notably by Alfred Kidder through huge excavations at Pecos pueblo, near Santa Fe.

The lure of Mesoamerica

The Maya civilization that dominated 260,000 square kilometres (100,000 square miles) of the Yucatán lowlands during the Classic period (c. AD 300–900) left behind in the rain forests spectacular ruined cities like Copán, Palenque and Tikal, with pyramids that reached dizzying heights as well as a rich inheritance of art and architecture. Stephens and Catherwood died early, in the 1850s, but the romantic legacy of their publications lived on, stimulating an interest in the ruins of Mesoamerica that has never since abated. So distinctive was Maya culture and so avid were its celebrants, that Maya archaeology rapidly became an enterprise in its own right – almost a separate strand in American archaeology – a situation that persists even today.

Exploration in the generation that followed Stephens and Catherwood focused, logically enough, on finding and systematically describing Maya cities. Among institutions, the Peabody Museum at Harvard took the lead, under the patronage of Charles Bowditch, a wealthy Bostonian fascinated by the Maya calendar. From the 1870s, numerous expeditions set off from Cambridge: to excavate at Copán in Honduras, nearly fifty years after the world was stunned by Catherwood's exquisite drawings of its stone carvings; to dig at nearby Quiriguá, one of the first Maya centres to be thoroughly studied archaeologically; and to explore the Maya lowlands, looking for new sites.

Other countries and institutions soon joined in, both in the study and in the field. The great German archaeologist Eduard Seler became the first to shed light on the prehistoric Maya by systematically combining archaeology with ethnohistory, the study of Spanish chronicles and native documents. His work on Maya stelae helped work out the basic details of the calendar and his carefully reasoned interpretations opened a new, more scientific era in Maya studies.

Among fieldworkers, it was, surprisingly, a self-funded Englishman, Alfred Percival Maudslay, who led the way. Arriving alone by steamship, a young ex-colonial official who wanted to pass the winter in a warm climate, Maudslay was so affected by the carved monuments he encountered at Quiriguá in 1881 that he devoted the

The Peabody Museum's Second Honduras Expedition, 1893. Mound 26 at Copán in the early stages of clearance.

rest of his life to the Maya. Although a graduate of the other Cambridge, he had no previous experience of American archaeology when he arrived and at first had to use Stephens' book as a guide. He visited Copán and then, putting his colonial experience to good use, hired local porters and made a seventeen-day trek through virtually uninhabited rain forest to the infinitely more remote Tikal. Arriving on Easter Sunday, he climbed one of five vertiginous pyramids he found overwhelmed by undergrowth, its broken stone steps slippery with tree roots and rotting vegetation. At the top he found himself floating on a sea of tree tops that stretched as far as the eye could see.

> Every house I entered had square doorways with beams of sapote wood across the top and all were built of stone and plaster. In the house at the top of the pyramid the beams were elaborately carved but too much eaten away to trace the figures … The forest was over everything. The work of clearing would be much more than I could do and there appeared to be very little hope of taking satisfactory photographs. No doubt I was on the site of a very large city, larger than anything mentioned by Stephens, but although the houses were large and numerous there was little sign of carving or ornamental work …

Maudslay spent five days clearing the pyramid, which proved to measure 51.2 metres by 55.9 metres (168 by 184 feet) at the base and to stand almost 36.6 metres (120 feet) high. The house at the top he took to be a temple. 'There is no trace of any idol or object of worship in these buildings', he noted in his diary, 'but I cannot doubt their being temples such as those so often mentioned by the Spanish conquerors'. Grouped around a once open plaza adorned with elaborately carved stone slabs representing figures in feathered headdresses, the pyramids evidently marked the centre of the city.

> The whole town had been laid out on a rectangular plan and wherever there are differences in elevation the ground has been terraced and the slopes faced with carefully-laid squared stones. Some houses are in a fair state of preservation … but the buildings can be seen in every state of decay and are often merely overgrown heaps of squared stones.

Among the first to use photography to record archaeological sites – despite the problems of transporting bulky equipment on mules and horseback through the rain forest – Maudslay continued to explore the Maya ruins of Guatemala, Mexico and Honduras for more than a decade. He described and mapped Copán, Chichén Itzá and Palenque and was one of the first to visit the remote Late Classic site of Yaxchilán on the Usumacinta river. He also made expert papier mâché and plaster casts of Maya carvings and inscriptions, shipping plaster from Europe and later employing an assistant to draw and colour the results. By the time his fieldwork ended in 1895, he had built up a huge collection of casts and moulds, as well as photographs, plans, drawings and written records that passed in time to the British

Machu Picchu: Lost City of the Inkas

While the Maya held great fascination for archaeologists and public alike, memorable discoveries were also being made in South America, particularly among the Andean civilizations of Peru. Most famously, in 1911, a young Yale historian called Hiram Bingham (1878–1956) rediscovered the lost Inka settlement of Machu Picchu, high above the Urubamba river in the Sacred Valley of the Inkas. Perched at 2,500 metres (8,000 feet) on a narrow saddle of rock between the great mountain, Machu Picchu, and a smaller vertical peak, Huayna Picchu, it remains even today the most spectacular archaeological site in the world.

Travelling north by mule and on foot down the Urubamba from Cuzco, Bingham worked on the simple, unromantic expedient of offering money to local Indians who could locate Inka ruins, doubling the price if the remains were particularly interesting. After a precipitous climb from the modern village of Puquiura, his expedition followed a stream through thick undergrowth, emerging eventually into a clearing. Ahead, rising above dense jungle growth, were the remains of some of the finest Inka buildings Bingham had ever seen.

> Before us was a great white rock over a spring. Our guides had not misled us. Beneath the trees were the ruins of an Inka temple, flanking and partly enclosing the gigantic granite boulder, one end of which overhung a small pool of running water ... It was late on the afternoon of August 9, 1911, when I first saw this remarkable shrine ... There was not a hut to be seen; scarcely a sound to be heard. It was an ideal place for practicing the mystic ceremonies of an ancient cult ... At last we had found the place where, in the days of Titu Cusi, the Inka priests faced the east, greeted the rising sun, 'extended their hands toward it', and 'threw kisses to it', 'a ceremony of the most profound resignation and reverence'.

Returning the following year, Bingham dislodged the native families living in the abandoned buildings and began to clear the site: no mean feat because when his workmen tried to cut back the vegetation, poisonous snakes fell from the trees. They eventually burned the trees off the site. What emerged was an Inka settlement no less magnificent for its exquisite architecture than for its dramatic and precipitous setting. Publicized from the first with photographs by the National Geographic Society, which provided funds for the expedition, the site rapidly became a universal symbol of Peru and the Inka Empire – an image that endures to this day.

Bingham's belief that Machu Picchu was the lost city of Vilcabamba, the last capital of the Inka Empire from which the Spanish were resisted until 1572, we now know to have been mistaken. Ironically, the real Vilcabamba was located by the explorer Gene Savoy in 1965 at a site called Espíritu Pampa, just a short distance from where Bingham himself gave up an earlier search in 1911. Wrong too was Bingham's identification of the settlement with Tampu-Toqo, the place of origin of the Inka dynasty. Machu Picchu's terraced fields, houses, tombs, and religious monuments are now thought more likely to be a country estate belonging to the first great Inka emperor, Pachacuti. Though Bingham claimed that the Spanish did not know the site, it is in fact listed in Spanish property records of the sixteenth century.

The fame Bingham won for his Peruvian exploits he later turned to political advantage. After serving as a pilot in France in the First World War, he became governor of Connecticut and a United States senator.

Alfred Perceval Maudslay (1850–1931) in the unique four-storey palace tower at Palenque, Mexico, the most westerly of all Maya cities. The palace with its many rooms and small courts was more ceremonial structure than secular residence. It carries both dedicatory plaques and stucco models of gods and humans. The tower was designed for making astronomical sightings.

Museum. In later life, in England, he devoted his attention to the Maya calendar and Maya writing – the enigmatic hieroglyphs only finally deciphered in the 1980s.

In the ancient Maya, archaeologists like Seler and Maudslay found a people whose concern with the passage of time was equal to their own. They left hundreds of stone monuments carved with seemingly indecipherable hieroglyphs, long inscriptions that covered pyramid walls, stairways, monuments and stelae, and even a handful of codices that escaped the book burnings of Catholic priests at the time of the Spanish conquest. Archaeologists soon recognized the use of numbers, depicted as bars and dots, always in the same configuration. They had discovered the Maya calendar – or, more properly, calendars. The dominant Long Count calendar reckoned time according to five cycles: *baktun*, 144,000 days; *katun*, 7,200 days; *tun*, 360 days; *uinal*, 20 days; and *kin*, 1 day, using the cumulative count to date monuments to the day. Thus Stela D at Copán, the subject of Catherwood's most famous lithograph, can be dated precisely to 26 July AD 736. It was a discovery that put Maya archaeology on a new footing.

Civilizations of the Andes
In the years immediately before the First World War, American fascination with the Maya gave way for a period to an almost equal passion for the Andean civilizations of Peru. The reason was the discovery, and early photographic coverage in *National*

Geographic magazine, of the spectacular Inka site of Machu Picchu, long hidden by dense jungle overgrowth. It was an event that fired the imagination of the world and launched Machu Picchu's discover, college professor Hiram Bingham, on a glorious career that ended on Capitol Hill.

While Bingham was growing famous for his exploits, less freewheeling archaeologists working on the coast of Peru were painstakingly reconstructing a long sequence of pre-Inka civilizations. Largely through the efforts of Max Uhle between 1892 and 1912, Peru became the first region in the world for which a broad archaeological synthesis was developed. Uhle's first encounter with Andean prehistory came when he met the traveller Alphons Stubel, recently returned from the impressive ruins of Tiahuanaco, near Lake Titicaca in highland Bolivia, at one time the capital of a short-lived empire that extended south into Chile and Argentina. The site had a substantial ancient population and its elaborate stone carvings of deities and supernatural creatures, ceremonial plazas and pyramids formed a sacred precinct that attracted pilgrims for centuries, between AD 300 and 1000. Together, Uhle and Stubel worked up Stubel's notes, publishing the results in 1892, the year Uhle left for Peru, the country where he spent the next twenty years researching for the universities of Pennsylvania and California.

When it came to building a regional chronology, Uhle proved as committed to stratigraphic excavation and the ordering of finds in their correct evolutionary sequence as he had been in California. Particularly important was his excavation in 1896–97 of the great ceremonial and urban site of Pachacamac, near Lima, home until the Spanish conquest of an oracle consulted by pilgrims from the entire Andean region. Digging stratigraphically, Uhle was able to document an orderly sequence of artifact styles that changed over time. Stratified beneath Inka remains, he found Tiahuanaco-like artifacts that he judged inferior in quality to the originals with which he was familiar; he called these 'Epigone', using them in his developing regional chronology to characterize the pre-Inka period on the Peruvian coast. Pachacamac in this way generated the first chronological sequence in Andean archaeology, one with far-reaching implications. Uhle moved on to Mochica and Chimú sites further north, later extending his work into the highlands and to Bolivia, Ecuador and Chile. The framework he established for Andean civilization revolutionized South American archaeology as a whole and has only recently been superseded.

The period from 1860 to 1920 can thus be seen in many ways as archaeology's 'golden age' of discovery, packed with pioneering finds, from palaeolithic art to Pachacamac and from Mycenae to Machu Picchu, and resounding with many of the greatest names in the history of the subject – Lartet, Schliemann, Evans, Petrie, Koldewey, Uhle. Yet it also saw the development of a more negative aspect, the rise of extreme nationalism – a spectre that was to cast ugly shadows in the years that followed.

CHAPTER 6

Archaeology Comes of Age, 1920–1960

The mid-twentieth century revolutionized archaeology in many ways. Major discoveries continued to be made, including such marvels as the tomb of Tutankhamen, the cemetery at Ur of the Chaldees and the cave of Lascaux, but advances in other fields and in science were of far greater importance to the maturing

'Wonderful things.' The sight that greeted Howard Carter and Lord Carnarvon in the antechamber of Tutankhamen's tomb in the Valley of the Kings on 26 November 1922. It was, wrote Carter, 'The day of days, the most wonderful that I have ever lived through, and certainly one whose like I can never hope to see again'.

He inserted a candle through a small hole in the blocking of the door and, slowly, as his eyes adjusted to the light, managed to make out 'strange animals, statues of gold, everywhere the glint of gold'.

The antechamber was small, just 8 metres (26 feet) deep and 3.7 metres (12 feet) wide, but solid with gifts for the afterlife. Immediately ahead lay a gilded bed in the shape of a cow with an arched tail, a jumble of furniture piled on top, a stack of wooden food boxes below, each one seemingly inscribed in ink with the name of its contents. Beyond lay a hippopotamus-headed bed bearing a large trunk, beneath it, in the shadows, a golden throne. On the left, dismantled to get them into the tomb, stood two richly decorated state chariots of gilded wood.

It was a discovery unparalleled in the history of archaeology, scarcely disturbed since the nineteen-year-old pharaoh's death in 1325 BC.

discipline: aerial photography, pollen analysis and, above all, radiocarbon dating had an immense impact. While in some countries its integrity was abused by totalitarian regimes, archaeology in this period enjoyed unprecedented success and popularity.

A NEW PROFESSIONALISM

In Europe, the decades between the two world wars were a period of new techniques and burgeoning discovery. One of the most exciting new ideas was photographic reconnaissance from the air. Its potential had first been recognized in the late nineteenth century – the first archaeological air photographs, of Stonehenge, were taken from a captive balloon as early as 1906 – but the invention of the aeroplane opened up new horizons, military as well as archaeological. During the First World War the technique was used by all sides to detect and record enemy positions. In peacetime it became clear that the aerial perspective laid out the landscape like a map, and made it possible to see regularities that were invisible to

an observer on the ground. In low light particularly, it could detect both earthworks and more subtle soil or crop changes that often proved to betray the existence of buried banks or ditches.

With such clear advantages, aerial photography soon came to be applied widely to ancient remains, both in Europe and the Near East. In England, its leading proponent was the geographer and archaeologist O. G. S. Crawford, who in 1928 published a classic album of prehistoric sites in southern Britain, *Wessex from the Air*. Aerial photography was also used by French and German archaeologists though, given the rarity of aircraft and the cost of flying, it did not achieve its full potential as an archaeological tool until after the Second World War. It was in the immediate aftermath of that war that aerial reconnaissance achieved what must be reckoned one of its most dramatic results: the discovery in 1945 by army officer John Bradford of more than two hundred enclosed neolithic village sites on the Tavoliere plain of southern Italy where none had been known before.

Ground-based archaeology became more sophisticated as professional archaeologists increased in number and more rigorous analytical and excavation techniques became available. One of the charismatic figures of the period was another army officer, the Englishman Mortimer Wheeler, who followed in the military tradition of Pitt-Rivers, demanding site discipline on his excavations and flexibility of response – the use of trowels rather than spades. He emphasized that digging an archaeological site meant destroying it, and insisted on careful record-keeping and the prompt publication of results. Particular stress was laid on a site's stratigraphic sequence – recorded principally in drawn sections – as the key to its dating and interpretation.

Wheeler was especially interested in military sites, and conducted excavations at a number of Iron Age hillforts in southern Britain and northern France: most famous of all were his excavations in 1934–37 at the enormous hillfort of Maiden Castle in Dorset, built *c.* 500 BC and occupied and remodelled for more than five centuries until it was overrun by the Roman army. Yet Wheeler's impact was far from restricted to western Europe. In 1943 he was appointed Director-General of Antiquities in India, and during his five years in that post dramatically improved techniques of excavation and recording in the sub-continent (p. 256). He also trained a whole school of Indian and Pakistani archaeologists to continue the good work after his departure.

Another way in which archaeology became more scientific in the 1930s and 1940s was by involving environmental specialists in excavation and fieldwork. In Scandinavia, interest in past environments dated back to the 1840s, when archaeologists like Worsaae studied the impact of changing glacial geology on prehistoric communities. By the end of the nineteenth century, Scandinavian archaeologists were able to produce the first landscape studies, comparing the distribution of sites of a particular period – initially the Neolithic – with that of specific types of soil. This 'landscape approach', correlating the geographical distribution of sites and

Opposite. Stonehenge, photographed in 1906 by Lieutenant P H Sharpe from an army war-balloon – the first known photograph from the air of any archaeological site in Britain.

The Stonehenge Avenue, which is invisible at ground level, and the circular ditches of the main enclosure show as dark ribbons of unparched grass. Notice also that one of the stone trilithons on the right is shored up with wooden props.

From 1908, comparable balloon photographs were taken in Italy by Italian army engineers. By 1911, both the Forum in Rome and the ancient port of Ostia had been captured from the air.

In America, the city of Cahokia, near St Louis, in 1922 became the first prehistoric site to be photographed from above.

spread of archaeological cultures with variations in the natural environment, struck a particular chord in Britain, where a long tradition of eighteenth- and nineteenth-century field studies emphasized the need to understand the landscape in which people lived as a prerequisite to understanding life in the past. The extent of forests and fields, the varieties of crops that were grown, the nature of the climate: all were vital concerns.

In northern Europe, pollen was the key that first unlocked the prehistoric environment. When it became clear early this century that a record of past vegetation survived in places in the form of buried pollen, the Scandinavian scientist, Lennart von Post, developed a technique for reconstructing ancient vegetation by counting the pollen grains in each layer of a core sample taken with an augur. From the 1930s, this played a leading part in archaeological projects, particularly those dealing with very early sites where finds were scarce and every last scrap of information needed to be wrung out. Together with careful study of animal bones and other organic remains, pollen analysis offered a startling glimpse of life in the distant past.

Mortimer Wheeler

Sir Mortimer Wheeler (1890–1976) was one the towering figures of twentieth-century archaeology, and one of its last great characters – a mixture of military officer, moustachioed dandy and roguish rake.

Much of his field-work concentrated on British sites occupied just before and during the Roman empire: at Colchester (*Camulodunum*) just after the First World War, and then at the legionary fortresses of Caernarfon, Brecon and Caerleon, and at St Albans (Roman *Verulamium*). After the Second World War, he explored the extensive Iron Age fortifications at Stanwick in Yorkshire.

Wheeler was a fastidious excavator, always happy to get his hands dirty, and he had an artist's eye for detail as well as a soldier's insistence on disciplined digging and recording. Though in many respects outmoded, his system of dividing sites into square excavated blocks with baulks left between for recording purposes – the so-called Wheeler grid – is still widely used around the world.

Besides his excavations, Wheeler worked hard to strengthen the institutional framework of archaeology in Britain. He ran the London Museum (now the Museum of London) between 1926 and 1944, and played a large part in the foundation in 1948 of the University of London's Institute of Archaeology, serving as first director of what he called that 'laboratory of archaeological science, wherein the archaeologist of the future may learn the essentials of his business'.

One of Wheeler's greatest assets was his enthusiasm, which infected visitors and volunteer diggers with his own passion for the subject. Always the leader of men, he realized the importance of *esprit de corps*. The excavators at Maiden Castle spent many a Friday night playing skittles in local pubs, while on fine nights after supper they would make a circuit of the hillfort's massive ramparts, singing songs.

But Wheeler was also a methodical fieldworker who thought carefully about the nature of archaeological excavation. What was the best way to excavate a site? What were the real – and realistically achievable – objectives? He was especially intrigued by the links that could be established between history and archaeology. During the excavations at Maiden Castle he came upon a group of burials, one with a Roman ballista bolt embedded in the spine. These he saw as the last defenders of the site against the invading Roman legions in AD 43, hastily buried in a war cemetery by the survivors. Earlier, at Verulamium, he had been looking for remains of the capital of Cassivellaunus, the British chieftain who opposed Julius Caesar in 54 BC.

Throughout his long career, Wheeler emphasized the public relations side of archaeology, insisting that archaeologists have an obligation to present their work and results in 'terse, vigorous, direct prose', as repayment of the debt owed to the taxpayers whose money ultimately funds most archaeological research. His own books, colourfully written and displaying a sharp wit, lived up to this standard. He conveyed the interest and excitement of his discoveries to a still wider

One important early use of pollen analysis was in the investigation of prehistoric agriculture. How had the first European farmers grown their crops? In forest clearings or open fields? The pioneer Danish palynologist Johannes Iversen sought to answer these questions by studying pollen sequences from peat bogs, and at Ordrup Møse found the answer: environmental change from thick forest to cleared land with grasses and cereals, followed by a reversion to forest. He concluded from this that early farmers had burned areas of forest, planted crops for two or three years, then moved on to clear fresh land as the fertility of the fields declined. The Ordrup Møse study – though qualified today by more recent work showing that this sequence of events was by no means universal in neolithic Europe – at the time had an enormous impact, showing how powerfully pollen analysis could reveal aspects of prehistoric life hitherto completely beyond our reach.

public through lectures and newspaper articles, and his personality and skill at popularization ensured that he was a huge success in the new medium of television.

His performances on the archaeological quiz *Animal, Vegetable, Mineral?* in the 1950s led to his becoming the BBC's first television personality of the year in 1954.

The 'Wheeler grid' in action at the eastern entrance of Maiden Castle, Dorset, 1926. The boxes were dug in parallel a layer at a time, all four sides being drawn in detail to provide a permanent record of the archaeological sequence.

Inset. Wheeler the ladies' man, with romantic novelist Barbara Cartland, 1965

The Roman fort at Bankhead, Dalswinton, in southwestern Scotland, recorded by the pioneer Cambridge air photographer Kenneth St Joseph (1912–94) on 12 July 1949.

Single handed, St Joseph found thousands of previously unknown sites.

In Britain, archaeologists trained originally as geographers adopted a rather different environmental approach. In the 1920s and 1930s, O. G. S. Crawford used aerial photography to plot the correlations between archaeological sites and features of the natural environment, while Cyril Fox pioneered detailed distribution maps that plotted finds of different periods against a background of physical geography, comparing successive periods region by region to chart the ebb and flow of early human culture. Beginning in the Cambridge region, he worked on an ever larger scale until, in *The Personality of Britain* (1932), he famously divided early

Britain into two, characterizing the Lowland Zone of southeastern England as more exposed to the diffusion of ideas from the continent of Europe than the communities of the Highland Zone of northwest Britain, which were culturally more conservative.

A more rounded view, tying archaeology firmly to environmental studies and ethnology, was developed by Grahame Clark, professor of archaeology at Cambridge from 1952 to 1974. From the 1930s Clark argued for an essentially economic approach to prehistory, insisting that the goal of archaeology was not to pigeon-hole artifacts in museums but to understand, comparatively and on a world scale, how people lived in the past. He envisaged prehistoric societies as operating in an explicitly ecological context but also as composed of different – though interconnected and interdependent – components such as economy, social organization and religious belief. Though internationally minded, Clark also believed that prehistoric life was best understood through the intensive study of individual sites. He pioneered the use of scientific techniques like pollen analysis, introduced to Britain from Scandinavia by his collaborator, the palaeobotanist Harry Godwin, most notably in 1949–51 at Star Carr, a ninth millennium BC mesolithic site in Yorkshire, northern England.

Star Carr was a milestone in archaeological documentation and analysis. Like the Swiss 'lake villages' (p. 94), it was a lakeside site at which waterlogging had preserved wooden tools and other organic objects that would otherwise have perished. Among the finds were carved bone and antler points, mattock heads cut from antler, and stag frontlets with antler stumps still attached that were interpreted as masks. Clark's careful analysis of the plant and animal remains allowed a detailed reconstruction of life at the site that concluded it had been occupied during the winter and spring by migratory hunters and gatherers. Red deer, roe deer and elk were hunted, and the bones of the domestic dog as well as forest animals like aurochs, wild pig, wolf and badger were found. Pollen analyses, as well as the waterlogged remains of tree trunks, indicated that the lakeside landscape after the ice sheets retreated was essentially forested, with birch the most common tree. As a reconstruction of human activity, Star Carr set new standards, not only for studies of hunter-gatherers but for delicate excavation and the analysis of slight archaeological remains. Archaeology had come of age.

Botanical work on plant remains also became established in this period, not only for reconstructing past environments but for winning information about prehistoric diet. The recovery after the Second World War, in Denmark and elsewhere, of well-preserved human bodies like Tollund Man, with stomach contents that could be analyzed, gave a new impetus to such studies: being able to reconstruct, cook and taste a gruel that matched a meal eaten in prehistory brought the reality of archaeology home to a new public.

Tollund Man met his end naked save for a belt and small cap, unaccompanied by any grave offerings. Far different was the lot of the Anglo-Saxon leader buried

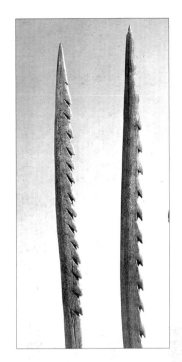

Some of the 187 barbed antler harpoons of the ninth millennium BC recovered from the mesolithic site of Star Carr.

Bog bodies

The peat bogs of northern Europe hold a grisly record of pre-historic times in the form of bog bodies, their skin, hair, finger-nails – even stubble and eyebrows – tanned and preserved by the acid waters: people who fell into the bogs and drowned, or more often were killed and thrown in intentionally.

The most famous such burial is Tollund Man, found in Denmark in 1950 and dating to the third century BC, a criminal or victim of ritual sacrifice who had been strangled and then cast into a bog. Analysis of his stomach contents revealed that his last meal had been a gruel containing barley, linseed, knotweed, dock and camomile, but no meat. This suggests that he had eaten gruel made from badly cleaned crops of barley and flax – crops in which the weed seeds had not been properly separated from the rest: just the sort of food one might expect to be fed to a prisoner destined for death.

'Traitors and deserters', commented the Roman historian Tacitus of the germanic tribes of the north 'are hanged on trees; cowards, shirkers and sodomites are pressed down under a wicker hurdle into the slimy mud of a bog'.

The number of bog burials recorded in Europe is considerable – Denmark has 166, Germany 215, the Netherlands 48 – though few have survived the circumstances of their discovery well enough to have ended up in museums. Britain and Ireland have yielded about 120, most notably Lindow Man, discovered in a Cheshire peat bog in 1984. He was around twenty-five when he was killed, probably in the first century AD, having been being struck twice violently on the head, garrotted, and finally having had his throat cut.

When Tollund Man was discovered, the techniques available meant that only the head could be fully preserved; through modern freeze-drying, Lindow Man has been conserved by the British Museum in his entirety.

Lindow Man, Britain's most recently discovered bog body, was recovered during commercial peat-cutting. One leg is missing, but the rest of the body, though distorted by pressure from above, is quite well preserved.

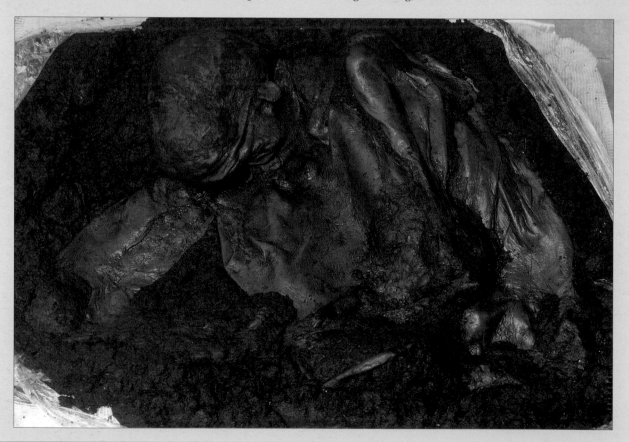

c. AD 625 in a barrow at Sutton Hoo, on the eastern coast of England – a discovery without which no account of European archaeology during these decades would be complete. Excavated by Cambridge archaeologist Charles Phillips in the shadow of war in 1939, Sutton Hoo proved to be both a ship burial and the richest archaeological find ever made in Britain. The ship itself had disappeared, but traces of its nailed, overlapping wooden planks were preserved, and from these the outline of the vessel could be reconstructed. Amidships lay the remains of the richly-furnished burial, complete with sword, shield and helmet, purse, a massive gold belt buckle, and cloak clasps decorated with blood-coloured garnet. There were also gold coins from France – one for each of the ship's phantom oarsmen – and silver dishes from as far away as Byzantium.

At Sutton Hoo – probably the burial of Raedwald of East Anglia, one of the early rulers of Anglo-Saxon England – it was careful techniques of excavation and recording that established archaeology not as the treasure hunt it would have been a century before, but as a controlled, scientific investigation of a unique discovery. In direct descent from Pitt-Rivers, Wheeler was the most influential British protagonist of scientific excavation between the wars. On the continent, however, his efforts were paralleled by German archaeologists who emphasized open area excavation: the stripping of large areas in their entirety to reveal the plans of buildings and other structures, and the spatial and chronological relations between them. This became a special feature of the German approach, intro-duced to Britain by Gerhard Bersu, a refugee from the Nazis in the 1930s, who demonstrated its effectiveness at Little Woodbury, an Iron Age farmstead of the fourth to second centuries BC which he dug in southern England in 1938–39.

Open area excavation was also influentially adopted by the Danish archaeologist Paul Nørlund in his excavations from 1934 at Trelleborg, a circular earthwork in southern Zealand; long the subject of historical and archaeological speculation, it proved to be a Viking military camp of the late tenth century AD. The large earthwork was obviously disciplined and symmetrical, divided into quadrants by four opposed gateways, but it came as a great surprise when Nørlund revealed the post-holes of bow-side timber barrack buildings within. The discovery threw a completely new light on the Viking period, dispelling the myth of disorderly barbaric armies and demon-strating that Viking Age Denmark was a centralized and organized state.

A comparable challenge to traditional prejudices about the barbarians – spawned, as we now see, by the partisan accounts left by classical and Early Christian writers – came from excavations in the 1950s at the early Iron Age fortress of the Heuneburg in southern Germany. This time the revelation concerned the Celts who occupied the 3 hectare (7.5 acre) site *c.* 600–500 BC. Defences had been recognized around the

Solid gold belt-buckle with interlaced animal ornament from the Sutton Hoo ship burial, Suffolk. Early seventh century AD. The design is picked out with a black inlay of niello (silver sulphide).

Measuring 13.2 centimetres (5 inches) long and weighing over 400 grams (14 ounces), the buckle ranks among the great masterpieces of European decorative art of all time.

triangular Heuneburg plateau, a bluff high above the Danube, in the late nineteenth century when excavations in neighbouring burial mounds unearthed bronze vessels and gold jewellery. However, it was not until 1950 that the first systematic excavation of the fortress began under the direction of Tübingen archaeologist Kurt Bittel. To his amazement, Bittel discovered that while the southern and eastern defences were of timber and rubble construction as he expected, on the long northwestern side there stood limestone footings for a wall of Mediterranean type, built of sun-dried mud brick and with a central gateway and square interval towers, ten in all. It was a defence recognizably Greek in inspiration, of a type otherwise unknown north of the Alps. Coupled with the discovery of Attic black-figure pottery and wine jars, it suggested that the ruler of the Heuneburg had close trading contacts with the Mediterranean world, perhaps through Massilia (modern Marseilles), a Greek colony at the mouth of the Rhône founded around 600 BC.

The Heuneburg data bore out other startling evidence of long-distance contact that had emerged immediately before the Second World War from the Hohmichele, a nearby burial mound 80 metres (260 feet) in diameter and 14 metres (45 feet) high. Here, in a timber burial chamber, lay the remains of a four-wheeled wagon accompanying a dead chieftain furnished with all the luxuries he needed in the afterlife: horse harness, bow and arrows, a bronze cauldron, and textiles embroidered with Chinese silk – the earliest documented occurrence in Europe.

Links between the Celts of the north and the eastern Mediterranean were demonstrated still more dramatically in 1953 in eastern France, when a modest stone cairn at Vix in Burgundy was excavated by a local schoolmaster, René Joffroy. It proved to be a princess's grave of the late sixth century BC, again containing a wagon, horse trappings and bronze bowls, but this time furnished in addition with jewellery, including a fine gold torc of Greek workmanship weighing a pound (450 grammes), Attic black-figure drinking cups and an Etruscan bronze wine flagon. Dominating the burial chamber was the prize exhibit, an enormous Greek *krater* (wine-mixing bowl), 160 centimetres (63 inches) in height. Decorated round the neck with an embossed frieze of Greek footsoldiers and chariots and topped by a lid bearing the statuette of a woman, it is the largest bronze vessel to have survived from the ancient world – probably a diplomatic gift to a powerful Celtic ruler.

STONE AGE PREHISTORY

In the first half of the twentieth century the palaeolithic sites of western Europe were intensively excavated. Bringing order to the past through chronology, typology and stratigraphy remained the key concerns, with little attention being paid at this time to what the finds meant in human terms. Digging techniques improved, but they remained unsophisticated by today's standards. Working fast, excavators noted only the more obvious layers, and in many cases collected only the bones of large mammals; scant attention was devoted to the relative positions of artifacts, and small bones and stone tool debris were often discarded.

One French pioneer far ahead of his time was Denis Peyrony, a schoolmaster who found the Magdalenian art of Font de Gaume in the Dordogne in 1901 (p. 124) and later became director of the National Museum of Prehistory in the village château at Les Eyzies. Digging stratigraphically, insisting on the near complete collection of artifacts a layer at a time, and with the benefit of many excavations behind him, Peyrony became the first to realise that among the distinctive stone tool industries of the Mousterian – the era of the Neandertals – were some that were clearly contemporary: a startling discovery at a time when each industry was assumed to be distinct in date and technology, and to follow its predecessor in a well-mannered sequence. He clarified the succession of industries in the Solutrean (c. 19,000–16,000 BC) and the Magdalenian (c. 16,000–10,000 BC), and through his work at the rock-shelters of La Ferrassie and Laugerie-Haute came to realize that the Aurignacian (c. 40,000–28,000 BC) was far less straightforward than Breuil had thought. Peyrony's solution was that it comprised two parallel developments, the Aurignacian and Perigordian cultures. In the 1930s at La Ferrassie, he also discovered the burials of two adult Neandertals and four children and babies, one of the graves associated with a rock pecked with cupmarks, a crucial example of very early 'art'.

While Peyrony was one of the first in Europe to publish plans of his sites – for example, at Le Fourneau du Diable (1932), showing post holes and stone arrangements – his understanding was limited by a reliance on small-scale digging: narrow cuts to bedrock that sampled a great many layers but left the wider context of any discovery unclear. The more suitable technique of horizontal, open area excavation, well established in Germany and eastern Europe and already in use in France for digging Roman sites and megalithic tombs, was not adopted for the Palaeolithic until well after the Second World War. The key postwar specialist, the stone-tool expert François Bordes, spoke for many when he acknowledged the suitability of the open area method for open-air sites with a single occupation level, but dismissed its value for caves and rock shelters like the ones he dug in the Dordogne; here, at sites like Pech de l'Azé and Combe-Grenal, he preferred to excavate in boxes of a square metre or less, only extending the area horizontally when some structure was encountered.

By the late 1950s palaeolithic excavations had become painstaking, large-scale dissections carried out by multi-disciplinary teams concerned with placing the occupants of a site in both biological and environmental context. The aim now was not so much to find objects as to solve problems: teasing out thin occupation layers, saving every artifact, and keeping representative samples of animal bones, pollen and sediments for laboratory analysis.

Typology – ordering stone tools in their proper evolutionary and chronological sequence – remained a fundamental preoccupation for specialists. The schemes devised by de Mortillet, Breuil and Peyrony classified tools primarily on the basis of shape: some labels referred to the object's assumed function (scraper or burin, for

Neanderthal male burial discovered in the Upper Palaeolithic rock-shelter of La Ferrassie, Dordogne, 1909. The bones lie in anatomical relation to each other, the knees drawn up to the chest, the head on one side.

Between 1909 and 1912, the fragmentary skeletons of four children, including a foetus and two newborn infants, were found at La Ferrassie, together with the complete skeletons of an adult male and female – presumably their parents. A seventh body, that of a child, was found at the site in later decades.

example), while others were simply descriptive (denticulate or laurel leaf). In other words, the inventories made of each tool 'assemblage' were catalogues that had no direct link with human activities. Assemblages – groups of related finds from a single layer or site – had their similarities and differences assessed, and they were then arranged into regional sequences that could be stylistically and chrono-logically correlated. The entire enterprise was based on the idea of *fossiles direc-teurs*: diagnostic tool-types – the archaeological equivalent of the type-fossils used by palaeontologists – selected as characteristic of each cultural tradition. In short, palaeolithic archaeology's origins in the natural sciences, and its geological frame of reference, led to artifacts being seen as 'fossils of history', comparable with those in the natural world. Indeed, it seemed to many that flints had come to be con-sidered as people, having their own evolution and producing hybrids, with little regard for the cultural context in which they were used.

By the 1950s, French palaeolithic specialists had evolved 'type-lists' that allowed large numbers of finds to be analyzed quantitatively. Classification according to the simple presence or absence of chosen 'type-fossils' was replaced by the study of whole assemblages of implements, and tools came to be defined more rigorously, not on the basis of shape but on their technique of manufacture. Simple cumulative diagrams showing the percentages of different tool-types in an assemblage could then be drawn up to facilitate comparisons between sites and between assemblages, with the differences and similarities presented visually.

Typology was also modified by experiments replicating stone tools, an occu-pation at which Bordes was expert, knapping razor sharp flints with enviable skill. His efforts won valuable insights into techniques of manufacture, and palaeolithic industries were shown to be far more complex than had been thought, with no orderly succession or correlation with environmental change. Far from being neatly descended in a single line one from another, flourishing traditions appeared to branch or peter out, more in the manner of a real family tree. Bordes was prompted in particular to redefine the Mousterian (c. 180,000–30,000 BC), rejecting the idea that it was a single, undifferentiated entity and dividing it into four distinct and overlapping traditions (characterized by differing types and percentages of tools) that he attributed to cultural and even ethnic differences – a theory hotly contested in later years (p. 289).

All the while, the discovery of new palaeolithic finds continued, the province still of amateurs as well as professionals. The cave excavations of Gustav Riek at Vogelherd in southwestern Germany in 1931 uncovered a remarkable series of Aurignacian ivory carvings of animals – including mammoth, bison and an exquisitely stylized horse – dating back at least 30,000 years and thus among the oldest such objects ever found. Equally memorable was the discovery in 1939 in a cave at Monte Circeo, south of Rome, of a Neandertal skull and jawbone, for decades mistakenly interpreted as evidence of ritual cannibalism. It now seems that the cave was a hyena den.

France yielded a whole series of Ice Age decorated caves of huge importance: in 1922 Pech Merle, with some sixty painted and engraved animal figures dating to c. 25,000–10,000 BC, including numerous mammoths and a famous panel of 'spotted' horses; and in 1923,

Lascaux

The French cave of Lascaux remains the most spectacular gallery of Ice Age art ever discovered. Located near Montignac, in the Dordogne, it was found in 1940 by four teenage boys exploring a hole they had discovered in the woods. Once deep inside, they lit a lamp and began to notice colour on the walls. What they had stumbled upon was an incredible collection of 600 paintings and nearly 1,500 engravings, preserved with astonishing clarity.

Lascaux's art is often thought of as a single composition of around 17,000 years ago, but it more probably comprises images of many different dates. The great 'Hall of Bulls' is dominated by four huge black bulls up to 5 metres (16 feet) long, the biggest figures known in palaeolithic art. The cave also has numerous horse and deer figures; and one narrow passage with paintings on its high walls and ceiling still preserves sockets that held wooden beams for scaffolding.

Lascaux was opened to the public in 1948, but ten years later it became obvious that the 100,000 annual visitors were damaging the art with their breath, body-heat and, especially, the algae and pollen carried in on their shoes. Green patches were growing and white crystals were forming on the walls. In 1963, the cave was closed. The algae were virtually

Down the 'shaft' at Lascaux. A disembowelled bison attacks an ithyphallic bird-headed man. Nearby is a bird on a stick. This may be a spearthrower – a simple device for hurling spears with added force.

eradicated and the crystals kept in check, but the public could never again be allowed in en masse. Instead a superb facsimile, Lascaux II, was opened nearby in 1983, a site that enthrals hundreds of thousands of visitors every year.

Montespan, in the Pyrenees, with engravings on the walls as well as clay statues and reliefs that include a sphinx-like bear over a metre (3.3 feet) long. Most famous of all, in the Free Zone of France during the German occupation, came Lascaux, the most richly decorated cave yet known anywhere in the world.

No rock art discovered in Spain in this period could rival the glories of Lascaux or Altamira. However, between 1929–31 at the Upper Palaeolithic cave of Parpalló on the coast of Valencia, Luis Pericot García carried out meticulous excavations that yielded scores of decorated bones, as well as over 5,000 small stone plaques engraved and painted with animal motifs including red deer, ibex and bovids. In the Basque country of the north, a tremendous programme of work began in 1916, dominated by José Miguel de Barandiarán, a Jesuit priest, Telesforo de Aranzadi, a physical anthropologist, and Enrique de Eguren, a geologist. Together they dug major sites such as Santimamiñe, an Upper Palaeolithic cave boasting a superb painted frieze of six bison and a horse. The Spanish Civil War of 1936 ended this work abruptly; when Franco's troops invaded the area, de Barandiarán had to flee by boat to the French side of the Pyrenees where he remained in exile until 1953.

ARCHAEOLOGY IN THE SERVICE OF THE STATE

Brought to a standstill by the Second World War, archaeology in Europe faltered for almost a decade. In the forces individuals continued to hone their skills in areas like aerial reconnaissance and discover through travel, to the long-term benefit of the subject, parts of the world – and languages – previously unknown to them. However, excavation came to a halt, with key figures like Wheeler returning to the army to command a tank battalion in north Africa. Museum collections were destroyed by bombing or looted, Schliemann's finds from Troy disappearing from Berlin in 1944 and only reappearing in Moscow fifty years later after the fall of the Soviet Union.

For all the destruction and disruption, western Europe was nonetheless spared the direct effects of the two major ideologies which, in the 1930s, had a brutalizing impact on archaeological discovery and thought in central and eastern Europe: Nazism in Germany and Stalinism in the Soviet Union.

The Party of the past

The impact of the October Revolution on archaeology in the Russian empire did not become apparent in Lenin's lifetime. The transformation accompanied the rise of Stalinism a decade later, a by-product of the first Five Year Plan, collectivization and 'dekulakization' – the liquidation of wealthier peasants as a class – in which at least six million people died. Archaeology – like all the historical and social sciences, and many areas of natural science also – was now at the service of the state.

With few exceptions, fieldwork in central and eastern Europe came to a halt with the First World War, in Russia a period also of two revolutions, devastating civil war and famine. Amid the civil conflict, during the spring of 1919, Lenin signed a decree establishing an organization to supersede the Imperial Archaeological Commission, which eventually became known as the State Academy for the History of Material Culture, or GAIMK (*Gosudarstvennaya Akademiya Istorii Material'noi Kul'tury*). Like its predecessor, it was located not in Moscow, but in St Petersburg (Petrograd, later Leningrad).

When excavation resumed in the 1920s, it initially followed the familiar path of pre-revolutionary archaeology. Work at Kostyonki was continued in 1922–23 by Pyotr Petrovich Efimenko, a palaeolithic specialist destined to play a major role in Soviet archaeology from the 1930s. During the period of Lenin's New Economic Policy (1921–28), which entailed a limited return to capitalism, the government did not interfere with the pursuit of archaeology, and considerable growth in regional archaeological organizations took place throughout Russia. The change came in 1928 with the first Five Year Plan, acceptance of which heralded the beginnings of industrialization and sweeping social and economic change. The following year, the Party seized control of the Academy of Sciences, dismissing or arresting members regarded as hostile to the regime, and attacked archaeology as a citadel of reaction and 'bourgeois science'. In the winter of 1929–30, regional organizations were shut down, and local archaeologists arrested by the secret police.

The Party exercised control through the GAIMK in Leningrad, making its director, Nikolai Yakovlevich Marr, the new head of Russian archaeology. Marr was not an archaeologist but a brilliant – if eccentric – linguist, who had established his reputation before 1917. One of the few prominent members of the Academy of Sciences enthusiastically to endorse the revolution from the outset, Marr was rewarded with the support of the Communist Party, of which he was now a member. He was among the first to denounce 'bourgeois science', calling for the reactionary field of archaeology to be swept away in favour of a 'history of material culture' based on Marxist principles.

With Marr's blessing, the ideological inititiative in Soviet archaeology passed in 1929 to Vladislav Iosifovich Ravdonikas. In an address called 'For a Marxist history of material culture', Ravdonikas took the first step in creating a revolutionary archaeology based on an explicitly Marxist history of material culture. A bitter debate ensued in which older archaeologists were vociferously condemned for their reactionary views, and taunted as 'Menshevik idealists' and 'bourgeois formalists'; some were arrested, and subsequently exiled or shot. With Leningrad triumphant, Vasili Alekseevich Gorodtsov, the most prominent archaeologist in Moscow, was dismissed from his post. Fieldwork almost ground to a standstill, and the pages of archaeological publications filled with polemical essays on theoretical issues. Contacts with foreign scholars and bourgeois archaeological literature from overseas were prohibited, and Russian researchers became increasingly isolated from the outside world.

Despite the strong central control Stalinism exerted, a modest amount of non-ideological archaeology continued even during this period. The Tsalka Archaeo-

Saddle cover of felt, leather, fur, hair and gold from Kurgan 1 at Pazyryk, showing an eagle-like gryphon attacking a mountain goat. The pendants at the edge are decorated with stylized rams' heads and horned tigers, and trimmed with horsehair dyed red. Fifth century BC.

The Siberian permafrost also preserved at Pazaryk a matchless array of organic materials: wood, leather, fur, horn, even silk. Pouches contained cheese, seeds, even hair and nail clippings apparently retained for magical purposes.

The presence at Pazyryk of flasks and goatskin bottles also recalls the horror Greek writers professed at the Scythian custom of drinking wine neat: for them, 'drinking the Scythian way' was merely a euphemism for getting blind drunk. As the poet Anacreon wrote in the sixth century BC:

Let us not again this evening
With our shouts and noisy uproar
Get ourselves as drunk as
    Scythians
Let's get moderately tipsy
And our best songs sing with
    fervour.

logical Expedition, for instance, conducted systematic research into the Bronze and Iron Age tombs of Georgia and the southern Caucasus between 1936 and 1940, presenting its excavation results in a wholly non-ideological framework, typical of the comparative, chronological approach archaeologists anywhere in the world would have taken at the time. It was during this period too that the extraordinary frozen tombs at Pazyryk in the Altai mountains of Siberia were excavated by Sergei Rudenko, first in 1929 and later in 1947–49. Renowned for the exceptional preservation of their contents – and some of the world's earliest evidence for gaming and cannabis smoking – the Pazyryk mounds, or *kurgans*, date from the sixth to the fourth centuries BC. Immediately after the burials, water seeped into the chambers and froze, preserving through permafrost the embalmed corpses, as well as some

5,000 objects, including clothes and footwear in leather, fur, wool, felt, even Chinese silk. In one kurgan, a wooden coffin contained the body of a man whose limbs and chest still bore tattoos of animals and fish; in another, within a burial chamber hung with decorated textiles, lay a wooden chariot and the carcasses of the horses that once pulled it, richly caparisoned with plumed headdresses and tasselled saddle cloths in bright colours. Excavated in the shadow of Stalinism, but among the most spectacular finds of the century, the Pazyryk kurgans probably belonged to nomadic chiefs related to the Scythians of southern Russia. The amazing finds they yielded are displayed in the Hermitage Museum, St Petersburg.

While the debate over Marxist archaeology raged in the early 1930s, a new east European archaeology began to take shape. Western goals and methods were rejected and the western emphasis on stratigraphy and typology was sharply criticized, especially among palaeolithic specialists. The Marxist goal was a history of material culture that avoided the western preoccupation with artifacts and sought instead to reconstruct the evolution of pre-capitalist societies in their entirety. This theoretical framework derived from the writings of Marx and Engels who, in turn, had drawn their ideas about 'primitive' or tribal societies from the anthropologists of their own era: the social evolutionists of the late nineteenth century, most notably the American Lewis Henry Morgan, who postulated a sequence of stages through which all societies were thought to evolve, from savagery, to barbarism, to civilization (p. 117).

Thinking big in the Soviet Union

The ambitious, if ultimately unrealizable, Soviet goal of reconstructing past society in its totality led to excavations on a hitherto unknown scale. Soviet archaeologists were the first to recover entire palaeolithic dwellings and complete neolithic villages, and expose great swathes of medieval towns. Throughout the 1930s they operated on a continental scale, recreating the cultural history not only of the Slavic-speaking republics but also of the Baltic region, the Caucasus, Central Asia and Siberia.

Excavations were extensive in number and immense in their horizontal exposures. Even today, archaeologists in the Soviet successor states tend to excavate far greater areas of a site than their western counterparts, depending less on statistical sampling and employing a more restricted range of laboratory techniques. It is not only the relative scarcity of statisticians, materials scientists, and environmentalists that determine modern excavation strategy; the manifold benefits of large-scale excavation also play their part.

The history of archaeological research in Central Asia well exemplifies the Soviet approach. Over the past ten years, excavations in Turkmenistan and Uzbekistan have uncovered an extensive but hitherto unknown Bronze Age culture dating to the late third/early second millennia BC, the 'Oxus civilization', named after the Oxus river near the present Afghan–Russian border. Major excavations on numerous sites have exposed acres of architecture, hundreds of burials and thousands of artifacts. Monumental buildings have been uncovered in their entirety, yielding statuary, distinctive seals, masses of metal-work and a veritable warehouse of complete pots.

Yet we know almost nothing of the environmental setting of the Oxus civilization, little about the plants and animals it exploited, and scarcely more about its stone, ceramic and metal technology. Western archaeologists are proud of their methods, their theoretical sophistication, and the scientific articles they write; Soviet archaeologists are proud of their excavations, the objects they discover, and the culture history they so prolifically present in their books. Clearly there is a great deal East and West could learn from each other.

CARL LAMBERG-KARLOVSKY

Palaeolithic specialists argued about how to apply the social evolutionary scheme to specific groups of archaeological remains, Efimenko and his student Pavel Iosifovich Boriskovskii eventually proving more convincing than Ravdonikas. Writing in 1932, Boriskovskii placed the revolutionary social transformation from 'humanity in its wild state' to the 'first defined social organization' at the beginning of the Upper Palaeolithic, a period we would now date *c.* 40,000 BC. Faithfully adhering to Morgan's writings, he identified this 'first defined social organization' as a clan society based on maternal descent, describing the transition from savagery as a 'dialectical leap' – an echo of collectivization and the ongoing upheaval in Soviet society – and denouncing as 'European bourgeois migrationists' western archaeologists who held opposing opinions. Such theoretical developments had a paradoxical effect. Soviet palaeolithic archaeologists surged decades ahead of their western European counterparts by paying more attention to society and economy, but they were left saddled with an outmoded interpretative framework derived from nineteenth-century anthropology that none dared modify or reject.

In the short-term, however, the strategic shift that now took place in Soviet archaeology – its avowed goal no longer material artifacts but the more slippery concepts of prehistoric society and economy – soon began to reap benefits. From the late 1920s, archaeologists began to expose extensive, horizontal areas of palaeolithic sites and record complex features such as 'living floors', pits and houses. While features like these were scarce further west, they were also a great deal harder to identify when they did occur because of the small scale on which caves and rock shelters were being dug.

In 1931–36, Efimenko uncovered at one of the Upper Palaeolithic sites of Kostyonki traces of a massive elongated structure that he identified as a 'longhouse': as much as 100 metres (330 feet) in length, it was marked by a linear arrangement of hearths surrounded by pits of various sizes. The longhouse was the type of structure most closely associated with matrilineal clan organization, as described by Morgan in his account of Iroquois Indian life, so for Efimenko the discovery validated the new Soviet theoretical framework. Discoveries of further palaeolithic 'longhouses' followed, by Boriskovskii in 1937–39 and then by other young Soviet archaeologists, but after the late 1930s, such discoveries ceased. Today, the reality of palaeolithic 'longhouses' remains unproven at best – more probably the result of ideological fervour than critical appraisal of the excavated remains.

The very real information obtained from the large-scale, horizontal excavation of east European open-air sites was, however, no more than minimally compromised by the occasional piece of disinformation. Other, more convincing, palaeolithic structures were encountered throughout the Soviet Union, the most memorable being the round shelters of mammoth bones and tusks subsequently discovered at Kostyonki, and at a number of east European sites. Central Europe itself was in general little affected by the ideological upheaval taking place further east, and competent excavations took place in increasing numbers. Particularly productive

were Karel Absolon's excavations in 1924–26 at Dolní Věstonice, an Upper Palaeolithic camp site on the Dyje river in Moravia, that yielded the famous 'Venus of
Vestonice', a masterly figurine of baked clay, just 11 centimetres (4.5 inches) high.
This was part of a growing body of portable art recovered from Upper Palaeolithic
sites in central and eastern Europe, following close on the heels of the first Kostyonki 'Venus' figurine, of mammoth ivory, found in 1923.

In 1935, the term 'archaeology', previously rejected for its western bourgeois
connotations, was formally reinstated at a meeting of the GAIMK. Theoretical discussions and shrill polemic ceased to dominate the archaeological literature and
fieldwork resumed on a large scale. After 1935, no archaeologists were arrested. The
period of revolutionary change came to a close, and the 'Marxist history of material
culture' evolved into a more stolid Soviet archaeology.

Cold War archaeology

Central and eastern Europe suffered immensely from the Second World War, Leningrad itself enduring a siege of two and a half years, the worst suffered by any
city in modern times, in which over a million people died. Museum collections
were destroyed, sites damaged, and archaeologists killed. In Poland, one in four

French prehistorian Count
Henri Bégouën (left) visiting
Karel Absolon at his excavations at Dolní Věstonice,
1928. They are examining a
collection of mammoth bones
that may have formed part
of a hut.

Opposite. 'Hitler's Stone-henge', probably the most comprehensive work of ersatz prehistory ever undertaken. Built on the orders of Heinrich Himmler in 1935, using slaves and forced labour, it constituted a huge megalithic monument to paganism at Sachsenhain at which Himmler could conduct solstice cere-monies with up to 10,000 followers.

The monument comprises 4,500 standing stones, aligned in double file to create avenues through woodland near the confluence of the rivers Weser and Aller at Verden, Lower Saxony. In places the avenues open out and the stones form circles.

The monument – intended to commemorate the 4,500 Saxon captives slaughtered at the site by the Christian emperor Charlemagne in AD 782 – was a gesture of defiance towards Christianity and a memorial to its pagan opponents.

prehistorians perished; and in Czechoslovakia, retreating German troops set fire in 1945 to Mikulov Castle, destroying collections from key Moravian sites like Předmostí.

The defeat of the Axis powers and the occupation of central Europe by Soviet armies brought to central Europe a new degree of political control. The communist regimes imposed after 1945 generally reorganized their research and educational institutions along the lines of the Soviet Union; though generously staffed and funded, academic institutions now came under the centralized control of the Party and archaeologists received training in Marxist theory.

Archaeology in central Europe fared relatively well in the post-war period be-cause its negligible political significance ensured minimal interference. Soviet influence to some extent shaped techniques and theory as well as organization and funding, but many new sites were discovered and excavated in this period in Poland, Czechoslovakia and Hungary. At Dolní Věstonice, large occupation areas were excavated for the first time in 1947–49, leading to the belated recognition of mammoth-bone dwellings.

In the Soviet Union, disputes about archaeological theory, dormant since 1935, revived suddenly with a spate of attacks on the work of Nikolai Marr. Since his death in 1934, Marr's work had continued to enjoy the approval of the political and academic establishment, but on 20 June 1950 Soviet citizens were startled to read in *Pravda* a denunciation by Josef Stalin himself. Universal condemnation of 'Mar-rism' by both linguists and archaeologists followed, Efimenko, for instance, in 1953 producing a new edition of his *Primeval Society* in which praise of Marr was re-placed by sharp criticism. At root a reflection of larger political trends and of the continuing struggle between Moscow and Leningrad, Marr's dethronement was unquestionably beneficial, liberating Soviet archaeology from many unwieldy notions imposed for political reasons. Because Stalin's denunciation originated among linguists and archaeologists in Moscow, the capital now regained control of Soviet archaeology. The Leningrad academy was reorganized as a branch of the Institute of the History of Material Culture in Moscow, and Ravdonikas was forced into retirement.

Nazi archaeology

The rise of National Socialism to the government of Germany in 1933 inaugurated the most discreditable episode in the entire history of archaeology: the closest connection ever between archaeologists and an extreme nationalist government. The prehistorians who let themselves be compromised were a mixture of disciples of the recently dead Kossinna (p. 136) and others, more cynical, who saw straight-forward career opportunities in the Thousand Year Reich. The central agencies that cultivated them were headed by Nazi ideologist Alfred Rosenberg and security-chief Heinrich Himmler, the *Reichsführer-SS* . Between 1933 and 1945, this unholy alliance brought about an extraordinary manipulation of the past for political ends.

Eight new professorial chairs in prehistory were established in Germany between 1933 and 1935, staffed largely by disciples of Kossinna, like Baron Bolko von
Richthofen in Königsberg. New popular journals such as *Heritage of the Germans*
were established, and films such as *The Flames of Prehistory* and *On the Trail of the
Eastern Germans* were made to celebrate German prehistory. Public money was
poured into archaeological research and the publication of finds; never before had
the study of the past enjoyed such official patronage. The aim of the exercise was to
establish both the antiquity of German settlement across a great swathe of the
continent and German superiority over the other peoples of Europe. While Kossinna had concentrated his attention on eastern and central Europe in the Iron Age,
attempts were made after his death in 1931 to show that German roots lay in neolithic times, perhaps even earlier, and that in this 'greater Germany' the Aryan
heritage ran as a pristine line over several millennia.

The first years of the Nazi regime saw many power struggles, and from these archaeology was not immune. Gerhard Bersu was sacked in 1935 as head of one of Germany's key archaeological institutions, the Römisch–Germanischen Kommission, for refusing to adhere to National Socialist ideology. Others were driven out on account of their Jewish ancestry. Of those archaeologists who remained silent, then and later, by no means all were co-opted by the Nazis; Kossinna's old adversary Carl Schuchhardt, worked quietly until his death, and many others maintained a low profile, avoiding political involvement. Yet as time passed and war grew closer, anything less than full-blooded involvement became increasingly difficult; by 1941, when Ernest Wahle, a student of Kossinna, put out a wartime critique of his old teacher's brand of 'settlement archaeology', dissent required considerable courage.

Within the Nazi party, internal power struggles eventually brought about a split in the official patronage for archaeology. On one side stood Rosenberg's propaganda office, the *Amt Rosenberg*, on the other Himmler's secret police headquarters, each man with his own agenda and ready to create organizations to carry out his goals. Rosenberg's main archaeological associate was Hans Reinerth, Kossinna's successor in Berlin, who headed the Confederation for German Prehistory, an agency established to make use of the past for political and patriotic ends. In his *Prehistory of the German Races* (1940), Reinerth wrote of German genetic superiority and the right of the modern German state to usurp any territory on which Germans had once lived. Like Kossinna, but now with the sinister backing of the Nazi state, he also made strident personal attacks on colleagues with whom he disagreed.

Eventually, Rosenberg and Reinerth proved so inept that most German archaeologists wanting official support turned to Himmler instead. Under Himmler, the *Schutzstaffel*, the secret police, had become a 'state within a state' that viewed the promotion of the German heritage as one of its key priorities. In 1935, to promote these interests further, Himmler established a completely new agency, the *SS-Ahnenerbe* (Ancestral Inheritance), a monument to Nazi bureaucracy replete with innumerable sections and subsections covering almost all the historical sciences, from philology and the humanities to geology and ethnography. Somewhere in all this was a mystic version of archaeology. While Rosenberg was interested in pursuing his racial theories, Himmler's instincts tended more towards the romantic and the occult, treating the German past as part of an all-embracing national creed with its roots in racial identity. The SS-Ahnenerbe sponsored large, well-funded, professional excavations, like those at the Hohmichele burial mound (p. 206) and at Haithabu in Schleswig-Holstein, a Viking trading centre with rich graves of *c.* 800–1050 and wooden buildings exceptionally preserved by waterlogging. It published monographs promoting German superiority through archaeology. Himmler also placed archaeologists, including Alexander Langsdorff and Werner Buttler, on his personal staff.

While the Second World War brought most archaeological research in Germany to a close, it also led to excavations in occupied territories. In Russia, for example, an *SS-Sonderkommando* unit was charged in 1942–43 with recovering prehistoric 'Germanic' remains in southern Russia and the Caucasus. Nazi archaeologists also took over museums in Poland and Czechoslovakia and reorganized the collections to reflect their own ideology. The new management of the museum in Łódź (Litzmannstadt during the occupation) 'evacuated' to Germany coin hoards and Bronze and Iron Age artifacts that have never been seen since, as well as the Biała urn, a local find of the third century AD, picked out because it was decorated with swastikas – an emblem with its origins deep in prehistory.

Major excavations

During the 1920s and 1930s, agrarian eastern Europe tried to catch up with the industrial age. Agricultural mechanization threatened buried remains and the earthmoving associated with new roads, railways and factories uncovered previously unknown sites. The result was that much emergency excavation took place in less than ideal conditions. Against this background, the period also saw 'big site' excavations involving the large-scale, horizontal stripping of key sites over months or even years. With an increased emphasis on how people lived, worked and fed themselves in the past, the logic of such excavations – geared to finding buildings and evidence of daily life rather than objects – became compelling. In the 1930s particularly, large excavations were used in both central and eastern Europe to provide unemployment relief.

Two of these great excavations, Köln-Lindenthal and Biskupin, had particular impact. At Köln-Lindenthal, discovered while landscaping a park on the outskirts of Cologne in 1928, the layout of an early farming village was revealed for the first time. In excavations by Werner Buttler in 1931–34, over one hundred workmen removed the topsoil from long trenches in which the archaeological features were then planned and meticulously dug. In the first year alone, over 21,000 square metres (5.2 acres) were exposed, revealing a complex, intercutting mass of rectangular timber buildings and large, irregular pits, partly enclosed by a ditch and wooden palisade. The 65 pits were interpreted as 'pithouses', the 40 buildings – regular patterns of five rows of postholes that once held vertical wall posts – as 'granaries': an interpretation strengthened in 1932 when the enter-prising Buttler went gathering 'ethnographic material from settlements peopled by primitive peasants in modern Europe', and found examples of semi-underground dwellings and post-built granaries in Hungary, Romania and Yugoslavia.

By the time excavation at Köln-Lindenthal was complete in 1934, a hitherto unimaginable 3 hectares (7.4 acres) had been dug within a site measuring 180 by 220 metres (590 by 720 feet). The recording of the finds and planning were exceptional for their time, and the monumental site report offered all the detail that specialists could want. Yet a fundamental problem remained. Buttler persisted in interpreting the pits as houses and the post-built buildings as granaries, in defiance of all common sense: as workmen digging a comparable site in Poland at around the same time remarked, 'If they had to live in slippery muddy holes, they'd break their legs'. Only after the Second World War did it become recognized that rectangular wooden 'longhouses' were typical of early neolithic sites and represented the habitations. The pits were no more than sources of mud plaster for the walls.

Nothing detracts from the skill and originality with which Buttler dug Köln-Lindenthal, a site that set new standards of excavation and publication. His instinctive condescension to the 'primitive peasants' of prehistory and of his own day nonetheless reflects a darker side. He joined the Nazi party in 1930, working subsequently on Himmler's general staff before taking up a professorship in Göttingen in 1938. In 1940 he was killed in action in France.

At Biskupin in central Poland, the key figure was Józef Kostrzewski, the first professor of archaeology at Poznań. From the mid-1920s, the Polish patriot Kostrzewski found himself in conflict with extreme German nationalist archaeologists such as von Richtofen, who rejected the view that the area between the Oder and Vistula was 'primeval Polish land'. Discovered in 1933, Biskupin proved critical in this debate because it fell chronologically into the late Bronze and early Iron Age, an era crucial for deciding whether the prehistoric inhabitants of the Oder–Vistula area were more 'German' or more 'Slav'.

Investigating the supposed 'roofs of inundated houses' seen amid the reeds on a lake peninsula at Biskupin, Kostrzewski found the piles of a wooden breakwater. By the following year, after exposing 500 square metres (600 square yards) of the site, he knew he was dealing with a considerable island settlement of the fifth and sixth centuries BC enclosed by a wood and earth rampart and a breakwater. A perimeter road ran within the rampart and from this parallel streets, surfaced with logs, cut across the settlement. Along the streets lay thirteen rows of houses – over one

Biskupin's principal timber gateway, reconstructed for modern visitors on the basis of the excavations of 1934–8. Elaborate timber-laced ramparts of box-construction encircle this early Iron Age settlement, a perimeter road for access immediately inside. Until the site was abandoned *c.* 400 BC, the interior contained over 100 houses laid out in regimented fashion along cross-streets of timber corduroy.

hundred buildings in all. Each contained a large room with a hearth and a smaller room with sleeping quarters; a small antechamber for storage stood by the entrance. Specialists were brought in. An army balloon was used to take photographs of the site from heights of up to 150 metres (500 feet), and botanists, zoologists and geo-morphologists arrived to analyze the rich organic finds and sediments. Biskupin also became the subject of one of the first films ever made about an excavation.

Kostrzewski believed that the inhabitants of Biskupin were ethnic Slavs, a view that incensed his German opponents but came to be widely publicized in Poland on account of the scale and exceptional preservation of the settlement, and the level of public interest it generated. The waterlogged conditions meant that an extra-ordinary range of wooden and bone artifacts were found, including ploughs, carts, dug-out canoes, looms, ladders, ladles and awls. And for the first time in eastern Europe, environment and economy were scientifically investigated, revealing the existence of wheat and other crops, and a range of domestic animals.

Polish excavations ended with the outbreak of the Second World War. Kostr-zewski fled underground and the Nazis took over, in 1940–42 putting the SS in charge of new investigations. Kostrzewski had concluded that Biskupin had been abandoned because of flooding, but SS archaeologists maintained, predictably under the circumstances, that its inhabitants had fled because of the 'violent southward expansion' of Germanic invaders of manifest military and physical superiority. After the war, the political connotations of the site at last faded, though excavations continued under the aegis of the Polish communist regime until the early 1950s. Biskupin was now developed as an archaeological tourist attraction, drawing busloads of Polish schoolchildren and increasing numbers of foreign tourists each year, its rampart, streets and some of its houses reconstructed in their original positions.

The same tradition of large-scale excavation continued in eastern Europe throughout the 1950s and 1960s, notably at Karanovo in southern Bulgaria and at Bylany in Bohemia. The tell at Karanovo was itself massive: over 12 metres (40 feet) high and up to 250 metres (820 feet) wide. Excavations by Georgi Georgiev from 1947 revealed seven periods of occupation spanning the period *c.* 6000–3000 BC – even today a key sequence for understanding the transition from the Neolithic to the early Bronze Age in the Balkans. Though extensive, Bylany was less massive. A neolithic settlement of the same early 'linear pottery' period as Köln-Lindenthal, it was revealed by deep ploughing in 1952 and dug by Bohumil Soudský between 1954 and 1967. It covered an enormous area: 85 hectares (210 acres), of which over 8 per cent was fully excavated. As in Dutch sites in the same period, large areas were exposed simultaneously, allowing individual groups of houses to be studied *in situ* in their entirety; in all, over one hundred houses were revealed and as many as 25 settlement phases identified. Like Köln-Lindenthal, it set a trend: the stripping of large areas henceforth became standard when excavating early agricultural set-tlements anywhere in eastern and central Europe.

THE RISE OF RADIOCARBON DATING

Radiocarbon dating has been the most significant development in twentieth-century archaeology, its revolutionary impact far more profound that of any discovery or ideological innovation. In providing an absolute age for organic materials like wood, charcoal and bone often found sealed in archaeological deposits, it released archaeologists from having to spend so much time organizing and dating their material. New ideas could now be pursued and more important questions asked.

Willard F. Libby (1908–80), the inventor of radiocarbon dating.

During the Second World War Libby undertook atom bomb research at Columbia University, New York, working on the separation of isotopes of uranium and studying cosmic radiation – the sub-atomic particles that constantly bombard the earth, producing high-energy neutrons.

The technique was refined after the war at Chicago University, where Libby was professor of chemistry 1945–54, and the first actual dates appeared in 1949. Over the next decade the immense potential of radiocarbon for archaeology throughout the world fast became apparent.

In 1959 Libby moved to the University of California, Los Angeles, and in the following year he was awarded the Nobel Prize for chemistry.

Developments in the years since have only served to emphasize the scale of Libby's achievement. The technique has been used to date relics of the past as disparate as the Avebury stone circle and the cave paintings of Altamira, the Turin Shroud and Lindow Man. Radiocarbon laboratories exist across the world and a single grain of wheat is today enough to provide a reliable date.

The radiocarbon technique was announced in 1949 by Willard Libby, a University of Chicago scientist interested in cosmic radiation and its effects on the earth's environment; archaeologists quickly realized its potential and Libby won a Nobel Prize. As a direct dating method, it can be used on any organic object and, theoretically at least, can provide dates up to 80,000 years old. Carbon 14 (14C) is a radioactive isotope, produced in the atmosphere, that is absorbed by plants during photosynthesis and passed on to the animals that feed on those plants, or indeed on other animals. All living things contain 14C. Because the isotope is unstable, it decays at a known rate, with a half-life of 5,730 years (in other words, half of the isotope is lost over that period). In living organisms, any 14C lost is replaced and the amount remains constant; but at death no more 14C is absorbed and the amount declines. As the rate of loss is known, Libby realized that he could measure how long ago an organism died by determining how much 14C was left.

Radiocarbon dating was an earth-shaking innovation for archaeology, but its impact from the outset has been much greater in the United States and western Europe than further east. Since the technique was a product of atomic bomb research, archaeologists in eastern Europe have always been particularly poorly served: although the first radiocarbon laboratory behind the Iron Curtain was inaugurated in Leningrad in 1955, it was not until 1961 that the East Berlin laboratory systematically began to date large numbers of samples. If access to western laboratories was wanted, hard currency or connections were required – both thin on the ground during the Cold War. More important still, eastern Europe was a region that had made a tremendous intellectual investment in artifact typology as a means of dating. For every major synthesis published in the west by a Schuchhardt or a Childe, there were hundreds of fine-tunings of regional pottery sequences and other diagnostic artifacts. Absolute dating therefore tended to be viewed as ancillary, even irrelevant, to the practice of archaeology.

Predictably therefore, the most sustained resistance to radiocarbon came from central and eastern Europe, most famously from the Heidelberg prehistorian Vladimir Milojčić. His monumental and meticulously documented book, *The Chronology of the Later Stone Age in Central and Southeastern Europe* (1949), rested on the then widely-accepted premise that the great late neolithic tell at Vinča, near Belgrade, excavated in 1908–12 (p. 132), was an outpost of Aegean early Bronze Age civilization – a harbinger of the copper and bronze metallurgy soon to sweep Europe. This belief lent support to Montelius' 'short chronology' for later European prehistory; through Vinča, Milojčić argued, innumerable central European cultures could be tied to an Aegean sequence underpinned by sound, historically documented dates.

However, it soon became clear that something was adrift. Some of the first radiocarbon dates in the 1950s came from Dutch early neolithic sites, which if the 'short chronology' were correct should have been dated *c.* 3,000 BC. In fact, they emerged over a thousand years older – a dating soon achieved so consistently that

Gordon Childe

Vere Gordon Childe (1892–1957) was one of the most influential archaeologists of the twentieth century. A lifelong socialist, whose earliest passion was the Australian Labour Party, he was born in Sydney, moving as a young man to England, where he took up archaeology. He eventually became professor of archaeology at Edinburgh (1927–46), and later director of London University's Institute of Archaeology (1946–56). Companionable, but an eccentric and profoundly lonely man, Childe returned to Australia on retirement, committing suicide soon after by throwing himself off a cliff in the Blue Mountains near his birthplace. A poignant note he left for publication spoke of his frustration at no longer being able to work effectively and his wish to avoid becoming a burden on society in old age.

Childe's archaeological renown stems from his fascination with big questions, such as the origins of agriculture and the rise of cities and civilizations, processes he named the 'Neolithic Revolution' and 'Urban Revolution' respectively. He argued that in three areas – Mesopotamia, the Nile and the Indus valley – surplus wealth grew faster than population, spawning cities. Population growth in these cities then brought about the creation of class-based political systems, whose élites were underpinned by their control of surplus wealth and the existence of agricultural irrigation systems that alone could feed growing urban populations.

It was Childe too who developed and popularized the concept of an archaeological 'culture', defined by him as a set of artifacts, restricted to a particular time and place, that appeared to be the archaeological manifestation of a distinct people or ethnic group. This notion had existed in Europe for more than twenty years (p. 135), but it was Childe who systematically defined and applied the concept, above all in *The Dawn of European Civilization* (1925). Variations in the compositions of cultures at different times and in different places were, he believed, due to contacts with other cultures – diffusion – or the migrations of people into new areas.

Childe's steadfast commitment to this view of culture was reflected in an insistence that social change in prehistoric Europe was caused essentially by diffusion, by way of the Danube, from the civilizations of the eastern Mediterranean. Over time, however, his belief in diffusion as the engine of cultural change was tempered by an increasing awareness of the importance of internal economic forces within societies – a position that became more solidly Marxist after his first visit to the Soviet Union in 1935.

Childe disliked being described as a Marxist prehistorian and the degree to which he embraced Marxism has been

Gordon Childe and teddy bear, a gift from students at Brno University, Czechoslovakia.

vigorously debated by his biographers. In the view of many, he failed to reconcile his commitment to Marxist materialism and simple, unilinear evolution with his emphasis on diffusion as the driving force of prehistoric social change.

What is clear is that Childe did not adopt a consistent Marxist framework: he chose rather to bring it to the fore in some books – like *Man Makes Himself* (1936) and *What Happened in History* (1942) – and push it into the background in others. Writings from his last two decades display little Marxist influence at all.

Although Childe's commitment to the politics of the left was sincere, he was, as conservative archaeologists pointed out, not at all above enjoying the creature comforts of the establishment. He was a member of the Athenaeum and seemed to enjoy his reputation as the 'Red Professor'. One, perhaps apocryphal, story relates to Childe's habit of conspicuously reading the communist newspaper, *The Daily Worker*, over breakfast at archaeological conferences; hidden behind its pages, the true object of his attention, was the right-wing, establishment paper, *The Daily Telegraph*.

One serious deficiency in Childe's work was his disdain for the prehistory and archaeology of certain regions beyond Europe, notably the Americas, that he did not believe were in the mainstream of human culture history. In other areas, the

changing world around him necessarily brought about a retreat. His early works were concerned with trying to understand the origins of the Indo-Europeans, and some of his conclusions in *The Aryans* (1926) were frankly racist; he successfully repudiated this position in later books.

Never a prolific or willing fieldworker – the neolithic stone-built village of Skara Brae in Orkney is his best known excavation – Childe is more justly famous for his massive syntheses of European archaeology, as well as some lively popular books. His interest in eastern Europe can be seen in his earliest work before the First World War. He made his first trip to the Danube valley in 1922, visiting sites and museums in Austria, Hungary and Czechoslovakia, and was to return to these regions many times in the years he spent preparing *The Dawn of European Civilization* and *The Danube in Prehistory* (1929), the latter a working through of his view of the transmission of culture from the Near East, through the Balkans, to northwestern Europe.

At the time, eastern Europe was *terra incognita*; for the genteel archaeologists of the west, the languages were unreadable and the travelling conditions unappealing.

Childe's encyclopedic knowledge of the archaeological literature was made possible by his ability to develop a reading knowledge of most central European languages. If enviable, the skills he acquired were workmanlike at best. His grammatical errors with place-names show that he was far from proficient and his pronunciation was apparently awful: he insisted in speaking to foreign archaeologists in their own languages, with frequently comic results.

Skara Brae, Orkney: Childe's best known excavation, *c.* 3100–2500 BC. Beyond the well preserved central hearth of House 7 is a stone 'dresser', on either side stone box-beds. Cupboard recesses are apparent in the walls.

Lasting twelve days, Childe's first visit to the Soviet Union was undertaken at a time when archaeology was just beginning to emerge from the Marrist purges of the early 1930s. Aarne Tallgren, a Finnish archaeologist who made the journey around the same time, wrote of these purges and was never allowed back. Childe took a more accommodating view, visiting the Soviet Union three more times after the Second World War, and becoming involved in the 1950s with the Society for Cultural Relations with the USSR, a Soviet 'front' organization.

In part at least, it seems to have been a pose. Childe was a man who enjoyed showing off his familiarity with things eastern European, right down to the gratuitous writing of Russian names in Cyrillic in his correspondence.

Childe did much to stimulate interest in the archaeology of central and eastern Europe among British and American archaeologists – an interest now burgeoning with the end of the Cold War. Since the 1960s his diffusionist notions have been overturned by new evidence for the independent origins of agriculture, trade and social stratification in prehistoric Europe. Yet his two major works of the 1920s, familiarly known as *Dawn* and *Danube*, endure still as archaeological classics despite the flood of new finds in the intervening decades.

Opposite. The Athenian agora, one of the triumphs of twentieth-century urban excavation.

Laid out around 600 BC, this great public square endured as the social, commercial and political heart of the ancient city until the sack of Athens by the Slavs in AD 582/3.

In Rome, the imperial forum was never lost to view, its battered principal buildings surviving throughout the Middle Ages. In Athens, the situation was very different.

For three years after the American excavations began in 1931, even the precise location of the agora remained unknown. Today over a hundred buildings have been identified and 180,000 objects – stored in the reconstructed 115-metre (375-foot) long Stoa of Attalos on the right – have been recovered.

it became clear that either the radiocarbon technique itself was flawed or the 'short chronology' was too short. Western Europe put its faith in radiocarbon and began to re-examine its archaeological data and chronologies. Further east there was consternation: some, like Milojčić, rejected the radiocarbon method, pitching in with some well-aimed thrusts at its early shortcomings; others simply chose to ignore it.

It was not until the 1960s, especially when the East Berlin laboratory began to date numerous samples from the Balkans and eastern Europe, that support for the 'short chronology' faded away. Vinča was shown to predate the Aegean early Bronze Age – specifically early Troy – by at least a millennium, its early bronze metallurgy evidently developed locally rather than borrowed from the eastern Mediterranean. Milojčić's scepticism long endured but most other archaeologists working in central and eastern Europe were quickly converted by the weight of the radiocarbon evidence to accept the new, 'longer' chronology. By 1970, the validity of the method was established to the satisfaction of almost all.

BIG PROJECTS IN THE CLASSICAL WORLD

Classical archaeology in the mid-twentieth century was characterized both by a renewed emphasis on 'connoisseurship' – the cataloguing and classification of material in museums – and by an increasing number of large-scale field projects designed to investigate the urban life and political institutions of the ancient world. Two campaigns of central importance were begun between the wars: the American excavations on the Athenian *agora* and the exploration of the Roman cities of North Africa, most notably Leptis Magna and Sabratha.

Athens had been the focus for work on classical Greece ever since the Greek War of Independence, but only piecemeal investigations had been made north of the akropolis, where lay the agora, the political and commercial heart of the classical city. The building of the Athens–Peiraeus railway in 1890–91 threw some light on the site but only in 1922, with the expulsion of large numbers of Anatolian Greeks who had been living in the area, was a decision made to excavate systematically rather than develop the area for housing. Funded by Rockefeller oil money, the American School of Classical Studies excavated from 1931 to 1940, resuming work after the Second World War.

Exposing so large an area, so central to the life of the ancient city, proved just as successful as had been predicted. The buildings of the agora were arranged around a central open space, rather in the manner of Manhattan around Central Park – albeit not so packed. Many have been identified thanks to the descriptions left by the ever-useful Pausanias who made his own tour of the site in the second century AD. Along the western side, beneath the Doric temple of Hephaistos (long known as the Theseion), lay the buildings where democracy itself was created: the square Bouleuterion, or Council House, of *c.* 500 BC, tiered seating for the five hundred senators who met daily to consider new legislation making up three sides of the

chamber. Elsewhere have been identified the lawcourts, committee rooms, even –
tentatively – the prison where Sokrates drank hemlock in 399 BC. So important was
the area that it continued to attract buildings well into Roman times. A concert hall,
the Odeion of Agrippa, was erected, the huge 25 metre (82 foot) span of its audi-
torium seating a thousand people. Augustus even seems to have moved to the agora
a fifth-century BC temple originally located in the Attic countryside to serve as a
focus for the imperial cult.

In 1952–6, to house the American School's finds and records, a colonnaded two-
storeyed building on the eastern side of the agora, destroyed in AD 267, was
reconstructed at full size; this was the Stoa, the original of which was given to the
city more than two millennia earlier by Attalos II (159–138 BC), king of Pergamum.

Across the Mediterranean on the North African littoral, it was the Italian
occupation of Libya in the 1930s rather than American oil wealth that prompted the
archaeological investigation of many well preserved classical buildings. Cyrene,
Leptis Magna and Sabratha were extensively excavated, the fine ruins that were
revealed serving as supposed historical justification for Mussolini's right to occupy
the region. Originally founded before *c.* 600 BC, Leptis was deemed particularly
important as the birthplace of the great military emperor Septimius Severus
(AD 193–211). Severan benefactions to the city included new public baths – the

Greek pots and potters

In the area of connoisseurship, the most notable work in classical archaeology undertaken in this period was by the Oxford art historian Sir John Beazley (1885–1970), a pioneer in classifying pots by identifying the anonymous artists who painted them.

Beazley's aim was to wring information from the large collections of Greek pots formed by Hamilton and others that had found their way into European museums like the British Museum and Louvre. It was not easy to make sense of such material: stylistically it was held to fall into no more than broad groups, meaninglessly classified as 'severe' or 'decadent'. However, German scholars had noted that some pots carried short inscriptions, including what appeared to be 'signatures': short texts giving the name of an artist followed by a verb, *epoiesen* or *egraphsen*, words taken to mean 'made by' or 'painted by'. This allowed a rudimentary categorization to be developed purely on the basis of signed works.

It was by identifying the unconscious details of individual artists – the way they portrayed eyes or chest muscles or chariot wheels – that Beazley changed the way ancient ceramics were perceived. He was able to add 'unsigned' pieces to the 'signed' corpus, and in time identify painters who never provided a signature, giving them names relating to features of style ('Elbows out'), the museum in which the pot resided ('Berlin painter'), the present or former proprietor ('Lewis painter'), or a key feature in one of the scenes ('Pig painter'). In this way tens of thousands of Attic black- and red-figure pots were grouped as the work of individual artisans.

Other categories of material have since been treated to the same sort of analysis. Beazley himself categorized Etruscan pots in this way, and Corinthian, East Greek and South Italian ceramics are now frequently attributed to anonymous painters by scholars using the same approach. Some have even attempted to extend Beazley's method to the exquisite Cycladic marble figurines of the third millennium BC, grouping known examples by 'artists' named after the collections in which they now reside. Because most were looted, unrecorded, from burials, names like the 'Goulandris master' have to stand in for any more precise attribution.

John Beazley was the son of a member of the Arts and Crafts movement, so it is little surprise that he wished, like Ruskin and William Morris, to celebrate craftsmen of an earlier era who produced masterpieces working in a humble medium. Yet Arts and Crafts values are not necessarily those of fifth-century Athenians or Capuans. Beazley's achievement in bringing order and dating to an unruly body of material was outstanding but, ever the connoisseur, he left no methodology that others could follow. We can appreciate the art better for his work but his 'artists', frustratingly, remain shadowy figures we can never know.

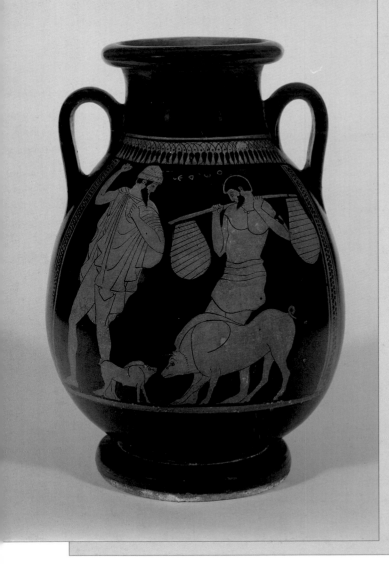

The Attic red-figured wine-flask that provided the name for Beazley's 'Pig painter'. The rural scene of two men, a pig and a piglet is popularly thought to represent Odysseus (left) and the swineherd Eumaios. On Odysseus' return from the Trojan War, it was Eumaios who helped drive from his palace the suitors of his wife Penelope. About 470–460 BC.

miraculously preserved 'Hunting Baths', so named from their stucco decoration – a forum and basilica complex, as well as a triumphal arch. Inscriptions on the marble imported to Leptis showing that it was specially selected for the city led to a major research programme on the Roman marble trade, work which continues today with isotopic analysis designed to reveal the identity of the principal quarries.

The end of the Second World War saw the removal of the Italians from Libya and new work undertaken under the aegis of a British protectorate. Notable projects included the first stratigraphic excavations at Sabratha in Tripolitania by the British archaeologist Kathleen Kenyon, revealing substantial remains of Roman civic and religious buildings.

THE MYCENAEANS STRIKE BACK

In 1905 Arthur Evans presented a chronological classification of the Bronze Age on Crete based on his excavations at Knossos. He defined three main periods – Early, Middle and Late Minoan – each subdivided into three phases. His model was the Old, Middle and New Kingdoms in Egypt which provided the absolute dates. For mainland Greece, a comparable chronology was devised in 1916–18 by Alan Wace and Carl Blegen, the three periods being designated Early, Middle and Late Helladic. Blegen was then Secretary of the American School of Classical Studies in Athens. His excavations at the prehistoric site of Korakou in the Corinthia in 1915–16 had produced the pottery sequence which formed the basis of the Helladic chronology. Subsequently he explored a number of Bronze Age sites in the Argolid. Wace, Director of the British School at Athens, had excavated in Laconia and Thessaly but would soon begin his meticulous analysis of the architectural history of Mycenae. In 1921–23 and 1939–55 he dated the construction of the fortifications, examined the palace, and excavated numerous houses and tombs.

Wace and Blegen soon became convinced that 'though Minoan in origin, the Mycenaean civilization is not merely transported from Crete, but is the fruit of the cultivated Cretan graft set on the wild stock of the mainland'. Arthur Evans, however, believed that the Minoans had conquered or colonized Greece; the Minoan civilization had been transplanted onto the mainland. The seeds of a fierce academic dispute had been sown. The suggestion that Mycenaean influence could be detected at Knossos greatly upset the Cretan faction.

Before this controversy could be resolved, Blegen had taken up the challenge of Troy, re-establishing its status as a key Aegean and Anatolian site. Schliemann and Dörpfeld had removed most of the mound but a number of untouched sections survived. In 1932–38 Blegen tested these and refined the site's stratigraphy, demonstrating that each of the nine 'cities' comprised a series of levels which spanned the Bronze Age. No excavator of Troy could ignore Homer, however. Blegen decided that Troy VI, which Dörpfeld had identified as the Homeric city, was destroyed by an earthquake. The period he called Troy VIIA seemed a much more plausible candidate: here, the houses were crammed together and had dozens of jars set in the floors, apparently an indication that the settlement was threatened by siege; the presence of skeletons implied that Troy had been sacked. Blegen therefore concluded:

> It can no longer be doubted, when one surveys the state of our knowledge, that there really was an actual historical Trojan War in which a coalition of Achaeans, or Mycenaeans, under a king whose overlordship was recognised, fought against the people of Troy and their allies.

He should have known that the doubts would not be dispelled. Excavations at Troy have recently resumed but Homer remains as elusive as ever.

In 1939 Blegen was in Greece once more: because king Nestor of Pylos was one of the most powerful Greek chiefs at Troy, he was convinced that a major Mycenaean centre existed in Messenia. Of eight possibilities identified by pottery during fieldwork, he chose the one where 'if you were a Mycenaean king, you would build a palace'. Excavating on the hill of Epano Englianos, even before lunch on the first day he had discovered substantial stone walls, fragments of fresco and inscribed clay tablets. His assumption that this was a Mycenaean palace proved correct although, because of the war, the excavation could not be completed until 1966.

Except in reconstructions, Pylos is not as spectacular as Mycenae or Tiryns, but it is much better preserved and was more carefully excavated. The presence of reception rooms, domestic apartments, magazines for oil and wine, archive rooms and a shrine recalls Minoan palaces, and this impression is not dispelled by the

The Mycenaean palace of Pylos, Messenia, *c.* **1300– 1200 BC. This reconstruction of the ornate throne room shows its columns, central hearth, throne and frescoes depicting mythological beasts; entry from the outer courtyard was through the monumental doorway on the right.**

Though ashlar-faced externally, the walls were constructed principally of timber and rubble. Floors, ceilings and interior walls were plastered and richly painted, the walls with frescoes drawing on both Mycenaean and Minoan motifs.

The Decipherment of Linear B

The sophistication of the civilization revealed by Schliemann had convinced Evans that the Mycenaeans must have been literate. On his travels in Crete he acquired engraved seal-stones, but it was when he commenced excavations at Knossos in 1900 that his assumption was proved correct. Evans discovered thousands of clay tablets, baked hard by the terrible fire that had destroyed the palace. Their study revealed that three different scripts in succession had been used at Knossos. From the early palace came documents in Cretan Hieroglyphic. This was replaced by Linear A, in turn superseded by Linear B, in use at the time Knossos went up in flames. Hieroglyphic and Linear A texts subsequently appeared on other sites in Crete, but Linear B proved to be the script used in the palaces of Mycenaean Greece.

Some of the signs incised on the tablets were obviously numerals and the scribes had also used pictograms, which could often be identified. So it was clear that most of these documents were the administrative records of the palace bureaucracy. Nevertheless the scripts defied decipherment despite furious assaults launched by successive waves of frustrated scholars. Hieroglyphic and Linear A have still not succumbed.

Linear B, however, was deciphered by Michael Ventris in 1952. An architect rather than an archaeologist, Ventris' interest in the Aegean had been fired when, as a fourteen-year-old, he heard a lecture by Sir Arthur Evans. In 1940, when just eighteen, he wrote an article arguing that the language of the scripts was Etruscan. After the war Ventris resumed his study of Linear B. Yet, writing in 1951, although he notes 'the remote possibility that the Knossos and Pylos tablets are actually written in Greek', he adds 'I feel that what we have seen so far of Minoan forms makes this unlikely'. It was not until June 1952 that Ventris seriously considered that the language might be Greek. He soon became convinced that he had broken the code. He enlisted the aid of a Cambridge philologist, John Chadwick, and together they published an article setting out details of what they had discovered.

Not everyone was convinced, but Blegen luckily tried out the new decipherment on a Linear B tablet he had discovered the previous summer at Pylos – a tablet that Ventris had never seen. The fact that he could read most of the tablet and confirm the identity of a number of the words through picto-grams persuaded Blegen, and in due course most scholars, that the decipherment must be fundamentally correct.

Not every Mycenaean text could at once be translated, of course; the decoding process had only just begun. The Linear B tablets themselves were just scratchpads – temporary notes

Linear B tablet, thirteenth century BC.

that would eventually have been destroyed; the scribes must have used a medium like papyrus for permanent records. This explains why no diplomatic treaties or letters are preserved in the archives. The texts nevertheless reveal unequivocally that the last rulers of Minoan Knossos were Mycenaean Greeks who controlled much of Crete. They throw particular light on a Mycenaean state economy whose bureaucratic complexity could never have been guessed at. The palaces supported a highly specialized workforce whose supply of raw materials and finished products was carefully monitored. These were no cottage industries: Knossos owned over 100,000 sheep bred for wool, while at Pylos four hundred bronzesmiths were dependent on the palace. The scribes even listed gifts offered to the gods, recording for us the names of their deities. The gods themselves were evidently unimpressed for the palaces were destroyed soon after the tablets were written.

Chadwick continues to work on Linear B to this day, though Michael Ventris died tragically young in a car accident in 1956. He had transformed Aegean archaeology.

frescoes that decorate the main rooms. Yet a glance at the plan of Pylos reveals the fundamentally Greek character of Mycenaean palaces: Wace and Blegen had accurately diagnosed the limited extent of Minoan influence on Mycenaean Greece. The decipherment of Linear B in 1952 provided the proof.

OUTSIDE EUROPE: THE PALAEOLITHIC PAST

In Africa, the first professional archaeologists were mainly interested in the Stone Age and in drawing up dated sequences of stone tools that could be compared with those in Europe. The hope was to trace the migrations of people and the diffusion of technology from Europe, seen at this time as the source of all knowledge and innovation. The need for local rather than European terminology was, however,

Olorgesailie in southern Kenya, one of the most important Acheulian sites in Africa, discovered by Mary and Louis Leakey in 1942. Dated *c.* 900,000–700,000 BC, the site has produced thousands of handaxes, cleavers and other artifacts.

appreciated by John Goodwin, who with C. van Riet Lowe, a civil engineer turned public relations man for archaeology, devised a simple Earlier/Middle/Later classification for the southern African Stone Age in their *Stone Age Cultures of South Africa* (1929). In East Africa, Louis Leakey began excavating in the Central Rift valley in 1926, and by 1929 had succeeded in framing a cultural sequence that remained in use until the 1970s, and survives in part today.

Exploration of the palaeolithic sites of western Asia began tentatively with surface fieldwork in the Levant before the First World War, but it was only in the 1920s and 1930s that significant excavations were undertaken, notably by the Cambridge prehistorian Dorothy Garrod at Shuqbah in Judea, where she revealed the Natufian, a late palaeolithic culture that played a major role in the origins of agriculture. In an early triumph for women in archaeology, she collaborated in 1929–34 with the animal bone expert Dorothea Bate in work at two cave sites, Tabun and el Wad, near Jaffa (Haifa) in the Mount Carmel area of Palestine.

Along with contemporary work at nearby Es-Skhul, these excavations laid one of the foundations of world palaeolithic archaeology. Garrod documented a long sequence of chipped stone industries from the Lower Palaeolithic to the beginning of the Neolithic, a span of more than 200,000 years. In form and technique the Mount Carmel finds showed many similarities with palaeolithic stone tools of western Europe, so Garrod categorized them using French terms like 'Acheulean', 'Mousterian' and 'Aurignacian'. Bate's faunal work was equally important. In addition to describing the animals that prehistoric people ate, she tried to understand the changing pleistocene climate to link Mount Carmel with the better-known framework of climatic change in western Europe, and so help date their discoveries. She examined the changing proportions of fallow deer to gazelle, arguing that high proportions of fallow deer reflected a more wooded landscape and therefore a wetter climate, while high proportions of gazelle implied open steppe vegetation and a drier climate.

Just as importantly, Tabun and Es-Skhul yielded the remains of eleven Neandertals and early modern humans. These were not the first such finds to be discovered in Palestine: the cave of Zouttiyah, near the Sea of Galilee, produced a Neandertal in association with Mousterian stone tools in 1925, and in the early 1930s early human fossils were found at Qafzeh, a cave near Nazareth. Yet the Mt Carmel specimens were intentionally buried flexed, in the foetal position, a very human reaction to death. Analysis at the time suggested that the bones belonged to a biological population 'in the throes of evolutionary change', since they displayed classic Neandertal features like heavy brow ridges mixed with modern human characteristics like a chin and higher forehead. They are specimens that even today play a key role in the debate about the origins of modern humans.

Complementary to the work at Mount Carmel in the 1930s were the meticulous German excavations of Albrecht Rust at Jabrud, near Damascus. Garrod, in common with others working in the Levant before the Second World War, classified her

Dorothy Garrod (1892–1968) shortly before her excavation, at the Devil's Tower rock-shelter, Gibraltar, in 1925–6.

The discovery of a stratified Neandertal child's skull in deposits that had earlier yielded Mousterian flints launched a career as a palaeolithic archaeologist that subsequently saw her excavating in Palestine, Lebanon, Kurdistan, Bulgaria and France.

In 1939 she became Disney Professor of Archaeology at Cambridge, the first woman professor at either Oxford or Cambridge. She was, wrote Glyn Daniel, one of her successors, 'a person of great integrity, a skilled excavator and an intrepid field worker'.

Opposite. Shanidar cave, Iraq, as Solecki's team uncover the Neandertal skull known as Shanidar I from beneath an ancient rock fall more than 4 metres (14 feet) below the cave floor.

Subsequent examination of the arthritic skeleton in the laboratory produced startling results. The right arm was so withered that the whole arm was crippled – evidence that more than 50,000 years ago a handicapped Neandertal who was unable to hunt could survive because others helped him.

The back part of the same individual's skull seems also to have been distorted by deliberate deformation in childhood, perhaps achieved by the anthropologically documented practice of tight binding with hard pads or bandages. Another possible explanation might be the carriage of loads using a head-strap, a practice well known in Kenya among the Kikuyu.

In addition, observed Solecki, 'We were puzzled by the marked worn character of the upper and lower front teeth … The likelihood is that this individual used his teeth to supplement his one good arm. We are reminded of the Eskimos, who used their teeth extensively in leather working.'

finds within the established palaeolithic sequence for western Europe. After the war, with Jabrud's publication, a reassessment was needed. Rust identified two chipped stone industries, placed at the end of the Lower and start of the Middle Palaeolithic, which Garrod had not identified at Mount Carmel and which did not correspond with any stage in the European sequence. Prompted to re-analyse the Tabun material, Garrod now discovered both industries, one showing such striking technological and typological similarities to Aurignacian blade industries of the Upper Palaeolithic that she named it 'Pre-Aurignacian'. As the 'Pre-Aurignacian' was dated over 50,000 years earlier than the Aurignacian proper, a hot debate sprang up over its significance.

In the 1960s, Moshe Stekelis threw remarkable new light on the earliest human occupation of the Levant when he dug at 'Ubaidiyah in the Jordan valley, recovering stone chopping tools, crudely fashioned by sharpening one edge of a natural pebble, that strongly resembled the very early stone tools found at East African sites like Olduvai Gorge, as well as animal bones and handaxes and tools made from simple flakes. The kinds of animals found suggest that the site may be as old as 1.4 million years.

In central Asia, palaeolithic archaeology developed more slowly than in other parts of the Near East. The breakthrough came in the 1950s when the American Ralph Solecki dug in Iraq at Shanidar cave in the foothills of the Zagros mountains. He identified broad similarities – though also significant differences in detail – between the palaeolithic in the Zagros and in the Levant, and discovered Neandertal burials in association with a Middle Palaeolithic flake industry. Study of the skeletons revealed that one of the Neandertals had in life survived a crushing blow to the side of his face, had lost the use of one arm and could not have fended for himself, yet lived to a respectable age – presumably sustained by family support. Another, as pollen in the grave fill suggested, had been interred with garlands of flowers. Impressed by this evidence of humanity, and with a nod to the popular culture of his time, Solecki gave the title *Shanidar. The First Flower People* (1971) to the popular account of his work.

In South Asia, the existence of palaeolithic culture had been established by pioneers like Foote in the nineteenth century, but dating remained unclear until systematic investigation of the geological context of palaeolithic tools began in the 1930s. A joint Yale–Cambridge expedition to the Potwar plateau in the north Indian Punjab identified pebble tool industries that could be placed in rough chronological sequence by their occurrence in successive gravel terraces and loess deposits along the Soan river. By correlating the Soan geological succession with episodes in the pleistocene glaciation in Kashmir that appeared to match the four phases of Alpine glaciation then known in Europe, the team was able to assign rough dates to the stone tools.

Palaeolithic archaeology in the Near East and South Asia concentrated until the 1950s, as it did in Europe, on caves with thick deposits of natural sediments and a

Opposite. Skulls of early modern *Homo sapiens* from Zhoukoudian, near Beijing (above, *c*. 28–18,000 BC) and from Předmostí, Czech Republic (below, *c*. 24,000 BC).

Debate still rages as to whether the Chinese specimens are descended from local populations of *Homo erectus* or from a population of modern humans who left Africa within the past 100,000 years.

The occurrence together at Zhoukoudian of *Homo erectus* remains and over 100,000 stone tools – mostly flakes, scrapers and choppers – makes the site one of exceptional significance, even though many of the best fossils, including fourteen skulls, were lost in unexplained circumstances at the beginning of the Second World War.

The site is complex, a maze of limestone caves with sediments so hard they often need loosening with pneumatic drills. Layers of ash from fires and the bones of deer, elephant, horse and water buffalo indicate that the caves were occupied extensively by early humans around 700,000–500,000 years ago.

In all, the remains of more than forty *Homo erectus* skeletons have now been found.

sequence of human occupation levels. Substantial layers corresponding to thousands of years of sporadic occupation were dug as a unit – often over a metre (39 inches) deep. Their tool industries were then characterized, not by the totality of the assemblage but by technique and the presence or absence of individual types such as handaxes. From the 1950s, accelerating thereafter, the standards of palaeolithic research became markedly more sophisticated. Bordes applied his Middle Palaeolithic typology to the analysis of complete tool assemblages from Mousterian sites in the Levant, and his approach soon became standard, maintained for chipped stone industries to the present day, across the world and for sites of all periods.

Equally important for twentieth-century understanding of the Palaeolithic has been the Far East, a region at the forefront of controversy about the evolution both of stone tool industries and of human beings – from our ancestral hominid species, *Homo erectus*, to modern humankind, *Homo sapiens sapiens*. In particular, the discovery of the world's largest group of *Homo erectus* fossils – more than forty individuals found at Zhoukoudian in northern China from 1929 – has generated a mass of new enquiries into the origins of humankind itself.

Homo erectus was first discovered in southeastern Asia in 1891 by a young Dutch doctor, Eugène Dubois, a man convinced that 'the fossilized precursors of man' would be found in Asia because 'all apes – and notably the anthropoid apes – are inhabitants of the tropics, and since man's fore-runners, as they gradually lost their coat of hair, must certainly have continued to live in warm regions …' Working in a hospital in the Dutch colony of Indonesia from 1887, Dubois spent his spare time searching the caves of Java. A fossil dug out of a marble quarry by local workers was his first 'discovery'. Thereafter he undertook his own dry-season excavations in the gravels of the Solo river at Trinil, where in 1890–92 he had the good fortune to find what he was seeking: the skull cap, femur and two molars of an ape-like man – a true 'missing link'.

In 1894 Dubois formally announced the discovery of *Pithecanthropus erectus* ('upright ape-man'), a transitional form between man and ape. Rapidly dubbed 'Java Man', *Pithecanthropus* soon became established across the world as the progenitor of humans. Finds proliferated in the years that followed: *Sinanthropus, Homo pekinensis* or 'Peking Man'; *Homo modjokertensis* or the 'Modjokerto Child'; *Homo soloensis* or 'Solo Man'; *Meganthropus*; and 'Wadjak Man'. All these Far Eastern fossils are now regarded as belonging to *Homo erectus*, a single species of early humans with stocky, muscular bodies, heavy faces with thick brow-ridges, and larger brains (*c*. 900–1225 millilitres) than their more remote predecessors. Far Eastern *Homo erectus* fossils are also central to the contemporary debate about how modern humans, *Homo sapiens sapiens*, emerged. Impressed by recent genetic research, many scholars envisage the worldwide replacement of *Homo erectus* by a new species that emanated from Africa and southwest Asia between 120,000 and 40,000 years ago – the so-called 'Eve' or 'Out of Africa' hypothesis (p. 324). However, some biological anthropologists familiar with Far Eastern fossil humans reject this replacement theory because of evidence for local evolution that has been observed in China. They see fossil finds like Maba Man and Liuchang Man, both from southern China, as transitional to modern humans, much like the Neandertals in the west, indicating normal evolutionary processes at work and regional continuity of population.

In the Far East, as elsewhere in the world, stone tools make up a larger part of the archaeological record than fossils. First to describe its palaeolithic assemblages systematically was the Harvard prehistorian, Hallam L. Movius Jr., who found them characterized 'by the presence of an overwhelmingly high proportion of core implements of the chopper, chopping-tool and hand-adze varieties, associated with plain, unprepared flakes and nuclei'. Movius coined the term 'chopper-chopping-tool tradition' for the stone tools of Asia north and east of the Indian subcontinent, a tradition he contrasted with those of western Asia, Africa and Europe, all of which featured distinctively well-worked handaxes.

Wanting both handaxes and refined flaking techniques, the Asian tradition of stone tool making was for decades treated as clumsy and unsophisticated, a poor relative of the traditions that prevailed elsewhere in the world. This condescending judgement has recently been rebutted. 'Handaxes', albeit crudely made, are known from several east Asian sites – particularly Chongok-ri in Korea – and it is agreed that in the east more Stone Age skills and labour were probably invested in bamboo or wooden tools than in elaborate handaxe flaking. On the Chinese mainland, at least two major stone tool traditions with a predominance of either heavy core or small flake tools appear to be specialized toolkits adapted to different sets of ecological resources.

The number and range of palaeolithic finds made in East Asia in the twentieth century vary markedly from country to country. Almost all fossil remains come from the karst areas of China: limestone terrain where chemical weathering formed caves and sinkholes that not only invited palaeolithic occupation but protected human fossils and occupation levels from subsequent erosion. In Japan by contrast, no bones can survive in the acidic volcanic soil. Most Early Palaeolithic tools also come from China. Japan, however, is rich in Late Palaeolithic sites, with over 2,000 now known; in China, only a few hundred palaeolithic sites are recorded in total; in Korea, only scores.

THE GOLDEN AGE OF EGYPTOLOGY

The period between the two world wars saw intensive archaeological work in Egypt. At Deir el-Medina near Thebes, excavations by Bernard Bruyère in 1922–51 brought vividly to life the village of the workmen who built the royal tombs of the Valley of the Kings during the New Kingdom (1550–1070 BC). Its documents of everyday life – many no more than brief notes scratched on potsherds or flat flakes of limestone – reveal a high degree of literacy and offer innumerable insights into such apparently modern concerns as personal relationships, disagreements between neighbours and problems in the workplace. Some documents are cheerfully salacious, as between lovers: 'If you come back drunk/and lie upon your bed/ I will rub your feet/and the children – shall hide behind the gate.' Others are plain angry.

> To Scribe Nekhenmut. Why are you falling into bad behaviour? Nobody's words penetrate your ears except your aggressive conceit. You are not a human being. You do not make your wife pregnant like other men. You are very, very rich but you do not give anything to anybody.

Bruyère needed light-railway wagons to shift huge quantities of rubble from the site, uncovering streets and over 70 houses as well as the 3000-year-old tombs of workmen and their families. Deir el-Medina in this way became one of the most richly documented communities of the ancient Near East.

Yet for the public at large archaeology in Egypt was still fuelled by death, gold and pharaohs – a perception now strengthened by two of the richest archaeological discoveries ever made: the royal burials at Tanis in the Nile delta, discovered in 1939; and the intact tomb of the boy king Tutankhamen (c. 1343–1325 BC), excavated by Howard Carter in the full glare of worldwide publicity between 1922 and 1928.

Tanis (San el-Hagar), the largest and most important archaeological site in the delta, had already been explored by Petrie (who planned the temples) and Mariette (who uncovered important royal sculptures of the Middle Kingdom) when the French Egyptologist Pierre Montet began work in 1928. Excavating within the precincts of the Temple of Amun in the period leading up to the Second World War, Montet was able to show the importance of Tanis as the seat of kings of the Twenty-First and Twenty-Second Dynasties (c. 1070–715 BC). The most dramatic phase of the work began in February 1939 when he discovered a deep shaft running down into what proved to be a stone-built tomb of four chambers. Inside, undisturbed, within a great sarcophagus of red granite, lay the burial of Psusennes I (1031–991 BC). Inside the sarcophagus was a coffin of black granite, re-used from an earlier era and already more than two hundred years old at the time the pharaoh died; and within that, a silver and gold inner coffin containing the decayed royal mummy, a fine gold mask over the face. Not far away lay the burials of Psusennes' wife, his son and successor, Amenemope (993–984 BC) and the later pharaoh Shoshenq II

Opposite. Pierre Montet (1885–1966) with the funerary mask of the pharaoh Psusennes I (1039–991 BC). Inlaid with lapis lazuli and black and white glass, it is made of sheet gold less than a millimetre thick.

Psusennes' richly-furnished tomb was intact when excavated in 1939, the only pharaonic tomb ever discovered wholly undisturbed. In addition to the pharaoh's own grave goods, the tomb contained those of one of his generals, Wendjebauendjedet; of his son and successor, Amenemope, buried nearby in a chamber originally prepared for his mother; and of the hitherto unknown pharaoh, Shoshenq II.

Among the richest finds were some thirty gold and silver vessels – bowls, dishes, goblets, flasks and pans.

(*c*. 890 BC), again provided with a gold funerary mask and encased in a falcon-headed silver coffin. Rich jewellery, including gold bracelets, pectorals and collars were also found.

Tanis, like Deir el-Medina, Tutankhamen's tomb and nearly all the other archaeological excavations taking place in Egypt at the time were still in the hands of foreigners. Only with the revolution of 1952 did this pattern slowly begin to change. This point is made with particular clarity if one looks at Nubia, the arid border area south of Aswan that lies today beneath the waters of Lake Nasser. As the height of the Aswan Dam rose in stages between 1902 and 1970, the rescue work undertaken to salvage sites soon to be submerged was largely in the hands of westerners. The American George Reisner inaugurated the First Nubian Archaeological Survey (1907–11), drawing on help from Philadelphia and Oxford, while the Second Nubian Survey (1929–34) was directed by two British-based archaeologists, Walter Emery and Leslie Kirwan. Only with the third and most dramatic raising of the dam (1960–70) did Nubian rescue work become at least notionally international, passing into the hands of UNESCO (p. 310).

For Egyptian archaeologists, the first notable triumph came just two years after the revolution, in May 1954, when Kamal el Mallakh of the Egyptian Antiquities Service, uncovered a stone-slabbed pit at the foot of the Great Pyramid which had been sealed to the air for more than 4,800 years. 'I closed my eyes,' wrote Mallakh

Tutankhamen and the glint of gold

For Howard Carter the discovery of the tomb of Tutankhamen was the culmination of a thirty-year obsession with ancient Egypt; his life was never to be the same again.

The son of an impoverished Norfolk animal painter, Carter (1874–1939) was an outstanding excavator and draughts-man, but a solitary, irascible man of little formal education. Dependent for much of his career on aristocratic patrons,

Howard Carter crouching at the doors of the second of the three shrines that enclosed Tutankhamen's mummy and sarcophagus.

The seals had remained unbroken for over 3000 years. With him are his assistant, 'Pecky' Callender, and an Egyptian foreman.

he began work as an artist at the age of seventeen copy-ing paintings on the walls of the rock-cut tombs at Beni Hassan for the pioneer British Egyptologist Francis Llewellyn Griffith. A year later he had his first taste of excavation under the direction of Flinders Petrie, appropriately enough at el-Amarna, the short-lived capital founded in upper Egypt by Tutankamen's probable father, the heretic pharaoh Akhenaten (d. 1337 BC).

In 1899 Carter was made Inspector-General of Monu-ments of Upper Egypt, an important new post in the Egyptian Antiquities Service. A similar appointment in Lower Egypt followed, but he was not to retain this post for long: in 1905 a brawl at the burial ground of Saqqara near Memphis between drunken French tourists and Antiquities Service guards ended with Carter ejecting the tourists by force. Affronted, they demanded an apology through the French consul in Cairo; Carter, with characteristic obstinacy, refused to provide one and resigned.

An experienced Egyptologist with negligible employment prospects, Carter was now lucky enough to meet George Herbert, fifth earl of Carnarvon (1866–1923), a languid and immensely rich English aristocrat whose early love of race-horses and fast cars had given way in middle age to an equal passion for archaeology. Carnarvon had dug in a small way at Thebes in 1907, but soon realised that he needed a profes-sional archaeologist like Carter to provide his work with credi-bility and technical direction. For five years (1907–11) Carter and Carnarvon together excavated in the private cemeteries on the west bank of the Nile at Thebes, extending their work to the Nile delta in 1912–13.

The delta excavations proved disappointing, so the acquis-ition in 1914 of one of the most sought-after excavating concessions in Egypt, that of the Valley of the Kings, was doubly welcome. Carter began work in the valley in 1915–16 by clearing the known tombs of Amenhotep III and Hatch-epsut, but by 1917 his activities were focused on the search for just one tomb, that of Tutankhamen.

Since no burial place was known, Carter concluded that the pharaoh's hidden and probably unrobbed tomb must exist somewhere nearby. Five barren years later anyone less cussedly determined and less well funded would have given up the search, but Carter persuaded Carnarvon to continue the concession for just one more season, offering to pay for the work himself if need be. He wanted to investigate the only remaining undug area on the floor of the valley, a small triangle in front of the tomb of Ramesses VI, left until then so as not to disrupt tourist access to the tomb.

The excavation season began on 1 November 1922. Three days later, beneath ancient workmens' huts, Carter found the first rock-cut step leading down to Tutankhamen's tomb; the following day he located the plastered blocking to the entrance and wired Carnarvon in England to announce his discovery – a sensation soon to grab headlines the world over. Finally, on 26 November, Carter, accompanied now by Carnarvon, broke into the tomb and gazed into the antechamber – one of the great moments in the history of archaeology.

> At first I could see nothing, the hot air escaping from the chamber causing the candle to flicker, but presently, as my eyes grew accustomed to the light, details of the room emerged slowly from the mist, strange animals, statues, and gold – everywhere the glint of gold. For the moment – an eternity it must have seemed to the others standing by – I was struck dumb with amazement, and when Lord Carnarvon, unable to stand the suspense any longer, inquired anxiously 'Can you see anything?', it was all I could do to get out the words 'Yes, wonderful things'.

More wonderful things were to follow for the antechamber was just one of four principal rooms heaped, as Carnarvon wrote, with 'beds, boxes and every conceivable thing'. The burial chamber itself proved to contain the mummy of the pharaoh encased in three coffins, the innermost of solid gold, as well as a massive quartzite sarcophagus and three shrines of gilded wood, one inside another.

Once the initial sensation had died down, Carter was left with the problem of how to deal with so stupendous a find. Money – some £36,000 – came from Carnarvon and an exclusive, though politically maladroit, newspaper deal with *The Times* of London. Carter was also able to put together a formidable team of specialists from museums around the world, notably the photographer Harry Burton from the Metropolitan Museum in New York, and from Cairo the chemist and conservator Alfred Lucas, who set up a field laboratory in the empty tomb of Seti II nearby. Slowly the work of recording, conserving, and removing to Cairo the thousands of objects from the tomb got under way. It was a task that occupied Carter and his team for the next ten years.

Within weeks of disturbing the tomb, on 5 April 1923, Lord Carnarvon died in Cairo of pneumonia following a septic mosquito bite. The legend of 'the curse of Tutankhamen' was born. Carter himself died peacefully some sixteen years later in his elegant London apartment close to Hyde Park, his retirement in England lonely and dogged by illness but his status in the archaeological pantheon secure for all time.

Linen-shrouded jackal, symbolising the god Anubis, guarding the entrance to the Treasury. Behind lies the gilded shrine that contained Tutankhamen's viscera.

later. 'And then with my eyes closed, I smelt incense, a very holy, holy, holy smell. I smelt time … I smelt centuries … I smelt history. And then I was sure that the boat was there.' It proved to be a perfectly preserved funeral boat of the pharaoh Khufu himself (2551–2528 BC), disassembled into 1,224 pieces of timber laid in thirteen layers, together with ropes, baskets and matting. Reconstructed over sixteen years by the restorer Ahmed Youssef Moustafa, as it is shown today in a specially-built museum on the site, the ship measures 44 metres (143 feet) long, with a beam of 6 metres (19 feet). Carrying six pairs of oars 6.5–8.5 metres (21–28 feet) long, and a pilot's cabin amidships, it displaces 45 tonnes. Another similar boat-pit alongside remains undisturbed, sealed by its line of massive limestone blocks for the archaeologists of the future.

THE SUMERIANS

The Near East saw an explosion of archaeological work in the two decades between the World Wars. Well-funded, long-term excavations made discoveries that caught public attention with an excitement unmatched since the early days of Layard and Botta. More popular archaeological books appeared than ever before, particularly from the pen of Leonard Woolley, a colourful and energetic writer who published several popular accounts of his work at Ur of the Chaldees and the riches of its royal cemetery, as well as a famous introduction to archaeology, *Digging up the Past* (1930).

Behind its public face, archaeology began to shift its attention away from the fine art of temples and palaces in favour of a broader view of life in the ancient world. At sites like Ur, expeditions managed for the first time both to expose large sections

of ancient cities and to trace variations in the city plan over time, revealing successive phases of prosperity and retrenchment. The new ability to cope with mud brick, developed at Babylon before the war, allowed properly stratigraphic excavations that could detect the changing styles of pottery and other household artifacts. Archaeologists rapidly determined the succession of pottery styles in different regions, sequences they used in the era before radiocarbon dating as a measure of relative age; with some, this even became a preoccupation, the stratigraphic sequence of pottery and other artifacts from many an excavation becoming its most significant result.

As the technical literature focused increasingly on pottery and its date, archaeology became less accessible to the lay person. The detective story writer Agatha Christie, who often accompanied her husband Max Mallowan during his archaeological work in Syria, made a character in *Murder in Mesopotamia* (1963) complain that archaeology seemed to be more about pottery than about the people that made it. In *Come, tell me how you live* (1946), she poked affectionate fun at her husband's obsession and at academic archaeologists in general:

> He said: 'I look for aged pots
> Of prehistoric days,
> And then I measure them in lots
> And lots of ways.
> And then (like you) I start to write,
> My words are twice as long
> As yours, and far more erudite.
> They prove my colleagues wrong!'

It was Leonard Woolley's Anglo-American expedition to Ur of the Chaldees that did more than any other excavation in the inter-war period to blow the academic dust off archaeology and excite a wider public. Woolley worked at Ur in the deep south of Mesopotamia from 1922 until 1934, winning a new understanding of the Sumerians and building up a comprehensive picture of the city's history from its prehistoric beginnings nearly seven thousand years ago to its final abandonment around the time of Christ. The technical publication of the site, filling ten fat volumes, was a triumph equal to Woolley's much-reprinted popular account, *Ur of the Chaldees* (1929).

The royal cemetery at Ur was Woolley's most memorable discovery, yielding one of the most spectacular treasures in the history of archaeology. The ancient inhabitants of the city for half a millennium had buried their dead in rubbish deposits filling an open space near the great ziggurat, or temple-tower. Woolley found 2,500 burials in this cemetery. Most lacked lavish grave goods, with only a few pots and everyday objects to accompany the body. Others held greater riches like copper tools and weapons, and imported stone jewellery. The few fantastically rich graves – the tombs of the Early Dynastic royal house of Ur – were contained in

Opposite. The so-called 'Standard of Ur', originally the sound box of a lyre, recovered by Woolley from the royal tombs in 1927–8. In the lower two panels, Sumerian infantry drive naked enemy prisoners before them, solid-wheeled chariots drawn by onagers bringing up the rear. In the top panel, the king receives the prisoners, his own empty chariot held by a dwarf-like groom. Dated *c* 2600–2500 BC, the mosaic is made up of engraved figures of mother-of-pearl set against a background of lapis lazuli.

Woolley wrote 'The wooden background had perished entirely, and the tiny pieces of inlay, though they kept their relative positions in the soil, were all quite loose … So delicate was the task of removing the dirt without further disturbing the mosaic that only about a square inch could be dealt with at a time – each section was waxed as soon as cleared, but so much of the surrounding dirt mingled with the hot wax that the face of the panel became invisible. When at last it could be lifted from the earth, I knew that we had found a very fine thing, but should have been hard put to say exactly what it was.'

sunken stone chambers with vaulted roofs, approached down a steep ramp cut into the earth.

Some of the royal tombs had been robbed of their contents in antiquity, but still held things of beauty and historical importance, like the Standard of Ur, a panel inlaid with mother-of-pearl and lapis lazuli. Others contained finely crafted gold and silver vessels and jewellery, an electrum helmet, weapons, lyres ornamented with golden bull heads and inlaid scenes of animals playing music, figures of rams caught in thickets, gaming boards inlaid with mother-of-pearl and precious stones, cylinder seals, cosmetic containers of shell and stone, and many other riches.

Still more dramatic were the funeral ceremonies that accompanied the royal burials. Woolley described what he found in *The Sumerians* (1928):

> The burial of the kings was accompanied by human sacrifice on a lavish scale, the bottom of the grave pit being crowded with the bodies of men and women who seemed to have been brought down here and butchered where they stood. In one grave the soldiers of the guard, wearing copper helmets and carrying spears, lie at the foot of the steep ramp that led down into the grave; against the end of the tomb chamber are nine ladies of the court with elaborate golden head-dresses; in front of the entrance are drawn up two heavy four-wheeled carts with three bullocks harnessed to each other, and the driver's bones lie in the carts and grooms are by the heads of the animals.

Another burial contained 68 female and six male attendants, still decked out in their court finery. Calling this the 'death pit', Woolley remarked that 'the sight of the remains of the victims is gruesome enough with the gold leaves and the coloured beads lying thick on the crushed and broken skulls, but in excavating a great death-pit such as that of last winter we do not see it as a whole, but have to clear it a little at a time'.

The royal cemetery greatly enhanced our understanding of the Sumerians of the third millennium BC. Yet although Woolley uncovered temples and common houses of later periods, including an entire residential district of the time of Hammurabi in the early second millennium BC, he was less successful at finding the Early Dynastic city. Another expedition to Iraq had better luck on this score. Backed, like contemporary work on the Athenian agora, by the wealth of John D. Rockefeller, the newly created Oriental Institute of Chicago excavated from 1930 to 1936 at Khafaje and Tell Asmar, in the Diyala basin northeast of Baghdad. Led by the art historian Henri Frankfort, the expedition uncovered densely occupied Early Dynastic quarters in which individual houses grouped around courtyards were crammed together along streets and alleys. Some of the dead were buried beneath the floors of their own houses, often accompanied by grave goods in vaulted brick chambers. Also excavated were temples and palaces built at different times between 3000 and 1800 BC. At Tell Asmar, most memorably, the temples of the god Abu contained caches of stone statues of gods and worshippers up to one metre (39 inches) high that communicate to the modern viewer a powerful sense of the wide-eyed awe Sumerians felt in the presence of their divinity.

At Uruk, the German archaeologist Julius Jordan initiated a long-term excavation continuing before and after the Second World War that focused particularly on religious architecture, notably the Eanna, the temple of the Sumerian goddess Inanna. This work revealed the very beginnings of Mesopotamian civilization, dating nearly a thousand years before the royal cemetery of Ur: the period in which Sumerian temples first developed cuneiform writing and cylinder seals to keep track of their affairs.

A PREHISTORY FOR NORTHERN MESOPOTAMIA

Max Mallowan, who had previously worked with Woolley at Ur, in 1927 helped to reopen the British excavations at Nineveh. Cutting a narrow trench to virgin soil, 26 metres (85 feet) below the mound surface, he revealed 21 metres (70 feet) of archaeological deposits below the level of the famous Assyrian palaces and temples and recovered from the lower levels early painted pottery of a type previously found at Tell Halaf and Carchemish. Wanting to find out more about these early cultures, Mallowan then dug the nearby site of Tell Arpachiyah. He was remarkably successful, uncovering the remains of an early farming village belonging to the Halaf culture that spread across northern Mesopotamia during the sixth and fifth millennia BC. At Arpach-iyah the houses were keyhole-shaped, with a single circular

Opposite. Limestone figures of worshippers, the eyes inlaid with shell, discovered in the Abu temple at Tell Asmar, Iraq (ancient Eshnunna) during the Chicago excavations of the 1930s. Around 2700 BC.

The arrival in the Near East of the Americans, hatless, bare-kneed and puzzled by the habitual beards, field-boots and solar topees of the Europeans, marked a sea change. European institutions at this time, noted the British archaeologist, Seton Lloyd, 'appeared to grudge every penny beyond the absolute minimum necessary to keep their expeditions in the field …

'The result was a tradition, particularly in English camps, of personal austerity and discomfort, as the only alternative to over-economy and improvisation in the actual fieldwork. In the early 1930s this circumstance was sharply emphasized by the arrival in the field of better equipped and more heavily subsidized expeditions sponsored by the richer American universities. Notable among these was Chicago's Oriental Institute, which was now engaged in establishing a chain of elaborate research stations throughout the Near and Middle East …

'At Tell Asmar, forty miles east of Baghdad, a desert station with fully-equipped photographic studio and laboratory provided a centre for the excavation of a whole group of most productive Sumerian sites, a score of miles from the nearest modern settlement.'

room up to 9 metres (30 feet) around, approached by a rectangular passage; outside, lanes of compacted gravel ran between the houses. The village also contained bread ovens that doubled as kilns for firing sophisticated pottery, painted with multiple colours in exuberant geometric designs.

Moving to northern Syria between 1935 and 1939, Mallowan excavated at the large tell of Chagar Bazar, where he identified evidence of links with the Sumerian world in the fourth and third millennia BC. His excavations also bore important prehistoric fruit. The lower layers at Chagar Bazar contained a village of the Halaf culture and, below this, occupation levels in which Mallowan discovered painted pottery of a type previously found at Samarra, north of Baghdad. This sort of discovery – that Samarran pottery, and therefore culture, was older than Halaf – was the basis on which an entire network of knowledge about the ancient Near East was now being built up.

As in Egypt, the French in Syria remained as active as the English in the interwar years. In the 1930s, André Parrot began digging the 600 hectares (1500 acres) of Tell Harari, the ancient city of Mari on the middle Euphrates in Syria. The project continues to this day. Parrot's work revealed two major periods of occupation: the mid-third millennium (Early Dynastic period) and the early second (Old Babylonian period). The 300-room Old Babylonian palace of Zimri-Lim (1782–1759 BC) and its archives made possible a new appreciation of the age of Hammurabi, the archives reflecting the administration and foreign relations of a major kingdom at a time when no single power dominated western Asia. Some 20,000 cuneiform tablets, a key source for the political and economic history of the period, revealed the state's shifting diplomatic relations and military strategies, its trading connections, economic organization and technology, and the sometimes uneasy relations that existed between settled and nomadic communities.

From 1929, Claude Schaeffer dug at the Bronze Age coastal city of Ras Shamra (ancient Ugarit), initiating another French research programme that continues to the present. Although Ugarit was occupied almost continuously from c. 6000 until c. 1200 BC, Schaeffer's attention focused particularly on the last two centuries of the city's history, when Ugarit was a vassal state of the Hittite empire. Over half of the city was excavated, exposing the palace and its elaborate burials, temples and private houses, as well as a contemporary port several miles away. Ugarit art, especially from the palace and temples, proved to unite Egyptian, Hittite and Mesopotamian elements into a distinctly Syrian style, as befitted an important long distance trading centre.

Also recovered from Ugarit were innumerable tablets carrying administrative accounts and religious and literary texts that greatly illuminate the political and economic conditions of northern Syria during a period of competition between the Hittite and Egyptian empires. They record in addition the mythology and religion of the culture from which Judaic monotheism eventually emerged. The gods of Ugarit represented natural forces, their myths concerning fertility and the cycle of life and death – crucial elements in the survival of any agricultural society. As god of storm and rain, Baal was the most important divinity at Ugarit, and many myths focused on his struggles with death and infertility. 'And Ahab, son of Omri, did evil in the sight of the Lord more than all that were before him ... He erected an altar for Baal in the house of Baal' (I Kings xvi, 30–32). The hatred of Baal and of graven images in the Old Testament shows how deeply this cult was ingrained in the religious culture of the ancient Levant.

BIBLICAL ARCHAEOLOGY

The methods of stratigraphic excavation that Petrie had introduced to Palestine in the 1890s now took hold, although his own return to the region in 1926 was not an unmitigated success. He picked up where he left off at Tell el-Hesy nearly forty years before, oblivious to technical developments that had emerged more recently in digging Palestinian tells. This was particularly apparent in his 1930–34 excavations at Tell el-Ajjul where his approach to the site was that of a previous generation; the giant of archaeology in the Near East now had 'an influence which in much of its technique ... [had] long outlasted its scientific usefulness'.

Opposite. Max Mallowan (1904–78) (third from left), during his archaeological apprenticeship at Ur, 1926. The three central figures beneath the verandah of the dig-house are Leonard and Katharine Woolley and the expedition's epigraphist, Eric Burrows.

They made an oddly contrasted trio, Mallowan recalled later. 'During the excavations, Woolley, always amiable, studiously polite and usually genial, was something of a tyrant as all successful heads of excavations have to be, but he was always just and never expected more than he gave himself ...

'His wife, Katharine Woolley, who always accompanied him, was a dominating and powerful personality ... Her first marriage had been a disaster, for not long after the honeymoon her husband shot himself at the foot of the Great Pyramid, and it was only with reluctance that she brought herself to marry Woolley – she needed a man to look after her, but was not intended for the physical side of matrimony. Katharine was a gifted woman, of great charm when she liked to apply it, but feline...'

The unworldly Father Burrows, a Jesuit priest from Oxford, was more endearing. 'Whenever I was conducting a visitor around Ur', Mallowan remembered, 'Burrows, wearing his little black hat, was invariably to be seen squatting in our unroofed open-air lavatory, clearly visible to visitors from the top of the ziggurat.'

Despite the technical sophistication of some early excavators like Reisner, excavation standards in the Levant remained depressingly low, as Wheeler sharply observed in his autobiography, *Still Digging* (1955):

> From the Sinai border to Megiddo and on to Byblos and northern Syria, I encountered such technical standards as had not been tolerated in Great Britain for a quarter of a century ... The scientific analysis of stratification, upon which modern excavation is largely based, was almost non-existent. And the work was being carried out upon a lavish and proportionately destructive scale.

James Breasted's Chicago expedition to Megiddo (the New Testament Armageddon) in 1925–39 was famously lavish, its dig house even equipped with tennis courts. Breasted began with the object of excavating the entire tell from top to bottom, layer by layer, but since Megiddo is a large site, about 17 metres (55 feet) high and covering over 5 hectares (12 acres), this proved impractical, especially when money ran short during the Depression. Even so, digging managed to uncover completely the upper five cities on the site (dating from 1000 to 350 BC), taking a few areas down to deeper levels as far back as the Early Bronze Age, nearly five thousand years ago. Some of the most spectacular discoveries dated to the tenth century BC, a period in which a large portion of the town was given over to buildings the excavators identified as King Solomon's stables, so illustrating the Bible's testimony that 'Solomon gathered together chariots and horsemen; he had fourteen hundred chariots and twelve thousand horsemen, whom he stationed in the chariot cities and with the king in Jerusalem' (I Kings x, 26).

In 1931–35, new excavations at Samaria, the capital of the northern kingdom of Israel, were undertaken by a British team that included Kathleen Kenyon, a famously indomitable lady archaeologist trained on Roman sites in Britain under Wheeler (p. 200). This training emphasised close control over stratigraphy, digging that followed the undulations of each newly exposed occupation level, and measured section drawing of the baulks that separated different excavation areas. It was now applied by Kenyon in the Near East, first at Samaria, and later at two of the most complex, and most excavated, sites in Palestine: Jericho and Jerusalem. At Samaria, the excavations amplified Reisner's earlier conclusions, uncovering the walled royal citadel that the kings Omri and Ahab built and decorated in the Phoenician style. These buildings yielded ornately carved ivory inlays that had once decorated wooden furniture, and also Hebrew ostraka, inscriptions on potsherds that recorded tax payments. The glories of the city ended in 721 BC when it was sacked by the Assyrian army and its people dispersed to Nimrud, Gozan (Tell Halaf) and elsewhere.

At Jericho, Kenyon in 1952–58 found evidence that pushed back occupation of the mound from the Bronze Age and Neolithic to the Natufian culture of the end of the Ice Age (*c.* 10,500–9,000 BC). However, it was the walled village of the neolithic early farming community that existed between *c.* 9,000 and 6,000 BC that produced such spectacular results that Jericho henceforth became commonly referred to as 'the earliest town in the world'. Immediately above the Natufian levels, Kenyon uncovered a farming village, whose inhabitants did not yet use pottery. This 'Pre-Pottery Neolithic' culture, as she called it, yielded a number of surprises. In its early phases, a stone wall, up to 3.6 metres (12 feet) high, and a large ditch cut into bedrock had surrounded the 4 hectare (10 acre) settlement. A tower, 9 metres (30 feet) high, of solid stone with an internal staircase, stood against the village wall – monumental stonework that Kenyon saw as a defence but which is now more plausibly interpreted as a device to divert flood water.

Human skull from Kenyon's excavations at Jericho, *c.* 8000–7000 BC. The features of the defleshed head were reconstructed in clay, plastered and painted. Cowrie shells have been inset for eyes.

Opposite. The caves at Qumran in which the Dead Sea Scrolls were hidden in the first century AD. Some of the scrolls have been radiocarbon dated to the last two centuries BC, and must therefore already have been old when secreted.

The large number of scrolls and fragments now known fall into three groups: copies of all but one of the books of the Old Testament; apocryphal works like the Book of Noah; and specifically sectarian works like the so-called Manual of Discipline, the War Scroll and the 8-metre (27-foot) long Temple Scroll. It is this last category that suggests the scrolls as a whole represent the library of the Essenes, a strict Jewish sect described among others by the Elder Pliny.

Interpretation of the scrolls has been dogged from the first by rancorous scholarly disputes, snail's pace publication and archaeological disagreement about the nature of the Qumran community.

The political potency of the Dead Sea Scrolls in the contemporary world is a good part of the problem, and it shows no signs of diminishing. To the fury of the Zionist community, the scrolls were in 1993 claimed as the cultural property of the Palestinian nation.

In the Pre-Pottery Neolithic's later phases, burials beneath houses sometimes contained skulls on which the face of the dead had been modelled in clay, with cowrie shells inserted for eyes. Earlier work at Jericho in the 1930s found several nearly life-sized clay statues with faces rendered in a similar manner; Kenyon recovered additional fragments, and recent excavations at the site of 'Ain Ghazal in Jordan have found further examples in the same style.

Between the campaigns at Samaria and Jericho, Kenyon continued to excavate, both in Britain and North Africa; but for her, as for other archaeologists, research in the Near East came to a halt with the Second World War. Iraq was one exception. Here the British archaeologist Seton Lloyd dug at Hassuna, an early farming village on the Zab river, revealing a neolithic culture still older than the Halaf culture identified by Mallowan at Arpachiya and Chagar Bazar. Some Hassuna pottery had painted decoration; some had cruder, incised designs; and some, just as in the lowest levels of Chagar Bazar, was painted in Samarran style. After the war, follow-up work at other sites established that the Hassuna culture had early beginnings in the seventh millennium BC, and that such farming villages represent the oldest known use of pottery in Mesopotamia.

The end of the Second World War brought a disturbed peace in the Near East, and a slow, difficult recovery. Archaeological work began again, but the 1940s and 1950s saw far fewer excavations than the inter-war period. Nor were the accomplishments of post-war archaeology in general as spectacular as those of previous generations. Excavators continued to find unlooted tombs with splendid wealth, hoards of precious objects and unexpectedly sophisticated early art. But after 1945, with the framework of knowledge established, more attention was devoted to filling in the gaps: to working out reliable chronologies in hitherto poorly researched regions, and to investigating more distant areas that never contained advanced civilizations like those of Mesopotamia.

ISRAEL: DIGGING FOR ROOTS

As early as 1914, with the creation of the Jewish Exploration Society, Jewish scholars took an active role in the archaeology of Palestine. During the years of the British mandate (1922–48), they concentrated primarily on the excavation of Jewish burial sites, synagogues and settlements. After the foundation of the state of Israel, the initiative passed firmly to Israeli archaeologists whose main focus was the Bronze and Iron Age occupation of the Levant, particularly the arrival and settlement of the Israelites. The most prominent of this first generation of Israeli archaeologists was Yigael Yadin, who made his mark in the early days of Israel as a soldier and archaeologist, and later as a politician. Yadin influenced a generation of Israeli archaeologists and shaped the Israeli archaeology presented to the wider world, selecting for excavation sites deeply symbolic in contemporary Israel for their position in biblical and post-exile history. The two most politically potent sites of all were Masada (p. 313) and Hazor.

The most important town in Middle and Late Bronze Age Canaan, flourishing from the eighteenth century BC, Hazor possessed a well-fortified akropolis overlooking a large 'lower city' covering 80 hectares (200 acres). Destroyed in the thirteenth century BC, it was later restored as a fortified Iron Age town. Reporting his excavations of 1955–58, Yadin interpreted the archaeology of Hazor in line with the Bible, ascribing its destruction to the entry of the Israelites into Canaan (Joshua xi, 13) and its Iron Age fortifications to king Solomon.

Of equally great interest to Jewish archaeology was the accidental discovery in 1947 and 1952–55 of a remarkable group of texts on parchment and leather, hidden in pottery jars in eleven caves near Qumran on the Dead Sea. These 'Dead Sea Scrolls' represent books of the Old Testament, and commentaries upon them, a thousand years older than previously known copies. Written mainly in Hebrew and Aramaic and dated *c.* 200 BC–AD 100, they are thought to represent the library, secreted in an emergency, of an ascetic Jewish sect known as the Essenes who were probably based at Qumran. The Essenes were crushed by the Roman army during the Jewish revolt of AD 66–73.

PERSIA AND CENTRAL ASIA

Except for the great Achaemenid centre of Persepolis itself, until the 1950s the archaeology of Persia remained little known, the few excavated sites pin-pricks of light on an otherwise dark map. During the 1930s Roman Ghirshman excavated at

Tepe Giyan, a prehistoric settlement mound of the fifth to first millennia BC in the Zagros mountains of Luristan, and later at Tepe Sialk on the Great Khorasan Road linking Mesopotamia with China. The traditional French monopoly of archaeology in Persia was finally broken by Ernst Herzfeld, excavator before the First World War of Samarra in Iraq, who dug at Fars in the southwest and later, in 1931–39, explored Persepolis.

The story in Central Asia was similar. It was only after the Second World War that Soviet archaeologists revealed the Bronze Age civilization of the third millennium BC that fringed the southern Kara Kum desert in Turkmenistan, excavating extensively at Altyn-depe, a walled town of 25–30 hectares (60–75 acres) with distinct residential, crafts and public areas. Altyn-depe was probably one of a small group of city-states each controlling a separate oasis. A stepped terrace, some 12 metres (40 feet) high, that presumably supported a temple at the top in the manner of a Mesopotamian ziggurat, formed the ritual centre of the community. Trading links with the Indus valley were attested by pieces of ivory and square stamp seals reminiscent of those found at Harappa (p. 254).

Over the Soviet border in Afghanistan, French archaeologists made important discoveries such as the Greek city at Ai Khanum on the banks of the Oxus river in Bactria. Founded c. 300 BC, perhaps by Seleucus I, heir to Alexander the Great's Asian conquests, it is the best known of the Hellenistic cities of the east. Excavation revealed a town laid out on the Greek model, with an akropolis, theatre and gymnasium, as well as a governor's palace with mosaic floors, and many of the objects found – pottery, sculpture, inscriptions and coinage – were Greek in origin. Yet other aspects of the town were Persian, or even Mesopotamian: for instance, one temple had both a traditional Mesopotamian floor-plan and architectural details. Ai Khanum thus gives archaeological expression to Alexander's intention of creating a new society that combined Greek and Persian cultures, and illustrates the Bactrian origins of the Greek influences on northern India that so preoccupied the Archaeological Survey of India during the days of Cunningham and Marshall.

Links between the Indus civilization and Central Asia came further into focus during the 1970s when the same team discovered Shortugai in eastern Bactria, a settlement with architecture, pottery, inscribed seals and other artifacts so similar to finds from Harappa that the site is thought to be a Harappan colony of the late third millennium BC, an outpost some 650 kilometres (400 miles) across the towering Hindu Kush from the Indus heartland. Ongoing French excavations in Pakistan have lent further support to this idea by revealing at Mehrgahr, and elsewhere in the Baluchistan hill country west of the Indus, a funerary cult that incorporates typically Central Asian objects datable to the period immediately after the peak of the Altyn-depe culture. Many archaeologists believe that these burials and hoards in Pakistan reflect the migration of Central Asian peoples southward, c. 2,000 BC.

Also at Mehrgahr, the French uncovered a long history of earlier occupation stretching back into the seventh millennium BC, revealing the development of crafts

Opposite. The citadel at Mohenjo-daro, from the north-west. Built on a great mudbrick platform and protected from the flooding of the Indus by a brick embankment 13 metres (43 feet) high, the citadel constituted the civic, religious and administrative core of the city. Its most remarkable feature was the Great Bath, in effect a brick-built and bitumen-sealed swimming pool for ritual purification, 3 metres (10 feet) deep and measuring 12 metres by 7 metres (39 by 23 feet) at ground level.

East of the citadel was a regularly planned lower city of two-storied houses for the bulk of the population, numbering perhaps 35–40,000.

In this photograph, a Buddhist shrine of the second century AD, built from the city's bricks several thousand years after it was abandoned, towers above the ancient structures.

and specialized occupations within a simple farming community. In its earliest stages, Mehrgahr was a farming village, cultivating wheat and barley, without pottery or domesticated animals but with established long-distance connections that brought it exotic materials like turquoise and sea shells. As early as the fifth millennium BC, the village supported crafts like metalworking that relied on imported raw materials, and over time started making pottery, eventually developing a specialized potting centre that, by c. 3,000 BC, was distributing its wares through the region. Above all, Mehrgahr threw particular light on the origins of the Indus civilization.

THE INDUS CIVILIZATION

Although Marshall's own interests lay with Taxila and the Greeks in the far north of India, his attention was dramatically diverted during the early 1920s by the recognition at Harappa and Mohenjo-daro of one of the great civilizations of antiquity, the Indus civilization of c. 2,500–2,000 BC. Both sites had been recognized as ancient cities in the mid-nineteenth century. At Harappa, in the Punjab, the civil

engineer William Brunton had ransacked the 80 hectare (200 acre) city for fired brick to use as railway ballast during construction of the Karachi–Lahore line in the 1850s, his workmen retrieving square steatite seals characteristic of the Indus civilization that Cunningham was able to buy when he visited the site in 1856. Although he suspected the site to be very old, his chronological notions of the Indian past and his preoccupation with historical archaeology prevented him from grasping its full implications; he assigned it to a date in the early first millennium AD.

Daya Ram Sahni's systematic excavations at Harappa from 1920 quickly identified its prehistoric character. Almost simultaneously, at Mohenjo-daro in the Sind, R. D. Banerji recognized prehistoric settlement below the Buddhist stupa, beginning excavations there in 1922. These first excavations at Harappa and Mohenjo-daro produced inscribed seals, painted pottery and other artifacts that matched nothing previously known from India. The knowledge of Indian archaeology that the Archaeological Survey had accumulated over the previous half century had not altered Cunningham's opinion that the subcontinent's earliest known monuments could be dated to c. 1,000 BC.

Faced with the puzzle of an apparently new civilization, Marshall in 1924 described the results of Sahni and Banerji's work in *The Illustrated London News*, in the hope, as he later wrote, that 'through the medium of that widely read journal I might succeed in getting some light thrown on their age and character by archaeologists in other countries. This hope, I am glad to say, was at once fulfilled.' In the next issues, several specialists in Sumerian archaeology drew attention to finds from Iraq that suggested a date for the new Indian civilization in the fourth or third millennium BC.

The Indus civilization received intense investigation over the next twenty years. Excavations at Mohenjo-daro spanned a decade, under the direction first of Marshall and then of Ernest Mackay, an archaeologist with experience of sites of comparable date in Iraq and Bahrain. Exploration in the same period by Aurel Stein and N. G. Majumdar discovered additional sites belonging not only to the Indus civilization but to its predecessors and neighbours in the Indus and surrounding hill country. Majumdar's trial excavations on the western edge of the Indus plain in the 1920s revealed at Jhukar a 'decadent' Indus pottery style stratified above typical Indus painted wares, and at Amri evidence of a pre-Indus (or Early Harappan) culture. Majumdar was killed by bandits in 1938, while looking for early sites in the Kirthar hills. Mortimer Wheeler, appointed Director General of Archaeology in India in 1944, rounded off this initial phase, digging until 1946 at both Harappa and Mohenjo-daro, concentrating on the cities' monumental architecture and deep stratigraphy, and seeking evidence to explain the end of the Indus civilization.

This first generation of work revealed the nature of the mature Indus civilization in a way that emphasized its cultural uniformity: notably burnt brick architecture and town layouts composed of distinct and physically separated citadel and residential quarters. At Harappa, Wheeler exposed an impressive defensive wall, some

9 metres (30 feet) high and 14 metres (46 feet) wide at the base, memorably shown in his excavation photographs as an abyss from which wiry labourers emerge with baskets of spoil balanced adroitly on their heads. 'The great walls of the citadel emerged for the first time in their majesty as our picks cut through the encumbering debris', Wheeler recalled, 'The historical character of the Indus civilization was changing and developing before our eyes. What mattered sweat and dust and a little cardiac overtime?'

At Mohenjo-daro – better preserved than Harappa – the buildings of the citadel were erected on a massive mud brick platform 6 metres (20 feet) high that covered 8 hectares (20 acres). The structures included a large, ventilated granary, a 3-metre (10-feet) deep asphalt-lined pool, the so-called 'Great Bath', probably used for ritual purification, and a complex of rooms that Marshall interpreted as priests' quarters. Extending over 100 hectares (250 acres), the lower town of Mohenjo-daro was laid out along a regular grid of major streets up to 9 metres (30 feet) wide around blocks of residential apartments and narrow lanes. The individual residential units, formed around courtyards, contained from one to dozens of rooms, with staircases leading to the roof or upper stories. In some quarters, workshops belonging to potters, shell bangle cutters, bead-makers, smiths and other craftsmen were interspersed among the houses.

The regularity of Mohenjo-daro's street layout and the residential architecture, sophisticated latrines, storage facilities and other municipal works gave the impression of town planning and indeed of a regimented society. Indus artifacts, both large and small, also seemed to be uniform: painted pottery, chipped stone and metal tools, steatite seals and other inscribed objects seemed to be identical across the Sind and the Punjab. Religion, moreover, seemed to be the central source of political authority in a society ruled by priest-kings. Struck by works of art that seemed to echo beliefs familiar from contemporary India, Marshall asserted that

> taken as a whole, their religion is so characteristically Indian as hardly to be distinguishable from still living Hinduism or at least from that aspect of it which is bound up with animism and the cults of Siva and the mother goddess – still the most potent forces in popular religion.

Indian independence and Partition in 1947 left most of the Harappan culture area in Muslim Pakistan, a circumstance that encouraged Indian archaeologists to explore more modest Harappan sites to the south and east of Sind and the Punjab. Excavations in the 1950s at sites in Gujarat exposed considerable sections of these Harappan settlements, including a large tank at the site of Lothal on the Gulf of Cambay that the excavator interpreted as a docking area for sea-going ships. At numerous sites in the Ganges drainage around Delhi parallel investigations also revealed an eastward extension of Harappan civilization. Later settlements shrank to village size, and lost many of the most advanced Harappan characteristics, such as the use of writing, weights and seals, and sophisticated art. Although the

Mortimer Wheeler and Indian archaeology

Regimenting the past. Wheeler's excavations at Arikamedu in southern India (right) and at Harappa in the Punjab, today in Pakistan (above). Although Harappa's massive ramparts were built of fired brick, which survives much better than mud-brick, the rising water-table today threatens the lower courses of the ruins with salts and corrosive minerals .

Mortimer Wheeler made a major impact on the practice of archaeology in India and Pakistan between 1944 and 1948, with echoes that endure to this day. Invited to review the state of the Archaeological Survey of India in 1938, becalmed since Marshall's retirement nine years before, the Near Eastern archaeologist Leonard Woolley had been scathing, identifying lack of training as the key problem. Excavation, wrote Woolley, was

> haphazard, initiated for no good scientific reason on new sites or carrying on the clearing of old sites which had already yielded their essential information ... On almost every site which I visited there was evidence of the work having been done in an amateur fashion by men anxious indeed to do well but not sufficiently trained and experienced to know what good work is.

In 1944, freed from military responsibilities by the fall of Libya, Woolley's nominee, Lieutenant-Colonel Wheeler, was named Director General of Archaeology in India, a position he was to fill until 1948. Wheeler's avowed aims were two-fold: to discover what followed the Indus civilization of northern India archaeologically, and to investigate Roman trade with southern India to put the cultural chronology of the region on a firm footing. To achieve these goals, he planned also to develop the technical excavation skills of 'the younger generation who will succeed us': the Indian staff of the Archaeological Survey.

Wheeler was largely successful in these endeavours, training students in stratigraphic excavation at Taxila and elsewhere, and digging sites in both northern and southern India. His first archaeological school, recalled the historian of archaeology Glyn Daniel,

> was a mixed bag of creeds and colours. Like the hot weather he proposed to ignore religious and eating prejudices. There was one dining room: some students complained. He addressed them in his best bloody brigadier manner. 'We are the same people here,' he said. 'I make no distinction between Sikhs, Parsees, Hindus and Moslems. We are all Indian archaeologists and if you don't like it you can go home.' No one left. Gradually he became a semi-divine guru figure to all his devoted and admiring pupils.

In the north, at the citadel of Harappa, Wheeler revealed traces of a settlement earlier than the Indus civilization, documented three phases of the city's great defensive wall, and between the defences and the Indus river excavated

massive granaries that covered some 840 square metres (1,000 square yards). To investigate Roman trade in the south, he dug in 1945 at Arikamedu, on the Coromandel coast of Tamil Nadu, where he found imported Mediterranean trade goods of the first century AD, including glossy red Arretine tableware, wine jars, glass, lamps and intaglio gems, in association with a warehouse and other buildings. These discoveries, concluded Wheeler, 'combine to indicate that Arikamedu was one of the regular "Yavana" or Western trading stations of which both Graeco-Roman and ancient Tamil writers speak'. Below the trading station, Wheeler found the remains of a settlement with polished black-and-brown pottery of a type previously found inland in so-called 'megalithic' tombs – a discovery that prompted him in 1947 to dig Brahmagiri in Mysore, a site with both 'megalithic' tombs and settlements of the same period.

In a South Asian context the term 'megalith' is misleading for European prehistorians because it is applied to burials in urns and pits as well as to those in stone-built cists. By Wheeler's time, many archaeologists had dug such tombs in southern India, notably Alexander Roa who in the early twentieth century dug Adittanallur, a vast cemetery covering over 400 hectares (1,000 acres), where the dead were buried in large urns accompanied by pottery and stone vessels, gold

diadems, iron swords, and bronze ornaments. Roa had no way of dating these burials, or any other megalithic tombs, but judged them no older than c. 250 BC.

Working at Brahmagiri, Wheeler showed that pottery found in the 'megalithic' tombs lay below the uppermost settlement levels, layers that contained a locally made pottery imitating imported Roman Arretine tablewares that could only date to the first centuries AD. This meant that the lower layers of the settlement and the 'megalithic' tombs must both be older than the time of Christ. On this basis, Wheeler dated the 'megalithic' culture of south India to the final two centuries BC, a date pushed back by later work to as early as c. 1,000 BC.

His four year term ended prematurely by Partition, Wheeler returned to Pakistan as a part-time archaeological adviser in 1949–50, a period in which, though less obviously successful than before, he managed to set up the National Museum in Karachi. His influence on the archaeology of the subcontinent was profound and lasting; most enduring of all was his emphasis on meticulous excavation and his insistence on an ethic of archaeological research. So thoroughly did he inculcate his method of digging within a tightly controlled grid of 'Wheeler boxes' that his students maintained these methods and high stratigraphic standards for a generation.

settlements themselves were small villages of farmers and artisans, local pottery in both Gujarat and the Delhi area had clearly developed from the Harappan painted style, implying a continuation of Indus traditions. Although confined to the second millennium BC, the Iron Age cultures of northern India emerged from these faded descendants of Harappan civilization, so forging a link between the Bronze Age cities of the Indus and the Indian cities of the time of the Buddha that Cunningham investigated more than a century before. It is this chain that helps validate the suggestion, made by Marshall and others, that many traditional aspects of Indian culture already existed in the civilization of the Indus valley in the third millennium BC.

THE FAR EAST

The modern discipline of Chinese archaeology began in this period with the work of Johan Andersson, a Swedish geologist working for the Geological Survey of China, a body established in 1906. In 1921, Andersson and his team identified the Chinese palaeolithic and neolithic periods through discoveries at the Zhoukoudian and Yangshao-cun sites. Zhoukoudian, some 100 kilometres (60 miles) southwest of Beijing, is a limestone outcrop with at least twenty-five named excavation localities where fossils of *Homo erectus* and modern humans have been recovered, together with stone tools, food remains and personal ornaments.

The geological origins of Chinese archaeology had both good and bad effects: fieldwork and stratigraphic excavation were instilled as proper field methods, but continuing use of Andersson's 'type fossil' approach to dating and comparing archaeological assemblages hampered the competent handling of complex cultural relationships. Within the field of physical anthropology, however, Andersson's international team of colleagues – including the Canadian Davidson Black, Franz Weidenreich and Teilhard de Chardin – made significant contributions to the study of the early Chinese populations. Pei Wenzhong, who unearthed the first *Homo erectus* fossil at the site, was a pioneer in studies of bone breakage to differentiate humanly made marks from destruction by carnivores or other natural agencies.

The Harvard-trained Chinese archaeologist, Li Chi, returned to China to conduct excavations at the spectacular Late Shang capital of Yin, northwest of modern Anyang. Comprising an unwalled complex of temple, royal burial grounds, craft workshops, and élite and commoner residences, Yin has produced the earliest written records in the Chinese language – divination inscriptions, mostly on cattle shoulder-blades and turtle shells, the so-called 'oracle bones'.

The fact that palaeolithic and protohistoric studies were conducted by separate institutes oriented towards different fields – the sciences versus historiography – meant that archaeology in China was a divided field, with the neolithic being neglected as a result. The discovery and excavation in 1953–55 of the neolithic village of Banpo near Xi'an, and its subsequent incarnation as a tourist attraction, helped shift the emphasis of research to the middle of the sequence. In the period of Marxist interpretation, which postulated a unilinear evolution of society from an early stage of matriarchy through patriarchy to a slave society, Banpo was used to illustrate early 'matriarchal society' and clan organization. The open excavation at the site museum, housed under a building as large as an airport hangar, reveals the ditched village with pottery kilns and burial grounds outside.

A similar division of interests is found in Japan, with protohistoric studies traditionally lodged in the west, centred on Kyoto University, and hunter-gatherer studies more focused in the east, centring on Tokyo University. This division was aided by the fact that most protohistoric mounded tombs are found in southwestern Japan, and that 80 per cent of Jomon sites are in the northeast. Interpretations of both Jomon and mounded-tomb cultures were traditionally keyed to the imperial chronology found in the eighth-century court records – the tombs belonging to the early kings and Jomon artifacts to gods, mythological beings and native peoples interacting with the early court. For example, Sekitei Kiuchi, a Confucianist scholar of the Edo period (1603–1868), referred to Jomon tanged scrapers as 'rice paddles of the mountain gnomes', stone maces as 'thunder clubs', and long projectile points as 'spears of the gods'.

Incredibly, the prehistoric age of the Jomon (10,000–300 BC) and Yayoi (300 BC–AD 300) cultures was not firmly acknowledged until 1936, even though the western discipline of archaeology had been practised since its introduction by Morse in 1879 (p. 174). The decisive event was the debate published in the Japanese journal *Minerva*, leading to the realization that 'anonymous' peoples, represented by archaeological cultures, could exist independent of – and earlier than – written records.

Between 1910 and 1945, Japanese archaeologists were heavily involved in work on the Korean peninsula, which was annexed to the Japanese empire. They excavated the Chinese commandery headquarters at Lelang (*c*. 108 BC–AD 220), south of P'yongyang, and many Silla kingdom tombs (*c*. AD 300–668) in Kyongju, the most glamorous of which was the Tomb of the Gold Bell.

Korean archaeology was thus begun under a non-western colonial regime, one of the few instances in the world of a secondary transfer of archaeological techniques. With the end of the Second World War, the freeing of academic thought from political control gave rise to competing theories of Japanese–Korean relations in the protohistoric period: that the fifth-century Yamato state in Japan was set up by conquering horse-riders from the Korean peninsula, or that Yamato established a fourth-century colony on the south Korean coast. These controversies are still with us today, and influence the interactions of Japanese and Korean politicians in terms of status and conduct.

AFRICA

After the First World War, systematic archaeological investigations began in many parts of Africa. At that time, no convincing early human remains had yet been found anywhere in the continent, and dating was a near impossibility. Workers

Opposite. Shang oracle bone. Such bones, commonly the shoulder-blades or ribs of pigs, oxen and sheep, sometimes turtle shells, were used for divination by the Shang monarchs of northern China in the later second millennium BC.

The patterns of cracks made by hot brands applied to the bones were read as guidance from royal ancestors, this information being recorded alongside using an ideographic script of 2,000 characters, the earliest known Chinese writing.

Oracle bones – normally inscribed with a divination request, the answer and the diviner's name – are thus China's earliest historical records. They provide a chronology of Shang kings and officials, and detail the prospects for such key royal concerns as sacrifice, war, hunting, childbirth, illness, rainfall and agriculture.

Since 1928, around 200,000 bones have been found around Anyang in Henan province. The first finds were recognized in apothecary's shops where inscribed shoulder blades and turtle shells delivered by villagers were being ground up for medicine. Tracking the bones to their source, scholars discovered great caches that had been disturbed by local residents in indiscriminate digging. Systematic excavation of the Late Shang capital followed.

therefore put their energies into elucidating regional cultural sequences. By 1960, however, discoveries of human ancestor fossils in southern and East Africa had established this region as the 'cradle of humanity' and dates could be provided by newly developed radiometric techniques. African archaeology had come of age.

The idea that Africa was the cradle of humankind goes back, like so much else in science, to Darwin. In one of his most important books, *The Descent of Man* (1871), he wrote: 'It is … probable that Africa was formerly inhabited by extinct apes closely allied to the gorilla and chimpanzee; and as these two apes are now man's nearest allies, it is probable that our early progenitors lived on the African continent'. Discovery by Dubois of the bones of early people in Asia in the 1890s led scientists to expect that early people originated in Asia. Europe was also seen as an important place in human development after the discoveries of Neandertals. Darwin's idea that evidence for human origins would be found in Africa was considered unlikely until discoveries of the bones of human ancestors in South Africa from 1924 and in East Africa from 1959 confirmed his prophecy.

Raymond Dart was an Australian-born anatomist who came to South Africa in 1923 to lecture in anatomy at the University of the Witwatersrand. In 1924, while dressing for a wedding, Dart received two large wooden boxes containing fossils from the Buxton Limeworks Mine near the village of Taung, 80 kilometres (50 miles) north of Kimberley. The nuptials forgotten, Dart eagerly opened the boxes and in the second found an endocranial cast, or mould of the inside of a skull, which fitted another limestone block containing a fossilized skull, face and lower jaw. 'I stood', he wrote later, 'holding the brain as greedily as any miser hugs his gold … Here, I was certain, was one of the most significant finds ever made in the history of anthropology'. Dart patiently chiselled away for weeks until, on 23 December, he managed to free the skull from its rock matrix. 'What emerged was a baby's face, an infant with a full set of milk teeth and its permanent molars just in the process of erupting. I doubt if there was any parent prouder of his offspring than I was of my Taung baby on that Christmas'. Dart's description of the Taung fossil appeared in February 1925 in the journal *Nature*. He named the fossil *Australopithecus africanus* ('southern ape of Africa'), claiming that it represented 'an extinct race of apes intermediate between living anthropoids and man'.

Dart became a celebrity overnight, but drew mixed reaction from the scientific community. While the prosecution of John Scopes for teaching evolution at a school in Dayton, Tennessee (the Scopes 'monkey trial'), was being reported in newspapers, the Taung 'trial' was being conducted in the leading scientific journals. Problems abounded, none more so than the fossil's anatomical 'inconvenience'. The prevailing opinion in 1925 was that the so-called 'missing link' would have a large brain but ape-like jaws and teeth – a view that had been reinforced by the fake Piltdown fossils from England discovered in 1912–15 (p. 127). The Taung fossil, on the other hand, had a small ape-like brain, but human-looking jaws and teeth.

Dart felt rejected by the scientific establishment and continued his work on early humans only at the urging of his student, Phillip Tobias – later to describe the first early *Homo* remains from East Africa – and after the public vindication of his stand on *Australopithecus* at the First Pan-African Congress of Prehistory and Quaternary Studies in 1947. This vindication was mainly due to the discovery in the 1930s and 1940s, by Robert Broom and others, of many more australopithecine fossils from Sterkfontein, Swartkrans and Kromdraai, near Krugersdorp in Gauteng province. These included a heavily-built variety currently called *Australopithecus robustus* or *Paranthropus robustus*.

In 1959, a century after Darwin's *On the Origin of Species*, yet another African fossil changed ideas about human origins. The first East African australopithecine came to light at Olduvai Gorge, after nearly thirty years of arduous research by Louis and Mary Leakey.

The formative period in African archaeology was heralded by the arrival of the first trained archaeologists, many of whom had studied under the prehistorian Miles Burkitt at Cambridge. One individual who played a central role in raising international interest in African archaeology during this period was the indefatigable Abbé Breuil, doyen of world let alone African prehistory, who travelled extensively in southern Africa promulgating his interpretation of rock art as sympathetic magic. Published in 1930, Breuil's *Prehistoric Africa* was the first overview of African prehistory. 'I well remember', recalls the Africanist archaeologist

Opposite. The man whose fossil came to him. Raymond Arthur Dart (1893–1988) holding the skull of the 'Taung baby', the first australopithecine known to science, a few days after its discovery was publicly announced in 1925. His correct interpretation of it as a form intermediate between apes and humans came at a time when comparable fossils had not yet been discovered.

Dart met at first with sceptical reactions. Most of the leading anthropologists of the day – many of them hoodwinked at the time by the Piltdown forgery – criticized both the scientific description of the fossil and Dart's evolutionary conclusions.

'An examination of the casts', the British anthropologist Sir Arthur Keith (1866–1955) assured readers of the journal *Nature*, '… will satisfy zoologists that [Dart's] claim is preposterous. The skull is that of a young anthropoid ape – one which was in its fourth year of growth, a child – and showing so many points of affinity with the two living African anthropoids, the gorilla and chimpanzee, that there cannot be a moment's hesitation in placing the fossil form in this living group.'

It was 1945 before the embittered Dart again took an interest in anthropological fieldwork, and 1947 before *Australopithecus africanus* won widespread acceptance among the scientific community.

Desmond Clark, 'the Abbé's telling one that, with his eyes closed and by merely *feeling* the bifaces from the Zambezi that I'd showed him, he could tell me which stage of the Acheulean they represented'.

The Leakeys at Olduvai

Louis Leakey (1903–72) was the Kenyan-born son of an English missionary, who took a doctorate in African prehistory at Cambridge. While at university, his head was injured during a rugby game and he took the medically recommended rest by joining a British Museum expedition to Tanzania to search for fossil dinosaurs. Thereafter, he decided to pursue a fossil-hunting rather than a missionary career, and in 1926 mounted his first expedition to look for early human fossils in East Africa – despite admonishment from the academic establishment that thought him a fool to look for such fossils in Africa rather than Asia.

With his second wife, Mary, Leakey worked for almost half a century at many sites in East Africa, switching his attention on occasion to other fields. He was known as an authority on subjects as diverse as the anthropology of the Kikuyu people of Kenya, intelligence work, dogs and tropical fish. He became curator of the Coryndon Museum in Nairobi in 1940, and honorary director of the ancillary Centre for Prehistory and Palaeontology in 1962.

Louis Leakey's favourite site was Olduvai Gorge, an ancient lake basin in northern Tanzania that forms part of the great East African Rift Valley. One July morning in 1959, he was ill and remained in camp while Mary went off to explore the gorge with her dalmatians. She caught sight of parts of a skull eroding from the side of the gorge and, after carefully recovering more than 400 fragments of bone from the place, could reconstruct the skull of an adult australopithecine, which Louis promptly named *Zinjanthropus boisei*: the genus means 'East Africa man', while the species name honours Charles Boise, who funded the research. The potassium-argon technique dated the fossil – today variously termed *Australopithecus* or *Paranthropus boisei* or *robustus*, or, more familiarly, 'Zinj', 'Dear Boy' or 'Nutcracker Man' (a reference to its large molar teeth) – to 1.79 million years.

Leakey is said to have been disappointed that the fossil was an australopithecine rather than early *Homo*, and he was delighted when the then earliest known *Homo* remains were found at Olduvai in 1961 and dated to 1.7 million years. These were attributed to *Homo habilis*, the 'handy man', as Louis believed he had at last found the maker of the first simple stone tools made at Olduvai.

The 'Zinj' find sparked intensive studies of early humans at sites throughout East Africa, which is now the key area for such studies. As Mary Leakey explains in her autobiography, *Disclosing the Past* (1984):

> The reason why 'Zinj' was so important to us was that he captured the public imagination rather than merely exciting the human palaeontologists and stirring up scientific controversy. If we had not had Des Bartlett and his film camera on the spot to record the discovery and excavation of the skull, this might have been much harder to achieve. Zinj made good television, and so a very wide public had the vicarious excitement of 'being there when he was dug up'. It was the ... popular impact of the skull, combined with the tremendous scientific importance of such a find *in situ* on a rich undisturbed living-floor ... that convinced the National Geographic Society in the United States that Louis and I and Olduvai were worth financial support on a scale that exceeded our wildest dreams ... There was probably no one in the world better able than Louis to exploit the publicity value, and hence the fund-raising potential, of a find like Zinj.

Louis and Mary Leakey delightedly display the palate of *Zinjanthropus boisei* shortly after its discovery in 1959.

OCEANIC ARCHAEOLOGY

Archaeological research in Australia during this period was limited and dominated by two men – Frederick McCarthy of the Australian Museum in Sydney, and Norman Tindale, based in Adelaide at the South Australian Museum. Their main achievement was to demonstrate that change had occurred in both culture and environment during the Aboriginal occupation of the continent.

In 1929, Tindale excavated at Devon Downs, a rockshelter on the Murray river in South Australia. It was to be a crucial breakthrough in Australian prehistory. He recognized a series of discrete stratigraphic layers each containing an assemblage of artifacts and bone remains, and demonstrated that the types of stone artifacts and

Charles McBurney (1914–1979), one of the pioneers of North African Stone Age archaeology, posing with friends in the manner of a Victorian expedition at Haua Fteah, Libya, 1951.

From right to left: John Blacking, Charles McBurney (seated), Charles Burney, David Perham, and Abdullah, the expedition's Arab cook.

animals changed over time – the first time in Australia that a sequence of changing cultures was recognized. In 1936, McCarthy also demonstrated change through time in the stone artifact sequence at Lapstone Creek, a rockshelter near Sydney. On the basis of these pioneering excavations, the two men proposed rival, but broadly equivalent, interpretations of prehistoric culture change in Australia.

Until the 1950s prehistoric archaeology in Australia was largely in the hands of museums, which by the early twentieth century were well established as research centres and holders of the major ethnographic collections. There were also many amateur artifact collectors, especially in New South Wales, Victoria and South Australia. Most were unaware of the potential of archaeological investigation and were strongly influenced by the belief that Aboriginal toolmaking was totally governed by the nature of the raw material.

McCarthy and Tindale dominated Australian prehistory in this period. Their careers were remarkably similar. Both began in their respective State Libraries, and, on moving to the museum, worked with natural history collections before entering the field of anthropology. Both recognized the potential of archaeological techniques for investigating the Aboriginal past and undertook programmes of excavation. Both forged intellectual links with academic institutions in Australia and overseas, especially America, Tindale, for example, collaborating extensively with the American physical anthropologist, Joseph B. Birdsell. Both recognized the relevance of Southeast Asia to Australian prehistory and investigated sites and artifacts in Malaysia and Indonesia. Their achievements are impressive: Tindale's tribal map of Australia, based on fieldwork and library research, is still widely used; McCarthy and his collaborators developed a classification for Aboriginal stone artifacts, which remains the standard today.

There was little other archaeological research before the 1950s. The American anthropologist, D. S. Davidson and the physical anthropologist N. G. W. Macintosh excavated sites in northern Australia, and at the Museum of Victoria the geomorphologist Edmund Gill carried out detailed studies with the aim of dating Aboriginal sites. He made two particular contributions. The first was his involvement in attempts to date an ancient cranium found in 1940 at Keilor, near Melbourne; from careful analysis of the area's geomorphology, Gill concluded that the remains were probably about 15,000 years old. The second was his pioneering use of radiocarbon dating: he published the first radiocarbon date for an Australian site and in 1955 presented a list of dates from both geomorphological and archaeological sites.

Museum curators and amateur artifact collectors also dominated archaeology in New Zealand. Henry Devenish Skinner was a key figure. His father, a government surveyor who was also one of the founders of the Polynesian Society, stimulated his interest in Maori sites. Following his discharge from the New Zealand Expeditionary Force after the Gallipoli campaign, he studied anthropology at Cambridge under A. C. Haddon, returning to New Zealand in 1918 to take up a position at Otago University as assistant curator of the University Museum and lecturer in

Opposite. Chipped stone tools from Riversleigh, northwestern Queensland, the most common and ubiquitous kind of Aboriginal stone artifacts.

ethnology. Skinner's Cambridge thesis was a study of the material culture of the Moriori of the Chatham Islands which demonstrated that the Moriori were a Polynesian people, debunking the theory that they were the remnants of a Melanesian group driven out by the later coming of the Maori. He finally visited the Chatham Islands himself in 1919, but as a stowaway because the ship was not allowed to carry passengers.

Skinner was primarily an ethnologist and he set new standards in the comparative study of material culture. He introduced the concept of culture areas to New Zealand under the influence of Haddon and American anthropologists, and established the basis of Polynesian adze classification. He also strongly encouraged field archaeology, although his own interests in material culture meant that he tended to regard excavation largely as a means of filling display cases. He did, however, learn field techniques both in the United States and with Wheeler at Maiden Castle.

Skinner's most prominent student was Roger Duff, based at Canterbury Museum. He conducted major excavations at Wairau Bar, an important moa-hunter site comprising both burials and middens which had been found by a schoolboy in 1939. Duff showed that the people of Wairau Bar were Polynesian in their physical characteristics and that there was no evidence that any other race had occupied New Zealand prior to the arrival of the Maori. He also proposed a division of New Zealand prehistory into two periods, the earlier of which was the moa-hunter period. Duff's work culminated in an important synthesis of New Zealand prehistory, *The Moa-hunter period of Maori culture* (1950).

With the 1950s came a period of radical changes in methods and approaches to archaeology in Australia and the Pacific. One important factor was the impact of the new technique of radiocarbon dating and the possibilities it opened up. But it was the new ideas and methods introduced to Australia by John Mulvaney and to New Zealand by Jack Golson that laid the foundations for a new approach to the archaeology of the entire region. In particular, there was an emphasis on rigorous excavation techniques. Sites likely to provide long sequences were chosen for excavation with a view to tackling basic questions of antiquity of occupation and culture change; there was also interest in a range of evidence other than stone tools.

In 1954, Golson took up the first university lectureship in prehistoric archaeology anywhere in the region, in the anthropology department at Auckland. He arrived in New Zealand from Britain with a wealth of field experience and promptly embarked on a programme of excavation and training in field techniques. He concentrated his activity in the North Island which had been neglected until then, although it was where most of the Maori population lived. His excavation of Moabone Point Cave, originally dug by Haast in the 1870s, was a demonstration of precise field techniques that revealed the unhappy effects of a century of uncontrolled digging. Golson also demonstrated the technique of large scale, open-area excavations at *pa* sites such as Kauri Point.

John Mulvaney confronts 5,000 years of occupation deposits excavated during the first season at Fromms Landing, on the Murray river in South Australia, 1956.

Though recognized today as a pioneer of Australian prehistory, in the late 1950s Mulvaney's efforts were hampered by his quite literal isolation.

'I had never experienced Aboriginal society and, in fact, I doubt whether I had even met an Aboriginal person', he recalled later.

'Except for a handful of museum curators and amateur stone-tool collectors (rugged individualists for the most part), I had few specialist contacts. The two leading authorities of the day, McCarthy and Tindale, were 600 miles and 450 miles distant, respectively. I relied upon advice from abroad ... [for] visitors to Australia in those days were a rarity. Gordon Childe was the first, on his lonely journey back to his roots.'

Though he left New Zealand for Australia in 1961, in those seven years he had transformed the country's archaeology. He greatly improved standards of field techniques and broadened attention from artifact studies and coastal shell middens to structures, settlement patterns and subsistence.

Fluted 'Folsom point'. Typical of the spear points hafted to wooden shafts used by Palaeoindians around 11,000 years ago, this is one of nineteen points from the type-site of Folsom, New Mexico, found with the remains of extinct long-horned bison (*Bison antiquus*) at an ancient marsh edge in 1926–7.

The Palaeoindian cultures of Folsom, and the more widespread and slightly earlier Clovis, are believed to be ancestral to the many human groups that existed in the Americas at the time of the first Spanish contact, from Alaska to Tierra del Fuego.

However, putting a date on these cultures only became possible with the advent of radiocarbon dating after the Second World War.

While archaeological field methods were being transformed, the Maori oral traditions that dominated accounts of New Zealand prehistory were being called into question. Spearheading this attack was Andrew Sharp, a civil servant, who questioned the historical basis of Maori traditions and the idea that there was deliberate voyaging between the Pacific islands. He proposed instead that New Zealand had been colonized accidentally, and that the traditions of the 'Great Fleet' were later fabrications. While Sharp's views about the nature of Pacific navigation have since been shown to be mistaken, his criticism of the authenticity of Maori tradition was widely accepted and helped to clear the way for a modern approach to New Zealand's prehistory.

In Australia, it was John Mulvaney above all who established prehistoric archaeology on a firm footing. Starting out as an historian at Melbourne University but excited by the potential of field archaeology, he went on to study at Cambridge, intending to return well versed in sound, modern archaeological techniques that could be applied to Australian prehistory. Back in Melbourne by 1953, teaching classical history, he introduced a course in prehistory and over the next decade embarked on a vigorous programme of field survey, excavation and analysis of earlier archaeological work, as well as documentary research into Aboriginal history. His first excavation in 1956 was at Fromms Landing on the Murray river, a few miles away from the Devon Downs site that Tindale had excavated.

In 1961, Mulvaney published a key article entitled 'The Stone Age of Australia' which thoroughly dissected all previous work and was highly critical of both McCarthy's and Tindale's earlier syntheses. So comprehensively did he clear the decks that this paper marks a clear break with the past and a new beginning for Australian archaeology; since then, Australian prehistorians have felt little need to pay attention to the efforts of his predecessors.

The 1950s also saw growing interest in Pacific archaeology. It had long been assumed that archaeology was a waste of time in the Pacific because human occupation of the region was too short to have left much trace, and because hurricanes, tidal waves and acidic soils would have destroyed what little archaeological material might once have existed. In 1950, however, radiocarbon dating of the abundant and varied artifacts from Kuli'ou'ou shelter on the island of Oahu demonstrated an unexpectedly early age of at least one thousand years for human settlement in Hawaii. In 1952, the distinctive Lapita pottery in New Caledonia was dated for the first time and, through comparison with scattered finds of similar pottery in Fiji, Tonga and Watom Island, a prehistoric archaeological culture was identified that straddled the ethnographically distinct culture areas of Melanesia and Polynesia.

RESEARCHING THE AMERICAS

During the 1920s and 1930s, key archaeological sites were excavated in New Mexico and Colorado that demonstrated conclusively that humans had lived in North

One of the spear points found with extinct bison at Folsom in 1926–7 that established the antiquity of humankind in North America.

America during the Late Pleistocene – how much earlier was still unclear. Sites like Lindenmeier and Dent in Colorado, and Blackwater Draw and Folsom in New Mexico were the bases for the definition of the Clovis and Folsom periods, the earliest well-defined Palaeoindian periods in North America, dating to *c.* 9,500–9,000 BC and 9,000–8,000 BC respectively.

The site of Folsom had been found by the black cowboy, George McJunkin, a former slave, in 1908; he had been checking fence lines when he encountered a deposit of prehistoric bison bones sticking out of an embankment. However, his report was not followed up until 1926, when Jesse Figgins, director of the Colorado Museum of Natural History and one of the great pioneers of early man studies in North America, sent a crew to Folsom to recover a mountable bison skeleton for display. An artifact, a fluted stone spear-point, was found in this pleistocene deposit with the bones. However, there was a continued reluctance on the part of many scholars to accept the validity of the find, until more spear-points were uncovered *in situ* at the site in 1927. The association of animals and artifacts was certain, and the 'pleistocene barrier' for a human presence in the New World had been broken.

In Mesoamerica, Maya research continued to occupy the attention of most archaeologists, but new investigations were also directed towards the highlands of central Mexico and Oaxaca in the south. The chronology based on the Maya calendar was extended to include all of Mesoamerica, despite the fact that the cultural sequences of those areas did not fit very well into the Maya model.

Research in the Maya area came to be dominated by the Carnegie Institution of Washington. In 1914 the energetic archaeologist Sylvanus Morley had persuaded the Carnegie to begin a long-term study of Maya prehistory. Rather than focus on a single site, like most projects then and now, this campaign attempted to study Maya sites of all periods, and in all parts of the region. In 1929, overall direction of the research was passed to Alfred Kidder, who had worked extensively in the American Southwest. Early this century, Kidder had famously pronounced Southwestern archaeology a 'sucked orange', and suggested – as one of the founders of the field – that archaeologists should abandon the Anasazi. He himself went off to the juicier environs of lowland Mexico – though he was to regret the decision. 'I only wish', he lamented later, 'I could return to that wonderful country and wet my aged lips once again on the rich juice of a fruit which a half-century of research has little more than begun to tap.' Under Kidder's direction the Carnegie project worked carefully and systematically, producing carefully illustrated and documented publications. It lasted until 1958, and succeeded in establishing the basic Maya sequence, defined on the basis of calendar dates, ceramic styles and architecture.

During this period Morley became the foremost figure in Maya archaeology, and his opinions of the Maya became established as the accepted view of the day. He saw the Maya as a peaceful society, under the control of a priestly ruling class who devoted most of their time to observing and recording the passage of time. The fact that all that had been translated of Maya writing were the calendar hieroglyphs and numbers certainly influenced this view. Morley discounted the possibility that there was also an historic content to the Maya glyphs. These views were adopted in even more extreme form by English archaeologist Eric Thompson, who eventually succeeded Morley as the most influential Mayanist of his time. Thompson had been hired by Morley to work at Chichén Itzá in the early 1920s, and spent the rest of his

life studying early Mexico and Guatemala. He was a vociferous opponent of every
suggestion that there was any historical content to Maya writings, or that Maya
glyphs might be phonetic in nature, and ridiculed all opinions to the contrary.

Although research in the Valley of Mexico lagged far behind Maya studies, it took
off with the formation in 1908 by Eduard Seler, along with Alfred Tozzer of Harvard
and Franz Boas of Columbia University, of the School of American Studies. Seler
became the School's first director, to be succeeded in 1910 by Boas who hired a
brilliant young archaeologist, Manuel Gamio, training him in the methods of scientific archaeology. Gamio conducted careful stratigraphic excavations in the Valley
of Mexico and produced the first regional ceramic chronology for highland Mexico.
In 1917 he began an ambitious project, unfortunately never completed, at Teotihuacán, the largest archaeological site in Mesoamerica and capital of a pre-Mexica state.
Gamio's work established the foundation upon which later research was based.

Another great Mexican archaeologist, who appeared on the scene in 1927, was
Alfonso Caso. Caso began work in the Valley of Oaxaca, the third great centre of
Mesoamerican culture, undertaking extensive excavations at the large site of Monte
Albán. He also took great interest in calendar studies, having seen how useful they
were to Mayanists. At about the same time, American archaeologist George Vaillant
worked in the Maya area, and then switched to the Valley of Mexico, so making
himself one of very few Mesoamerican archaeologists with knowledge of both
regions. He not only developed basic chronologies of the area, but was one of the
first archaeologists to attempt to relate events in one region to those in the other.
He also took an interest in new discoveries that seemed to predate both the Maya
and Teotihuacán.

In the 1930s the Olmec civilization was discovered on the Gulf coast. The first
evidence was the discovery of colossal heads: huge, hewn basalt boulders up to
3 metres (10 feet) tall, carved with the likeness of a human head. The features of the
heads were flattened to help roll the boulders, but their appearance gave rise to
fantastic theories of African influence in Mesoamerica. The first major Olmec
centre was San Lorenzo (1200–900 BC), 50 kilometres (30 miles) from the Gulf
Coast in Veracruz. Huge quantities of basalt were quarried from the Tuxtla mountains, 75 kilometres (45 miles) away, and brought by boat to the site. There they
were carved into the colossal heads, and hewn into great slabs, some of which were
used to build an extensive system of drains, in turn connected with a series of
artificial ponds. San Lorenzo was superseded as the primary Olmec centre in the
tenth century BC by La Venta (1000–500 BC), 100 kilometres (60 miles) to the
northeast, which had a major pyramid at one end of a sacred plaza flanked by two
lateral mounds.

Olmec culture is also known from carvings in jade of a distinctive motif – a
snarling half-jaguar, half-human baby; such pieces were traded far and wide in
Mesoamerica. Because the Olmec were the first complex culture with widespread
influence, archaeologists argued over whether or not this was the true 'mother

culture' of Mesoamerica, precursor of all the great civilizations that followed. Today, the Olmec are seen as just one of several related cultures that existed at that time, each unique in its own way, and each with its own separate history.

In Peru, research continued to focus on refining the chronological sequence established by Uhle, adding newly discovered sites and cultures. Alfred Kroeber in particular realized the importance of Uhle's work, and used it as the basis for his own regional chronology. After his work at Pachacamac, Uhle had continued to excavate in other areas of Peru, and most of his collections had been deposited at the archaeology museum of the University of California at Berkeley, where Kroeber and his colleagues spent years studying and publishing them. When Kroeber went to Peru in 1925–26 he was already very familiar with the artifact sequences from the coastal area. In this first trip he visited sites on the north and south coast, and excavated several in the Nasca region of the south coast. When he returned to Peru in 1942, he was able to visit parts of the coast and highlands that he had not seen before, and write the first major cultural synthesis of Peruvian prehistory. Based on Uhle's work, and adding his own observations and those of Peruvian archaeologist Julio C. Tello, Kroeber proposed the first outlines of a general sequence of three horizon styles (Chavín, Tiahuanaco, Inka), with regional cultures interspersed.

Tello was an extraordinary archaeologist, yet a source of frustration to his colleagues. A native Peruvian who had attended Harvard, he excavated sites from one end of the country to the other, and probably visited every major known site or area of interest. He knew more about Peruvian archaeology than the rest of the profession combined, yet rarely put his knowledge down on paper. He is best known for his excavations at Chavín, an impressive temple site in the Andes of northern Peru, apparently a religious centre to which pilgrims journeyed from great distances to leave offerings at its temple. The spread of Chavín-style artifacts and religious symbols provided the foundation for establishing the earliest widespread horizon style in the Andes. Tello also excavated the cemeteries of Paracas, full of tombs containing Chavín-related artifacts, which served to reinforce the importance of Chavín influence.

Wari, in the central highlands of Peru, was also subject to Tello's attentions, and discovered to be the source of Uhle's 'Epigone' style (p. 195). It is now known to have been the capital of the first great Andean empire, which controlled most of the coast and highlands of what is now Peru, seven centuries before the emergence of the better-known Inka empire. Tello dug in addition a major Wari offering site, Pacheco, in the Nasca valley. There he discovered a deposit of several tonnes of smashed ceramics – huge urns brilliantly painted in six or more colours with the images of Wari deities, vessels in the shapes of llamas or human heads or feet, and many other spectacular examples of Wari ceramic art. So busy was he that he had little time to publish his findings. Kroeber in particular chided Tello for not publishing his work, realizing that he was more apt to write short newspaper articles than scholarly monographs. As a result, much of Tello's work died with him. He did,

Opposite. Gigantic basalt head bearing the 'helmet' and scowl that are characteristic of the Olmec culture of the Veracruz lowlands of Mexico, c. 1200–400 BC. Such heads are thought to be portraits of Olmec rulers. The flat noses and thick lips are universal, but each padded helmet carries its own distinctive decorative devices. The helmets probably provided protection both in war and while playing the ceremonial ballgame, a basketball-like game of startling brutality played with a solid rubber ball on purpose-built courts throughout ancient Mesoamerica. Gauntlets, heavy belts and knee-guards were also required and the losing captain might be sacrificed by the victors.

The distinctive nature of Olmec culture as a whole went unrecognized until excavations by Matthew Stirling (1896–1975) in the 1930s, and it was only in 1955, with the appearance of the first radiocarbon dates, that its independence of Classic Maya civilization was established. Even today, the Olmec are known almost entirely from three sites discovered between the wars: La Venta (1925), Tres Zapotes (1938) and San Lorenzo (1945). La Venta, now largely destroyed by oil operations, yielded four giant stone heads, Tres Zapotes two, and San Lorenzo eight – the largest 2.85 metres (9.3 feet) high and weighing over 20 tonnes.

Opposite. Excavating the bones of a 2,500-year-old bison kill at the Smythe site, Oldman River Dam, Canada.

The site lies in southern Alberta only a few kilometres from Head-Smashed-In Buffalo Jump, a famous kill-site in almost continuous use from c. 3700 BC at which bison were slaughtered by being stampeded over a cliff.

however, make many of his finds available for others to study, and established three museums in Peru for this purpose, the most notable the National Museum of Anthropology, Archaeology and History in Lima. Tello humself lies buried in an interior courtyard.

Tello was proudest of his work at Chavín, and in 1940 established a small museum above the temple buildings in which to assemble many of the site's elaborate stone carvings. On the night of 16 January 1945, the nearby lake of Aywinlla broke its banks, and a deluge of water, mud and stones carried away the small museum and all its treasures, covered the streets and houses of the adjacent village, and deposited a thick layer of mud over the great temples of Chavín. Tello was devastated, lamenting 'Thus vanished the dreams of the artist and the archaeologist'. He died a short while later, the victim, it was said, of a broken heart.

The 1930s to 1950s saw a flurry of activity in the Andes, as American archaeologists applied the new principles of archaeological stratigraphy to excavation. Wendell Bennett conducted the first stratigraphic excavations at Tiahuanaco, and in 1946 a team led by Gordon Willey of Harvard undertook the first major regional survey in Latin America, in the Virú valley of Peru. From 1954 John Rowe undertook a series of projects on the south coast of Peru designed to amplify Kroeber's synthesis and refine the general chronology; using the temporal sequence of the Ica valley as a basis, he designed a master chronological scheme applicable to the entire Andean region that remains in use today.

While archaeologists were making great strides on the ground, aerial photography provided an important new view of prehistory. In the 1930s Robert Shippee and George R. Johnson embarked on an aerial tour of Peru, flying over the north coast, and discovering what they called The Great Wall of Peru in the Santa valley. They flew south and into the mountains, nearly losing one of their planes in the process, and flew over major ruins in the area of Cuzco, the old Inka capital. Several years later, the American Paul Kosok began to investigate ancient Peru from the air in great earnest; in doing so he focused the attention of the archaeological world on the extraordinary ground markings of Nasca.

Ecological studies, though long established in Britain, were slower to take root in North America. Some archaeologists began in the 1940s to look to the environment for explanations of human behaviour and, as the importance of environmental reconstruction became apparent, attention to faunal remains increased. Theodore White, for example, undertook butchering analyses of animal bones from sites in South Dakota during the early 1950s, and on the Great Plains of North America, where large catastrophic bison kills provide the investigator with massive bone samples, Waldo Wedel, in the late 1930s initiated studies of the effects of the environment on local populations. Slightly later, Emil Haury conducted intensive palaeoenvironmental reconstruction at the important site of Ventana Cave in Arizona, using botanists, geologists and other specialists. However, the shift to using environmental factors as an explanation for human behaviour only began in

The Nasca lines

Working in the Peruvian region of Nasca in 1925, Kroeber noticed what appeared to be a series of pathways extending across the broad desert plain. Paul Kosok saw them on aerial photographs in 1940 and went to investigate further. He was immediately impressed by their astonishing quality: it seemed clear to him that such long, straight lines, pointing towards the horizon, must have served some astronomical purpose. In 1941, Kosok was able to interest Maria Reiche, a German mathematician living in Peru, in coming to Nasca to begin a serious investigation of the area. She devoted her life thereafter to documenting and mapping the lines, and to searching for evidence of solar and stellar alignments.

Reiche was the first modern investigator to realize that some of the lines formed the figures of animals and plants and geometric shapes. Alone on the desert one day, she was mapping a series of marks she had noticed: a spiral and irregular lines associated with it. When she realized that they formed the shape of a monkey with a coiled tail, she sat down on the ground and laughed out loud.

After that, she could hardly contain her enthusiasm, discovering figure after figure. For years she worked alone in the desert, camping out and riding a rickety old bicycle into town for supplies, or living in a small run-down house nearby. At first the residents of Nasca were sure she was *loca* (crazy), but as the years went by they came not only to respect her and her devotion to her work, but also to treat her almost as a local saint, oblivious to worldly matters.

Thanks to Reiche's work, and that of subsequent investigators, we now know that there is order in the seemingly random profusion of straight lines criss-crossing the desert. The marks were made quite simply by removing the surface stones of the desert floor, coloured dark reddish-brown, to expose the light-coloured sand that lay beneath. Many straight lines begin at 'line centres', usually small hillocks or the ends of ridges, from which a number of lines radiate in different directions. While some align with points on the horizon at sunset on important days, most appear to be sacred pathways connecting sacred places on the plain. Still to be seen at the line centres are broken ceramics, left as offerings. These cover a very broad span of time, c. 200 BC to the sixteenth century AD, indicating that the straight lines were built and used for a very long period.

The animal figures resemble designs painted on ceramics dating to the period AD 1–400, suggesting that this subset of the lines had a much shorter period of construction. The figures usually comprise a single line that forms the outline of the animal, without ever crossing itself. Entrance and exit

points were provided so the lines could be used as pathways, allowing a person to walk onto a figure, all the way around it and out again. All these factors suggest that most of the lines served a ceremonial purpose. Yet many explanations have

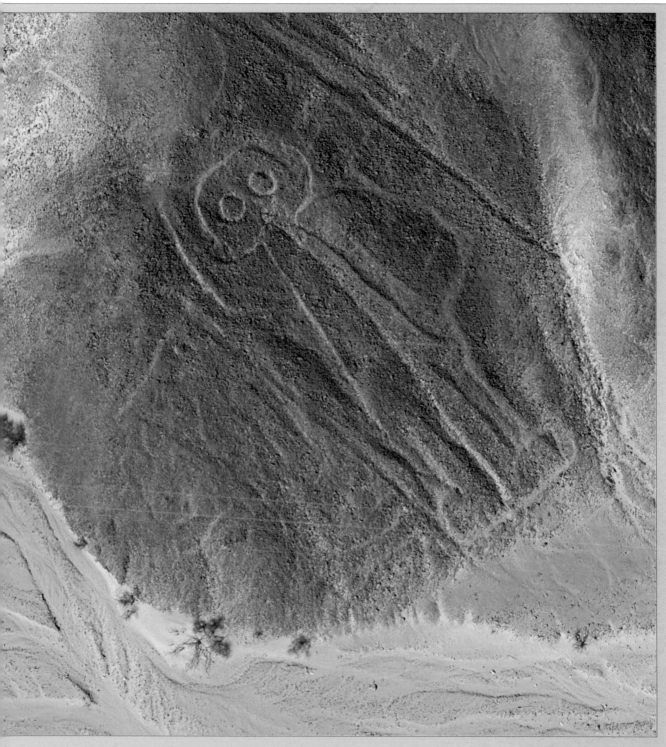

been offered in the past, ranging from the pseudo-practical – that the lines represent an irrigation system or were used for stretching thread for looms – to the outrageous: that they served as landing-strips for extraterrestrial visitors.

Waving human, 32 metres (105 feet) tall, marked out on a mountainside at Nasca.

Maria Reiche calls this the 'Owl-man' and suggests he represents the moon.

earnest with the more theoretical work of the anthropologists Julian Steward and Leslie White in the 1940s and 1950s.

Steward proposed that every culture had a core, 'the constellation of features which are most closely related to subsistence activities and economic arrangements, and thus were very much conditioned by the surrounding natural environment'. In particular, he promoted the concept of 'multilinear evolution' – the idea that the precise form a society would take in response to environmental constraints was not preordained by the environment itself. For White, any sociocultural system comprised three components: techno-economic, social and ideological; of these, techno-economic was the most important and determined the status of the other two. Human culture, on White's analysis, was therefore 'primarily a mechanism for harnessing energy and putting it to work in the service of man'.

By the 1960s, the time was ripe for a greater awareness of the importance of the environment in the social sciences, for during these decades the American public was faced with the consequences of its neglect of the environment. As its consciousness was raised, social sciences like archaeology began to pay more explicit attention to the important effects of the natural environment on human behaviour.

Parallel to the growth of environmental archaeology was the development of 'processual archaeology', from the 1970s the predominant mode of archaeological thought in North America. Its roots lie in the 1940s, in two key events: the invention of radiocarbon dating and the publication of Walter Taylor's *A Study of Archeology*. Tree-ring dating had been developed thirty years before, but its use had been restricted essentially to the American Southwest; with radiocarbon, archaeologists had for the first time an absolute, universally applicable, dating technique, and could begin to look seriously at problems other than chronology. In the New World, the appearance of the earliest settlement and subsistence studies – notably Gordon Willey's the Virú valley in Peru – followed close on the heels of the radiocarbon revolution.

In respect of archaeological theory, the revolution Taylor wrought with *A Study of Archeology* (1948) had a comparable impact. Taylor's book encapsulated all the discontent that anthropologists had been expressing about the development of North American archaeology. He emphasized that archaeologists should go beyond the analysis of artifacts, simply organizing them into spatial and temporal categories, and seek to understand the Indians who made them. Taylor advocated a 'conjunctive' approach in which the totality of a past culture was studied in order to understand it fully, a goal to be accomplished by very detailed studies of the quantities and distributions of artifacts and features within individual sites. Taylor's acerbic criticisms of such grand old men of American archaeology as Alfred Kidder resulted in his book not receiving the attention it deserved, but in the 1950s young archaeologists like Lewis Binford began to develop an approach that would in time take shape as processual archaeology: a fundamentally 'new' way of looking at the human past.

By 1960, archaeology was thus a strong and thriving discipline, with an arsenal of new techniques at its command, and an ever expanding body of material to work with. Yet many archaeologists, particularly in Britain and America, were beginning to express dissatisfaction with traditional approaches to the subject. Theory, for the first time, now became a major focus of attention that would lead over the next three decades to fundamental readjustments in the aims and practice of the discipline.

CHAPTER 7

New Techniques and Competing Philosophies, 1960–1990

Over recent decades, archaeology has seen a tremendous development in its ability to extract information from the material remains of the past, using a whole barrage of ever more sophisticated techniques, including computers, satellites, statistics and sampling, at the same time as it has found more and more of its resources

Gold funerary mask with emerald eyes and traces of red colouring. Peru, Chimú culture (twelfth-thirteenth century AD).

Over the last generation, archaeology has broadened its base away from elites to encompass the mass of the historic population, who subsisted by working the land or establishing themselves as artisans in rural areas or on the fringes of towns.

Developments in America and Britain have also emphasized anthropological, social, economic and cognitive issues at the expense of the more traditionally historical and art historical.

As a result, artistic masterworks like this that attract the general public to museums and galleries in huge numbers have come to be derided by many professionals as irrelevant to the mainstream of archaeology – a distraction best regarded as the province of museum curators, wealthy collectors and the vagaries of the international art market.

diverted from 'pure research' to salvage projects involving surveys and excavations just ahead of the bulldozers. Against this background, theoretical debates have led to a splintering of approaches, with a wide range of schools of thought now co-existing, particularly in Europe and North America.

SCIENCE AND ARCHAEOLOGY

The impact of the sciences can be observed today in nearly every area of archaeology. Although this impact is usually seen in terms of gadgetry, in hi-tech equipment for remote sensing or dating artifacts, archaeologists have in fact borrowed techniques from the hard sciences since the subject's inception.

Dating

The search for accurate dates has been central to the development of archaeology as a discipline. Archaeologists usually divide dating techniques into, first, relative and absolute; and, second, direct and indirect. A date is relative if it simply describes one object as older or younger than another; this technique is the oldest used by archaeologists. Absolute dates, in contrast, provide a calendrical date, usually measured using the BC/AD system or BP (before present, assigned as 1950). Direct dating techniques attribute a date directly to the artifact or feature, whereas indirect techniques can date only the surrounding matrix. Clearly, absolute techniques are preferable. The best-known are tree-ring dating and radiocarbon, the former because it was the first absolute dating method to be developed, the latter because it is the most widely-used technique and applicable anywhere in the world.

Dendrochronology or tree-ring dating was developed in the American Southwest by astronomer Andrew Douglass in the early twentieth century. It is based on the simple principle that each year a tree adds a ring to its growth, the size and composition of which is determined by that year's climate. Over the years a tree-ring sequence accumulates different rings since the climate changes slightly from year to year. Trees growing in the same areas will have matching sequences, so archaeologists have been able gradually to construct an absolute chronology by overlapping sequences of successively older trees from the same region. An archaeologist can send a sample of an ancient tree – say, from a roof beam – to a laboratory able to match its tree-ring sequence to a master chart and so establish a date for the beam itself. This technique is particularly well developed in the American Southwest, but shorter tree-ring sequences have also been developed elsewhere in North America and in parts of Europe.

Since Libby's discovery of radiocarbon dating in the late 1940s (p. 222), a number of modifications have been made to the technique. In the late 1970s, for example, gas counters were devised to enable smaller samples to be dated. More recently, the AMS (accelerator mass spectrometry) process has been developed to count the 14C atoms themselves. The technique is more expensive than the conventional system, but also much more accurate; it can date much smaller

samples, and should eventually push back the upper range of radiocarbon dating to c. 80,000 years.

After the initial euphoria of discovery died away, it became apparent in the 1960s that there were problems with the radiocarbon technique. For some periods, radiocarbon results were unreliable – differing significantly from definite ages fixed by documents or tree-rings – because atmospheric production of 14C proved to have been variable rather than constant through time. It therefore became necessary to correct some results to convert them from 'radiocarbon years' to calendar years. This 'calibration' had the effect of pushing back the ages of western Europe's prehistoric megalithic monuments, severing any possible links with the civilizations of the eastern Mediterranean; since megalithic tombs were now shown to be far earlier than their supposed Mediterranean prototypes, they could hardly have been built by visitors from these 'more advanced' cultures.

In eastern Europe the impact of radiocarbon calibration has still to be felt. Despite the efforts of western scholars, notably Colin Renfrew in his book *Before Civilisation* (1973), to reinterpret changes such as the beginnings of metallurgy in southeastern Europe in the light of these changed circumstances, the region's archaeologists have not yet embraced calibration themselves, and continue to construct chronologies on the basis of uncorrected radiocarbon dates. This is due partly to their isolation from the theoretical debates that accompanied the

The spectacular neolithic passage grave of Maes Howe in Orkney, Scotland, with its corbel-vaulted chamber, dates to c. 2700 BC. Only the calibration of radiocarbon dates in the 1970s proved that such megalithic monuments in western Europe owed nothing to eastern Mediterranean cultures such as Mycenaean Greece. They preceded them by centuries or even millennia.

calibration revolution, and partly to their late acceptance of the radiocarbon technique as a whole. The fact that radiocarbon needed to undergo a systematic correction offered a glimmer of hope to those who clung to belief in the historically-derived 'short chronology', but this was not enough to overturn the support for radiocarbon dating which had become widespread by the 1970s (p. 226).

Radiocarbon dating not only ushered in a revolution in archaeological interpretation but also encouraged the development of other radiometric and absolute dating techniques. Archaeologists can now get absolute dates for pottery manufacture, the use of hearths, the making of obsidian tools, and even the production of rock art. The adequate dating of materials is now scarcely ever an insuperable problem.

Plants and animals

The analysis of animal and plant remains from archaeological sites is crucial, providing insights into the environment of a site, the diet of the inhabitants and the ways in which the surrounding countryside was exploited for food. The full potential of animal bones in understanding the past was not, however, realized until the 1960s. Prior to this many archaeologists, intent on simply finding out how old a site was, paid little attention to bones, giving no more than simple species counts or, in some cases, differentiating between wild and domesticated forms. In Britain in particular, Grahame Clark's work (p. 203) gave an impetus to environmental and animal bone studies that eventually developed into a fully-fledged school of 'palaeo-economists' led by the Cambridge prehistorian Eric Higgs. 'Zooarchaeology' or 'archaeozoology' is now a highly respected specialization within archaeology. By the 1970s, the old adage 'you are what you eat' was being given new meaning with the reconstruction of the diets of past peoples through the study of the ratios of different forms of carbon retained in their bones. In recent developments, carbon studies coupled with measurements of strontium/calcium ratios are even extending these studies back into 'deep time', suggesting, for example, that heavily built or robust australopithecines such as *Zinjanthropus*, once thought to be specialized vegetarians, were in fact omnivores.

It was in the 1960s too that palaeobotany grew into a separate sub-discipline, making spectacular progress in understanding the development of agriculture throughout the world. Botanical studies now concentrated both on large plant specimens (macrofossils) and on microscopic remains like pollen. The former are not found at all archaeological sites, and are normally preserved only under particular climatic conditions, such as in the dry pueblo sites of the American Southwest where whole corncobs are commonly found. In contrast, pollen grains, the microscopic reproductive bodies of plants, have tough outer shells that allow them to survive for millennia. Archaeologists can now retrieve pollen from soils in archaeological sites, and even from tools such as grinding stones, and identify their family and often their genus.

Hochdorf

Rescuing sites from destruction at the hands of the farming, quarrying and construction industries is, unhappily, a key archaeological activity in the modern world. In central Europe, one of the most spectacular of all recent finds was made in this way.

The rich burial at Hochdorf, near Stuttgart in southern Germany, dates to the late Hallstatt period, c. 550–500 BC. It is one of a number of such burials from this period in central Europe that have been termed 'princely tombs'. In southern Germany, the Celtic mountain stronghold of the Hohenasperg was surrounded by a ring of such tombs, but almost all of them had been robbed in antiquity or modern times. In 1977, however, an amateur archaeologist reported a hitherto unnoticed burial mound 10 kilometres (6 miles) west of the Hohenasperg that appeared to be intact.

Although the Hochdorf barrow had been 6 metres (20 feet) high originally, it had become so eroded that it was hardly visible above the surrounding field surface; intensive archaeological prospection in this area since the nineteenth century had failed to identify it. By 1977, erosion and ploughing had placed the mound in great danger of destruction, and it was decided to excavate it completely. There was a good chance that it was a Hallstatt 'princely burial' that had survived unrobbed.

Excavation of the barrow, 60 metres (200 feet) in diameter, revealed a central burial shaft, 11 metres (36 feet) square and around 2.5 metres (8 feet) deep, containing two wooden structures, one within the other. The outer one was constructed of oak timbers and was 7.5 metres (25 feet) square. Inside was another box, 4.7 metres (15 feet) square and one metre (3 feet) deep. The space between them was filled with stones, which were also heaped over the whole tomb, about 50 tonnes in all. Unfortunately, this weight caused the roof of the grave chamber to collapse shortly after the burial, before the corpse had even decomposed. Finally, when the mound was built up, residues from the working of gold, bronze, and iron were included in its fill, indicating that workshops close by the tomb apparently produced many of the grave goods.

This burial chamber had extraordinary preservation, not only of metals but also of wood, leather and textiles. The primary burial was of a man about 1.80 metres (6 feet) tall. On his head was a conical birchbark hat, around his neck a gold hoop, and on his chest a small bag with a wooden comb, an iron razor, five amber beads and three iron fishhooks. He was lying on a bronze recliner with no known parallel in Celtic Europe, upholstered with furs and textiles. The seat was supported by bronze figures of eight women with upstretched arms. Scenes of wagons and dancers are embossed on the large bronze surfaces of the recliner's back and sides. Numerous gold ornaments decorated the clothes and even the shoes of the deceased, including brooches, cuffs and bands of hammered gold.

Nearby was a large bronze kettle, believed to have been manufactured in a Greek colony in southern Italy, which was decorated with three lions, while hung on the wall of the chamber were nine drinking horns. Residue in the kettle was from mead. Also inside the kettle was a small gold bowl.

On the other side of the burial chamber was a four-wheeled wagon of iron-sheathed wood, with harness for two horses. Wagons are common in Celtic princely tombs, but the iron sheathing is unique; including its tongue, the vehicle is 4.5 metres (15 feet) long, with massive ten-spoke wheels supporting a lightweight platform.

The Hochdorf barrow is in many respects the 'Tutankhamen's tomb' of Celtic archaeology, by any standards an extraordinary glimpse of aristocratic life and death in the Iron Age.

The Hochdorf prince's burial shoes were trimmed with geometrically impressed panels of gold foil, 0.2 millimetre thick. Notice the lace holes. Rather heavier sheet gold was used to make the prince's neck-ring and armband.

Medicine wheel in the Big Horn Mountains, Wyoming. From the central D-shaped stone cairn radiate 28 spokes made of individual stones. The outer circumference of this 'wheel' is surrounded by six smaller cairns.

Such medicine wheels are typical of the northwest Plains. They may have functioned as memorials to important people, played a role in vision quests and other ceremonies, acted as boundary or navigation markers, or served as calendars for the observation of celestial events like the summer solstice.

Some have been shown by radiocarbon dating to be 5,000 years old.

Statistics and sampling

Statistical techniques and computers have been used since the 1960s to facilitate archaeological interpretation. For archaeologists, the motives were twofold. The first aim was to assimilate a mass of data and reduce its patterns to something simpler and more comprehensible. The simplest example of this is the production of a graph that allows one to visualize differences in, say, the frequencies of different types of tools in a site; at the other extreme, multivariate computer techniques such as discriminant analysis allow the archaeologist to take ten measurements from each of 2,000 projectile points and search for patterns or clusterings in the points. Such patterns can then be used to generate new ideas about human behaviour in the past. The second aim was to test the validity of archaeological deductions. Two stone tool assemblages may, for instance, be statistically compared with each other to see how similar they are: significant differences will require investigation of the reasons for the contrast.

Early twentieth-century pioneers realized that some statistical competence was required to sample a site or a region properly, but it was the American Albert Spaulding's work in the 1950s which demonstrated the crucial relevance of such procedures to archaeological inference. Many of his arguments were picked up by the new, processual archaeology of the 1970s and 1980s. Sampling involves looking at or excavating only a portion of the total region or site, normally because time

and money will not stretch to a 100 per cent investigation. Properly conducted statistical sampling requires the archaeologist to give every different sample unit or environmental zone in the research area an equal chance of being examined, so the results of a sample survey will be an accurate reflection of the total area.

Computers and simulation

As computers became increasingly powerful and accessible during the 1960s, archaeologists were quick to realize their potential for simulation studies. A simulation is the construction of a complex model in which an archaeologist, by altering one variable, can gauge its effect in other areas of the system.

The construction of such models does not, of course, require a powerful computer, but for the types of modelling archaeologists had in mind in the 1970s, it was almost indispensable. David Hurst Thomas' simulation of Shoshonean subsistence in the Great Basin of western North America is a good example. The Shoshone were hunter-gatherers, able to live in an extremely harsh and arid environment. Thomas tested the validity of this model, derived from ethnography, against archaeological data obtained from an intensive study of the Reese valley of central Nevada. By altering the notional inputs of various foods, different results in terms of human behaviour could be predicted, each of them leaving a different type of archaeological record. Such predictions were then tested against excavated data on the ground. Thomas found that over 75 per cent of his model's predictions were borne out by the archaeological evidence, and was able to conclude not only that the theory was correct but also that the basic Shoshonean pattern of subsistence and settlement has been in existence since at least 2500 BC.

The use of computers has also generated some provocative ideas about human knowledge in prehistory. Astronomers and archaeologists have put forward propositions about the astronomical significance of sites such as Stonehenge, and archaeoastronomy is now a respected field in its own right. In the 1970s, for instance, the astronomer John Eddy investigated the possible astronomical significance of the prehistoric Moose Mountain medicine wheel, a large, 2,600-year-old stone cairn and boulder alignment in Wyoming, proposing that the alignments charted the direction of the summer solstice and the rising of the stars Aldebaran, Rigel and Sirius.

Archaeoastronomy

Archaeologists' enthusiasm for counting, weighing, and statistics over the last generation led by coincidence to renewed interest in archaeoastronomy – studying the relationship of prehistoric monuments to sun, moon and stars. Already in the eighteenth century, Stukeley realized that the major axis of Stonehenge was aligned on the midsummer solstice, a fact well known today to druids and festival-travellers. In the late nineteenth century, Petrie and the Astronomer Royal Sir Norman Lockyer both tried to find other astronomical alignments in the layout of the stones. But the idea did not really take off until the publication of American astronomer Gerald Hawkins' *Stonehenge Decoded* (1965), a book that used sophisticated computer calculations to propose that Stonehenge was a giant prehistoric calendar designed to predict when eclipses would occur.

This intriguing theory had serious shortcomings, and was rejected by many archaeologists. However, they could not easily dismiss the research of Alexander Thom, a distinguished engineer who spent many years taking exact measurements of prehistoric stone circles and rows in Britain and northwestern France. Thom assembled a formidable body of data to show that the builders of these monuments had used a common standard of measurement, which he called the 'megalithic yard', equivalent to 2.72 English feet (829 millimetres). He also argued that stone

circles which seemed to most observers to have irregular plans were really based on complex geometrical shapes, and showed knowledge of Pythagorean triangles. Finally, like Lockyer and Hawkins, Thom was convinced that these stone structures were really megalithic observatories.

The detailed case he set out for these conclusions between 1967 and 1978 generated furious debate. Many archaeologists ultimately rejected both the megalithic yard and the complicated geometry deduced from the plans of these sites, but Thom's work had one important merit that even hardened sceptics could not deny: it set people thinking in new and useful ways about the meaning of these impressive monuments, and the thoughts and beliefs of their builders.

ARCHAEOLOGICAL THOUGHT

Processual archaeology

The 'new archaeology' or 'processual archaeology' was first proclaimed to the world in an article by American archaeologist Lewis Binford in 1962. Forcefully argued and apparently with great potential, his views attracted the adherence of many younger archaeologists in the two decades that followed, and processual archaeology became for a time a juggernaut that threatened to dominate the subject entirely. The goal was simple: archaeology was to make an independent contribution to the anthropological understanding of human behaviour by developing itself as an explicit science, detached from the historical sciences that, according to Binford, had so far hampered its development.

To achieve this aim, processual archaeology drew on three main intellectual influences. The first was the emphasis on the environment and the model of cultural materialism that had been espoused in the 1950s by anthropologists like White and Steward (p. 278). The second influence was the use, as a model for how society works, of systems analysis. Any mechanism, whether a stereo system or a human society, operates through the interrelationships of its individual components. The relationships between these components mean that a change in one has a predictable and measurable effect on every other. In principle, a society could therefore be modelled in the same way as a computer system, a change to one component – say, the natural environment, population density or available technology – being related to a change in others – say, religious practices.

Leading proponents of this approach were Kent Flannery in the United States, whose analysis of the origins of corn agriculture in central America has achieved classic status; and, in Britain, David Clarke, whose *Analytical Archaeology* (1968) outlined a comprehensive, systems-based model for archaeological theory. Culture was now to be studied for its diversity, a diversity seen as a response to different functions and adaptive needs. Binford made this point in a celebrated reassessment of the stone tool industries of the Mousterian in France. Rather than seeing different assemblages as expressions of different cultural or ethnic groups as Bordes did, he suggested that variability was more probably due to tools having been used

Opposite: The Ring of Brodgar stone circle, one of the key sites surveyed by Alexander Thom in the early 1970s as part of his research into megalithic geometry.

Once there were probably 60 stones here, of which 27 thin slabs survive. The huge ditch surrounding the stones probably took 80,000 man hours to be battered out of the sandstone bedrock – three months of continuous labour for a hundred men.

Located on the Orkney mainland, in the far north of Britain, Brodgar was shown by Thom to be set out in a precise circle with a radius of 51.83 metres (170 feet), all but nine of the original stones lying within 0.5 metres of the circumference.

The 'Comet Stone' stands on a low platform, 150 metres (500 feet) southeast of the henge and stone circle, though any astronomical significance it might have had remains uncertain.

for different purposes. This insight was by no means new. As early as 1939, Donald Thomson demonstrated that if the remains of an Australian Aboriginal camp were analyzed on traditional assumptions, archaeologists would conclude that different peoples had existed simultaneously in the area; they would fail to recognize a single group that left different archaeological records in different seasons.

What was revolutionary about Binford's approach was the methodology he offered for testing archaeological interpretations. Its development was the outcome of the third, and perhaps most important, influence on the processualists: the model of scientific method advocated by the philosopher Karl Hempel. To arrive at a scientific explanation, Hempel insisted, hypotheses had to be deduced from general principles and then tested against empirical and independent data.

Early practitioners of processualism shared an insistence that the evaluation of archaeological interpretations needed to become more scientific. However, the method chosen by Binford, the deductive-nomological or hypothetico-deductive approach, was extremely controversial, even amongst philosophers of science, many of whom had already rejected Hempel's arguments. Many archaeologists were uncertain – if not downright ignorant – of the philosophical arguments being introduced to the discipline. This produced two intriguing reactions. One was to accept Binford's arguments, regardless of the validity of his scientific method; the other was to ignore both Binford and Hempel, and adopt an attitude of total scepticism to the innovations being proposed.

The new archaeology's approach was admirably demonstrated in 1974 in a study of northern Arizona by Fred Plog. The strategy was impeccable. First, Plog isolated a problem: the transition, *c.* AD 750, from Basketmaker to Pueblo cultures, a change marked by increasing sophistication in pottery technology, architecture and agricultural techniques based primarily on corn, beans and squash. He linked this question to a more general and universal transition, the origins of agriculture, and identified variables that he felt might explain this change: human population (size, composition, density); differentiation (measured by different activities and their specialization); integration (of different activities and roles); energy (expended and gained in subsistence and other activities). So far as was possible with archaeological data, Plog then measured these variables and their changes through time in an attempt to understand the change to Pueblo society. Although, on his own admission, he was unable to arrive at a conclusive explanation of the transition, he practised all the basic tenets of processual archaeology, laying out his assumptions, producing testable hypotheses, and allowing the reader to evaluate his logic and arguments objectively.

During the 1960s some of Binford's followers began to develop their own approaches beneath the overall processual umbrella, Plog and John Fritz, for example, seeking to define universal laws of human behaviour that can be deduced from archaeological analysis. However, no laws were ever developed other than those that Flannery in 1968 satirized as 'Mickey Mouse laws': ones that are self-evident, such as 'The size of a Bushman site is directly proportional to the number of houses on it' or 'As the population of a site increases, the number of storage pits will go up'.

Binford responded to this well-justified scepticism by advocating 'middle-range theory', an approach in which the focus shifted from *why* cultures change through time (explicable by laws or general principles, however limited) to *how* the archaeological record reflects past human behaviour. This aspect of understanding the past has consumed his efforts since, and he has published detailed works looking at hunter-gatherer societies and their material culture, in an attempt to understand how the archaeological record is produced.

Explanation of this sort is one of the most exciting areas of contemporary archaeology, its ultimate goal to understand behavioural processes: why ancient people did what they did. Before asking questions like this, however, archaeologists need to understand another matter: the transformational processes that a site goes through before it is excavated. The importance of such matters was acknowledged long before processual archaeologists came along, but it was they who systematically defined the methods by which transformational processes could be isolated. American archaeologist Michael Schiffer coined the term 'behavioral archaeology' for this branch of the discipline. Schiffer's concern is to isolate the impact on the archaeological record of what he calls transforms, both natural – for example, soil acidity – and cultural – such as later groups taking artifacts from a site.

Finally, in the 1980s, there developed 'off-site' archaeology, yet another branch of middle-range theory. Rather than concentrating on large – and often atypical – sites, 'off-site' research looks at the total distribution of artifacts and features over

Opposite. Cahokia, near St Louis, America's largest ancient city north of Mexico, as it was *c*. AD 1100-1150.

Central to any discussion of prehistoric change in the Midwest, the settlement may have achieved a state level of social organization.

The view in this reconstruction is from the south, across the Grand Plaza to Monks Mound. The dwellings and markets of the elite stood in the central district, enclosed by a log stockade; the homes and fields of the common citizens can be seen beyond, stretching a mile or more in every direction.

Many archaeologists label Cahokia a 'chiefdom'. Yet although no evidence of writing has been recovered, the arguments for it having been the capital of a state in the period AD 925–1200 are strong.

Well over 100 mounds arranged around filled and levelled plazas, and habitation evidence spread across the Mississippi floodplain indicate a dense population. There is also evidence that the social structure was strongly hierarchical in the shape of burials with grave goods drawn from the four quarters of the Midwest and more than 200 human sacrifices.

The city's plan, the pyramidal shape of the mounds and the iconography of Cahokia artifacts also imply links with Mesoamerica, likely in any case because of Cahokia's position on the Mississippi, the principal waterway to the Gulf of Mexico.

Object lesson. Establishing how the archaeological record reflects the vagaries of past human behaviour and how it is best interrogated are at the core of processual archaeology.

This Indian settlement in North Carolina, drawn *c.* 1585 by the Elizabethan explorer and artist John White, is an object lesson in the complexity of the physical remains archaeologists can expect to find, even within a simple settlement, and the subtlety of the traces they need to search for.

White described his snapshot of one fleeting moment of American Indian life before white settlement as 'The towne of Pomeiock and true forme of their howses couered and enclosed some with matts and some with barcks of trees; All compassed abowt with smale poles stock thick together in stedd of a wall.' He shows eighteen houses within a palisaded enclosure, as well as an Algonquian longhouse.

Add to the practical problems the requirement to find ways of elucidating a community's economic, social, cultural and spiritual life from a tiny and unrepresentative sample of what once existed, and the sheer scale of today's archaeological enterprise becomes clear.

the landscape, as in parts of East Africa where scattered camps belonging to early humans have been found. It seeks to understand the overall distribution of human behaviour in a particular region, and has contributed greatly to the understanding of how geomorphological processes affect the creation of the archaeological record.

Processual archaeology and its offshoots were characteristic of North America, and were never accepted to the same degree elsewhere in the world. In Britain, Cambridge prehistorian David Clarke was the closest archaeology came to having a heavyweight proponent of processual archaeology, and it is interesting to speculate how his brand of archaeology might have developed had he lived beyond the age of 38. Clarke was explicit in his desire to create a uniquely archaeological theory, based on systems theory; however, he never advocated the search for universal laws of human behaviour that characterized some elements of the processual school, nor did he wed himself to the Hempelian model.

While processual archaeology never dominated archaeology in the way that its adherents hoped, from the 1960s its influence permeated the subject to a marked degree. It gave archaeologists greater confidence in their subject's ability to make a unique contribution to the study of human behaviour – especially important in the United States, where archaeology has long been institutionally and intellectually subservient to anthropology; it also forced them to reconsider the quality and validity of their conclusions, injecting into their interpretation a much greater awareness of the need for objectivity. It is largely through Binford's advocacy of an explicitly scientific method that American archaeology in particular has spent so much time in the last three decades considering the status of archaeological knowledge.

Post-processual archaeology

The popularity of processual archaeology in North America fostered an inevitable reaction. In the late 1970s the interests of Ian Hodder, a Cambridge archaeologist whose early research under David Clarke had been scientific and positivist, began to shift substantially. With his students, he started to develop an explicitly political 'post-processual' archaeology that acknowledged the link between social mores and the practice of academic disciplines.

Although post-processual archaeology has its roots in Cambridge, it has come to subsume a number of approaches that were being developed independently by archaeologists elsewhere. The American Mark Leone, for example, has for years examined the role of ideology in how archaeologists frame their interpretation of the past. One of the most memorable of his studies looks at the layout of a natural-looking but carefully laid-out garden belonging to William Paca, a wealthy citizen of eighteenth-century Annapolis, Maryland. Leone argued that 'naturalizing' the garden's order was one way in which Paca was able to mask the contradictions inherent in his commitment to liberty and the fact that his own social position and wealth were based on slavery. Of course, such a reading of the garden may all be in the mind of the archaeologist; it can be argued that if the garden was private, its ideological message was confined to Paca and his friends and family. Nevertheless, Leone was able to demonstrate that a relationship between culture and sites like Paca's garden can at least be considered by archaeologists, who need not be limited simply to traditional studies of technology and subsistence.

Marxist archaeology

Marxist archaeology at its simplest level is the interpretation of the archaeological past using principles derived from Marxist thought. Thus, Marxist archaeology attempts to understand the mechanisms of social change by examining the contradictions between forces of production, such as technology and its control, and the relations of production, for instance social organization. These contradictions are expressed as a struggle between different socioeconomic classes. In classical Marxist thought, the economic base of a society determines the shape of its ideology, the latter being used to control the workers in society.

Marxist archaeologists openly proclaim the political nature of their archaeology, something which others would disavow, preferring to separate their professional work from their political beliefs. Neo-Marxist thought places less emphasis on the primacy of the economic base, stressing the importance of ideology in setting the tone of social change. Critical theory was developed by the 'Frankfurt School' and became popular in the social sciences in the 1970s, entering archaeological discourse about a decade later. It argues that no knowledge is politically innocent, and calls into question the objectivity of any archaeological statement. This has two potential repercussions. First, it denies the ability to rank claims about the past, rendering books proclaiming the extra-terrestrial origins of ancient civilizations just as valid as professional archaeologists' opinions. Second, and more sinister, it permits the rewriting of history as pure fiction, allowing the historical fact of the Holocaust to be dismissed as Jewish propaganda, as it has been by some anti-Semites. Archaeologists who are not totally wedded to a processual and positivistic viewpoint must deal with these objections.

NEW DIRECTIONS IN THE WEST

The essential paradox of archaeology is that it tries to understand the past but has only the present to study. Because all archaeological sites exist in the present, in order to construct their version of the past archaeologists have always had to rely on analogy and the replication of prehistoric behaviour through experimental tool manufacture and other techniques.

The use of analogy

The earliest use of analogy in archaeology is ethnographic analogy, which really began in the nineteenth century, when contemporary tribes were seen as 'living fossils' and thus representative of prehistoric people: northern peoples who exploited caribou were, for example, seen as sources of information on the reindeer-hunting people of the European Palaeolithic. As practised by such antiquarians as John Lubbock, ethnographic analogy was fundamentally racist. Subsequently, however, it has proved to be a fertile source of hypotheses against which archaeological data can be tested.

Other hypotheses for understanding the archaeological record have been provided by experimental archaeology and ethnoarchaeology. Experimental archaeology involves the replication and use of artifacts or even sites, so that testable hypotheses about function and methods of manufacture can be developed. The value of this approach was realized in the nineteenth century, when people like Lartet, Lubbock and Pitt-Rivers experimented with stone tools and digging implements. In North America, Kroeber undertook intensive studies, including replication of the traditional technologies used by Ishi, a Yahi Indian of California, forced in 1911 by the massacre of his band to enter the white man's world. Later, in the 1950s, Danish archaeologists like Iversen studied the efficiency of stone axes in cutting down trees: it was found that 500 square metres (600 square yards) of oak forest could be cleared by three men in four hours using flint axes hafted in a manner similar to actual prehistoric implements.

Today experimental archaeologists are involved in innumerable aspects of reconstructing the past. In North America, Donald Crabtree pioneered the replication of stone tools in the 1970s, like Bordes in France, while Lawrence Keeley revolut-

Opposite. Analogue system. An Inuit man and woman, photographed in 1914.

Once insultingly looked on, like other seemingly 'primitive' peoples, as living fossils still trapped in a prehistoric way of life, the Inuit have now – through ethnoarchaeology – become a precious source of observations and hypotheses about how the archaeological record comes into being and how it might best be interpreted.

ionized the analysis of edge-wear on tools by using the scanning electron micro-scope to characterize the types of wear encountered. Keeley reproduced different types of prehistoric stone tools, and then, by using them on different materials, was able to obtain 'signatures' illustrating the wear produced by different types of materials and tasks. These signatures could then be compared with the edge-wear on genuine prehistoric artifacts, and their functions identified. The results can be illuminating. Artifacts from the English Lower Palaeolithic site of Clacton, for example, were found to have been used on wood, hide, bone and meat.

Ethnoarchaeology emerged from the realization that ethnographic studies did not provide the data required by archaeologists trying to reconstruct behaviour from material culture. Before the Second World War Thomson's work on Aboriginal life showed the potential of this approach, but it was the 1970s before archaeo-logists began to mount ethnographic expeditions with the express purpose of observing what kind of archaeological record was produced by different types of human cultural behaviour. American archaeologist John Yellen's study of the !Kung in Africa, for instance, produced insights into the organization of activities around the camp, while William Rathje's 'garbology' project in Tucson, Arizona, has shown how an intensive study of garbage disposal in a modern American city can provide startling insights into urban behaviour.

Experimental archaeology

Over the same period, Europe has seen increasing interest in the experimental construction of buildings and farms. Archaeologists frequently recover the post-holes of prehistoric houses, and often have some idea how these houses would have looked when complete, and what they would have been like to live in. These remain mere ideas, however, unless put to practical experiment. This is what was done at Lejre in Jutland, where between 1965 and 1967 a series of six timber and thatch houses were built, their design based as closely as possible on the post-holes recov-ered at excavated sites. Close study of the houses made it possible to understand the advantages of different constructional methods and to appreciate the problems of heating and insulating such dwellings. In one dramatic experiment, one of the houses was deliberately burned to the ground in order to compare what was left with the remains that archaeologists usually encounter.

In southern Britain, a similar experimental project has attempted for over twenty years to reconstruct not only the buildings and structures of an Iron Age farmstead, but the fields, crops and livestock as well. The Butser Ancient Farm in Hampshire seeks to raise cereals and other plants of the kind used in the Iron Age, storing the produce in granaries and chalk-cut pits. The crops are grown in small rectangular fields of prehistoric type, with simple ploughs pulled by Dexter cattle, the modern breed closest in size to British Iron Age cattle. The Butser experiments are not limited to prehistoric farming, however, but also include the reconstruction of Iron Age round houses and the experimental firing of pottery kilns.

The value of experimentation extends even to such relatively well understood structures as Roman baths. At Xanten in Germany, a Roman bath building has been reconstructed. A trial firing showed that it took several days to reach the required temperature and consumed substantial amounts of wood fuel. One problem was regulating the temperature: more fuel and it continued to rise; less fuel and the fire went out. It therefore remains unclear how the Romans managed to achieve a steady temperature; even at a fairly modest 40 degrees Celsius the 100 per cent humidity created a powerful impact.

Urban archaeology

The years since the Second World War have seen an upsurge in urban archaeology, caused in part by the economic boom of the 1960s, in part by the clearance and rebuilding of wartime bomb damage. The results have been both a blessing and a

Viking Dublin. Recent excavations of waterlogged deposits at Wood Quay, Dublin, have revolutionized knowledge of the life and extensive trading relations of the Viking port that flourished between the tenth and twelfth centuries AD. The city was founded by the Vikings in 917. Finds have proved more varied and of higher quality than those from any other Viking town yet excavated.

Novgorod

Excavations at medieval Novgorod in northwestern Russia, about 100 miles (160 kilometres) south of St Petersburg, began in 1929 and since 1951 have been more or less continuous. For nearly fifty years, the Novgorod excavations have been among the largest in Russia.

The project has revealed extraordinary preservation, especially of wooden house walls and timber streets, but also of leather and wooden utensils, musical instruments, and even toys. Medieval Novgorod was built on compacted clay, which prevented the percolation of water and caused the wooden structures above to become waterlogged; analysis of tree rings in the larger timbers permits the dating of structures with a precision of fifteen to twenty-five years. About 140 workshops have been excavated which specialized in the manufacture of leather goods, jewellery, shoes, metal and glass objects, and other crafts. Novgorod was a key part of a trading network that encompassed much of northern Europe, extending even to the Indian Ocean.

Houses at Novgorod were log cabins, built using combinations of several basic modules, possibly with two or even three storeys. They were separate buildings, each with a yard enclosed by a stake or wattle fence. The streets were surfaced with timbers, using a method which involved laying three or four thin poles along the length of the street upon which were then laid split logs c. 40–50 centimetres (16–20 inches) in diameter, side by side across the width of the street. A total of 28 street levels identified at Saints Cosmas and Damian Street have been dated by dendrochronology: the earliest was laid in AD 953, the latest in AD 1462.

The most extraordinary finds at Novgorod have been over 700 manuscripts, known as *beresty*, dating between the mid-eleventh century and the early fifteenth century. Found also at towns like Pskov, *beresty* were pieces of birch-bark, boiled to remove the coarse outer layers and then inscribed without ink, using styluses made from bone or metal. The contents touch on numerous aspects of life in Novgorod, from mundane household records to legal, governmental and commercial discussions, and reveal an unexpected level of literacy.

Only 2 per cent of the area of ancient Novgorod has been excavated, so archaeologists estimate that there are over 20,000 *beresty* yet to be found under the modern town.

Timber town. Excavations near Holy Trinity church, Novgorod.

tragedy. On the one hand, we know more about the early development of centres such as London and Hamburg than we would ever have done had there been no such opportunities for excavation; on the other, excavations have made tragically clear the amount of destruction which new building has caused. Much of the evidence for the history of the world's cities is now lost for ever.

In partial recompense, the destruction of historic city centres has brought additional funds to pay for archaeological work in advance of redevelopment. In Britain, this has led to the discovery in London of the original timber quayside of the Roman port, and in York to the excavation at Coppergate of part of the Viking town, well preserved by waterlogging and rich in organic remains, including wooden implements and other objects of daily life. Other European countries have witnessed a similar spate of new information from beneath modern cities: in Paris the remodelling of the Louvre necessitated excavation beneath the foundations of the original medieval castle, now on display in the museum's basement. A little way downstream, in the Bercy area of Paris, excavations in advance of new development have discovered a neolithic riverside settlement and a series of wooden dug-out boats from the fourth millennium BC.

City-centre excavations have been most revealing where they have formed part of a long-term project that also encompasses documentary evidence. An excellent example is Winchester in Hampshire, southern England, where the plans of buried medieval buildings unearthed by archaeologists on Brook Street can be related directly to contemporary documents giving the value of the building and describing the activities carried on within it.

Wetland archaeology

One of the major innovations in archaeology during the last thirty years has been a renewed interest in wetlands. This has arisen in part from the realization that the well preserved remains buried in marshes and bogs are under serious threat from large-scale drainage works and other commercial operations such as peat-cutting. Major discoveries in Denmark, Britain and France have helped demonstrate the enormous potential of the European wetlands. In Denmark, the excavation of Tybrind Vig, a 6,000 year old fishing encampment, led to the recovery of logboats and a decorated wooden paddle. In the Somerset Levels in southwest Britain, a series of prehistoric timber trackways across the marshland has been traced and sections of them have been studied in detail to determine their date, their methods of construction, and the state of the local environment at the time they were built. One remarkable aspect of this work has been the use of tree-rings to date the trackways, showing that the oldest, the Sweet Track, was built in the year 3807 BC. Impressive results such as this have given wetlands a prominent profile in contemporary fieldwork, and have even led to talk of a 'wetland revolution' in archaeology.

Vindolanda

One of the most productive recent excavations in Rome's former western provinces has been at Vindolanda, just south of Hadrian's Wall, in northern England.

The remains of the fort of Vindolanda had been noted as early as 1702 although the first proper excavations did not take place here until 1930. Excavation in the 1970s started with the military bathhouse; debris from the drains contained hairpins and combs which suggested that the building was used not only by the garrison but also by females. Within the settlement was a *mansio* or inn that would have served officials travelling along Hadrian's Wall.

Vindolanda's waterlogged deposits yielded considerable environmental evidence. Meat was clearly consumed by the garrison: beef, mutton, pork, even deer. There is little evidence for agriculture, although cabbage was one of the vegetables and numerous hazelnuts were found. Organic items preserved included shoes and leather items as well as textiles.

The most significant find of all was a collection of over 1,500 documents, some consisting of wooden writing-tablets on which writing was cut through wax, and others comprising wooden slivers bearing writing in ink that can be read with the aid of infra-red photography. Such finds, especially in the northern provinces of the Roman empire, were virtually unknown before work at Vindolanda started.

Some documents are of a personal nature, such as one that mentions L. Neratius Marcellus ('that most distinguished man, my governor'), who is known to have been governor of the province of Britannia from AD 101 to 103. One of the most evocative of all is a letter to Sulpicia Lepidina, wife of Flavius Cerialis, the camp commandant at Vindolanda, from her friend Claudia Severa, wife of Aelius Brocchus, the commander of a neighbouring fort:

> Claudia Severa to her Lepidina, greetings. I send you a warm invitation to come to us on September 11th, for my birthday celebrations, to make my day more enjoyable by your presence. Give my greetings to your Cerialis. My Aelius greets you and your sons. I will expect you sister. Farewell, sister, my dearest soul, as I hope to prosper, and greetings.

One of the most important of the Vindolanda tablets lists military accounts, and provides information about the rations issued to the troops; this was especially significant as it could be compared to the evidence found in the excavations. The letters are important as they provide information about vulgar Latin, the spelling of words differing from that normally found in contemporary classical writers. They also allow comparison of handwriting in Britain with the hands found on Roman papyri from Egypt.

The dictated letter inviting Sulpicia Lepidina to Claudia Severa's birthday celebrations. The post-script in the lower right corner seems to have been written by Severa herself. If so, it represents the earliest surviving woman's hand-writing in Latin.

'If I have to spend the rest of my life working in dirty, wet trenches', wrote excavation director Robin Birley, 'I doubt whether I shall ever again experience the shock and excitement I felt at my first glimpse of ink hiero-glyphics on tiny scraps of wood'.

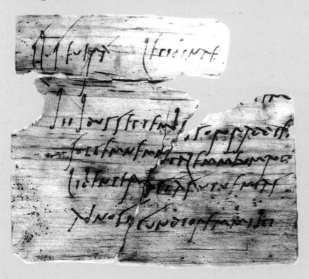

Underwater archaeology

Made possible only since the Second World War by the development of lightweight diving equipment, underwater archaeology involves the recovery of submerged archaeological finds and sites, particularly shipwrecks. Wrecks provide particularly valuable insights into ancient times, since they constitute time-capsules: 'snap-shots' of a brief moment in the past. Despite the bad reputation that treasure hunters have given such activities, underwater archaeology is conducted today by conscientious and trained professionals, its advent the result of the development of lightweight scuba gear that has given divers the manoeuvrability and independence properly to survey and excavate underwater archaeological sites.

As with terrestrial archaeology, sites must first be located using historical docu-ments or local informers. Remote sensing devices, such as a proton magnetometer or an underwater camera, can then zero in on the site itself. Excavation requires as much care in recording and removal as traditional field archaeology, the fact that everything takes place underwater obviously adding to the hazards and slowness of the operation. Finally, all recovered artifacts must be treated to slow down or stop deterioration as they are exposed to the air.

The earliest breakthroughs in underwater archaeology were made in the Medi-terranean, where pioneers like George Bass showed the potential of the technique by scientifically excavating classical and later ships, but it is now practised all over the world and in all climates, including the frigid waters of Lake Superior and Labrador. The rise in sports diving over recent years has meant that more sites have been recognized and reported – in the Mediterranean over 1,000 wrecks have been noted since 1945 – but it has also brought damage from illicit excavation. In recent years the development of remote cameras that can operate outside shallow coastal waters has meant that deep-water sites can now be identified also.

The large-scale movement of foodstuffs in the Roman period was mostly by sea, and the fact that wine and olive oil were transported in pottery jars, or *amphorae*, means that wreck sites are easily identified. The sixth-century BC shipwreck off Giglio Island, Italy, yielded a cargo of metal ingots and Etruscan amphorae contain-ing olives, as well as fine pottery from mainland Greece; and the fourth-century BC shipwreck of El Sec, Majorca, contained Athenian pottery inscribed with Punic graffiti, suggesting that although the cargo – which even included vine stocks – was mostly Greek, the traders were Phoenician. In contrast, ships containing grain or other organic cargoes are less likely to be discovered, so their numbers bear little relation to the amount of grain which ancient sources tell us was carried. Only one grain cargo has been found, and this dates from after the Roman period.

Shipwrecks have also led to theories about the distribution of archaeological artifacts having to be modified. It is clear that cargoes from different places could be found in the same ship. Certainly this is the case with the late fifth-century BC shipwreck off Porticello, in the Straits of Messina: its amphorae came from various cities in the east Mediterranean, while the fine pottery and silver nuggets found in

Ulu Burun: a Bronze Age shipwreck

In the fourteenth century BC, a ship set sail from Cyprus bound for the Aegean. Off Cape Ulu Burun, on the dangerous southern coast of Turkey, disaster struck, and the vessel foundered. In the late twentieth century, the wreck was rediscovered by sponge divers, and since 1984 it has been systematically excavated by George Bass and a team from the Institute of Nautical Archaeology in Texas.

For the archaeologist, shipwrecks have the immense advantage of being contemporaneous and accidental deposits. Furthermore, organic remains are often much better preserved underwater than on land. This is certainly true of the Ulu Burun wreck, which has produced almonds, acorns, pine nuts, thousands of olive, fig and pomegranate seeds, and a tonne of resin, possibly for making retsina or perfumed oil.

Metals formed the bulk of the cargo. There were around 250 oxhide-shaped ingots of Cypriot copper on board, weighing at least six tonnes, as well as tin and cobalt-blue glass ingots. The glass, elephant and hippopotamus ivory, and Egyptian ebony logs would have been turned into jewellery and furniture by Mycenaean craftsmen. Scrap gold and silver jewellery, bronze tools and weapons have also been recovered from the site.

Speculation about the 'nationality' of the ship is fruitless because the personal possessions of the crew included Mycenaean, Cypriot, Egyptian, Babylonian and Kassite seals, and pottery from Mycenaean Greece, Cyprus and the Near East. Although the presence of merchants on board seems certain, it has also been argued that this was a royal shipment destined for a specific port in the Aegean. The truth we will never know for sure.

Diver carrying one of the four-handled 'oxhide' copper ingots from the fourteenth-century BC Ulu Burun shipwreck, each of which weighs 60 pounds (27 kilograms). Several tin ingots were also recovered.

It was the heap of ingots, noticed by a sponge diver beneath a sheer cliff near Kas in southern Turkey, that first led to the discovery of the ancient shipwreck, its remains scattered across the sea bed at a depth of around 50 metres (165 feet).

Comparison of finds from the wreck with objects from land sites suggests that the ship was sailing from east to west, from Syria, or perhaps Cyprus, to Rhodes, the coast of Asia Minor or the Greek mainland. A coast-hugging sea route like this, minimizing the time spent at risk on open water, is thought to have operated for the transport of copper in the eastern Mediterranean throughout the Late Bronze Age.

the wreck originated in Attica. Ships and cargoes like this have provided an extra dimension to historical debates surrounding the economy of the ancient world.

STONE AGE ARCHAEOLOGY

During the 1960s and 1970s, Palaeolithic investigations in western Europe were dominated by the French prehistorians, André Leroi-Gourhan and François Bordes (p. 207). Interest in palaeoethnology was spearheaded by Leroi-Gourhan, an ethnologist who, in 1944, made his students excavate because he could not take them abroad to undertake ethnological fieldwork. He came to see prehistory as a branch of ethnology, and his interests lay in human behaviour and in ethnographic analysis; his aim was to make excavation a fundamental act, as reading a document would be for an historian.

Leroi-Gourhan's meticulous excavations in the caves of Arcy-sur-Cure (1946–63) and, from 1964, at the open-air reindeer-hunting camp of Pincevent, near Paris, pioneered the painstaking horizontal exposure, casting and preservation of activity areas, with every item left in place; the use of ethnographic analogy to study butchering patterns; and the study of *chaînes opératoires* (sequences in the production of tools) – that is, the investigation of artifacts as sources of human behaviour, from the selection of raw materials and the manufacture of tools to their abandonment. Analysis of traces of use-wear on tools and the refitting of flints and cores to study processes of production came into their own, with emphasis now placed squarely on the *life* of prehistoric people, not just on the classification and arrangement of bits of stone and bone. Although controversial, the identification of habitation floors representing a single, brief period of occupation provided the basis for finding out the things that palaeolithic groups did each time they stayed at a given site.

Leroi-Gourhan was equally influential in the field of palaeolithic art where, in the 1950s, in parallel with Annette Laming-Emperaire, he broke away from the traditional approach of Breuil which saw cave art as a random accumulation of images, and which applied to them such simplistic ethnographic analogies as 'hunting magic' or 'fertility magic'. Instead he considered each cave as a homogeneous composition, decorated according to a basic blueprint, and proposed a more rigorously defined series of styles as a chronological sequence for the art. He set out the hypothesis that the animals and 'signs' in the art could be divided into male and female symbols: developments which are rapidly becoming outmoded, but which at the time were nonetheless a major advance, stimulating a radical rethinking of all aspects of palaeolithic art.

Also in France, the American archaeologist Hallam Movius in 1958–64 carried out an exemplary excavation of the rich Upper Palaeolithic rock-shelter of Abri Pataud in Les Eyzies, extracting precise details about how different occupants had used and adapted the living area, and how they exploited their environment. Among countless other European developments in this period, one should mention

Above. Annette Laming-Emperaire (1917–1977) and André Leroi-Gourhan (1911–1986) in the cave of Pech-Merle, Quercy, 1975.

Above right. Some of the enigmatic 'signs' in the cave of El Castillo, northern Spain, dated *c.* 20,000–10,000 BC. Leroi-Gourhan saw these as 'full signs', and therefore female. Other paintings and engravings in the cave – evidently executed on repeated visits over a long period – include 50 red hand stencils, numerous quadrilateral signs and 155 animal figures. The nearby cave of La Pasiega, on the same hillside, contains a further 440 animal drawings.

the important excavations at Isernia, Italy, where a well-stratified Lower Palaeolithic open-air site of *c.* 730,000 BC produced thousands of stone tools associated with disarticulated animal bones; and the open-air Upper Palaeolithic campsite of Gönnersdorf, northwest Germany, where in 1968–76 hundreds of Magdalenian schist plaques engraved with images of animals and stylized females were found.

The 1960s and 1970s saw important cave excavations in northern Spain, some undertaken in collaboration with archaeologists from North America, while at Atapuerca, near Burgos, a cave dug since 1976 has yielded the remains of at least 24 individuals transitional between *Homo erectus* and Neandertals. The more than 1,000 human bones from the site represent about 90 per cent of all pre-Neandertal bones in Europe. Greece too – until after the Second World War a virtual blank on the palaeolithic map – witnessed its first large-scale investigations in the 1960s when Eric Higgs excavated key Middle and Upper Palaeolithic sites in the northwest, including Kokkinopilos, Asprochaliko and Kastritsa.

After Stalin's death in 1953 and the gradual decline of Cold War tensions, Soviet archaeology became less isolated from – and less hostile to – the ideas and methods of western archaeologists. With radiocarbon dating, Soviet archaeologists finally acquired a tool for addressing problems of chronology for a palaeolithic record poor in deeply stratified sites. However, their laboratories provided a very limited number of palaeolithic dates during the 1950s and 1960s; many they did provide proved

inaccurate owing to heavy reliance on bone from regions devoid of wood during the Ice Age. Many new Upper Palaeolithic open-air sites were discovered and excavated in European Russia and southern Siberia, and huts composed of mammoth bones and tusks, with associated hearths, storage pits and stone working areas, were uncovered at sites such as Mezhirich in the Ukraine.

THE MEDITERRANEAN WORLD

The growth from the 1960s of processual archaeology was thought largely irrelevant to classical archaeology, in part because of the prevailing view that material culture is only a minor part of the classical world. Slowly, however, new questions have begun to be asked and new strategies adopted. One important area has been the study of the rise of the Greek *polis* or city-state, through religion, literacy and urban survey. At the same time, more sophisticated ways of 'viewing' images have been borrowed from art history to enhance our understanding of the iconography of the ancient world.

Archaeology in the classical world has traditionally been seen as an integrated part of a classical tradition that includes language, literature and history. Processual archaeology was therefore perceived as challenging the role of the classicist – dismissing the work of classical archaeologists as no more than cataloguing – and criticizing their subject as one which 'describes everything, analyzes and synth-

Reconstructed Ice Age dwelling at Mezhirich, near Kiev, one of four mammoth-bone huts discovered since 1965. The huts are composed of several hundred mammoth bones and tusks arranged in a rough circle about 5 metres (16 feet) in diameter. The remains of a hearth typically lie near the centre, other hearths – often associated with concentrations of stone artifacts – outside. Nearby are large pits containing animal remains and artifacts.

Other mammoth-bone huts have been found in the Ukraine, Belorussia, Poland and Moravia. All appear to date to the coldest phase of the last Ice Age, roughly 25,000 to 14,000 years ago.

esizes a restricted range of aspects, and explains nothing'. In reality, however, the sheer amount of material available from classical sites that can be matched against literary and historical sources means that models and theoretical approaches in other branches of archaeology can be tested here; this is particularly important for the survival or loss of particular types of archaeological material, the role and function of craftsmen and women, and the long-distance movement of artifacts as part of trade and exchange patterns.

The ideas and techniques of the processualists have reached Mediterranean archaeology largely through the influence of prehistorians working on trade in the Bronze Age. It is clear from both documentary sources and archaeological evidence that the level of Bronze Age trade was considerable, and that it was conducted for the benefit of rulers whose status was enhanced by the acquisition of exotic goods. In the eastern Mediterranean in the later second millennium BC, trade frequently took the form of gift exchange rather than profit-driven commerce, but the gifts involved were much more than mere tokens – raw materials, for instance, were often sent in bulk. Much of the trade will be archaeologically invisible because the organic items concerned have perished, only being recovered under exceptional circumstances such as shipwreck.

Pottery in antiquity is unlikely to have been a major item of exchange. However, because it is virtually indestructible and has survived in quantity, trade routes in the ancient Mediterranean have traditionally been reconstructed and dated on the basis of pottery distribution. Sometimes the origin of a site's imported pottery is obvious but this is not always the case. The chariot krater from Enkomi in Cyprus is clearly Mycenaean in style, but most kraters of this type have been found in the eastern Mediterranean rather than in Greece, and it has therefore been suggested that they were made on Cyprus. But even if this were not so and the kraters were imported, the stylistic uniformity of Mycenaean pottery is such that the production centre could not be confidently identified.

The scientific analysis of pottery has revealed complex patterns of exchange that could not otherwise have been predicted. Examination of thin sections of sherds under a microscope, for example, has proved an efficient and inexpensive method of determining the provenance of coarse pottery. For fine fabrics, such as kraters, chemical analysis of minor and trace elements in the fabric can pinpoint the precise source of the clay; it has been demonstrated, for instance, that the chariot kraters were not in fact made on Cyprus but were imported from the Argolid.

The sheer volume of pottery and other excavated material from any classical site has made the computer an indispensable tool for today's classical archaeologist. Through the patronage of IBM, computer technology has also helped to enliven the archaeological remains of Pompeii by producing Computer Aided Design images of how the city and buildings within it would have appeared on the eve of its destruction in AD 79. Hotly debated by classical archaeologists, computer modelling has also helped to estimate the size of ancient cities, most notably Rome itself.

Vergina

Classical archaeology has often been in search of sites linked with historical events. Among the most spectacular recent discoveries are those made by Greek archaeologist Manolis Andronikos in northern Greece, the homeland of Philip of Macedon and his son, Alexander the Great.

Andronikos' exploration of Macedonian cemeteries caused him in 1977 to enter a large mound at Vergina that contained a substantial tomb with a decorated cornice showing a hunt scene. Both marble doors were still in place. As the earth was cleared, the remains of a small altar were found, with clear traces that horses had been sacrificed – an evocation of the heroic burial of Patroklos in Homer's *Iliad*.

When the tomb was opened the excavators could identify groups of silver vessels, armour and a marble box which they presumed contained the remains of the deceased. There were even fragments of furniture which once bore ivory and glass decoration. The most stunning discovery of all was made on opening the marble container for the ashes. Inside was a gold box or *larnax* on which was an embossed star-burst, symbol of the Macedonian kings. When it was opened, the cremated remains were found wrapped in a purple cloth; on top of them rested a gold oak wreath.

The tomb's second chamber was then opened to reveal a further marble sarcophagus as well as a gold wreath of myrtle leaves; this sarcophagus too contained a gold *larnax*, inside which lay bones wrapped in a gold and purple cloth.

The size of the tumulus, the richness of the finds, and the star-burst on the larnax pointed to this being the tomb of a member of the Macedonian royal family, especially if Vergina was, as is thought, the site of Aigai, home of the early kings. The stylistic date for the objects from the tomb pointed to c. 350–325 BC, and Andronikos therefore concluded that he had found the tomb of Philip II of Macedon (382–336 BC), the father of Alexander the Great.

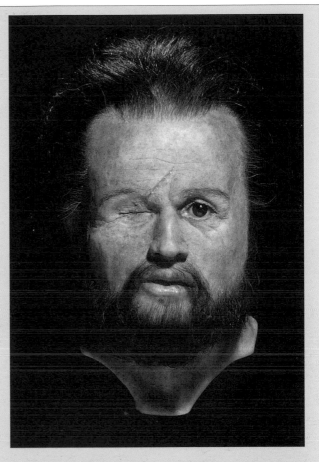

As a result of this suggestion, forensic scientist Richard Neave studied the bones of the deceased from the main chamber. From the remains of the skull he was able to reconstruct the face of a man who had at some point lost the sight of one eye – an injury Philip (above) is known to have suffered when he was struck by an arrow during a siege. This striking reconstruction, putting flesh on the bones of one of the key figures from the ancient world, lends additional support to Andronikos' identification.

Thera

In 1939 Greek archaeologist Spyridon Marinatos suggested that the collapse of the Minoan civilization of Crete should be attributed to the eruption of the Thera volcano. Few agreed, but Marinatos did not lose faith in his theory and began the search for a site on Thera which might offer proof. Eventually, in 1967, he started excavations at Akrotiri on the island's southern coast, discovering a 'prehistoric Pompeii' buried under volcanic ash.

Although Akrotiri is a Cycladic site rather than a Minoan colony, Cretan influence is strong. The excavated houses are impressive two- or three-storey buildings

incorporating features that recall Minoan architecture. Minoan too are the technique and style of the brilliant polychrome frescoes decorating the main rooms of the houses; the pottery, much of which was imported from Crete; and the Linear A script and system of weights and measures.

No skeletons have been found in the ruins: evidently the inhabitants fled before the pumice and ash buried their homes. That the eruption also devastated Crete, which lies 100 kilometres (60 miles) south of Thera, seemed likely. It has been suggested that tidal waves would have swamped sites on the coast, but most destructions were caused by fire, and tidal waves would not have affected sites on the southern side of Crete. It has also been thought that a blanket of noxious ash might have smothered Crete, but recent research indicates that most of the ash was in fact blown east. Seismic shocks no doubt accompanied the eruption, but Minoan Crete had suffered and recovered from severe earthquakes before.

It was not ultimately the problem of linking the effects of the eruption and the destructions on Crete which undermined Marinatos' theory; ironically, it was the excavation of Akrotiri itself. It soon became apparent that the settlement had been abandoned 30 to 50 years before disaster struck and that the eruption and destructions were not contemporary events. No proof exists, but most Aegean archaeologists now think it was the Mycenaeans who brought an end to Minoan civilization, possibly conquering Crete after the Minoans had been weakened by the effects of the Santorini eruption.

EGYPT AND THE NEAR EAST

The pace of archaeological work outside as well as inside Europe accelerated sharply in the 1960s, as the number of professional archaeologists rose substantially. Increased funds became available as the industrial world recovered from the economic disaster of the Second World War and as scientific achievement came to be regarded as an element in the Cold War arsenal. Archaeologists turned their attention more than ever towards trying to understand the ways in which ancient societies functioned, the ways in which people lived, and the reasons why complex societies evolved.

In Egypt, the period after the Second World War saw a return to 'business as usual'. Many long-term programmes of investigation at major sites, such as the French work at Tanis, resumed after an enforced period of abandonment. But an increasingly important engine driving fieldwork in Egypt was a concern for the recording as a bare minimum, and the conservation wherever possible, of the threatened sites and monuments.

Nubian rescue
Archaeologists working in northern Europe tend to believe that Egyptologists are unreasonably lucky because the sites they excavate are well preserved in dry, desiccating desert sand. This view is not entirely accurate. It is true that many of the sites

Opposite. Detail of a wall-painting at Thera, depicting a gatherer of saffron (crocus blossoms), from the large three-storey building known as Xeste 3.

in the south of Egypt (especially cemeteries) are situated on the fringes of the desert and are therefore beneficiaries of natural conservation. But this can be disturbed by the actions of people: just as construction work can destroy valuable archaeological sites in Europe and North America, so large-scale industrial and agricultural projects in the developing world can endanger its rich archaeological heritage.

A spectacular example of this process was the decision made in 1954 by the governments of Egypt and the Sudan to control the Nile by raising the dam at Aswan to massive heights. The purpose of the new dam was to control the seasonal rise and fall of the Nile in order to increase agricultural production and generate cheap hydro-electric power. Once constructed, it would create a large artificial lake immediately upstream of Aswan, up to 500 kilometres (300 miles) long and 10 kilometres (6 miles) wide. The downside was the submergence under Lake Nasser of Nubia, one of the richest archaeological treasure-houses in the world.

This was not a new problem. Lower dams built earlier this century had given rise to examples of what today would be called 'salvage' or 'rescue' archaeology. With the building of the new Aswan dam, and the subsequent 63 metres (207 feet) rise in the height of the Nile behind it, many more sites than before were threatened, including Abu Simbel and Philae, two of the best known and most visited ancient monuments in Egypt. For most, nothing practical could be done except to excavate and to record. Some of the most important Nubian sites, in particular a series of Middle and New Kingdom mud-brick fortresses in the area of the Second Cataract, such as Buhen, had to be left to disintegrate beneath Lake Nasser. However, the major aim of the Nubian rescue campaign was the physical removal from the danger zone of a famous group of New Kingdom temples, constructed by pharaonic Egypt in its southern colony.

Through UNESCO, an International Campaign to Save the Monuments of Nubia was launched with the participation of some 22 nations; it was in operation for twenty years, from 1960 to 1980. One group of Nubian temples was dismantled and re-erected close to the High Dam itself; another was re-sited on high ground close to the Wadi es-Sebua, and another close to Amada; a fourth group was placed in the gardens of the museum at Khartoum. However, the interest of the world focused on two of the most important buildings built by the ancient Egyptians: the temples of Abu Simbel and Philae.

The most problematic of the monuments was Abu Simbel. Unlike most of the others moved, the pair of temples here (both the work of Ramesses II, c. 1290–1224 BC) were not constructed of separate blocks that could be dismantled and re-erected on another site. They were rock-cut: each temple was, in effect, part of a mountain. In scale, too, Abu Simbel represented a huge problem. While the interior of the main temple is relatively modest in size, its exterior is monumental; dominated by three (originally four) seated colossi of the king, the facade 30 metres (100 feet) tall and 35 metres (116 feet) wide. Abu Simbel is also the single most important temple site in Lower Nubia, and while it was unthinkable that the friable

Opposite. Salvaging pharaoh Ramesses II's thirteenth-century BC temples at Abu Simbel in advance of the rising waters of Lake Nasser, 1964. The temples were moved 64 metres (210 feet) up a cliff to save them, an unprecedented feat of technology and one of the most ambitious civil engineering projects of modern times.

A huge concrete shell was built behind the reconstructed facade to enclose the main temple and sanctuary, and the exact alignment of the original structure was maintained. As a result, the rays of light from the sun that each summer and winter solstice for 3,000 years shone the length of the temple to illuminate the figure of Ramesses and the gods in the sanctuary still do so today.

sandstone monuments should be left to rot under Lake Nasser, it was less easy to come up with an obvious solution to the problem. From 1959 to 1963 suggestions about how best to tackle the problem were debated and rejected.

The solution finally adopted, at a projected cost of $32 million, was an Egyptian scheme to cut the temples out of the living rock and re-erect them above the lake. Work began on dismantling and re-erecting the temples on 1 April 1963, five months ahead of the first rise in the waters of the lake, and was completed in September 1968. It encompassed not just the re-erection of the Abu Simbel temples but, in the case of the larger temple, the creation of a huge concrete shell around and behind the temple, a shell later landscaped to recreate the original environmental context of the building.

Philae was a relatively simple proposition by comparison. An island in the Nile containing a group of related temples, the most important that of the goddess Isis, Philae was one of the most renowned centres of pilgrimage in the Graeco-Roman period (*c.* 380 BC–AD 400). As at Abu Simbel, the solution chosen was to recreate the context of the site by moving the temples to a new island. Transportation was relatively straightforward, lasting a little over two years, from 1977 to 1979. The major job was the landscaping of the nearby, flood-free island of Agilkia to make it look like Philae; it was this work that consumed the five years 1972 to 1977. Like Abu Simbel, the result was a triumph of human ingenuity, visited today by many thousands of tourists each year.

Israeli archaeology

In the aftermath of the Second World War, the creation of the state of Israel in 1948 brought conflict to the Near East. Four wars and perpetual low-level violence followed, and Arab opposition to Israel's existence caused tensions with western governments that, at times, limited archaeological access. Meanwhile, in Israel itself, archaeology became an ideological tool for legitimizing the Jewish claim to Palestine. Excavation became 'a revelation of the indissoluble bonds that link the ancient monuments of a people with their natural landscape, and therefore the community with its homeland'. The excavation of the cliff-top fortress of Masada was a case in point. It was not just an archaeological site: for the Israelis, the zealots' last stand 'elevated Masada to an undying symbol of desperate courage, a symbol which has stirred hearts throughout the last nineteen centuries ... it is this which brings the recruits of the armoured units of the Defence Forces of modern Israel to swear the oath of allegiance on Masada's heights: "Masada shall not fall again!"' Masada, like Zion, symbolizes both the past and the future of a people.

The Palaeolithic in the Near East

The Palaeolithic was the key beneficiary of archaeological excavation in the Near East during the 1960s and 1970s. The meticulous methods developed by French archaeologists in search of habitation floors were applied to sites in the Levant.

Masada

The most spectacular site ever excavated in Israel, Masada rises over 400 metres (1,300 feet) above the western shores of the Dead Sea. As William Albright has observed, 'from the standpoint of the impact of archaeology on national life Masada has no historical parallel; it remains unique'.

Masada is the late twentieth century's most potent example of a 'political' excavation, and was clearly recognized as such by its investigator, Yigael Yadin. Conducted between 1963 and 1965, his excavations concentrated on the fortress-palace complex built as a personal retreat and citadel by Herod the Great (37–34 BC). This comprises an elaborate villa and bath house, with fine frescoes, storehouses and an administrative building at one end of the plateau, a palace with mosaic floors, and several other large residential buildings. Byzantine monks reoccupied the site and added a chapel in the sixth century AD.

Yadin was particularly interested in the buildings associated with the Jewish defenders who held Masada against Roman military forces during the revolt of AD 66–73. He found the skeletons of the slain, an *ostrakon* or inscribed potsherd bearing the name Ben Ya'ir (probably the Zealot leader during the Roman siege), coins bearing the legend 'For the freedom of Zion' in Hebrew, and copies of the biblical books of Psalms, Leviticus and Ecclesiasticus written on scrolls of leather.

Yadin was a staunch nationalist, a member of the Haganah resistance organization before the creation of Israel, and then Chief of Operations of the Israel Defence Forces during the war of 1948; he then retired from the military and turned his full attention to archaeology. For him, as for every Israeli, the last stand at Masada was a crucial event.

The account of the siege, by the historian Flavius Josephus, describes how, when the capture of the fortress by the Romans was imminent and inevitable, the 960 defenders chose to commit communal suicide rather than surrender to the might of Rome. They resolved that:

> a death of glory was preferable to a life of infamy, and that the most magnanimous resolution would be to disdain the idea of surviving the loss of their liberty ... And so met [the Romans] with the multitude of the slain, but could take no pleasure in the fact, though it were done to their enemies. Nor could they do other than wonder at the courage of their resolution, and at the immovable contempt of death which so great a number of them had shown.

The excavations were important to New Testament archaeologists and caught the imagination of Jewish communities throughout the world. Later scholarship and study of the archaeological finds have cast considerable doubt on the mass suicide story and Yadin's interpretation of his finds, yet Masada remains a potent symbol of Jewish resistance to overwhelming odds that echoes down the ages.

The Amud I skull, found at Wadi Amud, northeast of Haifa, Israel: one of five Neandertals excavated at the site in the 1960s, and dating to 50–40,000 years ago. It belonged to a male, aged around twenty-five at the time of death. Anthropologically, the skull compares closely with Neandertal remains found at Tabun and Shanidar.

Jacques Tixier, for example, worked at Ksar Akil in 1969–75, defining a large number of very thin levels (fifteen in less than a metre of deposits) that he took to be 'living floors', each the product of a single episode of occupation.

Other interpretative advances came with more sophisticated methods of analysis. Arthur Jelinek reopened excavations at Tabun between 1967 and 1972, proceeding very carefully, with the three-dimensional position of all archaeological materials over 2 centimetres (0.8 inch) in size being mapped; the work of geologists, geomorphologists, and faunal and pollen analysts looked at the natural processes by which the cave deposits had formed. Jelinek defined over 80 'beds', whose archaeological assemblages helped to clarify the relationships between the Acheulean, Pre-Aurignacian and Mousterian industries of the Levant.

Most important of all was the discovery of more human fossils at sites in Israel. Work since 1960 at Qafzeh, Amud and Kebara has added to the fossil inventory accumulated in the 1920s and 1930s. The morphology of some specimens falls in the Neandertal pattern, but those from Qafzeh and Skhul present many modern human anatomical features along with other Neandertal-like characteristics. Most researchers emphasize the modern anatomical aspects of these specimens and distinguish them from the Neandertals.

Such fossils have become part of the heated debate about the African origins of anatomically modern *Homo sapiens*. Radiometric dating techniques have redated the Qafzeh and Skhul specimens from *c*. 40,000 to more than 100,000 years ago, to which period the Tabun Neandertals have also been assigned. This new chronological position, together with their many modern anatomical characteristics, have led many to argue that the Qafzeh and Skhul fossils represent an early population of anatomically modern *Homo sapiens* that co-existed with local Neandertals. Possibly the two populations were adapted to different climates – Neandertals to colder, moderns to warmer, conditions – and moved back and forth across the Levant in response to the changing climate of the Ice Age.

The roots of civilization

The archaeology of later periods in the Near East increasingly focused on two issues: researching the gaps – geographical or chronological – left by previous generations, and seeking to understand more fully the beginnings of farming and the origins of cities and state government – two key developments on the path to civilization. The pace of research increased particularly in countries striving to juggle the perils of modernization, new-found petroleum wealth and political alignment. Most of these countries now had national antiquities services and established university courses in archaeology.

Activity funded from overseas remained important nonetheless. In Iran, in 1975 alone, archaeological investigations included seventeen survey and thirty excavation programmes. At Siraf, on the desert coast of the Persian Gulf south of Shiraz, British excavations uncovered a famous port of Sassanian and Early Islamic times. Medieval Muslim geographers describe the flotillas of trading ships that annually left Siraf for Canton in China, stopping at Indian and Southeast Asian ports on the way. Siraf was a main cog in the great Indian Ocean trade that made the caliphs of Baghdad fabulously rich during the ninth century AD. Covering a square mile on this parched coast, the city was obliged to hoard its water in cisterns and import much of its food. The bazaars stretched a kilometre (0.6 mile) along the shore, and contained areas devoted to special crafts like copper-working. Siraf had residential areas too, some encompassing the palatial dwellings of rich merchants. Pottery included blue-green glazed jars of a type made in Iraq and found on the East African coast, along with vessels from India and Chinese stoneware.

While the radiocarbon revolution imposed wholesale revisions of the chronology and perceived relationships between cultures in Europe and Africa, its effects on Near Eastern archaeology were more limited. The accepted chronology for Assyria, Babylonia, the Hittites and their contemporaries was based on cuneiform king-lists and chronicles in which the dates of individual kings could be calculated backwards into the third millennium BC from a variety of fixed points, notably recorded observations of Venus and events in Greek and Egyptian history. The general precision of this historical chronology was far greater than that of radiocarbon dating, so Libby's technique tended to be regarded as superfluous in the Near East. Relatively few radiocarbon dates were obtained, and even today the best series of 14C dates for the fourth millennium BC Sumerians of southern Mesopotamia, who did not leave dated texts, comes from contemporary sites in Syria and eastern Turkey. Radiocarbon was more warmly received in prehistoric archaeology, which lacked this written framework for dating, and among archaeologists working on Mesopotamia's non-literate neighbours. In South Asia above all, it established dates between 2500 and 2000 BC for the Indus civilization – whose script remains undeciphered – far more precisely than traditional stylistic analysis could ever have done.

The origins of farming

Dissatisfied with traditional approaches to archaeology after the war, American archaeologist Robert Braidwood and his collaborator Bruce Howe 'envision[ed] not the familiar, old-fashioned archaeology of digging royal tombs for fine-art museums, but an "idea-archaeology", aimed at broad culture-historical problems, in which antiquities as such are meaningless save as tools for understanding the ways of mankind'. For Braidwood, this attitude expressed the need for inter-disciplinary thinking about the origins of food production that was ecological in focus, and expansive in geographical scope.

He expected to find evidence for the first farming villages in the hilly country between the Mesopotamian plain to the south and the high Taurus and Zagros mountains to the north. The wild ancestors of cultivated wheat and barley lived naturally in this 'nuclear zone', and rainfall and other climatic conditions allowed early farming without the need to irrigate or clear forests. Braidwood also believed that the inhabitants of the nuclear zone would not turn to farming until they had made certain necessary inventions, like equipment for grinding cereals into flour.

With these ideas in mind, he took a team of earth scientists, botanists and bone experts to the Zagros foothills of Iraq, where they found sites that showed the development of the tools needed for a farming way of life. Excavations at some of these sites, especially Jarmo, recovered unequivocal evidence of farming and animal herding in the early seventh millennium BC. Jarmo was a small village of nearly 1.6 hectares (4 acres) with a population of several hundred people who lived in small houses constructed of packed mud on stone foundations; they cultivated early forms of wheat and barley,

and herded goats and sheep, although wild foods still played an important role in their diet.

The explosion of interest in the origins of farming and herding from the 1960s led to remarkable discoveries across the region, from Greece to Central Asia and Pakistan, that ultimately eclipsed both Jericho and Jarmo. Excavators found fresh evidence for the very early domestication of plants and animals, and for early village life, creating a picture of the first farming as something not 'invented' but rather unwittingly developed as an economic reaction to environmental change and growing population.

In particular, the Cambridge prehistorian Eric Higgs argued in the 1970s that agriculture did not develop rapidly, its advantages over hunting and gathering manifest, as Childe's 'Neolithic Revolution' had assumed. It was rather the culmination of a long-term trend – apparent at least as early as the Upper Palaeolithic – towards a greater intensification of the human exploitation of plants and animals.

Burgeoning fieldwork stimulated the development of new ways of recovering information. Higgs and his team pioneered techniques like flotation, a method for separating from excavated soil the tiny seeds that revealed the genetic changes that the first agricultural experimentation brought about in wild wheat, barley and other plants. Somewhat later, in the early 1980s, chemical analysis of the changing levels of strontium and other elements in samples of ancient human bone began to support calculations of the changing amounts of cereals (wild or cultivated) in prehistoric diets. After several decades of work, the Neolithic in western Asia accordingly came to be perceived as a slow evolutionary process, in which at different times the entire region participated.

Tell Abu Hureyra, an early farming settlement in northern Syria, excavated in the 1970s. Flotation produced a mass of charred plant remains, while dry-sieving retrieved over 60,000 identifiable bone fragments.

The impact of processual archaeology in the Near East was similarly very limited initially: architecture, texts and the sequencing and chronology of pottery remained key concerns. From the 1960s, however, dissatisfied with the humanistic spirit of art history that underlay traditional techniques, a growing number of younger archaeologists sought to adopt the more explicitly scientific approach to research then increasingly being espoused in the United States and Britain. Many archaeologists now focused their attention on two major turning points in the evolution of ancient societies: why groups that had lived by hunting and gathering wild foods turned to farming and animal herding; and why independent villages of farmers and herders developed the bureaucratic supervision, tax obligations and social and economic inequalities of state government.

The most remarkable of the early farming settlements excavated in this period was Çatal Hüyük in central Turkey. A surprisingly large and sophisticated site dated *c.* 6250–5400 BC and covering 21 hectares (50 acres), Çatal Hüyük contained houses of mud brick and timber solidly packed around courtyards; the absence of

Wall-painting of the sixth millennium BC from the hunting shrine at Çatal Hüyük showing a dancing man with a bow in his right hand. He wears a white loincloth, black-spotted, pink leopard skin and a pendant round his neck.

The painted walls of the houses at Çatal Hüyük preserve an art form that rarely survives elsewhere. The designs were most often geometric shapes, and less often scenes of figures, whose intended meaning is unclear.

The exuberant frieze from which this detail is taken depicts a deer hunt, with 24 figures in all. Among the dancers are naked acrobats, a drummer and a strange figure, bi-coloured red and white, apparently headless.

streets indicates that access was gained through roofs. Many rooms were decorated with bright murals, and some were equipped with benches, platforms and modelled bull-heads. Clay figurines, notably of the mother goddess giving birth, offered additional insights into the beliefs of the community. The dead were buried beneath the house-floors, accompanied by many grave-goods, often of exotic origin, including turquoise, copper, sea-shells and fine flint. Çatal Hüyük probably controlled the trade in obsidian, or volcanic glass, that appeared in sites as far away as Jericho, and seems to have profited from the developing exchange relations that linked large areas of western Asia. The size, sophistication and wealth of the town contradicted many expectations about the nature of neolithic societies. When the British archaeologist James Mellaart excavated Çatal Hüyük, its only rival was Jericho; since then, other excavated sites have confirmed the sophistication and wealth of the period.

The origins of civilization and of the state as a means of government is the other great transformation in human history to have preoccupied Near Eastern archaeologists in recent years. The early Sumerians in southern Mesopotamia invented a state system of government which spawned cities, very large and elaborate temples, specialized occupations like weaving and account-keeping, cuneiform writing and other means of keeping track of property, and sharply defined hierarchies of social status. These advances toward civilization in Mesopotamia happened without any influence from other, already existing civilizations, making Mesopotamia one of no more than half a dozen 'pristine states' in human history.

The majority of Near Eastern states – whether the Hittites in Turkey or the Elamites in Iran – appear to have been 'secondary': to have developed by imitating more advanced neighbours, as is shown by their massive borrowings of the cuneiform writing system, styles of art and religious traditions. Much archaeological evidence for both pristine and secondary states now comes from technically out-moded excavations at places like Uruk, Ur and Susa in Mesopotamia, and Mohenjo-daro and Harappa in the Indus valley: sites that generated an enormous archaeological database that has been used to answer questions about the origins and workings of such early societies.

New ideas stimulated new work, as well as reanalysis of some older sites. For example, the German expedition at Uruk started looking outside the excavated temple areas, finding surface evidence that the city already covered 200 hectares (500 acres) by the late fourth millennium BC; and Italian and German archaeologists returned to Mohenjo-daro to map surface evidence for specialized craft areas in unexcavated parts of the site. Excavation of Bronze Age sites has in general become more detailed, digging small areas meticulously and using sophisticated retrieval techniques to recover animal and plant remains. One excavation spent two seasons digging a large rubbish pit at Sharafabad in western Iran, detecting individual seasons in which refuse was dumped, in order to gain information about the annual cycles of rural life.

Traditional excavations intended simply to discover what happened in a region, or to find new cuneiform tablets, works of art, and monumental architecture continue to yield major surprises. The Italian work at Tell Mardikh, the ancient Ebla, in northern Syria, is one such. Originally begun in the early 1960s to explore the second millennium BC city, the excavations eventually encountered the remains of an older city of the mid-third millennium, the centrepiece of which was a mud-brick palace built around a porticoed courtyard. Inside were remarkable artifacts: fragments of carved wooden furniture, stone inlay in Sumerian style, cylinder seals derived from Sumerian prototypes, stone vessels imported from Egypt, and a 23 kilogramme (50 pound) stock of lapis lazuli that must have come from eastern Afghanistan. Most memorable of all was a cache of 15,000 cuneiform tablets, most of them still in their original order on burnt and collapsed shelving. These administrative documents of the palace economy, written in Eblaitic, the local language of northern Syria, describe the economy of a very rich, powerful kingdom, whose wealth was based on textiles woven from the wool of enormous flocks of sheep, and on exchange with neighbouring settlements in southeastern Turkey and Mesopotamia. The Mardikh excavations revealed the unexpected early states of Syria, contemporaries of the city-states of Early Dynastic Mesopotamia, and their equals in sophistication and wealth.

But excavation itself has come to provide only part of the story, as other kinds of studies have come to the fore. Already in 1937, Thorkild Jacobsen, an Assyriologist whose main interest was the social interpretation of Mesopotamian religion, undertook a 'systematic survey of all existing tells in a region, dating the settlements by means of their surface pottery and plotting them on period maps, [to] show that they are grouped in linear patterns representing the lines of the major water courses of the region in antiquity'. Jacobsen originally wanted to gain topographic information useful for understanding the political and economic history of southern Mesopotamia, but the technique could equally provide information about the origins of Mesopotamian civilization. Chicago anthropologist Robert Adams later brought these methods to fruition through survey work in many parts of Babylonia. He was able to trace in detail the settlement history of many areas of southern Mesopotamia, from the earliest occupation around 7000 years ago to medieval times, showing how strongly Mesopotamian civilization was based on cities: by the mid-third millennium BC, roughly three-quarters of the people in the heartland of southern Mesopotamia lived in cities at least 40 hectares (100 acres) in size. Similar studies in the Indus valley reveal a more even pattern in which villages and smaller towns balanced the populations of cities like Mohenjo-daro and Harappa.

As in the Mediterranean, the physical and chemical characteristics of artifacts also provided new kinds of information about long-distance trade in exotic raw materials. The development of physical and chemical techniques suited to identifying the sources of raw materials and technologies of producing finished goods has allowed increasingly sophisticated conclusions about the ancient economy. The classic example is obsidian-sourcing, in which the chemical characteristics of obsidian flows in Anatolia are matched against those of obsidian stone tools from neolithic sites in Syro-Palestine and Mesopotamia. This work, begun in the 1960s, revealed patterns of neolithic exchange, and similar studies have since been undertaken of more complex societies of the third millennium, and of the circulation of pottery, metals and stone vessels throughout the Near East.

THE FAR EAST

New developments in Far Eastern archaeology over the last generation have been technological rather than theoretical, with tephrachronology (dating from volcanic deposits), experimental archaeology, underwater archaeology and conservation techniques of primary interest.

In Japan in particular, computers are increasingly used to store huge databases for all known shell-mounds, keyhole-shaped mounded tombs, bronze mirrors, Jomon figurines and rooftiles. The last is particularly useful for the palace excavations in western Japan, such as Fujiwara

Celadons or green stoneware jars from the fourteenth-century AD Sinan shipwreck, discovered in 1976. Many were covered with incised lotus and arabesque (right) or ribbed (above) designs. The ship's huge and varied cargo of ceramics – some 17,000 pieces in all – was destined for the markets of Japan and the Philippines.

(occupied AD 696–710) and Nara (AD 710–84), where over 6,000 types of rooftiles have been documented, many tiles being shifted from site to site during rebuilding projects. The shell mound database focuses on Jomon-period sites, but even scarce medieval shell mounds are being evaluated for new information on dietary habits. Keyhole-shaped tombs are thought to be burials of protohistoric rulers; lesser aristocrats used round- or square-shaped tombs. Analyses of their relative distributions give clear pictures of regional developments of territorial hierarchies, while analyses of their bronze mirror deposits shed light on specialist craft production and patterns of exchange among the wealthy.

Environmental archaeology is now being taken up in East Asia, with analyses of plant and animal remains leading the field. Near Shanghai, for example, ancient paddy fields are being sought by analysing densities of 'plant opal' (phytoliths) in soil core samples: these microscopic silica particles exist in all grasses and, according to a methodology pioneered by the Japanese, if phytoliths exceed 5,000 counts per gram of soil, then that soil was probably from a paddy field. Flotation in northern Japan has also recovered seed remains indicating the domestication of 'barnyard millet', a weed grain not ordinarily used elsewhere.

Underwater archaeology is extremely important for shipwreck investigation, pursued by Far Eastern groups interested in historic trade routes and ceramic cargoes. The Sinan site, the wreck of a Chinese Yuan-dynasty (AD 1271–1368) ship off the western Korean coast, yielded porcelain, celadon (stoneware vessels) and an astonishing quantity (18.6 tonnes) of Chinese coins. The convergence of environmental, wetland and underwater archaeology is represented by the Awazu site at the bottom of Lake Biwa, Japan. Consisting of two shell mounds packed with botanical data as well as wooden artifacts and lacquer ware of Jomon date, Awazu has been investigated since 1980 by the Kyoto City Archaeological Centre, using many innovative techniques, including surrounding the site with iron shuttering and pumping it dry for excavation.

Innumerable major finds have been made in Far Eastern archaeology, including extraordinarily rich graves in both China and in Korea, where Silla kingdom tombs of the period AD 300–668 – including the Tomb of the Heavenly Horse and the Great Tomb at Hwangnang – were excavated in Kyongju in 1973–75. The Tomb of the Heavenly Horse derives its name from a painting of a flying horse on a sewn birch-bark mud-guard. The deceased himself wore a gold crown and belt decorated with gold pendants and jade beads.

As the main aim of Far Eastern archaeology is historical and nationalistic, describing everyday life in prehistoric times is a major objective of research and museum display. Museums incorporate many reconstructions of houses, rooms and workshops using life-sized mannequins or dioramas of sites – all of which allow the viewer to 'enter into the past'. The new National Folk Museum in Seoul, for example, has large-scale models of the imperial capital of ninth-century Seoul and a diorama of a Bronze Age village among its displays, while the National

Museum for Japanese History near Narita offers a full-sized model of a Yayoi-period raised storehouse for the storage of rice sheaves, with mannequins illustrating the use of a two-person saw on a large timber. Each province and prefecture in China, Korea and Japan has its own museum, focusing on the past life of the area, giving its residents a concrete feel for their own history. Increasingly, such museums are highly imaginative architecturally. The actual Tomb of the Heavenly Horse in Kyongju can be entered to view the gorgeous gold finds, as can the Chinese Ming tombs north of Beijing.

The Terracotta Army

Often referred to as the Eighth Wonder of the World, the 'Terracotta Army' was discovered near Xi'an, in China's Shaanxi province, in 1974 by peasants digging a well. It comprises around 7,000 life-size figures in fired clay, representing the troops who were to guard China's first emperor, Qin Shihuangdi, after his death in the third century BC. He lies undisturbed in an immense burial mound some distance from his terracotta troops.

Each warrior's head is different, and much has been learned from the figures about hairstyles, weaponry, horse trappings and the positioning of categories of soldier. The enormous Pit 1, containing most of the figures, had been destroyed by fire; it is now enclosed within a hangar and forms one of China's – and the world's – major tourist attractions. Chinese archaeologists found that Pit 3, discovered in 1976, had collapsed naturally, damaging its contents badly. Though far smaller than the immense Pit 1, it is still 21.4 metres (70 feet) long, 17.6 metres (58 feet) wide, and more than 5 metres (16 feet) deep. It contains 68 warriors, four horses and a war chariot, as well as 34 weapons. This pit seems to represent the headquarters, the army's commanders, together with their personal guard. The warriors are at least 13 centimetres (5 inches) taller than average, and they are drawn up in battle formation.

Each warrior's head is individual, fitted to a standardized body, and with a very wide range of facial expressions. Every racial group in China seems to be represented. More than half have round earlobes, but nearly 20 per cent have square ones, a proportion similar to modern Chinese. There are 25 styles of beard, corresponding to the age, character, facial shape and post of the figure represented.

Much has also been learned from the figures about hair-styles, clothing and armour, weaponry, horse trappings and the positioning of categories of soldier. There are generals, officers, infantrymen, kneeling archers, and cavalrymen; more than 600 clay horses and over 100 war chariots have also been uncovered.

Most warriors are muscular, nearly 90 per cent are tall, and every general is depicted as a stalwart with thickset bones and well-developed muscles. This is clearly a combat-ready army of strong, healthy soldiers, arranged in ancient Chinese battle formation.

AFRICAN ARCHAEOLOGY

The 1960s and 1970s were boom years for African archaeology, with more funds, more professional archaeologists, and more university departments and museums than ever before. This growth levelled off in the 1980s. Numbers of indigenous archaeologists increased and there was a growing interest in the African past in newly independent states, especially in the Iron Age, partly in reaction to the colonial denial that it existed at all and partly in a new search for roots. Yet important though these developments were, they rate only as a sideshow in comparison with the headline-grabbing impact of the discovery in East Africa and Ethiopia of thousands of early human and hominid fossils from the 1960s onwards. *National Geographic*'s coverage of the Leakeys was read by millions, and for the first time television brought palaeoanthropology into living rooms all over the world.

New orientations

The impact of processual archaeology in Africa in this period was limited to South Africa, in part at least because the processualists' emphasis on understanding change from within a cultural system and their rejection of migration and diffusion from elsewhere as explanations of change, mirrored trends already under way in a post-independence African archaeology that sought to celebrate indigenous African creativity and innovation.

Environmental archaeology, however, was more warmly welcomed and it is now widely used in African archaeology. The palaeoeconomic work of Cambridge archaeologists like Clark and Higgs; better standards of fieldwork; the increasing use of quantitative methods; the systematic recovery of animal and plant remains;

Harvard archaeologist Glynn Isaac (1937–1985) working at Koobi Fora in northern Kenya, a vast stretch of fossil-rich sandstone sediments extending some 40 kilometres (25 miles) from the edge of Lake Turkana to the volcanic slopes of the Rudolf basin. Astonishingly, this wilderness has produced a larger number of early hominid remains datable between 2.5 and 1 million years old than any other site in the world – in all the remains of more than 150 individuals.

Isaac himself was particularly interested in the social behaviour of early people, such as the possibility that they shared food communally and roamed the landscape in a structured fashion, travelling considerable distances from their home base with no more than lightweight tools.

increased interest in foraging behaviour and the origins of African food production; and the excavation of Stone Age 'living-floors' at early sites like Olduvai Gorge and Koobi Fora, followed by studies of the animal and plant remains found on them and the reconstruction of past environments: all contributed to a burgeoning environmental emphasis in archaeological research. The natural science component that entered African archaeology as a result probably accounts for environmental rather than social and historical reasons being used to explain cultural change and choice even in the 1990s. Only in the Iron Age did migration and diffusion remain important explanatory concepts.

South African archaeology has traditionally stood apart, part of world archaeology rather than an aspect of the 'nationalist' archaeology prevalent elsewhere on the continent that tends to focus on the recent past, particularly the Iron Age. It will be interesting to see what course South African archaeologists chart for themselves in the new, post-apartheid era.

Absolute dating

Radiocarbon and potassium-argon dating are the cornerstones and chronological basis of modern African archaeology. From the 1950s onwards, potassium-argon dating – based on the radioactive decay of Potassium 40 to Argon 40, and used primarily on lava flows and volcanic tuffs – established the unexpected antiquity of the hominids found at Olduvai and elsewhere, and established East Africa as the key area for the study of human origins. At the same time, radiocarbon dating showed that successive African Stone Age cultures and technologies were as old as, or older than, those in Europe. As a result, Africa came to be seen as central rather than peripheral to the human story.

In some instances, however, radiocarbon dating has been a mixed blessing. West African archaeology in particular is a 'child of the radiocarbon age' as nearly all major excavation and research projects there postdate 1960. The ease with which radiocarbon dating could be used to establish a chronology meant that detailed

Was Eve an African?

Until the 1970s, physically modern people (*Homo sapiens sapiens*) were thought to have evolved at about the same time as the appearance of Upper Palaeolithic blade technology in Europe, around 35,000 years ago. Then new dating techniques and new fossils from southern and East Africa as well as Israel showed that modern, or near-modern, people were present in these areas from 120,000 years ago, at a time when archaic Neandertals occupied western Europe. In a further development in the late 1980s, genetic studies based on mitochondrial DNA – genetic material only inherited from the mother – were interpreted as indicating that all modern people evolved from a single ancestor, appropriately dubbed 'Eve', who lived in an African 'Garden of Eden' 200,000 years ago.

In 1992, however, these studies were shown to be statistically flawed, to the delight of proponents of the so-called 'multi-regional hypothesis': the idea that modern humans evolved gradually from archaic humans in many parts of the world, not only in Africa. The 'Out of Africa' hypothesis according to which modern people arose in Africa and spread from there to replace archaic people elsewhere nonetheless still enjoys some support from the fossil record and other genetic studies.

temporal sequences based on pottery or other material remains were not produced. Recent developments in the high precision calibration of conventional radiocarbon dates, however, produce a real calendar date range no better than three to four hundred years. This means that independent dating evidence from (often neglected) detailed pottery sequences and stratigraphy remains important in establishing temporal relationships, especially in the Iron Age.

Human origins

In the wake of the Leakeys' 1959 discovery of the unexpectedly ancient 'Zinj' remains at Olduvai, a flood of funding for human origins research – especially in East Africa – produced thousands of fossils and an explosion of information. The players in the story include at least three kinds of australopithecines, and three species of our own genus, *Homo*, as well as the scientists who study them, and whose rivalries in a field where key fossils are few but the stakes in respect of international recognition are high, have influenced ideas about the development of our species as much as the fossils themselves.

Following the discovery at Olduvai Gorge in 1961 of the earliest known human remains, a 1.7 million-year-old specimen ascribed to *Homo habilis*, in 1972 another

Bernard Ngeneo, the man who found the controversial 1470 fossil at Koobi Fora in August 1972. The relatively large brain size of the fossil, about 800 millilitres, and the three-million-year-old date initially assigned to the find generated almost a decade of anthropological controversy. The fossil is now redated to about two million years ago and the brain size reassessed at 752 millilitres.

The skull was badly crushed when found and had to be reconstructed from over 300 fragments. Sieving of the surrounding deposits over weeks was necessary to retrieve splinters that had washed down the slope of the steep-sided ravine from which the fossil was eroding out.

key fossil of early *Homo* was discovered by Bernard Ngeneo, a member of the team headed by the Leakeys' son, Richard, that had been working in northern Kenya on the Koobi Fora peninsula of Lake Turkana (formerly Lake Rudolf) since the 1960s. Despite his teenage avowal that he 'very definitely was not going to follow in the Leakey tradition', Richard found himself drawn into the world of fossils from his twenties, eventually becoming the director of the National Museums of Kenya 1968–89, and director of Kenya Wildlife Services 1989–94.

The Turkana fossil was catalogued as KNM-ER 1470 (Kenya National Museum, East Rudolf) and has since become known to the world simply as '1470'. Its relatively large brain size, initially estimated at 800 millilitres, was more than 100 millilitres larger than estimates for *Homo habilis*, then believed to be the earliest human, for whom palaeoanthropologists such as Phillip Tobias claim human abilities like the power of speech. On these grounds, 1470 was human and Richard Leakey cautiously named it *Homo* (species undetermined). Initial estimates of its age were nearly 3 million years. Since this was older than many australopithecine fossils, its great age initially cast doubt on the view that *Homo* evolved from australopithecines. However, this dating has now been revised to *c.* 1.9 million years, the same order of age as *Homo habilis* from Olduvai, so ending its reign as 'the world's oldest man.' Apart from brain size, other features of 1470 are more typical of australopithecines, so its classification remains the subject of debate.

In the 1970s and 1980s, Leakey and his colleagues continued fieldwork in the Turkana region and made a remarkable series of discoveries of *Homo erectus*-like fossils, until then found mainly in Asia. The most astonishing is the 'Turkana Boy' (WT-15000), discovered at Nariokotome in 1984. This twelve-year-old, who died *c.* 1.6 million years ago, left an unusually complete skeleton (only the feet are missing) which indicated that he had a powerful physique and would probably have grown to over six feet tall. Turkana Boy is one of the earliest known *Homo erectus*-like fossils, remarkably similar to modern humans except for differences in the spine, hips and legs. The striking difference between this strapping lad and his *Homo habilis* predecessor, who would have been much shorter than the average modern European or North American, has focused attention on the period between 2 and 1.5 million years ago, now seen as a time when crucial human anatomical changes occurred.

In the 1970s, attention was directed also to the Afar region in northeastern Ethiopia. Here, on a rocky slope on Christmas Eve 1974, Cleveland palaeoanthropologist Donald Johanson found a piece of hominid arm and, after intensive exploration, uncovered several hundred more pieces of bone which made up about 40 per cent of the skeleton of a 1.1 metre- (43 inch-) tall, upright-walking female. Scientifically named *Australopithecus afarensis* in 1978, she is better known to the world as 'Lucy', after the Beatles' song 'Lucy in the sky with diamonds' that was being played in the field camp on the night of the discovery. Lucy created intense excitement because she was the most complete and oldest known hominid found

Our most famous relative: the three million year old partial skeleton of 'Lucy', *Australopithecus afarensis*, discovered at Hadar in the Afar region of Ethiopia in 1974, with her finder, American anthropologist Don Johanson. It was the discovery of 'Lucy' which showed that the ability to walk on two legs preceded a large brain or toolmaking.

"'Jesus Christ', said [Tom] Gray. He picked it up. It was the back of a small skull. A few feet away was part of a femur: a thighbone. "Jesus Christ", he said again. We stood up, and began to see other bits of bone on the slope: a couple of vertebrae, part of a pelvis – all of them hominid … *A single individual.*

"I can't believe it", I said. "I just can't believe it".

"By God, you'd better believe it!" shouted Gray. "Here it is. Right here!" His voice went up into a howl. I joined him. In that 110-degree heat we began jumping up and down. With nobody to share our feelings, we hugged each other, sweaty and smelly, howling and hugging in the heat-shimmering gravel, the small brown remains of what now seemed almost certain to be parts of a single hominid skeleton lying all around us.'

up to that time, with a potassium-argon date of around 3 million years. In 1975, also at Hadar, Johanson and his colleagues discovered a collection of fossils of at least thirteen hominid individuals, a mixture of adults and children, males and females, bigger than Lucy and more than 3 million years old. Although it is uncertain how these bones came together, they were dubbed the 'First Family'.

The Laetoli footprints

Before the 1970s, it was thought that two-legged walking evolved at roughly the same time as the development of large brains and the use of stone tools. One of the sites that has produced startling evidence to the contrary was Laetoli, just south of Olduvai Gorge in northern Tanzania.

One September day in 1976, a group of scientists visiting Mary Leakey's excavations there were letting off steam by hurling dried elephant dung at each other. One of them, Andrew Hill, stumbled and found himself on the ground staring at strange indentations. They turned out to be fossil animal tracks made in damp volcanic ash more than three million years before.

Exciting as this was, it was nothing compared with the astonishing discovery in 1978 of two trails of fossilized hominid footprints made c. 3.7 million years ago. The prints are remarkably human in that the pattern of weight distribution is almost exactly the same as that of a modern person walking along a beach: the big toe lies alongside the other toes and is only slightly longer, not splayed from them or considerably longer as in apes. Fossilized hominid bones found at Laetoli suggest the prints were made by australopithecines and confirm the evidence of upright walking inferred from fossils like Lucy.

Cleaning the hominid footprint trail. Prints of two individuals, one large and one small, walking close enough to have been touching, can be seen.

'The discovery of the trails was immensely exciting', Mary Leakey recalls. 'It was a quite different feeling from the discovery of a major hominid fossil – *Proconsul* or *Zinjanthropus*, for example – because that happens all at once, and within a short time you know exactly what you have got. The Laetoli hominid trails were something that grew in extent, in detail and in importance over two seasons.'

The discovery of the Laetoli footprints and the Hadar fossils showed that creatures that were very ape-like, especially in brain size, were already walking on two legs before 3.5 million years ago, well over a million years before the earliest known stone tools, which are dated to 2.5 million years ago in sediments of the Middle Awash valley in Ethiopia. This changed the previously-held assumption that the evolution of walking on two legs was linked to the development of the brain and the use of stone tools – the idea that as the brain became bigger and more complex, hands were used less for moving about, became more manipulative, and started making tools. Now walking on two legs is considered to have been the first step on the road to humanity.

Although the details remain controversial, most of what is known about human origins has been learned in the last thirty years and has firmly established Africa as the cradle of humanity. Hominids, the biological family to which people belong, emerged at least five million years ago, and shortly thereafter split into separate lineages. One was a heavily-built group of creatures with ape-sized brains and large teeth, the so-called robust australopithecines, who became extinct about 1 million years ago or shortly after; the other was a more lightly built, or gracile, group of australopithecines, thought to be closely associated with the later rise of several species of humans, *Homo*, beginning about two million years ago. These creatures seem to have initiated the technological and social behaviour that characterizes our species today.

Mighty hunters or lowly scavengers?
Scatters of animal bones alongside remains of early people and their tools were once thought to be the remains of big game hunts conducted by early menfolk. Works such as Robert Ardrey's *African Genesis* (1961) helped popularize the view of early people as bloodthirsty killers, while the legends of modern 'Stone Age' foragers also suggested that hunting large or fierce animals was very important in prehistory. However, the fact that the men of these societies more often caught small animals was not mentioned in their heroic campfire tales. In fact, ethnographic studies showed that plants gathered by women provide most of the food eaten by surviving foragers in most parts of the world. Hunting was important only in the Arctic, where there is little plant food – but people did not reach the Arctic until about 30,000 years ago. Studies of animal bones and stone tools from African Stone Age sites such as Klasies River Mouth on the southern coast of South Africa showed, moreover, that people were ineffective hunters until the appearance of fully modern behaviour around 40,000 years ago. Studies of the damage caused by animal teeth and stone cutting on the animal bones found with early stone tools suggest instead that animal predators rather than early people were generally first in at the kill.

This new understanding owes a great deal to the post-1960s development of 'taphonomy' – what happens to a bone between the death of a living animal and its discovery by an archaeologist – a study that was spurred into life by the challenge of interpreting early human behaviour from remains found at early sites in South and East Africa. One of the pioneers of such investigations, C. K. 'Bob' Brain of the Transvaal Museum in South Africa, studied the damage caused to animal carcasses by leopards, hyenas and porcupines to show that early hominids at cave sites like Swartkrans in South Africa were probably the hunted rather than the hunters.

Recent work on the African Iron Age has concentrated particularly on documenting the origin and spread of Bantu-speaking black farmers through eastern and southern Africa. Radiocarbon dating and pottery used to develop detailed culture-historical sequences for the area had by the 1980s established the basis on which the history of black people could be written. Though couched too often in

Igbo Ukwu

The second millennium AD saw the emergence of many complex societies in West Africa, involving major developments in art and technology as well as social and political structures. However, their roots in the first millennium AD

Fabergé-like virtuosity. A richly decorated, cast-bronze altar stand excavated by Thurstan Shaw at Igbo-Ukwu. On opposing sides, male and female figures are shown flanked by openwork panels containing snakes and spiders.

remain poorly understood. A notable contribution towards explaining the origins of the remarkable bronze craft tradition of West Africa and its accompanying evidence for the concentration of social authority and accumulation of wealth was made by British archaeologist Thurstan Shaw.

Although a cache of remarkable bronzes was uncovered at the site of Igbo Ukwu in the natural forest area of southeastern Nigeria in 1938, the first systematic excavations there, undertaken by Shaw in 1959–60, led to the discovery of one of the world's most extraordinary archaeological sites. He describes it as 'the most nerve-wracking excavation I have undertaken ... partly because I very soon realized I was into something unique and important, partly because of the hazards of the physical circumstances under which the excavation was undertaken ... dysentry most of the time ... [and an] attempt in the night after the first bronze was discovered to steal it from under my bed'.

Shaw uncovered a remarkable collection of bronze objects, cast by the 'lost wax' process, and finely smithed and chased copper objects, dated to the ninth or tenth century AD by radiocarbon. The burial chamber and regalia repository of one high-ranking individual yielded a bronze staff and whisk, a copper pectoral and crown, and over 100,000 glass and carnelian beads, some perhaps acquired by trade from India.

Also significant is the evidence for exceptionally accomplished indigenous craft specialists at this time. Although the exact source of the copper and tin used at Igbo Ukwu remains uncertain, studies of the chemical composition of the metals, as well as of the techniques used to smelt and cast them, indicate that they were not of Arab or European origin.

Crudely worked tin bronze and arsenical leaded copper of mid-first-millennium AD date recently found at Jenne-jeno in the Middle Niger region support the case for indigenous West African metallurgical innovation.

the neutral terms of archaeological ceramic sequences, these studies were influential in discrediting the myth propounded by Afrikaner nationalism and apartheid education that black and white farmers arrived in a nearly 'empty' South Africa at about the same time, in the fifteenth or sixteenth centuries AD. Rather, they showed conclusively that black farmers were already settled in southern Africa by AD 200.

OCEANIA: COLONIZING AN ISLAND WORLD

Interest in Australian archaeology took off during the 1960s and within ten years the subject had been transformed. The resulting explosion of information produced revolutionary new data on the antiquity, nature and origins of the initial colon-

Harald Pager (1923–1985) duplicating the images of three hartebeest at Sebaaieni Cave in the Natal Drakensberg, South Africa's richest rock art area.

Pager devoted his skills as a graphic designer to the painstaking recording of Drakensberg and Brandberg rock paintings, documenting thousands of paintings in the rock shelters.

Aerial view of the 'Walls of China', an eroding shoreline dune on the eastern side of the now dry Lake Mungo, western New South Wales, that has produced the oldest dated human remains yet found in Australia. Since 1969 the area has yielded a wide range of sites including middens, burials, and hearths dating from more than 30,000 years ago to recent times. The female burial known as Mungo 1, dated *c.* 24,000 BC, is the oldest cremation in the world.

ization of Australia and New Guinea. The ethnographic and historical records of traditional Aboriginal life provided a rich source of information for a better understanding of archaeological evidence, both from Australia and from other hunter-gatherer societies around the world. Study of how Aborigines managed their environment, and especially their use of fire for this purpose, overturned images of a miserable struggle for existence and replaced them with a picture of 'fire-stick farmers' with a deep concern for the land. New Guinea emerged as a centre for the early development of agricultural systems. The discovery of 20,000 year old ground-stone axes in Arnhem Land in northern Australia, and art and underground flint-mining of about the same date at Koonalda Cave, on the Nullarbor plain, challenged traditional Eurocentric views of prehistory. Within a decade, Australian prehistory was firmly established on the world stage.

Although older sites were claimed – notably Keilor, in the suburbs of Melbourne – the oldest firm radiocarbon date for the human occupation of Australia in 1960

was 8,700 years old. Within three years Mulvaney's excavations at Kenniff Cave, a Queensland rockshelter with stencilled rock art, had produced a stratified series of dates taking occupation there back to about 16,000 years ago. The field team received the news of the first pleistocene dates by telegram relayed by the Royal Flying Doctor Service. Mulvaney was so surprised that he asked for confirmation, thinking that an extra zero might have been added. Word came 'at porridge time' the next morning – 'twelve thousand confirmed'. By the end of the decade, the discovery of human remains, stone tools and animal bones in the 'Walls of China', eroding sand dunes bordering Lake Mungo, a dry lake bed in western New South Wales, had pushed human occupation back beyond 30,000 years. Mungo, and other lakes in the region, were then full of water and people enjoyed a rich and varied diet based on fish and shellfish, and hunting animals on the surrounding plains. These dates were confirmed at several other sites in Australia and New Guinea over the next ten years, ranging from Devils Lair, a limestone cave in the far southwest corner of the continent, to Kosipe, an open camp site in the New Guinea highlands. By 1980, 40,000 years ago was widely accepted. In the 1990s, 60,000 years ago and earlier is being confidently claimed.

It was already known that some of the fossil human bones from Australia had archaic features reminiscent of *Homo erectus* fossils from Java. In 1968, physical anthropologist Alan Thorne found some ancient-looking bones in the Museum of Victoria. He tracked down the original find spot at Kow Swamp in northern Victoria and excavated a series of burials of robust, archaic-looking individuals dated between 9,000 and 13,000 years ago. The human remains from Lake Mungo proved to be quite different. They were much more delicate and showed no evidence of 'the mark of ancient Java'. These discoveries triggered a controversy about the biological affinities and origins of pleistocene Australians and their relationship to modern Aborigines. Thorne has argued that the bones represent two separate groups of colonizers, one from China and one from Indonesia. However, his view has been strongly criticized by other workers who feel that the differences between fossils have been exaggerated and that some of the archaic features may be a result of cultural practices such as the head-binding of infants.

Excavations in the 1960s, beginning with Mulvaney's work at Kenniff Cave, focused on caves and rockshelters likely to yield long stratigraphic sequences and established the main outlines of the Australian cultural sequence. Mulvaney's *The Prehistory of Australia* (1969) identified an early Adaptive phase and a more recent Inventive phase, distinguished mainly by the appearance of hafted tools about 5,000 years ago; the earlier assemblages were subsequently lumped together as the Australian Core Tool and Scraper tradition, while the more recent assemblages have come to be known as the Australian Small Tool tradition. These terms have not been revised, although they are losing their usefulness.

The excitement of these discoveries about pleistocene Australia has tended to dominate research, but archaeologists have also taken a broader interest in under-

John Mulvaney's 1962 excavation in Kenniff Cave, Queensland, named after the bush-ranging Kenniff brothers.

The excavation deposits, dating back 19,000 years, went down 3.3 metres (11 feet) and yielded more than 800 stone artifacts and 22,000 waste flakes. The radiocarbon dates from the site provided the first evidence that Australia was occupied during the Pleistocene.

standing human use of the environment. Australia was the only continent entirely occupied by hunter-gatherers until the European invasion, a circumstance that led to an early development of interest in ethnoarchaeology and ethnohistory as a way of interpreting the Australian archaeological record and understanding evidence from hunter-gatherer societies elsewhere in the world. Aboriginal art, too, has attracted great interest as the world's oldest known and longest-lasting art tradition, originating over 40,000 years ago.

Both Tindale and McCarthy had been interested in how observations of traditional Aboriginal life could contribute to interpreting the archaeological record. Although Thomson's influential work before the Second World War described how differences in the stone tools discarded at different camp-sites reflected seasonal variation in activities, Australian archaeologists were generally slow to recognize these possibilities, which were first explored by anthropologists and by American archaeologists working with traditionally-oriented Aboriginal peoples in northern and central Australia. Mulvaney recognized the value of historical sources for illuminating aspects of traditional Aboriginal life, especially in the heavily-settled southeast where traditional life was disrupted early. Many archaeologists have made use of historical accounts in interpreting recent sites, and a number of important ethnoarchaeological studies have also been conducted in New Guinea, most notably on stone tool manufacture.

In New Zealand, Golson had made a great impact on archaeology by 1961, stimulating an improvement in field techniques and a shift of interest away from traditional material culture studies towards looking at evidence of structures and subsistence. A key concern of archaeological research was whether the earliest colonists introduced agriculture to New Zealand or whether they largely abandoned it in favour of hunting and gathering, particularly in view of the hunting opportunities afforded by the moa. Equally controversial were the development of warfare, an important aspect of Maori society at the time of European settlement, and the investigation of the spectacular *pa* or fortified sites. Detailed material culture studies have largely gone out of fashion as a result of the new interest in economy and society. Although Golson was himself concerned with artifacts, the sites he excavated, with their complex stratigraphy, were not particularly rich in material culture; stone artifacts have remained important, but the emphasis has moved away from typological studies to the technology of making stone artifacts and to distribution studies of raw materials.

Public archaeology

During the 1960s there was strong pressure for Australian states to enact legislation to protect Aboriginal archaeological sites and, later, historic sites and shipwrecks. By the mid 1970s all states had some legislation and the federal government had established the Australian Heritage Commission. With legislation came the establishment of state bureaucracies to administer it and the development of contract archaeology.

Rock engravings in soft limestone at Mount Cameron West, in northern Tasmania. Located near the ocean beach, they were excavated from the sand in 1968 by Rhys Jones.

Once thought to be very ancient, and linked with archaic petroglyphs in Australia, they are now believed to date to *c.* 1350–850 years ago.

In the beginning the emphasis was primarily on archaeological sites. Over time, however, Australian archaeology came increasingly under attack from Aborigines. State governments responded with various attempts to incorporate Aboriginal people into the bureaucracy and to take account of their views in decisions about the management of sites, requiring researchers to consult Aboriginal communities as a condition of excavation permits.

Archaeology in Australia has been closely associated with the broader conservation movement, most obviously in the successful battle to prevent the damming of the Franklin river in southwest Tasmania in 1982–83. The issue dominated the federal election in 1983 and the significance of the archaeological sites was crucial in the High Court case that followed.

In New Zealand, legislation to protect archaeological sites was passed in 1975 and is administered by the New Zealand Historic Places Trust. As in Australia, this has greatly expanded the role of the public sector and resulted in the development of contract archaeology. The Maori Buildings and Advisory Committee has also played an increasing role in matters relating to both archaeological and traditional sites. This has been formalized by the establishment of a Maori Heritage Council under a revised Historic Places Act in 1993.

Historical archaeology

The use of archaeology to investigate historic rather than prehistoric sites in Australia and the Pacific is relatively recent. Historical archaeology complements documentary sources and is at its best depicting the lives of ordinary people who go largely unrepresented in official records. A wide range of Australian colonial sites has been investigated, from remote rural settlements to city houses, from grand mansions to convict huts, and from Chinese market gardens to Aboriginal missions. The many shipwrecks that are found in Australian waters are a topic in themselves, the oldest dating back to the seventeenth-century Dutch trade with the East Indies. Historical archaeology in Australia began in the mid-1960s. Mulvaney was quick to recognize its potential, and on his arrival at the Australian National University in 1965 began encouraging students to research in this area. Among the first projects was a study of Macassan sites in the Northern Territory, which showed that Macassan traders, from what is now Indonesia, had been visiting the northern Australian coast for centuries in search of trepang (sea-cucumber), much in demand in China for cooking and as an aphrodisiac.

Other pioneering excavations in the 1960s and 1970s were at Port Essington, a failed colonial frontier outpost in the Northern Territory, Irrawang pottery in New South Wales, and the settlement at Wybalenna, on Flinders Island, established in 1832 for the few surviving Tasmanian Aborigines.

The investigation of shipwrecks, especially seventeenth- and eighteenth-century Dutch wrecks along the west coast, also got underway in the 1970s, often with spectacular results. The excavation of the *Batavia*, for example, a Dutch East

India-man lost in 1629 off Western Australia, produced a wealth of material including a complete portico probably intended for the new fort at Batavia. In the 1970s the penal settlement at Port Arthur in Tasmania was the site of a major long-term archaeological research project. During the 1980s the first major urban excavations were conducted in Sydney on the site of the first Government House, and in the centre of Melbourne a complete nineteenth-century city block was dug, uncovering 'Little Lon', a notorious red light district. The excavations revealed a more diverse community than had been expected from contemporary literary descriptions.

Papua New Guinea

During periods of low sea level, a land bridge connected New Guinea and Australia. Excavations in the 1960s showed that, like Australia, the highlands had been occupied for at least 30,000 years. More recently, sites of similar age have been found in the islands of the Bismarck archipelago, off the northwest coast and in the Solomons. Over the last 10,000 years, however, New Guinea's prehistory has diverged markedly from that of neighbouring Australia. While Australia remained a continent of hunter-gatherers, the development of agriculture in New Guinea in some areas supported very large and dense populations.

There was little archaeological work in Papua New Guinea before 1959–60 when two rock-shelters in the central highlands were excavated. This is still the case for Irian Jaya which is now incorporated into Indonesia. Golson began fieldwork in the highlands himself, and encouraged student research in Papua New Guinea, soon after he was appointed to the Australian National University in 1961. Much of the fieldwork during the 1960s and 1970s, mainly by Australian National University staff, was therefore exploratory and conducted in remote areas under very difficult field conditions.

Apart from establishing that the occupation of New Guinea went back to the pleistocene, archaeologists have concentrated on two major themes: the development of agriculture and the growth of trade. Golson's work at Kuk produced evidence of large channels for swamp drainage dating back about 10,000 years and traced the development of field systems over that period. The great age of these drainage systems makes the New Guinea highlands a candidate for an independent centre of plant domestication. Elaborate trading systems were well established along the south coast by the time Europeans arrived in the region, with communities producing and exchanging pottery, obsidian, sago and shell ornaments. Some of these systems are well known from oral history, but archaeological research shows that they began as much as 2,000 years ago.

Colonizing the Pacific

An important theme of archaeology in the Pacific has been how and when the many small island groups were first settled. By the 1960s, it was generally thought that the ancestors of the present-day Polynesians had come into the Pacific from the west, from the islands of southeast Asia, and that they were the makers of the distinctively decorated Lapita pottery known from sites in Melanesia and western Polynesia. During the 1960s and 1970s, archaeologists were particularly interested in establishing the distribution and age of Lapita pottery and understanding the way of life of its makers. Lapita pottery seems to have first appeared just under 4,000 years ago and finally disappeared about 2,000 years ago, by which time both Tonga and Samoa had been settled. Within the next few centuries Polynesian voyagers had reached the Marquesas, the Tuamotus and the Society Islands. Finally, they colonized Hawaii, New Zealand and Easter Island.

There has been considerable debate among archaeologists about how the Polynesian voyages were accomplished and whether they were intentional or accidental. Studies of traditional navigation systems and canoe technology have led to computer simulations and experimental voyages. The voyage of the *Hokule'a* from Hawaii to Tahiti in 1976 was a spectacular demonstration of the effectiveness of traditional navigation techniques and the ability of Pacific peoples to mount voyages of discovery and colonize new islands.

THE AMERICAS

The date of the earliest human occupation of the American continent remains today as controversial as it ever was. The great sandstone rockshelter of Pedra Furada in Brazil, excavated by N*i*ède Guidon and Fabio Parenti in the 1970s and 1980s, has produced radiocarbon dates of 40,000 years ago and more, while Tom Dillehay's open-air site of Monte Verde in Chile has occupation dated to 13,000 and perhaps 33,000 years ago. Other sites, like the deeply stratified Meadowcroft rockshelter in western Pennsylvania excavated by James Adovasio between 1973–77, provide more conservative results, with very good evidence for human occupation 12,000 years ago, perhaps much earlier. The continuing controversy arises from such factors as the sparseness of the archaeological remains, their alleged disturbance by geological activities, the lack of artifacts that can be tied to a specific period, and – last but not least – the egos of the archaeologists involved in the debate.

In the Yukon, stone artifacts and Ice Age animal remains have been excavated in the Bluefish Caves, south of Old Crow Basin. Richard E. Morlan and Jacques Cinq-Mars found a small quantity of tools, including microblades, in deposits containing bones dated to 23,000–10,000 BC; however, the relationship between the bones and artifacts remains unclear. Between 1980 and 1993, several sites were also investigated in the northern foothills of the Alaska range and the Tanana valley. For the first time, Alaskan archaeological remains were firmly dated by radiocarbon to the same period as the early Palaeo-Indian sites of the North American Plains, that is *c.* 10,000–9,000 BC. At present, unless the early dating of the artifacts from Bluefish Caves is accepted, it appears that the microblade industry was preceded by one containing projectile points that may be linked to the Palaeo-Indian cultures of the

The huge sandstone rock-shelter of Pedra Furada, north-eastern Brazil, dug from 1978 to 1988, originally in the hope of dating the rock paintings on its back wall.

The excavations eventually uncovered what is claimed to be human occupation dating back at least 50,000 years – a direct challenge to the prevailing orthodoxy that the Americas were only settled 15,000, or even 12,000, years ago, the earliest bands of hunters and gatherers reaching Alaska from Eurasia by way of the ice-free Bering land bridge.

Debate still rages over whether the hundreds of crudely flaked quartzite pebbles from Pedra Furada are humanly worked artifacts or naturally occurring 'geofacts', and whether the scores of excavated 'structures' – arrangements of sandstone plaques, or pebbles or both – are artificial or natural.

Great Plains and further south. Although archaeologists in other parts of the New World continue to report the discovery of significantly older occupation, unequivocal evidence of earlier occupations has yet to emerge from the far north.

Cultural Resource Management

Cultural Resource Management (CRM) is the term used in America for the protection and study of archaeological sites on public land. The first law passed by the federal government to protect archaeological sites was the Antiquities Act of

Chaco Canyon and Pueblo Bonito

Chaco Canyon is today a dry and inhospitable canyon on the Navajo Indian reservation of northwestern New Mexico. The canyon walls rise 15 to 45 metres (50–150 feet) above the wide, sand-covered bottom cut by the intermittent Chaco Wash. About one thousand years ago, this canyon was the centre of one of the most remarkable and sophisticated cultures in prehistoric North America. The florescence of Chaco began just after AD 1000, and it remained an important centre of Anasazi culture until its abandonment between AD 1130–1150, primarily because of drought.

The canyon, 24 kilometres (15 miles) in length, is dominated by thirteen large Anasazi villages, the largest of which is Pueblo Bonito. These free-standing architectural structures each contain as many as 700 rooms and 34 kivas: circular, semi-subterranean structures that were a combination of ceremonial and social centre. Over 200,000 wooden beams were used in the construction of these villages, all of which had to be transported from mountains some distance away. To get to the uplands above, the Anasazi cut steps into the steep canyon walls.

Astronomical observation was important to the Anasazi. The supernova of July AD 1054 is recorded in rock art close to the Anasazi village of Penasco Blanco, and many other Chaco sites have astronomical significance: the best documented is Fajada Butte, a winter and summer solstice marker.

Radiating from Chaco Canyon are numerous well-made and remarkably straight roads, some of which are 96 kilometres (60 miles) long and 13 metres (43 feet) wide. Many are invisible to the observer standing on them, since they are often only slight depressions of a few centimetres, but, once their location is known, more intensive ground survey reveals the actual stone kerbs of the roads themselves. These roads connect the main canyon sites to smaller Chacoan sites called 'outliers', which probably served specialized functions within the overall system. The purpose of the road network, like that of the Chacoan system itself, is still unclear. Some archaeologists have suggested that the system was an economic bloc, others that it was part of a religious movement, still others that it was built by a feudal or militaristic society.

The existence of Anasazi roads was mentioned by the earliest American military expeditions in the area. However, it was only in the 1970s, using intensive aerial survey, that their full extent became clear. At first, archaeologists used existing aerial photographs that showed previously undiscovered roads. Enthused by the potential of aerial reconnaissance, the Remote Sensing Division of the Chaco Center then arranged for new photography, this time using more sensitive equipment with infra-red and electronic image enhancement. Over the years new aerial surveys have been completed, each backed up by site survey and recording. The result today is that archaeologists have a complete picture of one of the most extensive and fascinating engineering achievements of prehistoric North America.

Chaco Canyon, New Mexico (opposite), and (above) the enormous 700-room Anasazi village of Pueblo Bonito from the air.

1906, although Congress did not make available funds for its enforcement. The modern era of site protection only began in 1966, when the National Historic Preservation Act was passed to develop a national programme of site preservation, administered through both federal and state agencies. The Archaeological Resources Protection Act of 1979 sanctioned criminal and civil penalties for the looting or destruction of sites on federal lands. American laws protecting sites apply only to federal lands, although states and even some cities have enacted laws to protect sites under their jurisdiction. Significantly, these laws do not apply to sites on private land; a landowner is pretty much free to do what he or she will with a site. In respect of shipwrecks, Congress in 1987 passed the Abandoned Shipwreck Act, which makes it illegal for wrecks to be salvaged by commercial enterprises and defines them as historical resources.

Because of these laws, no development on, or alteration of, federal lands, whether initiated by the government or by a private entity, can proceed without the project's impact on archaeological sites being assessed or in some cases mitigated through excavation. This is accomplished by private archaeological companies, working for the developer and under the supervision of the appropriate federal archaeologist.

The impact of CRM on American archaeology has been incalculable. It has massively increased the information available to researchers and contributed significantly to the understanding of both culture history and culture process. There is also a much better publication record now, since federal law demands that no project can be concluded until a final, professional-quality report has been submitted to, and accepted by, the appropriate federal agency. CRM is now the single largest employer of archaeologists in the USA, although the quality of those jobs, in terms of salary, benefits and security is still highly variable. In North America today, most fieldwork is CRM-related, but excavation is considered the court of last resort, being so very labour-intensive and so expensive in costs and time.

The New Archaeology and Latin America

In both Mesoamerica and South America, the era of processual archaeology ushered in a new set of research problems. While efforts continued to provide basic regional chronologies and culture histories, attention was also now devoted to explaining the changes observed in the archaeological record, not just describing them. The processual revolution of the 1960s, generally attributed to Binford (p. 289), had been foreshadowed nearly a quarter of a century earlier by Clyde Kluckhohn. Viewing the field of Mesoamerican archaeology essentially as an outsider, Kluckhohn was appalled by its backwardness. 'I should like to record,' he wrote, 'an overwhelming impression that many students in this field [Middle American studies] are but slightly reformed antiquarians. To one who is a layman in these highly specialized realms there seems a great deal of obsessive wallowing in detail of and for itself.'

Three decades of research by the Carnegie Institution had produced a published record that was still preoccupied with factual details rather than synthesis and interpretation. By 1960 the Carnegie had abruptly ceased its Maya research, and new concerns arose in Mesoamerican studies: understanding the origins of agriculture and the domestication of maize, studying trade and the interaction between different cultures, and reconstructing the settlements and daily life of people at all levels of power and wealth. Research in highland areas including the Tehuacán valley, Oaxaca and the Valley of Mexico was to move rapidly beyond the confines of traditional Maya studies, which until then had established the agenda in Mesoamerican archaeology.

Binford called upon archaeologists to deal with the three great problems of human prehistory that archaeology was uniquely suited to study: the origin of humans, the origins of agriculture, and the emergence of complex societies. While the first goal was attainable only in the Old World, in the New World archaeologists quickly began to grapple with the second and third problems.

Maize agriculture formed the basis of subsistence throughout the New World, yet its origins were unknown. It seemed likely that the earliest cultivated maize should be found in Mesoamerica, where the closest living wild relative of maize, *teosinte*, still grew. After several preliminary searches, American archaeologist Richard MacNeish settled upon the Tehuacán valley as a likely location in which to seek evidence for the transition to maize cultivation. Rather than focus on a single site, he first conducted a survey of the region, looking for dry caves in which he might find long stratigraphic sequences reaching back thousands of years, as well as conditions conducive to good preservation of botanical remains. He then excavated a series of caves, and was able to document a shift from hunting and gathering to the gradual inclusion of cultivated plants in the diet, and finally a reliance on agriculture. He estimated that maize had first been domesticated in what he called the Coxcatlán phase, around 5200–3400 BC. While newer techniques of radiocarbon dating have moved the earliest domesticated maize to a somewhat later date, MacNeish's project still documents the earliest transition to life based on domesticated plants.

In the mid-1960s Flannery, who had worked in Tehuacán with MacNeish, and also with Braidwood studying early agriculture in the Near East (p. 316), began a series of investigations in the Oaxaca valley. His work combined excavations of individual sites with broad surveys of the entire region, providing a fuller and richer picture of the prehistory of that area than had existed for any other at that time. His research addressed the origins of agriculture, the evolution of settled life, and the emergence of social complexity, and in many ways set the standard for more recent investigations in Mesoamerica and elsewhere.

Regional surveys and carefully designed excavations were undertaken not only in Tehuacán and Oaxaca, but also in the Valley of Mexico. With Jeffrey Parsons and Robert Santley, William Sanders undertook to survey the basin and elucidate the

Teotihuacán, Mexico. The view down the 'Street of the Dead' from the summit of the Pyramid of the Moon, with the Pyramid of the Sun on the left. A planned urban centre from its inception, Teotihuacán was amongst the largest cities in the preindustrial world.

processes of emerging cultural complexity. Perhaps no more ambitious regional survey has ever been undertaken anywhere. Through careful identification of different types of sites at different periods of time, they were able to document the development of village life, the first small ceremonial centres, the rise of the first great urban site, Teotihuacán, its collapse, and the emergence of the Mexica empire. Finally, archaeologists were able not only to document what happened in prehistory, but also to offer explanations as to why those events took place.

Flourishing during the period AD 300–800, Teotihuacán was one of the largest prehistoric cities in the New World, covering 20 square kilometres (8 square miles), with a maximum population of about 150,000 people. Its central street was anchor-

ed by the Pyramid of the Moon at one end, the Pyramid of the Sun along one side, and the Temple of Quetzalcoatl and the Great Compound flanking the other end. Teotihuacán not only controlled the entire central valley of Mexico; it may also have been the capital of an empire ruling large portions of Mesoamerica, extending east to the Gulf of Mexico, and south beyond the Maya region in southern Guatemala. Teotihuacán became in this period the focus of a major research project designed systematically to map its ground-level features, as well as excavate specific areas. Under the direction of the Americans Rene Millon and George Cowgill, the site was rigorously surveyed, using surface techniques as well as aerial photography. One of the research goals of the project was to document the growth and eventual collapse of the city, so pottery fragments on the surface were recorded with great care. It was seen that once the site emerged as an urban centre it grew tremendously in size. Regional settlement data indicated that the countryside was largely depopulated: everyone had moved to the big city. It was even possible to define a section of Teotihuacán where foreigners – people from Oaxaca – apparently lived. Finally, and suddenly, the city was abandoned. Millon turned his attention to the collapse and determined that it was violent, with ramifications that shook all of Mesoamerica.

Archaeologists in the Maya area pursued new interests in settlement patterns, and the agricultural basis of Maya society. Mayanists are at a distinct disadvantage compared to their highland counterparts, because it is impossible to conduct settlement surveys in dense jungle in the manner of surveys on high, dry terrain with little vegetation. However, archaeologists, for example on Patrick Culbert's Tikal project, did move beyond the ceremonial core of the site, looking at outer areas and the humbler habitations of the thousands of common people living there. Others determined that Maya subsistence, long thought to be based simply on slash-and-burn agriculture, was in fact much more complex and varied.

Maya studies also took a new twist in the 1970s and 1980s, with a series of breakthroughs in the translation of Maya hieroglyphic writing. Thompson, through the sheer strength of his personality, not to mention his acerbity, had for decades squashed all attempts to treat the glyphs as phonetic writing. The work of Yuri Knorosov, although championed by some Mayanists, had not been given the attention it deserved, and even the work of Tatiana Proskouriakoff had been held back by Thompson's prejudices. Then, in the early 1970s, Linda Schele and Peter Matthews broke the code of the tomb inscription of Pacal, the ruler of Palenque.

The reverberations of this breakthrough are still echoing through the Maya world. It now became clear that the Maya had indeed recorded details of their own history on carved stones; the information was not limited to dates and place names. One of the most remarkable of the new generation of epigraphers was David Stuart, an archaeological child prodigy, who had been participating in archaeological projects in the Maya region since the age of eight; by the age of eleven he was working with Schele on the Palenque data, and by thirteen presenting his first professional paper.

Proskouriakoff and the Maya

Tatiana Proskouriakoff (1909–85) was born in Siberia of a family whose ancestors had been exiled there by Peter the Great. Her father was in America, supervising the manufacture of munitions, when the 1917 revolution broke out and the family elected to stay. Tatiana attended an American high school, losing her accent but not her Russian, and gaining the nickname that would remain with her for the rest of her life: 'Duchess'. Unemployed after graduating as an architect in 1930, she ended up working as a museum artist in the University of Pennsylvania in Philadelphia.

A visit to the Maya site of Piedras Negra for the purpose of drawing architectural reconstructions changed Proskouriakoff's life, and she devoted the rest of her days to Maya architecture and hieroglyphs. A skilled draughtsman, quick witted and independent minded, she worked on the architecture of Chichén Itzá and Copán, producing drawing after drawing, plan after plan. The rigours of fieldwork proved a revelation after her lady-like upbringing, as one obituarist commented.

She travelled alone to Copán, and once there, found life at the camp distinctly wild. Having been brought up in a very proper European household, she was surprised considerably by the battery of bottles displayed on a table in the camp *sala*, and more so on finding how much the consumption of their contents enlivened the nightly games of poker, especially on Saturdays. One Sunday morning, annoyed with the men for sleeping so late, she opened the door of Gustav Stromsvik's room and let his parrot in. Soon there was a duet of squawking, the parrot having gotten Stromsvik by the mustache.

Proskouriakoff later moved with Alfred Kidder to the Peabody Museum at Harvard, where, largely self-taught, she worked alone until her death on the intricate problems of Maya hieroglyphic writing. Sympathetic to the possibility of a phonetic component – an idea championed by the Russian Yuri Knorosov – she was, like so many others, discouraged by the opposition of the leading Mayanist Eric Thompson.

Chacmool altar in the Temple of Warriors, Chichén Itzá, a Maya site with which Proskouriakoff is particularly associated.

Maya archaeologists continue to reconstruct prehistoric ways of life, to study subsistence and exchange, and to seek to understand the settlement patterns of all the prehistoric Maya. However, as a result of the recent strides made by epigraphic studies in deciphering Maya history, archaeology has taken something of a back seat recently when it comes to the reconstruction of prehistoric events. It will be some time before the written histories are known, and it will then remain to be seen whether the archaeological record conforms to those records. We have, after all, no way of knowing if Maya rulers were proclaiming the truth in their inscriptions, or if what they wrote was – as seems more likely – revised history and political propaganda.

In South America, while many archaeologists continued to be concerned with chronologies and culture histories, new concerns with documenting and explaining the origins of agriculture and the emergence of social complexity also became apparent. After his success in obtaining evidence of the transition to agriculture in Mesoamerica, MacNeish set his sights on the high Andes, undertaking a very similar project in the Ayacucho valley of central Peru. Here again he began with a regional survey, designed to locate dry caves, and then proceeded to excavate. MacNeish did not find evidence of early domestication, but he was able to document the gradual adoption of domesticated plants and animals through several phases, a sequence remarkably similar to that of Tehuacán. Moreover, excavation directed his attention to a new problem: the earliest evidence of human occupation in South America. In the cave of Pikimachay he found what he judged to be crude stone tools associated with the bones of extinct megafauna radiocarbon-dated to 20,000 years ago. Given the orthodox view that humans did not arrive in the New World before about 15,000 years ago, and the possibility that the 'stone tools' might be of natural origin, MacNeish's interpretation failed to win general acceptance.

The Ayacucho valley was also the setting for an enormous urban site, Wari, capital of Peru's first empire. As part of MacNeish's project, Peruvian archaeologist Luis Lumbreras undertook a survey of Wari-related sites in the area and, with the American Gary Vescelius, excavated at Wari itself. Research at the site unfortunately ceased abruptly in the early 1980s when the Shining Path terrorist group took control of the area. Similarly, on the north coast of Peru, in the Moche valley, Michael Moseley began in the 1970s to study Chanchan, the enormous capital of the prehistoric Chimú – the site that long before had caused Humboldt to wonder about the lack of rain on the Peruvian coast (p. 111). Moseley undertook a detailed study of the site and documented its growth, studying the organization of the regal compounds, and identifying different residential types and functions at the site. A systematic regional survey was also begun of the lower Moche valley, site not only of the Chimú capital, but also of the capital of the Moche in much earlier times.

The Virú valley survey of the 1940s was the first major regional survey in Latin America, and regional surveys have continued to the present. While the goals of

that early survey were couched in terms of the research questions of the time – chronology and culture history – modern surveys have focused on processual questions closer to the hearts of today's archaeologists: the transition to settled life, the emergence of complexity, the effects of imperial control, and the impact of changing climate on human adaptation.

In both Mesoamerica and South America there are probably few major sites to be discovered: certainly no lost civilizations remain hidden in the jungles. Year by year, our picture of the region's prehistory becomes progressively more detailed. Ever more refined regional chronologies and culture histories are being developed, and much archaeological research is still being aimed at the excavation of single sites, with a bias towards their major architectural monuments. However, the diversity of prehistoric culture is now seen to include not just those things done or built by rulers and élites, but also the life of common people, women, those not in power. The processual approach has opened up considerably beyond its earlier focus on explanations that relied heavily on environment and technology as limiting human actions; new focuses on ideology and less material aspects of culture are being added all the time to archaeological investigation.

Regional approaches are also providing a much-needed complement to single-site projects. The big Mesoamerican surveys of the Mexico and Oaxaca valleys have spawned a new generation of investigations moving beyond the core areas of the major states and into those regions that bore the brunt of their expansion. Finally, across all Latin America there is new interest in what came before the great civilizations. The millennia of occupation prior to the building of the first platform mounds or pyramids have in the past been neglected by archaeologists; now investigators are looking more closely at the roots of those later developments, and the initial development of social inequality, which took on such grandiose proportions in the three millennia before the Spanish conquest.

Some forty years ago, in *Archaeology from the Earth* (1954), Mortimer Wheeler wrote:

> We have … been preparing time-tables; let us now have some trains.
>
> Cultural catalogues are all very well, so far as they go. But they do not, of themselves, go very far. They are a means to an end. An admitted need of the present day is the methodical exploration of the *social unit* on a more expansive scale than has been normal in the past.

The following generation of scholars responded with the archaeology of research questions, questions that asked not just when and where, but how and why the human past took the directions it did. These questions, in turn, required new ways of gathering and looking at archaeological information, new ways of digging, of seeing ancient landscapes, of using the information that previous generations of archaeologists left behind. The result has been a fuller appreciation of the social and

Opposite. Chimú ceremonial knife representing a divinity, probably Naymlap, of gold decorated with turquoises. From Lambayeque, Peru, twelfth to thirteenth centuries AD. Length 40 centimetres (16 inches).

The power of the prehistoric Chimú extended from the central coast of Peru nearly to Ecuador. Their memorable art and architecture, particularly the huge coastal capital of Chanchan, impress modern visitors to Peru as much as they did Humboldt two hundred years ago.

Occupied from c. 1000 AD to the Inka conquest c. 1470 AD, Chanchan itself covered 19 square kilometres (7.3 square miles), with a population of around 30,000. The monumental centre 6 square kilometres (2.3 square miles) in area is notable for its ten huge rectangular enclosures or *ciudadelas*, apparently royal residences and administrative centres of the kingdom during successive reigns.

On the death of a king, his residence became a mausoleum and a new *ciudadela* was built, a response that over time took the boundaries of the city progressively further inland.

economic arrangements of ancient societies, going beyond the palaces, temples and treasures that preoccupied earlier archaeologists and continue to hold enormous popular appeal.

Today, new studies in 'cognitive archaeology' or the 'archaeology of the mind' are even attempting to get inside the heads of ancient peoples, to understand the meanings that they invested in their art and cities, their religion and their social identities. Yet much still remains to be accomplished in these directions, and much basic research remains unfinished – the train schedules for many parts of archaeology are not yet fully prepared. The future offers exciting prospects and daunting challenges for this still very young subject.

Opposite. Cognitive mapping. The archaeology of human cognition – reconstructing past ways of thought from material remains – is one of the most exciting areas of contemporary archaeology. Actual maps of the ancient world are rare, but there are myriad ways in which mental maps, the mind-sets through which the people of the past viewed the world around them, can be reconstructed: for example, through studying language and literacy, mensuration and mythology, the layout of villages and cities, the symbolism of power, or the representation of gods and humans in art.

Getting a sense of the way space was conceived in the ancient world makes the few maps that do survive of particular interest. This clay tablet, known as the 'Babylonian map of the world', dates to the seventh century BC. It shows a circle labelled the 'Salt Sea'. Outside it are wondrous regions 'where the sun is not seen', described in the text above. In the middle is the known world, with west at the top. The rectangle in the upper part of the circle is inscribed 'Babylon'; on the right are names including Assyria and, at the bottom, Susa. The vertical lines across the centre of the map are thought to represent the Euphrates. The mountains at the source of the river are shown and, to the south, the country of Bit-Yakin and the marshes at its mouth.

CHAPTER 8   *Current Controversies and Future Trends*

Archaeology is now a truly international discipline which has even extended into Antarctica, where several expedition huts of early explorers such as Robert Falcon Scott are being carefully preserved and inventoried. Thanks to the power of the media, major discoveries such as the miraculously preserved 'Iceman' of 3300 BC,

Interrogating archaeological finds and the visual images of the past to see what light they throw on the role of women – or other less favoured groups like children, craftspeople, or slaves – has become a prominent aspect of archaeological interpretation in recent years.

Classical Athenian society, in which women were confined to the home and excluded from public and political life but frequently represented on fine pottery, offers particular scope.

This boudoir scene of the fifth century BC represents the preparation for a wedding, placed very clearly in the domestic space of the home in which upper class women were immured in almost oriental confinement.

A seated girl, Thalea, is being adorned with jewellery, a mirror on the wall behind her. The room is otherwise sparsely furnished. In front, a woman stands with a trinket box; behind, Glauke is about to place a necklace around her neck.

The entire scene serves to convey the elite ideal of proper female behaviour, of companionship and seclusion.

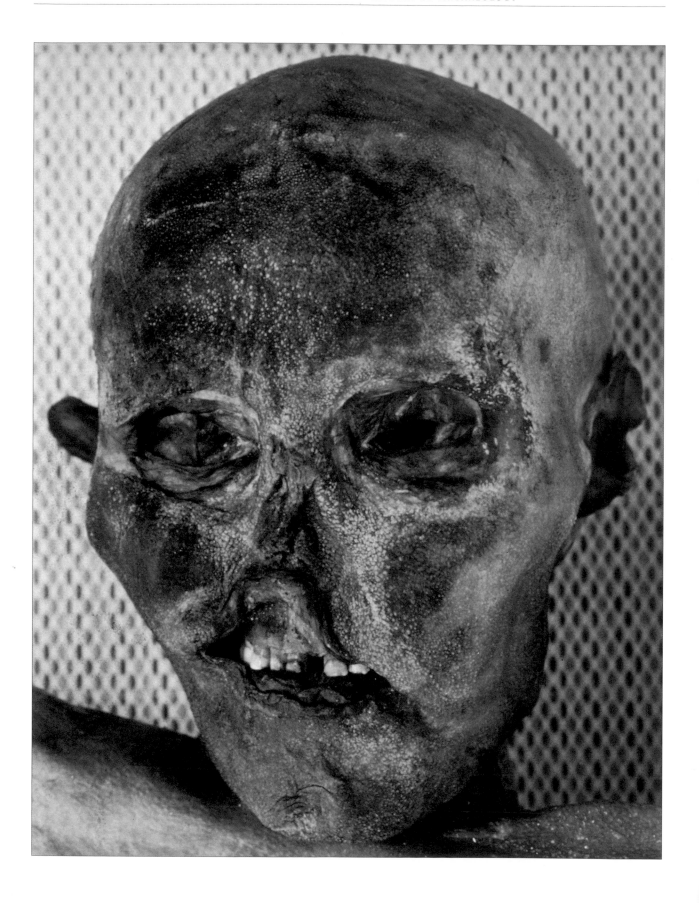

found high in the Italian Alps in 1991 with his clothing and equipment, are instant news all around the globe.

At the same time, paradoxically, archaeology has become a fragmented discipline, crowded with players and overflowing with a diversity of research, ideas and strategy. Specialization – 'a preparation of opium distilled by a minority for a minority' – compounds this fragmentation. The age of the Renaissance or Victorian polymath is long gone. The enormous volume of information inhibits, even in those scholars inclined to try, a full command of one continent's archaeology, much less world archaeology. This can sometimes result in a failure to communicate, a blockage in the transmission of important results and ideas even between archaeologists. But in recent years, archaeology – already reeling from self-doubt caused by some of the theoretical avenues it has explored – has become painfully aware of some stark realities: that it has often grossly neglected the role of women; that indigenous peoples have strong opinions about, and claims to, the material remains of the past; that politics and economics continue to affect the subject in many different ways; and that the subject's very future is threatened by the rapidly growing, often unscrupulous and occasionally murderous market in antiquities.

On the brighter side, archaeologists are not only learning to accommodate the claims of indigenous peoples, but are experiencing public interest in their subject on an unprecedented scale. The future of the subject is extremely promising: with new finds will come big surprises; and with new techniques for finding, analysing and dating evidence, new ideas will emerge that will change and adapt our picture of the past. This is one of the fascinations of archaeology: it never ceases to evolve.

ARCHAEOLOGY AND WOMEN

A close alliance has developed between post-processual archaeology and a more gender-aware archaeology. American researchers in particular have argued that archaeology has traditionally been male oriented, not only in its basic terminology – 'early *man*' – but also in its emphasis on what have traditionally been considered male activities: hunting, say, or making tools such as projectile points. They have argued that archaeology must fight against gender-bias both in its professional practice and also in its interpretations. It is to be hoped, at least, that we have progressed from the tone set in 1915 by the archaeologist J. P. Droop, who argued against having women on excavations on the grounds that men could not in moments of stress give vent to their true feelings in the presence of ladies!

The explicit emphasis placed today on gender studies is welcome not only for its attempt to create a much greater awareness of the need to extend gender equality into all aspects of contemporary life, including academia, but also for the substantial contribution that it is making to our understanding of how ancient societies may have worked.

Opposite. The face of the 'Iceman' discovered high in the Tyrolean Alps in September 1991. Aged between 25 and 40 at the time of his death *c.* 3300 BC, he stood only about 5 feet 2inches tall (156–160 centimetres).

Brain, muscle tissues, lungs, heart, liver and digestive organs remain in excellent condition. The lungs are blackened by smoke, probably from open fires. The body also has eight rib fractures, which were healed or healing when the Iceman died.

Groups of tattoos, mostly short parallel vertical blue lines half an inch long, can be seen on both sides of the lower spine and on the left calf and right ankle; on the inner right knee is a blue cross.

The body's nails had dropped off, but one fingernail was recovered. Its analysis revealed both that the Iceman undertook manual labour and that he underwent periods of reduced nail growth – linked to episodes of illness – four, three and two months before death.

Particular interest attaches to the clothing, tools and weapons found with the Iceman – a unique 'time-capsule' of the stuff of everyday life, many of the items made from normally perishable organic materials here preserved by the cold and ice. An astonishing variety of woods, and a range of very sophisticated techniques of work with leather and grasses, can be seen in a collection of 70 objects which have greatly added to archaeological understanding of life in the late Stone Age.

Womens' work

Women have traditionally been at a disadvantage in archaeology, but the twentieth century has nonetheless brought them considerable achievements in a subject once dominated by the likes of Belzoni, Layard and Wheeler.

Many of the most prominent women archaeologists have been British. Dorothy Garrod, daughter of a prominent academic family, became in 1939 the first woman to hold a professorship in Cambridge. After studying with Breuil, she specialized in palaeolithic and early neolithic archaeology, establishing the Palestinian sequence through her innovative work with archaeozoologist Dorothea Bate in the caves of Mount Carmel (p. 233). Beginning under the direction of Petrie, one of the few project directors to give women professional opportunities, another Cambridge graduate, Gertrude Caton-Thompson, later worked in the Fayum, Arabia, and in 1929 excavated Great Zimbabwe, authoritatively demonstrating its African origin (p. 176).

Winifred Lamb, once excluded because she was a woman from university lectures in her speciality of Greek archaeology, in 1920 undertook important Bronze Age excavations in the Aegean, notably on Lesbos, home of Sappho, the greatest woman poet of antiquity. In Palestine, Dame Kathleen Kenyon (p. 248), daughter of a director of the British Museum, carried out major excavations at Jericho and Jerusalem, earning a reputation as a 'formidable Dame' who, in archaeological myth at least, could throw a shovel-load of soil to the top of a deep trench without losing the ash off the end of her cigarette. In Africa, the achievements of Mary Leakey are remarkable: marrying Louis Leakey as a young archaeologist, she collaborated with him in Olduvai Gorge and herself discovered footprints of australopithecines nearly four million years old at Laetoli (p. 328).

American women archaeologists, such as Florence Hawley Ellis and Frederica de Laguna, often complemented archaeological investigations with ethnographic enquiry. De Laguna worked in southern Alaska, devising in 1947 the concept of a prehistoric–historic North Pacific cultural continuum; the Yakutat Tlingit Indians of Alaska honoured her work with a potlatch feast. Hawley Ellis worked extensively with Pueblo Indians in the American Southwest, seeking to interpret prehistoric features through familiarity with historic Pueblo and Mesoamerican cultures, and making available her researches in support of Pueblo claims to land and their own religious practices.

Partnering archaeologist husbands enabled many women to carry on field research. Sophie Schliemann, wife of Heinrich, is an early example. Ann Axtell Morris and Linda Braidwood collaborated with their husbands, co-authoring reports, but also writing popular books recounting their fieldwork adventures; and Agatha Christie, not herself an archaeologist, used her experiences in the field camps of her husband, Max Mallowan (p. 243), for whodunnits like *Murder in Mesopotamia*.

Countless women have also worked as non-professional archaeologists, locating and recording sites and collections near their homes. Frequently, they organized and staffed local museums combining historic and prehistoric information and displays. A notable example is Mary Butler Lewis, the first woman archaeologist to receive a Ph.D. from the University of Pennsylvania. After marrying in 1942, she shifted from research on Mesoamerican ceramics to prehistoric and historic investigations in her home area of New York and Pennsylvania.

Gertrude Bell (1868–1926), founder of the antiquities service of Iraq, *c.* 1910. Working with Leonard Woolley, Bell laid down rules that required all excavators to match current technical standards and include epigraphers, architects, photographers and other specialists in their digging teams.

From the 1970s, women were more visible in archaeology, especially in the United States and western Europe. The US Civil Rights Act of 1964 barred discrimination by sex, ending the routine exclusion of women from employment on federally-funded projects or in university faculties. The rise of cultural resource management and rescue archaeology created staff research positions that valued women's commitment to interpreting sites for the public and their conscientiousness in carrying out routine investigations. Even so, women archaeologists still obtained significantly less research support than men from the US National Science Foundation.

From the late 1980s, 'gender archaeology' attracted attention. Women challenged the standard depiction of 'Man the hunter' that dominated prehistory, arguing that more artifacts and features resulting from women's activities should be sought in fieldwork and excavation. There has also been feminist interest in discovering female deities and the history of women. Recognition of the presence of women in ancient societies is not new: in 1949 Breuil published delightful watercolours of palaeolithic camps with women flint-knapping, while Arcelin's palaeolithic novel of 1872 featured a young woman who was both chief and artist in the group at Solutré. However, there is now much more systematic consideration of how gender roles might be reflected in archaeological assemblages. Concern with more equitable representation of women in the profession of archaeology thus correlates with efforts to discern women in the past – a history of humanity rather than of mankind.

ALICE KEHOE, WITH MARY ANN LEVINE

Frederica de Laguna at the Alaskan site of Palugvik, Prince William Sound, 1933. On the left are R. Matrona Tiedemann, an Eskimo interpreter, and her father Chief Makari.

The Danish ethnologist Kaj Birket-Smith and de Laguna took turns excavating and recording ethnographic data from Chief Makari, who also identified artifacts for them.

ARCHAEOLOGY AND MINORITY GROUPS

Over the last fifteen years, archaeology across the world has become more sensitive to the rights of indigenous peoples whose past is being studied. Much of the debate has revolved around the treatment by archaeologists of aboriginal buried remains, but this important issue is only one part of the overall problem of who owns and controls the past.

At one extreme are scientific archaeologists who believe that they can legitimately and ethically treat all past remains, including human skeletons, as scientific data to be analysed. They point out that benefits – for example, in tracing the histories of infectious diseases – can accrue to aboriginal peoples from these studies. They also argue that many archaeological sites date back long before contemporary aboriginal groups appeared on the scene, and so belong to human-kind rather than to any single tribe or ethnic group. Finally, such archaeologists assert that any attempt by aboriginal groups to control archaeological data and their interpretation is academic censorship.

Aboriginal groups, on the other hand, make the simple point that archaeological remains are the remains of their ancestors, not those of Europeans. Cleverly, North American Indians have further argued that since Whites first came to North America, Indians have been lumped together as a group and their ethnic and cultural differences ignored: Indians cannot therefore be blamed if they follow the example of Whites and treat all prehistoric remains as Indian, regardless of specific ethnic affiliation. Many aboriginal groups also feel that they know all there is to know about the past, and that the spirits of the dead should not be disturbed by having their bones or their artifacts dug up and treated disrespectfully. For American Indians, time is not construed lineally as it is for Europeans, so there is no need for the detailed studies of the past that constitute archaeology. Moreover, for many indigenous groups, the control of archaeology is part of a wider power struggle with the dominant European ideology. They feel that their lives and culture are in danger of being completely lost or weakened: defining history their way is one means of preventing this.

These issues have sparked intense and acrimonious charges from both sides. Compromises are, however, being reached. One such is the Native American Graves Protection and Repatriation Act of 1990, which defines the ownership of Native American remains and objects on federal or tribal lands, and sets up procedures for analysing and returning such goods to the appropriate tribe.

Archaeologists working in the Americas have overwhelmingly been of European descent, and antagonism between archaeologists and Native Americans has in the past been common. For Native Americans, archaeological excavations are disrespectful to their ancestors' remains, and unnecessary because legendary histories provide them with sufficient knowledge of their pasts. Since the 1980s, however, there have been encouraging signs of rapprochement between the two groups: archaeologists have realized that prehistoric American remains are more than sci-

Opposite. Horse head from the chariot of the moon goddess, Selene, from the 'Elgin Marbles', the Parthenon frieze now housed in the British Museum.

Of the 111 panels that originally made up the frieze, some 97 survive, intact or broken; 56 are in the British Museum, 40 *in situ* or in the Acropolis Museum, and one in the Louvre. The British Museum also holds 15 of the original 92 metopes – 39 survive in Athens – and 17 pedimental sculptures.

Efforts, notably by the late Melina Mercouri, the Greek actress and politician, to have the marbles returned have come to nothing because the British Museum is prevented by statute from giving away its collections.

entific data, and increasingly acknowledged the right of contemporary Native Americans to participate in the study and disposition of their archaeological heritage. Because many skeletons and artifacts could be shown to have been stolen during the heyday of collecting a century ago against the wishes of Indian communities, legislation has also been passed – at both state and federal level – to oblige museums to repatriate skeletons and objects upon request from descendants.

Some Indian nations, including the Zuni, Navajo and Hopi nations in the Southwest, and the Makah in northwest Washington state have now appointed their own staff archaeologists and historians to research and protect their heritage. The Makah even employed archaeologists to excavate Ozette village, buried in a mudslide in the fifteenth century AD, and built a museum to exhibit their remarkably preserved history. Other communities employ archaeologists to carry out research that will train their own young people in archaeological techniques and understanding.

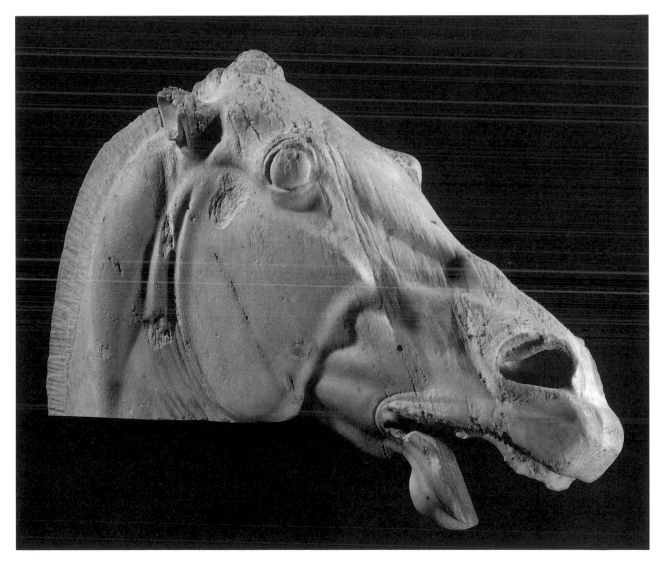

Whose past? Archaeologists versus Aborigines

The past has considerable symbolic power and can be used for political and social purposes. Since the 1970s, dispossessed indigenous peoples have increasingly challenged North American, Australian and New Zealand archaeologists, rejecting the view that archaeological sites are the common heritage of humanity and insisting that this is merely a pretext to justify cultural domination by more powerful invaders. They accuse archaeologists of direct complicity in colonization by portraying indigenous peoples as primitive and doomed to extinction. They object also to the excavation of burials and other sites – especially sacred sites – and the collections of human bones and cultural artifacts held by museums.

In Australia, Aboriginal people are increasingly asserting their right to own and control their own culture and their own past, and have strongly criticized the activities of archaeologists and anthropologists. Since the European invasion Aborigines have been driven from their traditional land, often violently and with great loss of life. Introduced diseases like smallpox and measles have taken their toll of the population, and government policies of assimilation have led to the removal of children from their parents and the destruction of family life. Over the last 25 years, however, Aborigines have become increasingly successful in their struggle for social justice and political recognition, and there has been a considerable change in attitude. The campaign for land rights has been the most prominent part of this struggle, but pressure to take control of Aboriginal heritage has also been important. As a consequence, white Australian archaeologists have had to reconsider how they conduct research and how they should relate to Aboriginal people.

There is a wide spectrum of opinion on both sides of the debate. On the one hand, archaeological information has been used for political purposes by Aborigines to support their long-term occupation of Australia. On the other, there has been vigorous controversy about issues like access to sites, excavation and the control of museum collections. In Western Australia, Aboriginal communities were greatly

offended when a female archaeologist visited ceremonial sites forbidden to women, and withdrew permission for archaeological work.

The excavation and study of human remains have been the most public and bitter areas of dispute, and Aborigines have campaigned vigorously for the return and reburial of skeletal materials now in museums around the world. Aborigines make no distinction between recent burials and very ancient ones, or between scientific excavation and the indiscriminate violation of graves to collect anatomical specimens – a common practice in the past. Most archaeologists are happy to support the reburial of recent remains, especially those of named individuals like Truganini, the so-called 'last Tasmanian'. However, many have strongly opposed the return of more ancient remains such as the unique series of burials from Kow Swamp, dating back to between 9,000 and 13,000 years ago; these were finally handed back to the Aboriginal community in 1990 and reburied. More recently, the first burial found at Lake Mungo, which is the world's oldest known cremation,

has been voluntarily returned to the custody of the Aborigines of the Mungo area.

Archaeologists in Australia have found it difficult to cope with the idea that they are not detached scientific objective observers but actual participants in a social drama. Some have abandoned Aboriginal archaeology, although others have sought active collaboration with Aboriginal groups. Generally, the trend has been towards greater consultation and discussion and there have been successful cooperative research ventures.

The public sector, both federal and state, has moved to involve Aboriginal people in the management of sites, through membership of advisory committees, the regulation of research, or through recruiting Aboriginal staff and providing training for them. In 1991, a code of ethics was adopted at the annual conference of the Australian Archaeological Association. It explicitly acknowledges members' obligations to respect and consult with the living people whose ancestors' lives are under investigation.

Ultimately, these issues can only be resolved in the broader context of reconciliation between Aborigines and the general Australian community. In 1992, a decision of the High Court recognized the existence of native title and overturned the legal fiction of *terra nullius*, that there was no indigenous system of land ownership, which had underwritten the dispossession of the Aboriginal population. The implications of this decision are far-reaching and are forcing all non-Aboriginal Australians to re-examine the history of their relations with Aborigines.

In New Zealand, the Maori challenge to the Pakeha (white) community over the control of Maori heritage, including archaeological sites, has been equally strong. Archaeology is often seen as a threat to the Maori world view, undermining Maori traditions. Unlike in Australia, the invading British did recognize Maori sovereignty and the Treaty of Waitangi was signed in 1840.

As a result, the Maori have increasingly used this treaty to assert their traditional rights over land and over sites.

'Mungo Lady returns to her people' read the headlines. In 1992, an important step in the process of reconciliation between Aborigines and archaeologists occurred when the remains of the Mungo 1 cremation were returned to the keeping of the Aboriginal elders of western New South Wales.

POLITICS AND ARCHAEOLOGY

It has long been accepted that archaeology can serve the public interest, beyond providing an objective and accurate representation of what happened in the past. In particular, it can be used to serve partisan national or political interests: a possibility seen at its most sinister in Nazi Germany and Stalinist Russia (p. 210), or in White-ruled Rhodesia where Great Zimbabwe was used to uphold racist views about Africa's past (p. 176). Such abuses of interpretation are object lessons for those who insist on regarding archaeology as an objective and verifiable science of the human past.

Nowhere is the illusion that archaeologists can write a 'scientific' and unbiased history of past societies shattered more poignantly than in the story of archaeology in Africa. Perhaps more than any other part of the world, Africa emphasizes the fact that archaeology is a critical contemporary discussion of the past. Absolute objectivity is impossible, because all archaeologists, either implicitly or explicitly, draw on their own backgrounds in their work. This does not mean that there are no facts in archaeology, or that archaeologists write political propaganda at worst, fairy stories at best. Indeed, the relevance of archaeology lies in its connection between present and past. As Grahame Clark wrote in the shadow of Nazism, in *Archaeology and Society* (1939), archaeology 'finds complete justification if it enriches the experience of [people] and helps them to live more abundantly as heirs of all ages and brothers to one another'.

The liberalization of Soviet society under Khrushchev led to some hope of greater connections between Soviet and western archaeologists, although these were dashed by the sharpening ideological confrontation between West and East in the 1960s. Some western archaeologists succeeded in establishing important links, but it was not until after the Vietnam War in 1975 that any greater opening up occurred. Most contacts consisted of western archaeologists visiting the Soviet Union; restrictions on Soviet citizens travelling abroad meant that most Soviet archaeologists were not exposed to the diversity of archaeological scholarship and recent technical advances in western archaeology. In the 1970s and 1980s, some Soviet archaeologists travelled abroad and published in western journals, but their numbers remained small, and they still tended to write defensively of a self-contained 'Soviet archaeology', when in reality East and West by then had much more in common.

As a result, the lingering caricature of pre-1991 Soviet archaeology held in the West is that Soviet archaeologists mindlessly applied Engels' scheme of social evolution and ignored other approaches. While the tendency to put an ideological cast on prehistory may have persisted to varying degrees, after the death of Stalin Soviet archaeology was not monolithic. Instead, it sought to recover archaeological information and interpret the results in ways that were just as valid as – if different from – the approaches espoused in the West. At the same time, Soviet archaeology was adversely affected by limitations on international contacts and the general impoverishment of society. Perhaps now that most of the barriers between the former Soviet republics and the rest of the world have been eliminated, it will be possible to examine the history of Soviet archaeology in greater detail.

Soviet withdrawal from central Europe at the end of the 1980s was followed by the collapse of the USSR itself in 1991. Once again, major political events had profound effects on archaeology – most notably a sharp reduction in funding for field research and publication. By the early 1990s, research had been severely curtailed as archaeologists of the former Soviet bloc struggled to obtain funds within a new – often decentralized – system. Overstaffed institutions were forced to trim their payrolls. Journals and monographs became expensive to produce; many have been suspended or ceased publication.

The revolutions of 1989–91 caused major changes in archaeological personnel in many countries. Since 1989, some have banned former Party members from holding positions, which has had the effect of removing previously influential scholars. The result has been temporary disorientation and the dislocation of

Modern ideology and ancient monuments. The Shah of Iran at the tomb of Cyrus the Great (d. 529 BC) to celebrate the '2,500th anniversary of the Achaemenid monarchy' in 1971.

Opposite. Cycladic folded-arm figurine, *c.* 2500-2000 BC.

Cycladic marble figurines stand at the beginning of western art and for almost a thousand years, throughout the third millennium BC, they constituted the main form of artistic expression in the Aegean region. Unhappily, in this century their striking similarity to modern works of art – notably by Brancusi and Giacometti – has attracted not just art lovers but also international art dealers driven by profit rather than a thirst for archaeological knowledge.

The result, during the 1960s, was an upsurge in illicit digging in the Cyclades, particularly Naxos, which caused immense damage. Thousands of prehistoric graves were rifled – not just those holding figurines – and a mass of information about the creators of this unique art form was lost.

More recently, in the 1970s and 1980s, the importunate demands of the international art market have been satisfied by the wide diffusion of fakes, many of them apparently made in Paris. Collections made up almost exclusively of counterfeit figurines were assembled – divine retribution, archaeologists like to think, by the gods of the Cyclades.

research programmes. Nonetheless, there is a mood of optimism as the 1990s move along. Support for archaeology is expected to come from construction projects as the road and pipeline system of eastern Europe is modernized, and archaeologists are learning about competing for grants, instead of relying on state support. Most institutions have survived the upheavals and are continuing their research, albeit at a reduced level. Best of all, the intellectual climate in many former communist states has become revitalized. Telecommunication via fax and electronic mail has linked hitherto isolated research centres to the global archaeological community, and young archaeologists can both speak their minds and feel free to try new interpretative approaches. More disturbing is the fact that, since 1989, eastern Europe and the former Soviet Union have seen the re-emergence of extreme nationalist elements whose influence may eventually be felt once again in archaeological interpretation, moving the subject back in the direction of Kossinna's 'settlement archaeology' as new states attempt to establish territorial legitimacy.

Nationalist manipulation of the past thrives too in other parts of the world, with modern ethnic communities often focusing on a glorious past as a means of constructing a national myth. The short-lived Armenian kingdom of Tigranes the Great in the first century BC, for instance, extended from the Caspian to the Black Sea, and southward across Syria; displayed today by many Armenians, maps of Tigranes' conquests appeal implicitly both to extinguished political power and to potential land claims. Further back in time, the Armenian national myth traces descent from the Iron Age Urartian kingdom that controlled territories from northwestern Iran to the Euphrates in Turkey, despite the complete linguistic and cultural rupture between Urartians and Armenians.

Another variant of the nationalist myth involves claims of legitimate inherited power through which a modern ruler claims descent from glorious kings of the past. One current example is Saddam Hussein's appeal to the mantle of Nebuchadnezzar and the reconstruction of Babylon as a symbol of national identity. Iran under the Pahlavis offers an equally instructive example. Reza Khan, an army officer, seized power after a coup in 1921, styled himself Pahlavi – after the language of Sassanian Persia, fifteen hundred years before – and renamed the country Iran ('Aryan') as a further reference to the linguistic and ethnic identity of Persia. The Russians and British seized the country in 1941, forcing Reza Khan into South African exile. His son Mohammad Reza was placed on the throne, and by the 1960s had emerged as an autocratic ruler, taking such ancient titles as 'King of Kings' and 'Light of the Aryans'. In 1971, the Shah spent $300 million in celebrating the 2,500th anniversary of the Achaemenid monarchy – although 529 BC marked no known founding event in Achaemenid history – firmly identifying himself as the successor to Cyrus the Great.

As far as Africa is concerned, most regions lack written records from before the nineteenth or even twentieth centuries, so archaeology is the major source of information on Africa's past. The growth of African history and the archaeological study of later periods occurred with the rise of African nationalism and the desire to provide Africans with an indigenous past. Collaborative studies involving archaeological and documentary sources as well as oral traditions have done much to banish colonial myths of a 'dark continent', but not without the danger of creating new ones, such as a 'merrie olde Africa' in which people lived in harmony with nature in simple rustic villages without strife or poverty. Indeed, African nationalist historians have begun writing histories that authenticate 'nationhood', despite the ethnically artificial boundaries of most modern African states.

African archaeology today is international, unlike European and North American archaeology, where it is difficult for foreign researchers to undertake fieldwork. However, archaeology is an expensive luxury on a continent plagued by war, famine, disease and poverty, and only a few African countries have an institutional framework conducive to active research. Nevertheless, almost every country in Africa funds embryonic archaeological research and, especially in West Africa, the training of indigenous archaeologists. The rise of 'nationalist' archaeology in the post-independence era after the 1960s, in many cases still practised mainly by expatriate archaeologists, has resulted in the replacement of the migration and diffusion theories of colonial ideology with models emphasizing indigenous innovation. However, as in other parts of the world, the close relationship between subject, interpretation and today's political economy remains all-pervasive. One challenge is to search for a balance between the practice of western 'critical' archaeology and a post-independence African 'contextualized' archaeology, increasingly seen as a vehicle for appropriating the real and imagined glories of the past for political gain.

LOOTING AND FORGERY

Tragically, in some areas of eastern Europe, notably parts of the former nation of Yugoslavia, archaeological sites and museums, and archaeologists themselves, are today threatened by war and a collapse of civil order. The museum in Vukovar in Croatia, for instance, housing materials from the Copper Age tell at Vučedol and other sites, was destroyed in the Serbian siege of 1991. Elsewhere, the looting of archaeological sites and museums is feeding an emerging antiquities market, for instance in Bulgaria; collectors seem to find bronze specimens from the Bronze and Iron Ages particularly attractive. Tight enforcement of national antiquities laws previously kept such activity in check, but with open borders and scarce funds, there is now little to look forward to except looting and trafficking in illicit antiquities for years to come.

The outlook for archaeology in eastern Europe and the former Soviet Union is at once optimistic and grim. In regions where stable economies are emerging, such as Poland, the Czech Republic and Hungary, archaeological research is proceeding apace. Where there is poverty, hyperinflation and food shortage, there is every

Grave-robbing and the international art trade

The placing of artifacts with the dead has always attracted the interest of the living. Even in antiquity, graves were desecrated in the search for precious metals, as an incident retailed in the *Life* of the Byzantine saint Theodore of Sykeon illustrates: around AD 600, the governor of Galatia Prima tried to arrest men who were variously suspected of treasure-hunting, of disturbing tombs, and of enlarging a threshing-floor as a cover for illicit digging. Things were little improved by the eighteenth and nineteenth centuries when the unscientific opening of graves in Tuscany and southern Italy involved little attempt to understand the original context: the tombs merely offered beautiful objects, with Greek vases perceived as 'truffles'. With the rise of national collections, sources of ancient art had to be discovered to fill galleries in London, Paris and Berlin with excellence from the past. Finally, in the twentieth century, temples and architectural monuments came to be seen as sources of sculptural reliefs, while objects with slighter intrinsic value became collectibles, recovered and displayed in comfortable living rooms from Tokyo to Turin.

The rise of the private collector has undoubtedly encouraged the destruction of archaeological sites to supply the market. Whereas in the eighteenth century country houses made appropriate settings for life-size marble sculpture, the mantelpieces of opulent Manhattan apartments have created a market for pretty portable objects. One classic case is the acquisition of third-millennium BC marble Cycladic figurines from the Aegean. Following the Second World War, private collectors began to perceive their links with the sculpture of modern artists like Brancusi. This led to such unprecedented looting of Cycladic cemeteries to supply growing international demand that less than 10 per cent of all figurines known today come from a recorded archaeological context. The archaeologist is therefore faced with a near impossible task when it comes to interpreting the figures and the society that created them.

In addition to looting, there is the problem of forgeries. If demand outstrips supply consistently enough, objects will be created for the market. It has recently emerged that craftsmen employed in recreating the Minoan palace at Knossos (p. 150) were also engaged in creating 'Minoan' works of art which not only convinced Evans, the excavator, but were purchased through the Paris market by European and North American museums. In a field where beauty is all-important and meaning resides in the object itself, the archaeological context is irrelevant. Indeed its absence permits many happy

Luigi Perticarari, 'King of the Italian grave-robbers', slips through a hole revealed by the plough to discover yet another Etruscan tomb in the hillside of Tarquinia.

One of Italy's hundreds of *tombaroli* and *clandestini* (tomb robbers and illegal excavators), he is known as 'the magician' for his extraordinary ability to find unrifled tombs. In 1986, he even published his autobiography, *The Secrets of a Tomb Robber*.

Cesnola's legacy. Luigi Palma de Cesnola, was the first director of the Metropolitan Museum of Art, New York. This masterly silver dish was among a total of 35,373 objects he acquired in pre-Metropolitan days while United States consul in Cyprus, 1865–76. On hearing that he had sold the collection at auction to the Metropolitan, the Cypriot authorities issued an order forbidding export of the art – but too late. Cesnola, forewarned, had shipped his treasures off the island.

hours of fruitless speculation; connoisseurship alone allows the 'expert' to decide if an object is genuine. Thus in recent years there have been many cases where museums have bought objects which one group of connoisseurs has announced to be genuine, only to find a second group condemns it as a forgery. This was the case with the over life-size marble *kouros*, or statue of a youth, bought recently by the J. Paul Getty Museum in Malibu. The multi-million dollar purchase was soon condemned as a forgery, and scientific techniques are unable either to confirm or deny its authenticity.

An equally disturbing trend in recent decades has been the theft of antiquities from museums: one of the most celebrated was the removal from Corinth of 271 objects, including a portrait head of Julius Caesar. Objects which have been published and are known to the archaeological world are unlikely to surface on the antiquities market without being recognized, a fact which suggests such thefts are occurring at the order of private collectors. The phenomenon is linked to

the growth of new professions such as 'ancient art consultants' and the appearance of investment portfolios that contain antiquities. There has thus been a marked move towards promoting the intrinsic beauty of an object and ignoring its context: a decorated Athenian wine-mixing bowl, relatively cheap in its day and almost certainly not viewed as 'art', can be plucked from an Etruscan tomb, sold on the international art market for a million dollars, and displayed in a museum as a major work of art.

The regular appearance of unprovenanced objects in the auction houses of London and New York is a continuing source of concern for all archaeologists. Each sale represents loss of knowledge through the previous year's pillaging of sites. More worrying still is the fact that some of these objects may prove to be creations of the late twentieth century, whose appearance in scholarly reference works will only serve to corrupt our interpretation of the past.

Opposite. Mass tourism presents a huge conservation challenge to the world's historic as well as natural environment in the twenty-first century.

This abraded pillar painting from the tomb of Seti I (1306–1290 BC) in the Valley of the Kings, shows the pharaoh with the ibis-headed Thoth, god of wisdom, writing and learning.

Like all the tomb's paintings, it was in pristine condition when discovered by Belzoni, in October 1817:

'I perceived immediately by the painting on the ceiling and by the hieroglyphs in *basso relievo*, which were to be seen where the earth did not reach, that this was the entrance into a large and magnificent tomb …The paintings became more perfect as we advanced further into the interior. They retained their gloss, or a kind of varnish over the colours, which has a beautiful effect. At the end of the corridor we descended ten steps into another. From this we entered a small chamber to which I gave the name of the Room of Beauties; for it is adorned with the most beautiful figures in *basso relievo*, like all the rest, and painted.'

reason to believe that advances in archaeology will be limited to accidental discoveries. Indeed, it will be a challenge simply to conserve existing collections and to protect sites from looting and destruction. Regions of ethnic warfare, such as the former Yugoslavia, Georgia and Azerbaijan, are archaeological wastelands for which there is very little hope in the foreseeable future.

Looting is now a worldwide phenomenon. Not having the money to enforce laws protecting archaeological sites, Thailand, for example, is struggling with the wholesale bulldozing of sites for their glass trade-beads from India, while China haemorrhages artifacts daily into the Hong Kong antiquities market through collusion between grave-robbers and local officials.

TOURISM AND CONSERVATION

In many parts of the world, like the Far East, the current importance of archaeology lies in the context of tourism and the national heritage. As a tool of government, archaeology is seen as a means of generating income as well as strengthening the indigenous identity of the people, and money for the subject depends on these overarching interests. In China, for example, archaeological research projects are chosen for their tourism potential. In places like Xi'an, a former capital of several dynasties, heritage-driven economic investment has led to the building of a new airport as well as several western-style luxury hotels, so we shall certainly see more sites like Banpo and the Terracotta Army presented for public display in the near future.

In other places, like Hong Kong and Osaka, airport construction is likewise demanding new archaeological investigations. The budget for construction-related excavation in Japan stands at £300 million per year, exactly three hundred times the sum annually available for archaeology in England. This amount is not provided from taxation but mostly extracted from the developer, who passes the cost on to the consumer. The rule that 'the developer pays' is not inscribed in Japanese law; it is a custom based on 'gentlemen's agreement' and correspondingly difficult to institute in other countries. This developer-paid pre-construction excavation on both private and public land is undertaken by the largest archaeological bureaucracy in the world, comprising over 5,000 public archaeologists.

The laws requiring archaeological involvement in the Far East are quite different from those in the West. In Japan, any disturbance of the earth – whether on private or public land – requires notification to the authorities who must then by law investigate the archaeological remains before construction. Often this investigation is confined to field survey or a watching brief during construction, but theoretically nothing is allowed to go undocumented. In the United States, the laws apply only to state-owned, not private, land (p. 342); in England, only treasure trove needs to be reported and only work on listed sites needs permission in advance. Thus, laws not only generate different levels of economic expenditure and labour involvement, but different quantities of archaeological information too.

Many archaeological initiatives are funded by the Japanese media, especially outside Japan. Several projects in China and Russia have recently been carried out with Fuji television or *Yomiuri* newspaper. Japan supplies the specialists in hi-tech analytic techniques, the local countries provide fieldworkers and permissions, and the media get exclusive access to the results, fuelling the public appetite for heritage news.

In Australia and the Pacific, the development of cultural tourism means that many archaeological sites now have economic value for indigenous people, but at the same time those sites are threatened by pressure of visitors. Conflict between the economic imperatives of development and traditional practices is thus increasingly a problem. Kakadu National Park in the Northern Territory well illustrates these difficulties, demanding a balance between conservation of the natural and cultural environment, tourism, the requirements of the mining industry, and the wishes and aspirations of the traditional owners of the land. Such issues are far from straightforward, with some Aboriginal people supporting new mining ventures destructive of archaeology for the economic benefits they would bring their community.

As archaeology has grown more popular and mass tourism has come into existence with the advent of easy air travel, so a number of towns, regions – even whole countries such as China, Peru, Egypt – have become heavily dependent on archaeological tourism. According to the United Nations, tourism will be the most important activity in the world by the year 2000. This trend is healthy in some respects, since public awareness and enjoyment of archaeology are crucial to the subject's development in an era of financial stringency. There are nonetheless two unfortunate consequences. First, the sites and even the tourists themselves can become targets for terrorism, as has occurred in highland Peru and the Nile valley. It has proved easy to scare away huge numbers of tourists in this way, making a major impact on the country's economy: for example, by 1994, attacks by Islamic fundamentalists had cost the Egyptian government more than £650 million in lost tourist revenues, one of the ailing economy's main sources of hard currency. Second, we are in danger of 'loving archaeology to death'. The ever-increasing numbers of tourists are causing immense, and often irreparable, damage to many sites through pollution, body-heat, condensation, and general wear and tear, quite apart from accidental damage, vandalism and theft. Mesa Verde, for instance, had around 666,000 visitors in 1993 and 742,000 in 1992. And in 1989–90 over 3.4 million visitors descended in a single year on the newly excavated Yoshinogari site in Kyushu, Japan, to view a moated settlement erroneously publicized as belonging to Himiko, an ancient queen.

Some of the world's most famous sites have had to be protected from tourism: Lascaux cave was closed in 1963 when bacteria threatened the paintings, and other decorated caves have seen visits stopped or severely curtailed. The interior of Stonehenge is now closed to the public, thanks to the effects of millions of feet treading on the paths and stones. Most recently, reports have appeared of the catastrophic condition of some major Egyptian sites: the Sphinx succumbing to the terrible effects of pollution, and Tutankhamen's tomb – visited by hundreds of thousands every year – in serious danger of collapse. Simple neglect, as with the footprint trail of Laetoli (p. 328) being destroyed by tree roots, is another major threat.

The central problem is how to weigh the public's entitlement to see its common cultural heritage against the well-being and survival of that heritage. One solution, as at Lascaux, is an exact replica which, though never as satisfying as the original, can nonetheless meet the aspirations of most tourists. However, it is clear that conservation – of tombs, sites, rock art and monuments – is now, and will increasingly become, a crucial part of archaeology's future, with less emphasis on new excavation and research, and more on looking after what has already been found.

EDUCATING THE PUBLIC

Archaeological information can often be used as a means of benefiting modern society. Scientists from Israel's Ben-Gurion University, for example, have been able to study how ancient peoples farmed the arid Negev desert and apply this knowledge to modern farm practices. Similar projects are being carried out in South America, where the reintroduction in highland Peru and Bolivia of ancient forms of raised-field agriculture has revolutionized crop-yields.

In southwest Colorado, the Crow Canyon Center for American Archaeology is a private educational and research institution that concentrates on the archaeology of the Anasazi, providing educational experience for members of the public able to pay for the privilege of learning a little about archaeology. While some archaeologists criticize this commercialization of the subject, in these days of severe restrictions on archaeological funding it remains true that the important research accomplished in recent years by Crow Canyon archaeologists would simply not have been undertaken had it not been done for financial gain. The Center has been highly successful in bringing archaeology to a wider segment of the American public.

Radical archaeologists on both sides of the Atlantic have criticized the 'heritage industry' – profit-making museums and heritage centres that charge the public for admission – for what they see as a whitewash of the past that indulges in sanitized recreation rather than historically accurate reconstruction. There are nonetheless good reasons for the rise of heritage parks and reconstructions around the world, not least the challenge of making the results of – usually publicly funded – research available in palatable form to a wide, and in some parts of the world illiterate, audience. Rapidly growing populations, economic development and urbanization accentuate the need to create an archaeologically informed public that will stimulate a climate of conservation and give teeth to such rudimentary conservation laws as currently exist.

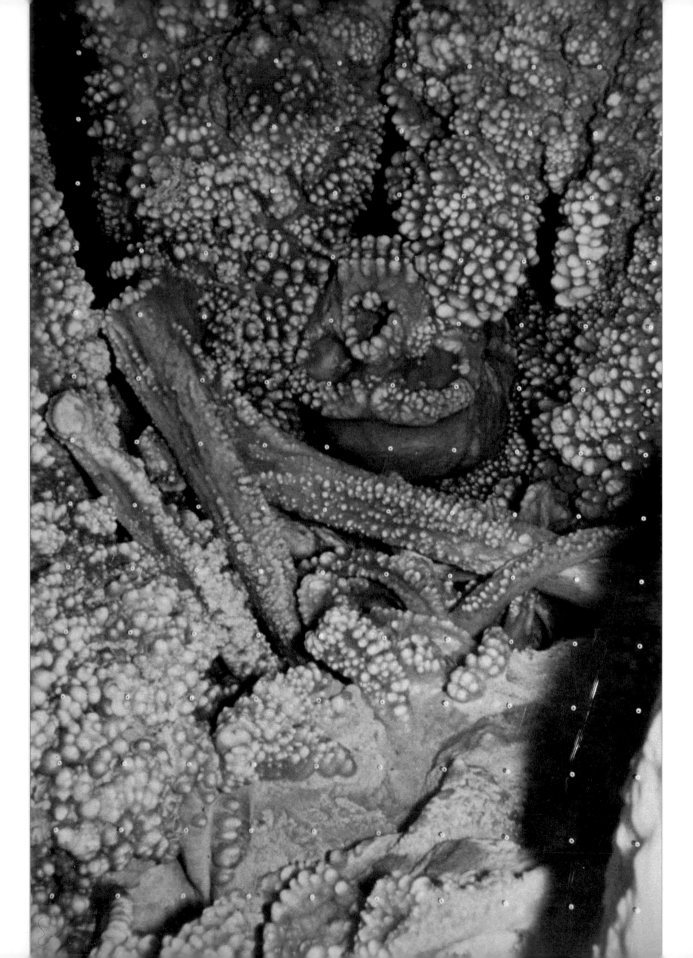

ON THE HORIZON

What will archaeology be like in fifty years time? Archaeologists of all people should know the dangers of predicting the future, but it seems safe to say that changes will continue on a wide range of fronts.

First, it is likely that indigenous groups will continue to see archaeology as a means by which their own political goals can be realized. This does not necessarily mean that archaeology will be seething with discord. Rather, it has the potential to become a vehicle for promoting ethnic and racial harmony through which minority groups can promote greater respect and understanding of their culture. That archaeology studies and serves *all* humankind is more than a simple truism.

Second, archaeology will radically alter how it obtains its data. This does not simply mean that the discipline will increasingly take into account the wishes of the peoples whose ancestors it is studying – though this will undoubtedly occur. Rather, that more non-invasive survey procedures will be developed so that sites can be examined in depth without being destroyed.

Third, archaeological theory will continue to evolve. It is highly unlikely that archaeology will ever be able – or even want – to settle on a single and unified approach that will guide all its investigations. Rather, it will continue to entertain highly divergent and often contradictory ways of studying the past, remaining true to its disciplinary roots and continuing to be part anthropology, part history, part science. It will also continue to capitalize on its unique emphases on material culture and long time depth.

Finally, archaeology must continue to keep itself relevant. It has been supported by the public because of their interest in the past. Local archaeological societies thrive throughout the world. The popularity of television programmes or articles in magazines such as *National Geographic*, and the interest with which new finds are greeted – whether they be as grand as 'Lucy' or as apparently mundane as a site found during highway construction – speak well for archaeology's continuing existence. Shrinking central government budgets, on which archaeology ultimately depends, mean that vigilance will remain crucial. Professional archaeologists must make public involvement and interest in their work a priority, while continuing to emphasize that archaeology has a serious purpose that goes far beyond being, in Grahame Clark's magnificent phrase, just an 'intellectual game for the meritocracy'.

Archaeology, we can boast, has already provided partial answers to many fundamental questions about the development of our species. It is important to know why humans began to turn to agriculture 12,000 years ago or why cities developed 5,000 years ago. Archaeology is the only discipline that can shed light on human antiquity so far back in time. If it is true that the present is defined by the past, archaeology's role should be secure for all time.

Opposite. A constant flow of new discoveries continues to invigorate archaeology as humankind moves into the third millennium of the Christian era.

This skeleton, found deep inside a cave system at Altamura, Italy, in 1993, may be the oldest intact human skeleton in Europe. Its archaic features such as heavy brow ridges are hard to make out because of the thick encrustation by stalagmites, but suggest that the skeleton may be 300,000 or 400,000 years old – perhaps a link between Homo erectus *and* Homo sapiens.

Reference guide to
The Cambridge
Illustrated History of

Archaeology

A Chronology of
Archaeology from 1500

Further Reading

A Chronology of Archaeology from 1500

1506 Laocoön of *c.* 200 BC rediscovered in Rome; influences Michelangelo

1521 Cortés conquers Mexica empire; captures Tenochtitlán

1524 Pizarro conquers Inka empire; captures Cajamarca

1533 Leland becomes King's Antiquary to Henry VIII

1534 da Orta visits Elephanta and rock-cut temples near Bombay

1542 Coronado searches for seven cities of Cibola in American Southwest

1558 First Etruscan tombs discovered in Perugia

1568 Camden's *Britannia* published

1585 White's drawings of Native Americans

1603 Stow describes Roman cemetery at Spitalfields, London

1610 Cartwright visits Babylon and Persepolis

1612 Howard digs for classical sculpture in Rome

1615 della Valle visits Babylon, Ur, Persepolis

1630 Bure becomes Royal Antiquary to Gustavus Adolphus

1650 Ussher calculates date of Creation: 23 October 4004 BC

1652 Browne's 'Urne Burial', prompted by Anglo-Saxon pots found in Norfolk

1663 Aubrey plans Stonehenge

1677 Conyers observes Roman pottery kilns during building of St Paul's

1685 Le Prévôt digs megalithic tomb at Cocherel, Normandy

1690 Conyers finds palaeolithic hand axe at Gray's Inn Lane, London

1691 First archaeological expedition in Near East: to Palmyra

1717 Mercati's *Metallotheca* published

1718 Society of Antiquaries of London founded, Stukeley first president

1722 Roggeveen visits Easter Island

1723 First known excavation of a British barrow: near Stonehenge by Stukeley

1727 First medieval excavation: Châtenay-Malabry, by de Clérambault

1738 Excavations at Pompeii and Herculaneum inaugurated

1744 Frederick of Denmark and Pontop-pidan excavate barrow in Zealand

1759 British Museum founded at Montagu House, Bloomsbury

1763 Hamilton begins collecting Greek pottery in Naples

1764 Winckelmann's *History of Ancient Art* published

1765 Niebuhr visits Persepolis; identifies sites of Babylon and Nineveh

1768 Cook's *Endeavour* explores east coast of Australia

1771 Esper finds bones of humans and extinct animals at Gaillenreuth

1776 First excavation in sub-Saharan Africa: Sparrman at Cookhouse

1784 First excavation in North America: Jefferson at Monticello

1788 First excavation in Australia: Hunter at Port Jackson

1797 Frere finds palaeolithic axe with bones of extinct animals at Hoxne

1799 Rosetta Stone discovered; von Humboldt visits Chanchan

1802 Denon's *A Journey through Upper and Lower Egypt* published

1804 Elgin's Parthenon Marbles arrive in London

1810s First excavations at Persepolis, by Morier

1811 Claudius Rich plans Babylon

1812 Burckhardt reaches Petra

1813 Napoleonic *Description of Egypt* published

1815 de Jouannet at Combe Grenal and Pech de l'Azé; first excavations in Palestine: Stanhope at Ashkelon

1817 Belzoni discovers tomb of Seti I at Thebes; Thomsen organizes Danish National Museum, Copenhagen, according to the Three Age System

1819 First excavation of south Indian megalith, by Babington

1821 Colt Hoare's *Ancient Wiltshire* published

1822 Champollion deciphers Egyptian hieroglyphic

1823 Buckland discovers 'Red Lady of Paviland'

1825 MacEnery at Kent's Cavern

1826 Tournal attributes human bones from Bize to 'antehistoric' time

1829 Blouet at Olympia

1831 Darwin's *Beagle* voyage

1833 Lyell's *Principles of Geology* published; Schmerling finds early human burials at Engis

1836 Thomsen's *Guide to Northern Archaeology* published

1839 Stephens and Catherwood explore the Maya cities of central America; Rawlinson deciphers cuneiform script

1840 Lepsius surveys antiquities of Nubia

1841 Wilkinson's *Manners and Customs of the Ancient Egyptians* published

1842 Boucher de Perthes digs at Menchecourt-les-Abbeville.

1843 Botta at palace of Sargon II at Khorsabad; Worsaae's *Primeval Antiquities of Denmark* published

1844 British Archaeological Association founded

1845 Layard at palace of Assurnasirpal II at Nimrud; Squier and Davis investigate Ohio moundbuilders

1846 Ramsauer at Hallstatt

1850 Loftus at Warka

1851 First excavations in Jerusalem, by de Saulcy; Wilson's *Archaeology and Prehistoric Annals of Scotland*; Crystal Palace exhibition, London

1852 First excavation in New Zealand: Mantell at Awamoa; Römisch-Germanisches Zentralmuseum, Mainz, founded

1854 Keller identifies Swiss lake dwellings; Taylor tunnels into the ziggurat at Ur

1855 Smithsonian Institution opens in Washington DC

1856 Neandertal remains first identified at Feldhofer, near Düsseldorf

1858 Schwab at La Tène; Mariette becomes Director of Egyptian Monuments

1859 Charles Darwin's *Origin of Species* published; antiquity of humankind established through Boucher de Perthes' discoveries at Abbeville

1860 Lartet at Massat and Aurignac; Fiorelli at Pompeii

1863 Lartet and Christy at Le Moustier and La Madeleine; first Indian palaeolithic hand axe found at Pallavaram, Madras (Foote); Cairo Museum opens at Bulaq; Lyell's *The Antiquity of Man* and Huxley's *Man's Place in Nature* published

1865 Pengelly at Kent's Cavern; Lubbock's *Pre-Historic Times* published

1866 Arcelin at Solutré; Westropp coins 'mesolithic' for middle stone age; Palestine Exploration Fund and Peabody Museum, Harvard, established

1867 Musée des Antiquités Nationales, St Germain-en-Laye, inaugurated

1868 Louis Lartet excavates palaeolithic burials at Cro-Magnon

1870 Cunningham becomes Director General of Archaeological Survey of India

1871 Schliemann at Troy; Mauch discovers Great Zimbabwe; Darwin's *Descent of Man* and Taylor's *Primitive Culture* published

1872 First classification of palaeolithic sites by stone tools, by Mortillet

1873 Smith at Kuyunjik

1875 German excavations at Olympia begin

1876 Schliemann discovers shaft graves at Mycenae

1877 First excavation in Japan: Morse at Omori; de Sarzec at Tello

1879 de Sautuola discovers cave art of Altamira; first excavations at Kostyonki; Bureau of American Ethnology established

1880 Gokstad ship discovered; Pitt-Rivers begins excavating on Cranborne Chase; first excavations at Předmostí; Bandelier explores pueblos of New Mexico; Montelius' *On the Dating of the Bronze Age* published

1881 Petrie's Pyramid survey at Giza; Maudslay's expedition to Tikal

1882 Delta Excavation Fund (later Egypt Exploration Society) and Naturhistorisches Museum, Vienna, founded

1884 Schliemann at Tiryns; Petrie at Tanis and Naucratis; Dieulafoy at Susa; first excavations at Willendorf

1886 Museum für Völkerkunde, Berlin, founded

1887 Discovery of Amarna letters; Piette at Mas d'Azil

1888 Wetherill discovers Cliff Palace, Mesa Verde; Peters at Nippur

1890 Petrie at Tell el-Hesy

1891 Siret brothers at Los Millares

1892 Bulleid at Glastonbury Lake Village

1894 Dubois discovers 'Java Man'

1896 Uhle at Pachacamac

1897 Vesselovskii at Maikop; Benin punitive expedition

1898 Pitt-Rivers' *Excavations in Cranborne Chase* completed

1899 Koldewey at Babylon

1900 Evans at Knossos

1902 Authenticity of palaeolithic cave art established; Marshall becomes Director General of Archaeological Survey of India; Hal Saflieni hypogeum discovered; Andrae at Ashur

1903 Uhle at Emeryville

1905 Reisner excavates Pyramid of Menkaure at Giza

1906 First archaeological air photograph, of Stonehenge; Winkler at Boghazköy

1907 Reisner's First Nubian Survey; Stein at Caves of a Thousand Buddhas, Dunhuang

1908 Vasić at Vinča; Hogarth at Carchemish; School of American Studies established

1911 Bingham reaches Machu Picchu; first Piltdown 'fossils' found

1912 Marshall at Taxila; Kossinna's *German Prehistory* published

1915 Hrozny deciphers Hittite script

1919 Schuchhardt's *Early Europe* published

1921 Andersson discovers first *Homo erectus* fossils at Zhoukoudian

1922 Carter discovers tomb of Tutankhamen; Bruyère at Deir el-Medina; Woolley at Ur

1924 Indus civilization identified at Mohenjo-daro and Harappa; Dart discovers Taung skull of *Australopithecus africanus*; Absolon at Dolní-Věstonice; Caton-Thompson at the Fayum; Kidder's *Study of South-western Archeology* published

1925 Childe's *The Dawn of European Civilization* published; Reisner discovers tomb of Hetepheres; Breasted at Megiddo; Kroeber discovers Nasca lines; Scopes 'monkey trial' in Dayton, Tennessee

1926 Folsom bison-kill, New Mexico, excavated; first Leakey expedition to East Africa

1927 Mallowan at Nineveh; Caso's valley of Oaxaca survey

1928 Crawford's *Wessex from the Air* published; Li Chi at Anyang

1929 Childe's *The Danube in Prehistory* published; Caton-Thompson establishes black African origin of Great Zimbabwe; Garrod and Bate at Mount Carmel; Schaeffer at Ras Shamra; Tindale at Devon Downs; Novgorod excavations begin; Emery and Kirwan's Second Nubian Survey

1930 Frankfort at Tell Asmar; Garstang at Jericho; Breuil's *Prehistoric Africa* published

1931 Herzfeld at Persepolis; Crowfoot at Samaria

1932 Blegen at Troy

1933 Kostrzewski identifies Biskupin; Broom at Sterkfontein

1934 Wheeler at Maiden Castle; Norlund at Trelleborg; Stirling discovers Olmec civilization

1935 Mallowan at Chagar Bazar; Yale–Cambridge North Indian expedition

1936 McCarthy at Lapstone Creek

1938 Bersu at Little Woodbury

1939 Phillips at Sutton Hoo; Blegen at Pylos; Hohmichele excavated; Montet at Tanis; Thomson's Aboriginal ethnoarchaeology; Clarke's *Archaeology and Society* published; Garrod first woman professor of archaeology

1940 Lascaux cave art discovered

1941 Reiche's surveys at Nasca begin

1944 Wheeler Director General of Antiquities in India

1945 Wheeler at Arikamedu

1946 Willey's Virú valley survey

1947 Dead Dea Scrolls discovered; Rudenko at Pazyryk; Georgiev at Karanovo; Hittite hieroglyphs deciphered; Heyerdahl's Kon-Tiki expedition

1948 Taylor's *A Study of Archeology* published

1949 Libby publishes first radiocarbon dates; Clark at Star Carr

1950 Tollund Man discovered; Solecki at Shanidar; Bittel at the Heuneburg; National Museum, Karachi, inaugurated; Daniel's *A Hundred Years of Archaeology* published

1951 McBurney at Haua Fteah

1952 Kenyon at Jericho; Ventris deciphers Linear B; Cousteau explores Le Grand Congloué shipwreck; Clark's *Prehistoric Europe* published

1953 Vix discovered; Piltdown fakes exposed; Banpo, Xi'an, discovered

1954 Khufu's funeral boat discovered at Giza

1955 Yadin at Hazor

1956 Mulvaney at Fromm's Landing

1958 Movius at Abri Pataud

1959 Mary Leakey discovers 'Nutcracker Man' (*Zinjanthropus boisei*) at Olduvai; Shaw at Igbo Ukwu

1960 International Campaign to Save the Monuments of Nubia; Libby wins Nobel Prize for Chemistry

1961 *Homo habilis* found at Olduvai; Mellaart at Çatal Hüyük; Biddle at Winchester; *Wasa* raised; Clark's *World Prehistory* and Mulvaney's *The Stone Age of Australia* published

1962 Binford proclaims 'New Archeology'; Leroi-Gourhan at Arcy-sur-Cure; Mulvaney at Kenniff Cave

1963 Yadin at Masada

1964 Leroi-Gourhan at Pincevent

1965 Lepenski Vir first excavated; Hawkins' *Stonehenge Decoded* published

1967 Marinatos at Akrotiri

1968 Clarke's *Analytical Archaeology* and Binfords' *New Perspectives in Archeology* published; Abu Simbel reconstructed

1969 Tixier at Ksar Akil; world's oldest cremation found at Lake Mungo

1972 Ngeneo discovers '1470' at Koobi Fora

1973 Coles at Somerset Levels; Renfrew's *Before Civilisation* published

1974 Terracotta army discovered near Xi'an; Johanson discovers 'Lucy' (*Australopithecus afarensis*) at Hadar

1976 Coppergate excavations, York

1977 Hochdorf discovered; Vergina excavated

1978 Mary Leakey exposes Laetoli footprints; Maya hieroglyphs deciphered

1979 Philae temples reconstructed

1982 *Mary Rose* raised

1984 'Turkana Boy' discovered at Nariokotome; Bass at Ulu Burun; 'Lindow Man' discovered

1991 5,000-year-old 'Iceman' found in Similaun Pass, Italian Alps; Cosquer Cave rock art discovered

1994 Grotte Chauvet rock art found; *Ardipithecus ramidus* identified

Further Reading

Bahn, P. G. (ed.) 1995. *The Story of Archaeology: 100 Great Discoveries*. New York: Barnes and Noble; London: Weidenfeld & Nicholson

Bernal, I. 1980. *A History of Mexican Archaeology*. London: Thames and Hudson.

Ceram, C. W. 1951. *Gods, Graves and Scholars: The Study of Archaeology*. New York: Knopf.

_____, 1971. *The First American. A Story of North American Archaeology*. New York: Harcourt Brace Jovanovich.

Chakrabarti, D. K. 1988. *A History of Indian Archaeology from the Beginning to 1947*. New Delhi: Munshiram Manoharlal Publishers.

Clark, J.G.D. 1989. *Prehistory at Cambridge and Beyond*. Cambridge: Cambridge University Press.

Daniel, G. 1967. *The Origins and Growth of Archaeology*. Harmondsworth: Pelican.

_____, 1975. *150 Years of Archaeology*. London: Duckworth.

_____, 1981. *A Short History of Archaeology*. London: Thames and Hudson.

_____, (ed.) 1981. *Towards a History of Archaeology*. London: Thames and Hudson.

_____ and Chippindale, C. (eds.). *The Pastmasters. Eleven Modern Pioneers of Archaeology*. London: Thames and Hudson.

_____ and Renfrew, C. 1988. *The Idea of Prehistory*. Edinburgh: Edinburgh University Press.

Daux, G. 1966. *Histoire de l'Archéologie*. 'Que sais-je?' No. 54. Paris: Presses Universitaires de France.

Duval, A. (ed.) 1992. *La Préhistoire en France. Musées, Ecoles de Fouille, Associations du XIXe Siècle à nos Jours*. Actes du 114e Congrès National des Sociétés Savantes (Paris 1989). Paris: Editions du Comité des Travaux Historiques et Scientifiques.

Elliott, M. 1995. *Great Excavations: Tales of Early Southwestern Archeology, 1888–1939*. Santa Fe: School of American Research Press.

Fagan, B. 1975. *The Rape of the Nile: Tomb Robbers, Tourists and Archaeologists in Egypt*. New York: Scribner.

_____, 1977. *Elusive Treasure. The Story of Early Archaeologists in the Americas*. New York: Scribner.

Gräslund, B. 1987. *The Birth of Prehistoric Chronology*. Cambridge: Cambridge University Press.

Grayson, D. K. 1983. *The Establishment of Human Antiquity*. New York: Academic Press.

Groenen, M. 1994. *Pour une Histoire de la Préhistoire*. Grenoble: Jérôme Millon.

Horton, D. 1991. *Recovering the Tracks. The Story of Australian Archaeology*. Canberra: Aboriginal Studies Press.

Klindt-Jensen, O. 1975. *A History of Scandinavian Archaeology*. London: Thames and Hudson.

Laming-Emperaire, A. 1964. *Origines de l'Archéologie Préhistorique en France*. Paris: Picard.

Lartet, Breuil, Peyrony et les autres. Une histoire de la préhistoire en Aquitaine. Paris: Ministère de la Culture, 1990.

Lloyd, S. 1980. *Foundations in the Dust. The story of Mesopotamian Exploration*, (2nd edn). London: Thames and Hudson.

Malina, J. and Vašíček, Z. 1990. *Archaeology Yesterday and Today*. Cambridge: Cambridge University Press.

Marsden, B. M. 1974. *The Early Barrow-Diggers*. Princes Risborough: Shire Publications.

_____, 1984. *Pioneers of Prehistory. Leaders and Landmarks in English Archaeology (1500–1900)*. Ormskirk: Hesketh.

Norman, B. 1987. *Footsteps. Nine Archaeological Journeys of Romance and Discovery*. London: BBC Publications.

Piggott, S. 1976. *Ruins in a Landscape: Essays in Antiquarianism*. Edinburgh: Edinburgh University Press.

Reyman, J. E. (ed.) 1992. *Rediscovering our Past: Essays on the History of American Archaeology*. Aldershot: Avebury.

Robertshaw, P. (ed.) 1990. *A History of African Archaeology*. London: James Currey.

Schnapp, A. 1993. *La Conquête du Passe. Aux Origines de l'Archéologie*. Paris: Editions Carré.

Silberman, N. A. 1982. *Digging for God and Country. Exploration, Archaeology, and the Secret Struggle for the Holy Land, 1799–1917*. New York: Knopf.

Sklenar, K. 1983. *Archaeology in Central Europe: the first 500 Years*. Leicester: Leicester University Press.

Stiebing, W.H. Jr. 1993. *Uncovering the Past: a History of Archaeology*. Buffalo: Prometheus Books.

Trigger, B. G. 1989. *A History of Archaeological Thought*. Cambridge: Cambridge University Press.

Van Riper, A. B. 1993. *Men Among the Mammoths. Victorian Science and the Discovery of Human Prehistory*. Chicago: Chicago University Press.

Willey, G. R. (ed.) 1974. *Archeological Researches in Retrospect*. Cambridge, Mass: Winthrop.

_____, 1988. *Portraits in American Archeology. Remembrances of some distinguished Americanists*. Albuquerque: University of New Mexico Press.

_____ and Sabloff, J. A. 1993. *A History of American Archeology*, (3rd edn). New York: Freeman.

There are innumerable biographies and autobiographies of individuals mentioned in this book. References can be found in the more general works listed above.

Acknowledgements

The publishers gratefully acknowledge the help given towards compiling the illustrations for this volume by the many individuals and organizations who cannot all be named. Every effort has been made to obtain permission to use copyright materials; the publishers apologise for any omissions or oversights and would welcome these being brought to their attention.

The following abbreviations have been used:
b: bottom; t: top; l: left; r: right; AAA – Ronald Sheridan/Ancient Art and Architecture Collection; AM – Ashmolean Museum, Oxford; BAL – Bridgeman Art Library; BL (British Library) – by permission of the British Library; BM (British Museum) – © British Museum; CUL (Cambridge University Library) – by permission of the Syndics of Cambridge University Library; RMN – Réunion des Musées Nationaux, Paris; MNHN – Muséum National d'Histoire Naturelle, Paris; UC – University of Cambridge.

i AM. ii/iii Royal Collection, Belgium/BAL. viii Biblioteca Apostolica Vaticana. x Národní Galerie v Praze. xi A. von Morlot 'Underwater excavation 1854'/Bernisches Historisches Museum, Bern. xiii Benelux Press, Brussels. xiv BL, MS Harley 4337 folio 2. 3 BM. 4 AAA. 5 Bibliotheca Hertziana, Rome. 6 Mary Evans Picture Library. 7 BL Cotton MS Nero DI. 8 'St. Geneviève Gardant ses Moutons'; © DACS 1996. 9 BL, MS Egerton 3028 folio 30. 10 Bibliothèque Nationale, Paris. 12 Life File; photo Emma Lee. 14/15 © 'Leiv Erikson oppdager Amerika'; by Christian Krohg 1893/photo © Nasjonalgalleriet, Oslo. 16 National Palace Museum, Taipei, Taiwan, Republic of China. 18 The Whitworth Art Gallery, University of Manchester. 20 AM. 23 Map from Eduardo Matos Moctezuma The Great Temple of the Aztecs, Treasures of Tenochtitlán Thames and Hudson 1988. 24 From Felipe Guaman Nueva Corónica y Buen Gobierno Université de Paris 1936. 25 Werner Forman Archive/Biblioteca Universitaria, Bologna, Italy. 26 E. T. Archive. 28 Gemaldegalerie, Kunsthistorisches Museum, Vienna/BAL. 30 BAL. 32 Life File; photo Nigel Sitwell. 34 By courtesy of the National Portrait Gallery. 36t The Bodleian Library, Oxford. 36b CUL. 37 BL, MS Harley 4339 folio 2. 39 BM/BAL. 41 CUL. 42/3 BM. 44/5 By courtesy of the Board of Trustees of the V&A/BAL. 47 BM. 48/9 Städelsches Kunstinstitut Frankfurt/Artothek, Peissenberg; photo Blauel/Gnamm. 51 The Office of Public Works, Dublin. 52t CUL. 52b CUL; engraving taken from Metallotheca. 53 Landesmuseum Oldenburg; photo H. R. Wacker. 55 Wiltshire Archaeological and Natural History Society, Devizes. 57t City Museum and Mappin Art Gallery, Sheffield. 57b County Archive Service, Humberside County Council. 58 Fitzwilliam Museum, UC. 59 National Trust Photographic Library; photo John Hammond. 61 Townley Hall Art Gallery and Museum, Burnley/BAL. 63 Museum of Classical Archaeology, UC. 64 BM. 65 Bibliothèque Centrale MNHN, Paris. 68l Louvre/BAL. 68r From C. Hobson The World of the Pharaohs Thames and Hudson. 69 CUL. 70 BM. 72 Comstock; photo Dr George Gerster. 73 Cecil Higgins Art Gallery, Bedford/BAL. 74 BM. 77 Private Collection/BAL. 78 Art Gallery of Western Australia, Perth. 79 The Saint Louis Art Museum MO. 80/1 Gustave Boulanger, 'La Répétition du "Joueur de Flûte" et de "la Femme de Diomède" dans l'atrium de la Maison Pompeienne du Prince Napoléon en 1860, Versailles; © photo RMN 83 Hamburger Kunsthalle. 84 Bibliothèque Municipale, Amiens. 85 AM. 86 Mary Evans Picture Library. 88, 89 The National Museum, Copenhagen. 90 Det Kongelige Bibliotek, København. 91 CUL. 92 Royal Ontario Museum. 93 BM/BAL. 95 Swiss National Museum, Zürich, LM-30486; photo Schweiz, Landesmuseum. 96 Museum Hallstatt; photo Max Singer. 97 CUL. 98 Stapleton Collection/BAL. 100 Mary Evans Picture Library. 101 O'Shea Gallery, London/BAL. 105 Christie's Images. 106 BM. 107 Comstock. 108 BM. 110 Staatliche Museen zu Berlin/Preussischer Kulturbesitz Nationalgalerie; photo Klaus Göken, 1992. 112 CUL; from Frederick Catherwood The Views of Ancient Monuments of Central America, Chiapas and Yucatán 1884. 113 Comstock. 115 National Museum of American Art, Smithsonia Permlet Art Resource/BAL. 116/17 Robert Harding Picture Library/Robert Frerck. 118 CUL. 120 MNHN, Paléontologie; photo D. Serrette. 121 Robert S. Peabody Museum of Archaeology, Andover, MA. 122 Musée des Antiquités Nationales, Paris. 123 Institut de Paléontologie Humaine, Paris. 124/5 Jean Vertut, Issy-les-Moulineaux. 126 The Illustrated London News Picture Library. 127 The Natural History Museum. 128 Alexander Marshack, New York.

130 University Museum of National Antiquities, Oslo. 132 By kind permission of G. A. Pitt Rivers. 134 University Museum of National Antiquities, Oslo. 136/7 Saalburgmuseum, Bad Homburg. 138 Staatliche Museen zu Berlin – Preussischer Kulturbesitz/Museum für Vor– und Frühgeschichte. 140 Robert Harding Picture Library; photo Adam Woolfitt. 141 Deutsches Archäologisches Institut-Athen, Athens. 143 Hulton/Syndication. 144 AAA. 146 AM. 147 Tony Stone Worldwide; photo Trevor Wood. 148/9, 151 Petrie Museum of Egyptian Archaeology, University College London. 152 AM. 153 Louvre/RMN 156 Robert Harding Picture Library. 159 CUL; from William J. Hamilton Researches in Asia Minor, Pontus and Armenia 1842. 161 BM. 163 Tony Stone Worldwide; photo Sarah Stone. 164 Hulton Deutsch Collection. 165 The Semitic Museum, Harvard University. 168 Robert Harding Picture Library. 171 BL. 173 CUL; from Aurel Stein Ruins of Desert Cathay 1912. 175 CUL. 177 Comstock; photo Dr George Gerster. 179 BM. 180 The University of Cape Town. 181 Hulton Deutsch Collection. 183 Canterbury Museum, New Zealand, ref: 3047. 184/5 National Maritime Museum Picture Library. 188 Werner Forman Archive. 191 Peabody Museum, Harvard University. 193 Tony Stone Images; photo Ed Simpson. 194 BM. 196/7 The Griffith Institute, AM. 198, 201 Society of Antiquaries of London. 201r Popperfoto. 202 British Crown Copyright/MOD. 203t/b Michael Holford. 204 BM. 205 Michael Holford. 208 Photothèque Musée de l'Homme, Paris. 209 Jean Vertut, Issy-les-Moulineaux. 212 AAA. 215 Archives du Musée Bégouën, Montesquieu-Avantès. 217 The Times Magazine, London; photo Graham Wood. 220 Anthony Harding. 222 From Glyn Daniel A Short History of Archaeology Thames and Hudson 1981. 224 Institute of Archaeology, University College London. 225 Event Horizons – David Lyons. 227 Michael Holford. 228 Fitzwilliam Museum, UC. 230 Archaeological Receipts Fund, Athens. 231 AAA. 232 Bruce Coleman Limited; photo Kim Taylor. 233 Antonia Benedek. 235 The Illustrated London News Picture Library. 237 The Natural History Museum, London. 239 Keystone/Sygma. 240, 241 The Griffith Institute, AM. 242 Michael Holford. 244 Courtesy of The Oriental Institute of the University of Chicago. 246 BM. 249 AM. 251 Ministry of Culture/Garo Nalbandian, Jerusalem. 253 Robert Harding Picture Library. 256, 257 Mortimer Wheeler. 258 BM/BAL. 260 University of the Witwatersrand Medical School, Johannesburg. 262 Bruce Coleman Inc., New York. 263 Anne McBurney. 264 Kathie Atkinson, Pymble NSW. 267 D. J. Mulvaney, Canberra. 268 Werner Forman Archive/Maxwell Museum. 269 Photo Archives, Denver Museum of Natural History, all rights reserved. 272 Werner Forman Archive/Anthropology Museum, Veracruz University, Jalapa. 275 Archaeological Survey, Provincial Museum of Alberta. 276/7 Comstock. 280/1 Michael Holford. 283 Mick Sharp, Caernarvon. 285 Württembergisches Landesmuseum Stuttgart. 286 Comstock; photo Dr George Gerster. 288 Event Horizons – David Lyons. 290 Cahokia Mounds State Historic Site, Collinsville IL; painting Lloyd K. Townsend. 292 BM/BAL. 295 Hulton Deutsch Collection. 297 The Irish Times, Dublin 298 Novosti (London). 300 The Vindolanda Trust, Hexham. 302 Bill Curtsinger, Yarmouth ME. 304l Brigitte and Gilles Delluc. 304r Jean Vertut, Issy-les-Moulineaux. 305 Paul Bahn. 307 The Manchester Museum. 308 Idryma Theras – Petros M. Nomikos, Piraeus, Greece. 311 VBB, Stockholm. 313 Comstock. 314 Israel Antiquities Authority, Jerusalem. 316 Gordon Hillman, Institute of Archaeology, London. 317 Courtesy James Mellaart; photo Arlette Mellaart. 322 Paul Bahn. 323 Glynn Isaac. 325 Bob Campbell, Nairobi. 327 Nanci Kahn, Institute of Human Origins, Berkeley CA. 328 John Reader/Science Photo Library. 330 Thurstan Shaw, Cambridge. 331 Shirley Ann Pager. 332 Jim Bowler. 334 D. J. Mulvaney, Canberra. 335 Rhys Jones. 339 Paul Bahn. 340, 341 Comstock; photo Dr George Gerster. 344 Robert Harding Picture Library; photo Adina Tovy. 346 Robert Harding Picture Library; photo Michael J. Howell. 348 Michael Holford. 350 AAA. 352/3 Michael Holford 354 Universität Innsbruck. 356 Gertrude Bell Archives, University of Newcastle, Department of Archaeology. 357 F.H.E Archives, Albuquerque NM; photo Frederica de Laguna. 359 BM. 360/1 The Age, Melbourne. 363 Associated Press, London. 365 Michael Holford. 366 The Times Newspapers Limited; photo Graham Wood. 367 The Metropolitan Museum of Art, New York; The Cesnola Collection, Purchased by subscription, 1874–1876 (74.51.4554). 369 Giraudon/BAL. 372 Courtesy of Bari State University, Italy.

Index